T0171791

Beginning the Linux Command Line

Second Edition

Sander van Vugt

Beginning the Linux Command Line, Second edition

Copyright © 2015 by Sander van Vugt

This work is subject to copyright. All rights are reserved by the Publisher, whether the whole or part of the material is concerned, specifically the rights of translation, reprinting, reuse of illustrations, recitation, broadcasting, reproduction on microfilms or in any other physical way, and transmission or information storage and retrieval, electronic adaptation, computer software, or by similar or dissimilar methodology now known or hereafter developed. Exempted from this legal reservation are brief excerpts in connection with reviews or scholarly analysis or material supplied specifically for the purpose of being entered and executed on a computer system, for exclusive use by the purchaser of the work. Duplication of this publication or parts thereof is permitted only under the provisions of the Copyright Law of the Publisher's location, in its current version, and permission for use must always be obtained from Springer. Permissions for use may be obtained through RightsLink at the Copyright Clearance Center. Violations are liable to prosecution under the respective Copyright Law.

ISBN-13 (pbk): 978-1-4302-6830-7

ISBN-13 (electronic): 978-1-4302-6829-1

Trademarked names, logos, and images may appear in this book. Rather than use a trademark symbol with every occurrence of a trademarked name, logo, or image we use the names, logos, and images only in an editorial fashion and to the benefit of the trademark owner, with no intention of infringement of the trademark.

The use in this publication of trade names, trademarks, service marks, and similar terms, even if they are not identified as such, is not to be taken as an expression of opinion as to whether or not they are subject to proprietary rights.

While the advice and information in this book are believed to be true and accurate at the date of publication, neither the authors nor the editors nor the publisher can accept any legal responsibility for any errors or omissions that may be made. The publisher makes no warranty, express or implied, with respect to the material contained herein.

Managing Director: Welmoed Spahr
Lead Editor: Michelle Lowman
Technical Reviewer: Stewart Watkiss
Editorial Board: Steve Anglin, Louise Corrigan, Jim DeWolf, Jonathan Gennick, Robert Hutchinson, Michelle Lowman, James Markham, Susan McDermott, Matthew Moodie, Jeff Olson, Jeffrey Pepper, Douglas Pundick, Ben Renow-Clarke, Gwenan Spearing
Coordinating Editor: Mark Powers
Compositor: SPi Global
Indexer: SPi Global
Artist: SPi Global

Distributed to the book trade worldwide by Springer Science+Business Media New York, 233 Spring Street, 6th Floor, New York, NY 10013. Phone 1-800-SPRINGER, fax (201) 348-4505, e-mail orders-ny@springer-sbm.com, or visit www.springeronline.com. Apress Media, LLC is a California LLC and the sole member (owner) is Springer Science + Business Media Finance Inc (SSBM Finance Inc). SSBM Finance Inc is a Delaware corporation.

For information on translations, please e-mail rights@apress.com, or visit www.apress.com.

Apress and friends of ED books may be purchased in bulk for academic, corporate, or promotional use. eBook versions and licenses are also available for most titles. For more information, reference our Special Bulk Sales–eBook Licensing web page at www.apress.com/bulk-sales.

Any source code or other supplementary material referenced by the author in this text is available to readers at www.apress.com/9781430268307. For detailed information about how to locate your book's source code, go to www.apress.com/source-code/. Readers can also access source code at SpringerLink in the Supplementary Material section for each chapter.

This book is dedicated to Florence. Your love is making me invincible.

Contents at a Glance

Contents

About the Author

Sander van Vugt is a Linux expert working from the Netherlands as an author, technical trainer, and consultant for clients around the world. Sander has published several books about different Linux distributions and is a regular contributor to major international Linux-related web sites. As a consultant, he is specialized in Linux high availability and performance optimization. As a technical trainer, Sander is an authorized trainer for SUSE Linux Enterprise Server and Red Hat Enterprise Linux. More information about the author can be found at his web site at www.sandervanvugt.com.

Introduction

This book is for anyone who wants to master Linux from the command line. When writing it, I had in mind system administrators, software developers, and enthusiastic users who want toget things going from the Linux command line. For beginning users, this may be a daunting task, as Linux commands often have many options documented only in man pages that are not that easy to understand.

This book is distribution agnostic. That is, while writing it, I've checked all items against Ubuntu, Red Hat, and SUSE. Since most distributions are quite similar to one of these three, this book should help you with other distributions as well. There is only one item in the book that is not distribution agnostic: the Appendix, which explains how to install either CentOS or Ubuntu.

The book begins with an introduction to exactly what I'm talking about when discussing Linux and its different appearances: the distributions. In Chapter 1, you'll also find essential information on how to log on to the computer and how to find out more about the way a command should be used. Chapter 2 follows with some essential Linux commands. After reading this chapter, you'll already start to feel at ease on the Linux command line; among other things, it teaches you how to work with files and directories and how to communicate with other users. Chapter 3 moves the focus to one of the most important tasks you'll perform whenworking with Linux: working with files. In this chapter, you'll learn not only how to copy files and make directories, but also how to mount devices to your Linux system.

Working with Linux from the command line means working with text files. In Chapter 4, you'll learn about the tools that are at your disposal to do this. You'll get familiar with some of the classic tools, such as find and grep, and also with some of the more advanced tools, such as awk and sed. Following that, in Chapter 5 you'll learn more about partitions, logical volumes,and other advanced file system management tasks. After reading this chapter, you'll start feeling at ease on the Linux command line. Chapters 6 and 7 move on to two other essential subjects: the management of users and permissions.

Chapter 8 covers a topic that seems to be handled differently by all the Linux distributions: software management. This chapter teaches you about generic ways to install and manage software packages, such as rpm and dpkg, and also about some of the distribution- specific ways to deal with these tasks, such as apt-get, rpm, and zypper. Chapters 9 and 10 cover tasks that are important for system administration. In these chapters, you'll learn how to manage processes and how to handle logging on your computer.

By the time you reach Chapters 11 and 12, you're ready to explore network-related tasks. In these chapters, you'll learn how to configure anetwork interface and how to set up the Samba and NFS file services. Chapters 13 and 14 cover two advanced but useful topics: kernelmanagement and shell scripting. After you finish the last chapter, you'll have all the knowledge you need to work with Linux from the command line.

In Appendix B you'll find some additional exercises, which help making this book an excellent study guide that can be used in classroom environments.

I hope you enjoy reading this book and that it prepares you for getting things done from the Linux command line!

■ ■ ■

## CHAPTER 1

Starting Linux Command-Line Administration

To unleash the full power of Linux, as a Linux administrator you will spend most of your time typing commands on the Linux command line, the so-called shell prompt. For someone who is new to the command line, the things that advanced users do there may look like magic. In this chapter, you'll learn about the following topics:

- History of the Linux operating system

- What is open source?

- What are distributions?

- Logging in to Linux

- Command basics: working with commands, options, and arguments

- Using piping and redirection

- Getting help with --help and man

- Working with the shell

Linux Distributions

For someone new to Linux, the operating system may appear a little bit strange. Due to its open source character, there are different versions (the so-called distributions) of Linux. After some Linux history, this chapter teaches you about the differences and similarities between these distributions so that you'll be able to pick the Linux distribution that fits your needs in the best possible way.

Linux History

Linux started around 1991 all because the Finnish student Linus Torvalds wasn't too happy with Minix, the educational version of the UNIX operating system that he had to work with at the University of Helsinki. In particular, the ability of the kernel (which is the heart of the operating system) of this Minix distribution didn't please him much. He decided to create a better kernel and gave it the name Linux.

Possibly the smartest thing that Torvalds did when starting his initiative was deciding not to do it alone. To find other people who wanted to work with him, he posted a message on Usenet, a major social media platform in those days that could be used to exchange information with other people and get help from other people.

1

The initiative by Torvalds didn't stand on its own. Many other software developers had already started initiatives to create free software for the UNIX operating system. The only thing that really was missing at that moment was a kernel that was stable enough to go into production and offer a complete and free alternative to the expensive UNIX operating system.

Open Source

Right from the start, Torvalds released his software as open source software—that is, software whose source code is freely available to anyone. This brings a major benefit: other programmers have access to the source code and thus it becomes much easier to fix issues in the code, with the result of getting code that is more stable and reliable. This open source initiative fitted well into many other open source programs that were a part of the GNU initiative. The acronym GNU stands for GNU is Not UNIX, which means that this is about software written for the UNIX platform but doesn't use UNIX licensing. This GNU initiative was a part of the Free Software Foundation (FSF), which wanted to create free software for a better operating system experience.

When it came to licensing, Torvalds released his software under the GPL. In those days, GPL stood for GNU Public License, but nowadays it means General Public License. The details of this license are quite complex, but in essence it means that software released under the GPL can be used and modified by anyone, as long as the person modifying this software makes sure that his or her modifications will be released under the GPL as well. In brief: once software has a GPL, it will always stay GPL software. This prevents companies from making small modifications and then taking the software out of GPL and selling it for a lot of money.

In current Linux versions GPL still is very important. Most distributions consider it an essential property of the Operating system and will refuse software that doesn't comply with the conditions in the GPL license. By being so strict about the licensing, Linux distributions ensure that the software that is released as Open Source software will always stay Open Source software. Some distrubutions do also allow non-open source softare to be included, such as binary code for specific firmware. You will notice a different philosophical approach in this between the different distributions.

The First Distributions

Apart from the Linux kernel, lots of other programs were available under the GPL as well. In the early days, people who wanted to start using Linux had to go on the Internet and download these software programs themselves. Often, after downloading them, they even had to compile them for themselves. This compilation process was necessary to convert the program files, which were published as source code files only, to executable programs that users could execute on their computer.

Software compilation is not very easy to do, and for that reason, different people started to create collections that consisted of the Linux kernel and some other useful programs. One of the first persons to do so was Patrick Volkerding, who started his Slackware distribution in 1993. In those days, this distribution consisted of different software categories, all put together on no fewer than 43 diskettes. Volkerding was perhaps the first who made a successful Linux distribution that started to get used on servers all around the world, and his Slackware distribution still exists, although new releases are not published very frequently.

Linux Turning Mainstream

The years between 1993 and 1998 marked the rise of the Linux operating system. One of the most important reasons that it took of so rapidly, is that it provided a very affordable alternative for the expensive UNIX operating system that was used on many mission-critical server systems. In the early days of Linux, no support was available, but that didn't prevent scientists at different institutes around the globe to start working with it. Linux also acquired huge popularity rapidly in educational environments. Due to this popularity, during this period the most important Linux distributions were created.

Whereas Slackware was just a collection of software programs with an installation program that made working with Linux easy, other Linux distributions soon started to add value to the open source software. Some did this by adding commercial support to their software collection, others by creating programs and adding that to their distribution, and some hired developers to optimize the open source programs. The result is that nowadays dozens of Linux distributions are available for new Linux users. Of all these Linux distributions, only some really matter. In this book, I've focused on the three most important distributions: Red Hat, SUSE, and Ubuntu. By focusing on these three only, I am not making a statement about the quality of the other distributions; however, it makes sense to focus on these three as they make up more than 90% of the Linux market. Following are short descriptions of these three distributions.

Red Hat

North Carolina–based Linux distribution Red Hat had a major role in bringing Linux to the data center of many companies. The reason for the success of Red Hat was that this distributor added support for Linux. At one level, this is support of different hardware and software programs, which means that users of the supported hardware and software programs were guaranteed that they would work on Linux. Red Hat also added help for Linux users, available as a commercial added value to Linux.

Because Red Hat offered Linux with support, companies started putting aside their old flavors of UNIX and replacing them with the much cheaper Linux. This made Red Hat the most successful Linux distribution on the planet. Even though Ubuntu is widely adopted in environments where people don't want to pay for a supported Linux distribution, Red Hat by far is the leader of the commercial Linux distributions.

Currently, there are three product lines related to Red Hat. The most important of these is Red Hat Enterprise Linux (RHEL), which consists of two server versions and a desktop version. RHEL is a commercial product, so it is not available as a free download. It is open source software, however, but the only reason you can't download it for free is because Red Hat has added the Red Hat logo to the RHEL software, and this is something that users have to pay for.

Red Hat also founded the Fedora open source project. Basically, you can see this as the development environment for RHEL. Most new software components are first used and tested in Fedora, and if they are successful there, they will make it into RHEL as well. Fedora Linux is available for free download at www.redhat.com/fedora.

Since the only thing that is not free in Red Hat Enterprise Linux is the Red Hat logo, the CentOS (Community ENTerprise Operating System) distribution offers Red Hat Enterprise Linux software from which the Red Hat logo has been removed. This sounds illegal, but it isn't, as Red Hat is completely open source software. In fact, Red Hat has integrated the CentOS community within the Red Hat business, so that they can provide a freely available Linux distribution with the quality of Red Hat Enterprise Linux to those people and companies who aren't ready to pay for their Linux support yet. So if you want the stability of Red Hat Enterprise Linux, but don't want to pay for it, CentOS provides a good alternative. You can download CentOS at www.centos.org.

SUSE

The SUSE Linux distribution was founded in Germany. It became popular quite fast because from the beginning SUSE Linux came with lots of software packages that were shipped on DVDs in a large box, that contained installation manuals and even a stciker. SUSE was one of the first distributions that only sold their distribution and just delivered a demo system as freely available software, thus trying to make money out of it.

In 2004, Utah-based network software company Novell purchased SUSE and developed it into an enterprise-ready Linux distribution that could compete with Red Hat, which in that period still dominated the market. Currently, SUSE is an independent brand again.

Currently, there are two directions in SUSE Linux. SUSE Linux Enterprise is the commercial software that offers support, and it exists in two different flavors: SUSE Linux Enterprise Server, SUSE Linux Enterprise Desktop. With SUSE Linux Enterprise Desktop, SUSE has some success in bringing Linux to the enterprise desktop, whereas Red Hat, for example, still focuses on server versions. Interestingly, the SUSE Linux Enterprise products are freely downloadable at downloads.suse.com Notice however that in order to download updates and patches, a subscription is required. So even if you can download and install it for free, you'll need a subscription if you want to continue using it.

Apart from the SUSE Linux Enterprise products, there is OpenSUSE, which is a fully open source product. This version also offers a stable Linux distribution, but at the same time is used as a development platform for new software. You can download OpenSUSE at `www.opensuse.org`. All versions of SUSE Linux Enterprise Server are based on OpenSUSE.

Ubuntu

Ubuntu has become quite successful because its founder, the South African millionaire Mark Shuttleworth, made it an extremely user-friendly distribution and in the early days of Ubuntu even gave away CDs with the Ubuntu Desktop for free.

Apart from the Ubuntu Desktop, Ubuntu has a server edition as well, which due to the success of the desktop version has become quite. Both versions of Ubuntu Linux are available for free; customers who are interested in getting support can purchase it from Canonical, the company that has been created by Ubuntu founder Mark Shuttleworth to provide professional support services on Ubuntu.

Remarkable about Ubuntu Linux is the fact that there is a new software release every 6 months. By looking at the name of the distribution, you can see when it was released; for instance, Ubuntu 15.04 was released in April 2015. As enterprise users normally don't like upgrading their operating system every 6 months, there is also a Long Term Support (LTS) version that currently is released every 2 years. The special thing about this version is the extended period of support that is offered. For desktops and servers this is 7 years. For setting up a server that is based on Ubuntu Linux, it is highly recommended to use the LTS version.

■ **Note** This book focuses on Red Hat, SUSE, and Ubuntu Linux. You will notice, however, that 98% of the commands and configuration files covered in this book are available on other Linux distributions as well. This means that no matter what Linux distribution you use, the information in this book will be useful for you.

Logging In and Out

Now that you know about Linux in general, and about the Linux distributions more specifically, it's time to move on and get familiar with the essential tasks while working with Linux. Before you can do anything on a Linux computer, you have to log in. In this section, you'll learn about usernames and different ways you can use to make yourself known to your Linux computer.

Different Login Interfaces

Before starting to work on your Linux computer, you need to tell it who you are. The person that installed your Linux version has created a user account, and you must use this account and the associated password to make yourself known. To do this, Linux offers you a login prompt. This can be either a graphical or a nongraphical prompt. If you are working on a Linux desktop, you are likely to see a graphical environment. If, however, it is a server you a working from, you'll just see a shell login prompt.

In Linux, there often is a choice between different solutions. This means there is not just one unified graphical login prompt, but many, depending on the distribution that you are using and on the graphical environment that you have installed. You will notice that the graphical login screen for that reason will be different between the distributions. In Figure 1-1, you can see what it looks like on CentOS Linux.

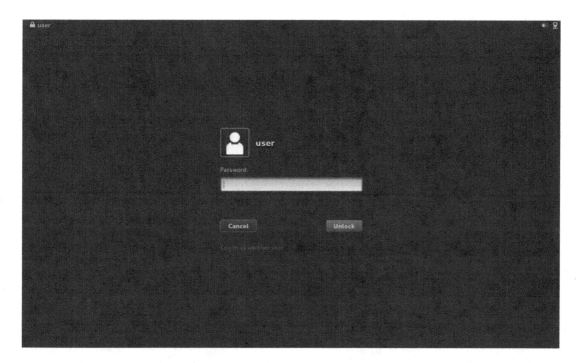

Figure 1-1. *The graphical login screen on CentOS*

When working with a graphical environment, it is the graphical environment that provides you with the login screen. More specifically, it is the gdm process that starts the graphical login screen. So what you see in Figure 1-1 is really the result of this xdm process. On specific graphical desktop environments, alternatives may be used, such as the gdm process which is the default on the GNOME graphical desktop.

Note: Historically, different graphical desktops have been offered on Linux. Currently, the GNOME desktop is used as the default on most Linux distributions. It runs on top of the X Windowing system, which is the generic system that provides a graphical screen, but with very basic functionality. GNOME adds functionality such as menu's to that screen. KDE is an alternative graphical desktop.

If you are working on a server, the graphical environment doesn't matter and is normally not started by default. That is because the graphical environment consumes resources, and these resources on server systems are better reserved for other purposes. Therefore, servers normally offer a text-based login prompt only. In Figure 1-2, you can see what this sort of login prompt looks like.

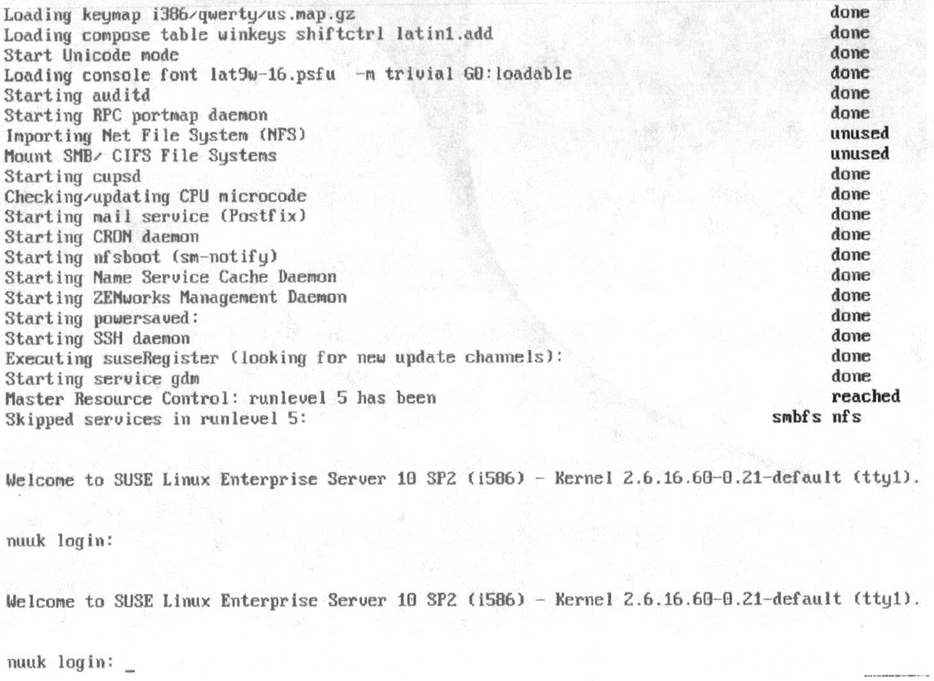

```
Loading keymap i386/qwerty/us.map.gz                                        done
Loading compose table winkeys shiftctrl latin1.add                         done
Start Unicode mode                                                         done
Loading console font lat9w-16.psfu  -m trivial G0:loadable                 done
Starting auditd                                                            done
Starting RPC portmap daemon                                                done
Importing Net File System (NFS)                                          unused
Mount SMB/ CIFS File Systems                                             unused
Starting cupsd                                                             done
Checking/updating CPU microcode                                            done
Starting mail service (Postfix)                                            done
Starting CRON daemon                                                       done
Starting nfsboot (sm-notify)                                               done
Starting Name Service Cache Daemon                                         done
Starting ZENworks Management Daemon                                        done
Starting powersaved:                                                       done
Starting SSH daemon                                                        done
Executing suseRegister (looking for new update channels):                  done
Starting service gdm                                                       done
Master Resource Control: runlevel 5 has been                            reached
Skipped services in runlevel 5:                                    smbfs nfs


Welcome to SUSE Linux Enterprise Server 10 SP2 (i586) - Kernel 2.6.16.60-0.21-default (tty1).


nuuk login:


Welcome to SUSE Linux Enterprise Server 10 SP2 (i586) - Kernel 2.6.16.60-0.21-default (tty1).


nuuk login: _
```

Figure 1-2. *The text-based login prompt*

There are other ways of connecting to a Linux machine as well. If you are a server administrator, your server will probably be installed in an air-conditioned and cold server room that you enter only if really necessary. Alternatively, your Linux server may be hosted somewhere remotely in the cloud, or as a Virtual Private Server (VPS) at somehosting provider. No matter how it is running, often your server isn't physically accessible. Therefore, as a server administrator, you may use a remote access tool like the Windows utility PuTTY to get shell access to the server. In Figure 1-3, you can see what the PuTTY login screen looks like.

Figure 1-3. PuTTY is the de facto standard for accessing a Linux console remotely from a Windows workstation

■ **Note**   PuTTY is the de facto standard for accessing Linux machines from a Windows desktop. You can download PuTTY for free from `www.putty.org`. To use it, you need an SSH server running on your Linux computer as well. SSH is covered in detail in Chapter 11. On Linux workstations and Apple computers a native SSH client is integrated in the operating system, and you won't need PuTTY to establish a remote session with your Linux server.

As you can see, there are many ways to connect to a Linux machine. In all cases, you do need to provide user credentials. The next section gives more information about that.

Working with a User Account

To log in to a Linux machine, you need a user account name and a password. You should already know what username to use if you installed the machine yourself. If someone else installed the machine for you, ask him or her what username you should use. This username will also have a password. At the login prompt, you need to provide the username and password to make yourself known to the machine. This procedure is also known as *authentication*.

■ **Note**   There are alternatives to passwords for authentication. For instance, you may use a smart card to authenticate on your machine. However, this requires additional hardware, and for this reason, in this book I will focus on password authentication.

When authenticating for the first time, you have to decide what user account to use. You can authenticate as a normal user, but you can authenticate with the account of the system administrator as well. The username for this account is root. On every Linux computer, there is a user with the name root, and this user account has no restrictions. The user root really is almighty. If you are connecting to Linux to perform system administration tasks, it makes sense to authenticate as root; after all, you need to do system administration, and for that purpose you need all the permissions there are. If, however, you are a normal user, you shouldn't make a habit of logging in as root by default. Just log in with your normal user account, and use su or sudo to become root when needed. In Chapter 2, you'll learn how to do this. At this time, just make sure that you are authenticated.

Command-Line Basics

The command line is important, because a system administrator can do anything from it. Even if your Linux installation is running a graphical interface as well, you'll need command line access to unleash the full power and potential of Linux. The only reason why many administrators are using a graphical interface on Linux, is because it allows them to run many terminal windows simultaneously, which makes it easy to read the documentation in one window, configure in another window and test the configuration in a third window for instance.

Linux has many, many commands, more than you will ever know, and new commands are added on a regular basis. All of these commands, though, share a common way of working. In this section, you'll learn about common elements that you will encounter in any Linux command. First, you'll learn about the common structure that every Linux command has. Next, we'll talk about characters that you can and can't use in Linux commands. Figure 1-4 shows what a command line looks like, when started as a terminal from a graphical environment.

Figure 1-4. *The command line as seen from a terminal window*

The command line offers you a prompt that consists of different parts. The first part of the prompt, as you can see in Figure 1-4, is the name of the computer you are working on. In this case, the computer name is server1. Next, the prompt refers to the current directory in the file system where the user is at right now. In Figure 1-4, you can see a ~ sign instead of the name of a directory. This sign refers to the home directory, which is the folder in the file system where the user can store his or her personal files. Last, the # sign in this prompt indicates that the current user is *root*, the mighty system administrator. If you see anything other than #, the current user is not root, but a normal user with normal privileges. Be aware that if this is the case, some commands have limited use. For instance, on Linux a normal user cannot format hard disks, and many other tasks cannot be accomplished by non-root users.

■ **Note** Since in open source there are no rules that are strictly enforces to everyone, a developer can do as he or she likes. Therefore, words like "always" and "every" are not applicable in Linux, as there are often exceptions to the rules that are used in Linux. To keep this book readable, I will, however, use these words anyway. Just keep in mind that when you see the terms "every" and "always," it should read "almost every" and "almost always."

Bash: The Command Interpreter

When working on the command line, as an administrator you will be dealing with the shell. The shell is the command interpreter: it is responsible for making something out of the things that you type on the command line. How you work with commands is largely defined by the abilities of the shell. The shell itself is a program that your server starts automatically after you log in on your server, no matter if you've done so directly on the server console or via a remote session that you've started from PuTTY on your Windows workstation. Two shells are used quite often: Bash and Dash. Bash is the default shell on the current SUSE and Red Hat versions, and Dash is available on Ubuntu. The good news is that as a beginning command-line administrator, you don't really care which shell is used—both work in the same way. In the section "Working with the Shell" later in this chapter, you'll learn about some of its most important and most useful features.

Commands, Options, and Arguments

A Linux command normally consists of three parts: the command itself, the command options, and its arguments. For instance, the following example shows what a Linux command looks like:

```
useradd -m -G sales linda
```

This example consists of three parts, useradd, which is the command; -m and -G sales, which are both options; and linda, which is a generic argument. Notice that the word "sales" behind the -G is also a special item, it is an argument to the option -G. Further on in this section, I'll explain these components in more detail.

The command itself is the character string you type to activate a certain task. For instance, the command ls (see Listing 1-1) lists files. In Listing 1-1, you see the result of this command when used in the home directory of the user root (the Linux system administrator). Certain functionality is defined for this command. Linux has many commands, as mentioned previously; later in this chapter, in the section "Using man to Get Help," you'll learn how to get detailed usage information about them by using the man command.

Listing 1-1. Using the ls Command Without Options Shows Files in the Current Directory

```
nuuk:~ # ls
.ICEauthority   .exrc    .gnome2_                  private          .metacity
.Xauthority     .fvwm    .gnupg                    .nautilus        .wapi
.bash_history   .gconf   .gstreamer-0.10           .qt              .xsession-errors
.config         .gconfd  .gtkrc                    .recently-used   Desktop
.dmrc           .gnome   .gtkrc-1.2-gnome2         .skel            Documents
.esd_auth       .gnome2  .kbd                      .suse_           register.log bin
```

Options

Most commands have options as their second part. By using these options, you modify the behavior of the commands. Options are a part of the program code, they are fixed and the software programmer that created the program has provided the available options. For instance, the ls command just shows the names of files in the current directory, as you can see in Listing 1-1. If you want to see details, such as the file size, the permissions that are set for it, and information about the creation date, you can add the option -l. In Listing 1-2, you can see how this option modifies the behavior of the ls command.

Listing 1-2. By Adding an Option to a Command, You Modify Its Behavior

```
nuuk:~ # ls     -l
total 120
-rw-------    1    root    root     777    Dec   5    10:43    .ICEauthority
-rw-------    1    root    root     115    Dec   5    10:43    .Xauthority
-rw-------    1    root    root     2558   Nov   24   13:39    .bash_history
drwx------    3    root    root     4096   Nov   7    11:04    .config
-rw-------    1    root    root     24     Nov   7    11:03    .dmrc
-rw-------    1    root    root     16     Nov   7    11:03    .esd_auth
-rw-r--r--    1    root    root     1332   Nov   23   2005     .exrc
drwxr-xr-x    2    root    root     4096   Nov   7    10:47    .fvwm
drwx------    5    root    root     4096   Dec   5    10:43    .gconf
drwx------    2    root    root     4096   Dec   5    11:03    .gconfd
drwxr-xr-x    3    root    root     4096   Nov   7    11:04    .gnome
drwx------    6    root    root     4096   Nov   7    11:04    .gnome2
drwx------    2    root    root     4096   Nov   7    11:03    .gnome2_private
drwx------    3    root    root     4096   Nov   7    11:03    .gnupg
drwxr-xr-x    2    root    root     4096   Dec   5    10:43    .gstreamer-0.10
-rw-r--r--    1    root    root     123    Nov   7    11:03    .gtkrc
-rw-r--r--    1    root    root     134    Nov   7    11:03    .gtkrc-1.2-gnome2
drwxr-xr-x    2    root    root     4096   Nov   7    10:47    .kbd
drwx------    3    root    root     4096   Nov   7    11:03    .metacity
drwxr-xr-x    3    root    root     4096   Nov   7    11:04    .nautilus
drwxr-xr-x    2    root    root     4096   Nov   19   15:03    .qt
-rw-------    1    root    root     325    Dec   5    10:43    .recently-used
drwxr-xr-x    2    root    root     4096   Nov   7    11:03    .skel
-rw-r--r--    1    root    root     795    Dec   5    10:44    .suse_register.log
drwx------    3    root    root     4096   Nov   7    11:04    .thumbnails
drwxr-xr-x    2    root    root     4096   Dec   1    05:27    .wapi
-rw-r--r--    1    root    root     1238   Dec   5    10:43    .xsession-errors
drwxr-xr-x    2    root    root     4096   Nov   7    11:04    Desktop
drwx------    2    root    root     4096   Nov   7    11:04    Documents
drwxr-xr-x    2    root    root     4096   May   3    2007     bin
```

Options provide a method that is defined within the command code to modify the behavior of the command. This means that as a user or an administrator, you cannot add options yourself. The only way of doing this is to change the source code of the command and recomplie the command, which is not something that you want to be doing as a Linux user or administrator. Options are very specific to the command you use. Some commands don't have any options, and other commands can have more than 50. The man command normally gives you a complete list of all options that are available. Alternatively, many commands support the option --help, which will show a summary of all available options.

Many commands offer two different methods of working with options: the short option and the long option. For example, you can use the command ls -lh, which makes the ls command present its output in a human-readable way by showing kilobytes, megabytes, and gigabytes instead of just bytes. You can also use the short option -h in a long way, written as --human-readable. In Listing 1-3, you can see this option at work, combined with the option -l, which makes sure that the output of ls is given as a long listing. (Unfortunately, there is no long alternative for the short option -l.) Notice that if more than one option is used, all options can be specified together, without a - in front of each option. So the command **ls -lh** is valid, and so is the command **ls -l -h.**

Listing 1-3. Most Linux Commands Work with Short As Well As Long Options

```
nuuk:/somedir # ls -l -h
total 4.0M
-rwxr-xr-x 1 root root 1.5M Dec 5 11:32 vmlinux-2.6.16.60-0.21-default.gz
-rw-r--r-- 1 root root 1.3M Dec 5 11:32 vmlinuz
-rw-r--r-- 1 root root 1.3M Dec 5 11:32 vmlinuz-2.6.16.60-0.21-default
nuuk:/somedir # ls -l --human-readable
total 4.0M
-rwxr-xr-x 1 root root 1.5M Dec 5 11:32 vmlinux-2.6.16.60-0.21-default.gz
-rw-r--r-- 1 root root 1.3M Dec 5 11:32 vmlinuz
-rw-r--r-- 1 root root 1.3M Dec 5 11:32 vmlinuz-2.6.16.60-0.21-default
```

Short options are preceded by a sign, and you can add more than one short option after the sign. For instance, you can combine the options -l and -h from the example in Listing 1-4 as ls -lh. Long options are preceded by the -- sign. For instance, ls --human-readable executes the ls command with just one option, which Is --human-readable. If by mistake you put just one in front of a long option, the long option is not interpreted as a long option, but as a collection of short options. This means that ls -human-readable would be interpreted as ls -h -u -m -a -n -- -r -e -a -d -a -b -l -e.

Arguments

Apart from options, many Linux commands have arguments. These are additional specifications that you can add to the command to tell it more precisely what to do, but the argument is typically not defined in the command code itself. For example, consider the command ls -l /etc/hosts:

```
nuuk:/somedir # ls -l /etc/hosts
-rw-r--r-- 1 root root 683 Nov 7 10:53 /etc/hosts
```

In this example, /etc/hosts is the argument. As you can imagine, you can use any other file name instead of /etc/hosts, and this is typical for arguments. They are not fixed, and you can use any argument you like as long as it is relevant in the context of the command. In this book, I'll make a very clear distinction between options and arguments.

You should be aware that not only commands have arguments, but also options have arguments as well. For example, consider the following command:

```
mail -s hello root
```

This command consists of four different parts:

- `mail`: The command itself
- `-s`: The option that tells the `mail` command what subject it should use
- `hello`: The argument of the option `-s`, which specifies what exactly you want to do with the option `-s`
- `root`: The argument of the command, which in this case makes clear to whom to send the mail message

As a rule of thumb, arguments at the end of the command are normally command arguments, and arguments for options are placed right next to the options. You may wonder now how to find out the differences between command arguments and arguments for options, but later in this chapter in the section "Getting Help," you'll see that it is fairly simple to differentiate the two argument types.

Piping and Redirection

To unleash the full power of Linux's many commands, you can use piping and redirection. By piping, you can send the result of a command to another command, and by using redirection, you can determine where the command should send its results.

Piping

Piping offers you great benefits in a Linux environment. By using piping, you can combine the abilities of two or more commands to create a kind of super command that offers even more capabilities. By creating the right pipes, you can really do amazing stuff. For an advanced Linux administrator, a command such as the following is pretty common (after reading all the chapters in this book, you should be able to understand what this command is doing):

```
kill `ps aux | grep y2 | grep -v grep | awk '{ print $2 }'`
```

As a Linux administrator, you absolutely need to know about piping, so let's start with an easy example. If you try a command like `ls -R /`, you will see that it gives a lot of output that scrolls over your screen without stopping. On Linux, there is a very useful command, named `less`, that you can use as a viewer for text files. For example, try `less /etc/hosts` (see Listing 1-4); this will open the `/etc/hosts` file in `less` to show the contents of the file (use q to quit `less`).

■ **Note** The `/etc/hosts` file contains a list of IP addresses and the matching host name. In a small network, you can use it as an alternative to using DNS for resolving host names.

Listing 1-4. You Can Use less As a Viewer to Read Text Files

```
nuuk:/ # less /etc/hosts
#
# hosts          This file describes a number of hostname-to-address
#                mappings for the TCP/IP subsystem. It is mostly
#                used at boot time, when no name servers are running.
#                On small systems, this file can be used instead of a
#                "named" name server.
# Syntax:
#
# IP-Address     Full-Qualified-Hostname Short-Hostname
#

127.0.0.1       localhost

# special IPv6 addresses
::1             localhost ipv6-localhost ipv6-loopback

fe00::0         ipv6-localnet

ff00::0         ipv6-mcastprefix
ff02::1         ipv6-allnodes
ff02::2         ipv6-allrouters
ff02::3         ipv6-allhosts
127.0.0.2       nuuk.sander.gl nuuk
/etc/hosts lines 1-23/23 (END)
```

The less command can be very useful in a pipe as well. By using piping, you'll send the result of the first command to the second command. So if you use ls -R / | less, the ls -R / command executes and sends its result to the less command. less will function as a pager in this situation and show you the output of the first command screen by screen (see Listing 1-5). It will also show you the current position that you are at; this is indicated by lines 1-23, which you see at the end of the example file. Press the spacebar to proceed to the next screen of output.

Listing 1-5. By Piping to less, You Can Display the Results of a Command That Gives a Large Amount of Output Screen by Screen

```
nuuk:/ # ls -R / | less
/:
.rnd
bin
boot
dev
etc
home
lib
lost+found
media
mnt
opt
proc
```

```
root
sbin
somedir
srv
sys
tmp
usr
var

/bin:
lines 1-23
```

Redirection

Another operator that is very useful in the Linux command shell is the redirection operator, >. By default, a command will show its result on your computer monitor. In Linux slang, you can also say that the shell will send the result of a command to standard output, abbreviated to STDOUT, which is usually your computer monitor (but can be something else as well. A long time ago, printers were often used as STDOUT instead of monitors). Using redirection, you can send it anywhere else.

■ **Tip**   If possible, try all commands described in this section immediately after reading about them. Without trying them yourself, it may be quite hard to understand what they are doing.

Let's use the command ls -l once more as an example. If you just type the command, you will see its result on STDOUT. However, if you type ls -l > somewhere, you'll tell the command to send its output somewhere else, in this case to a file that has the name somewhere. This file will be created in the current directory if it doesn't exist. If a file with this name already exists, you will overwrite it by using this command. In case you want to add to an existing file instead of overwriting it, use ls -l >> somewhere. The double redirector tells the command to append to the contents of the file instead of overwriting it. If the file doesn't already exist, the command will create it. So if you want to be sure never to overwrite an existing file by accident when using redirection, use >> at all times instead of >.

Some commands give you error messages apart from output. The good thing is that you can redirect these error messages also. To do this, use 2> instead of >. So if ls -l gives you a lot of error messages as well (which isn't very likely, but you never know), you can send all of them to the file errors, which will be created in the current directory if you use ls -l 2> errors. And it is even possible to redirect the standard output of a command in one direction, while sending the error output somewhere else. For instance, the command ls -l > output 2> errors will create two files, the file output for the regular output and the file errors for the error output.

Instead of sending the results of a command to a file, you can redirect to some of the Linux special devices as well. Every piece of hardware in Linux can be addressed by using a device file. For instance, there is the device file /dev/null, which can be used as a digital waste bin. Everything that you send to /dev/null will immediately disappear into thin air. So if you just don't want to see any error messages at all, instead of saving them somewhere on your system, you can redirect the error messages to the /dev/null device. The following example shows how to do so:

```
ls -l 2> /dev/null
```

In this example, the regular output is still written to your current terminal, but you just won't see error messages anymore.

Apart from output, you can also use redirection on input for a command. This is used not as often, but can be useful for commands that open an interactive prompt where you are expected to provide input for the command. An example of this is the Linux mail command that you can use on the command line.

■ **Tip**   You can use the mail command for some simple mail handling from a terminal screen, but if your server is configured properly, you can even use it to send mail to other users on the Internet. The only thing you need to do is set up DNS on your server.

Consider the command mail -s hello root. This command opens a command prompt that will allow you to compose a mail message to the user root (whose name is provided as the argument to the command). The option -s hello specifies the subject, in this case hello. In Listing 1-6, you can see the result of this command.

Listing 1-6. Composing a Mail Message with mail

```
nuuk:/ # mail -s hello root
Hi root, how are you.
.
EOT
```

Now the problem with the mail command is that when used in this way, it opens an interactive prompt where you type the message body. When finished typing the message body, you have to provide a dot on a separate line and press Enter. By using input redirection, you can feed the dot immediately to the command, which allows you to run the command without any interruption from the command line.

```
mail -s hello root < .
```

The difference between Listing 1-6, where mail opens a command prompt, and the preceding example, where input redirection is used, is that in the example with input redirection, you cannot enter a message in the body of the mail. To send the mail, there is just one line to use, and that's all.

EXERCISE 1-1: WORKING WITH LINUX COMMANDS

1. Log in to your Linux machine as root and open a shell.

2. Type **useradd lisa** to create a user with the name lisa.

3. Type **passwd lisa**. This command will prompt you for the password that you want to use. Enter the password "password" and when asked for confirmation, enter it again. Notice that this command will give you a warning about the password being too simple, which you can safely ignore.

4. Use **Ctrl-D** to close the shell you are currently logged in to. If it was a non-graphical shell, you'll now see a login prompt. If you're working from a graphical environment, find the option that logs you out of your current session.

5. Log in again, this time as user lisa and open a shell.

6. Type **ls -l iwehig**. This should give you an error message.

7. Type **ls il iwehig 2> ~/errors**. This command redirects all errors to a file with the name errors that is created in your home directory.

8. Type **cat ~/errors** to view the contents of this file.

9. Type **ls --help** to view a list of options that can be used with the **ls** command. You'll notice that the list is too long and doesn't fit on the screen.

10. Type **ls --help | less** to pipe the output of the **ls** command to **less**. You can now use the arrow keys to move up and down in the output.

11. Press **q** to quit the less viewer.

Getting Help

Linux offers many ways to get help. Let's start with a short overview:

- The man command offers documentation for most commands that are available on your system.

- Almost all commands accept the --help option. Using it will display a short overview of available options that can be used with the command.

- As with every shell, the Bash shell also has internal commands. These commands can't be found as a program file on disk, but they are built in the Bash shell and available in memory as soon as the Bash shell is loaded. For these Bash internal commands, you can use the help command to find out more about them. For example, use help for to get more information about the Bash internal command for.

■ **Note** Want to find out whether a command is an internal command or not? Use type. For example, try type cd; the result will show you what kind of command cd is, in this case a Bash internal command.

Using man to Get Help

The most important source of information about commands on your Linux system is man, which is short for the System Programmers Manual. The basic structure for using man is to type man followed by the command you want information about. For example, type man passwd to get more information about the passwd item. You'll then see a page displayed by the less pager, as shown in Listing 1-7.

Listing 1-7. Example of a man Page

```
PASSWD(1)                     User Commands                     PASSWD(1)

NAME
       passwd - change user password

SYNOPSIS
       passwd [options] [LOGIN]
```

```
DESCRIPTION
        passwd changes passwords for user accounts. A normal user
        may only change the password for his/her own account, while
        the super user may change the password for any account.
        passwd also changes account information, such as the full
        name of the user, the user's login shell, or his/her
        password expiry date and interval.

    Password Changes
Manual page passwd(1) line 1
```

Each man page consists of the following elements.

- *Name*: This is the name of the command. It also includes a short description of the purpose of the command.

- *Synopsis*: Here you can find short usage information about the command. It will show all available options and indicate whether an option is optional (shown between square brackets) or mandatory (not between brackets).

- *Description*: This describes what the command is doing. Read it to get a clear and complete picture of the purpose of the command.

- *Options*: This is a complete list of all options that are available, and it documents the use of all of them.

- *Files*: If it exists, this section provides a brief list of files that are related to the command you want more information about.

- *See also*: This is a list of related commands.

- *Author*: This indicates the author and also provides the mail address of the person who wrote the man page.

man Sections

In the early days, nine different man volumes documented every aspect of the UNIX operating system. This structure of separate books (nowadays called sections) is still present in the man command. Table 1-1 lists the available sections and the type of help you can find in them.

Table 1-1. *man Sections and What They Cover*

Section	Topic	Description
0	Header files	These are files that are typically in /usr/include and contain generic code that can be used by your programs.
1	Executable programs or shell commands	For the user, this is the most important section because it normally documents all commands that can be used.
2	System calls	As an administrator, you will not use this section on a frequent basis. The system calls are functions that are provided by the kernel. It's all very interesting if you are a kernel debugger, but normal administrators won't need this information.

(continued)

Table 1-1. (*continued*)

Section	Topic	Description
3	Library calls	A library is a piece of shared code that can be used by several different programs. Typically, man pages that are documented in section 3 are relevant for programmers, not so much for Linux users and system administrators.
4	Special files	In here, the device files in the directory /dev are documented. These files are needed to access devices in a computer. This section can be useful for learning more about the workings of specific devices and how to address them using device files.
5	Configuration files	Here you'll find the proper format you can use for most configuration files on your server. If, for example, you want to know more about the way /etc/passwd is organized, use the entry for passwd in this section by using the command man 5 passwd.
6	Games	On a modern Linux system, this section contains hardly any information.
7	Miscellaneous	This section contains some information on macro packages used on your server.
8	System administration commands	This section does contain important information about thev commands you will use on a frequent basis to change settings on your Linux machine.
9	Kernel routines	This is documentation that isn't even included as part of the standard install and optionally contains information about kernel routines.

So the information that matters to you as a system administrator is in sections 1, 5, and 8 Mostly you don't need to know anything about the other sections, but sometimes an entry can be found in more than one section. For example, information on an item called passwd is found in section 1 as well as in section 5. If you just type man passwd, you'll see the content of the first entry that man finds. If you want to make sure that all the information you need is displayed, use man -a <yourcommand>. This makes sure that man browses all sections to see whether it can find anything about <yourcommand>. If you know what section to look in, specify the section number as well, as in man 5 passwd, which will open the passwd item from section 5 directly.

Now man is a very useful tool for getting more information on how to use a given command. On its own, however, it is useful only if you know the name of the command you want to read about. If you don't have that information and need to locate the proper command, you will like man -k. The -k option allows you to locate the command you need by looking at keywords.

■ **Note** man -k is very useful. Instead of using man -k, you may also use the apropos command, which does exactly the same thing.

---

man -k often produces a very long list of commands from all sections of the man pages, and in most cases you don't need to see all that information; the commands that are relevant for the system administrator are in sections 1 and 8. Sometimes, when you are looking for a configuration file, section 5 should be browsed as well. Therefore, it's good to pipe the output of man -k through the grep utility, which can be used for filtering. Just add the text you're looking for as an argument to the grep command, and it will show you only those lines that contain that specific text. For example, use man -k time | grep 1 to show only lines from man section 1 that have the word "time" in the description.

■ **Tip** It may happen that man -k provides only a message stating that nothing is appropriate. If this is the case, run the mandb command (**makewhatis** on some Linux distributions). This will create the database that is necessary to search the man indexes.

Using the --help Option

The --help option is pretty straightforward. Most commands accept this option, although not all commands recognize it. But the nice thing is that if your command doesn't recognize the option, it will give you a short summary on how to use the command anyway because it doesn't understand what you want it to do. Although the purpose of the command is to provide a short overview of the way it should be used, you should be aware that the information is often still too long to fit on one screen. If this is the case, pipe it through less to view the information page by page. In Listing 1-8, you see what happens when you do that.

Listing 1-8. Displaying Information Screen by Screen by Piping Through less

```
nuuk:/ # ls --help | less
Usage: /bin/ls [OPTION]… [FILE]…
List information about the FILEs (the current directory by default). Sort entries
alphabetically if none of -cftuSUX nor --sort.

Mandatory arguments to long options are mandatory for short options too.

-a,     --all               do not ignore entries starting with .
-A,     --almost-all        do not list implied . and ..
        --author            with -l, print the author of each file
-b,     --escape            print octal escapes for nongraphic characters
        --block-size=SIZE   use SIZE-byte blocks
-B,     --ignore-backups    do not list implied entries ending with ~
-c                          with -lt: sort by, and show, ctime (time of
                            modification of file status information)
                            with -l: show ctime and sort by name
                            otherwise: sort by ctime
-C                          list entries by columns
        --color[=WHEN]      control whether color is used to distinguish file
                            types. WHEN may be `never', `always', or
                            `auto'
-d,     --directory         list directory entries instead of contents,
                            and do not dereference symbolic links
-D,     --dired             generate output designed for Emacs' dired mode
-f                          do not sort, enable -aU, disable -lst
-F,     --classify          append indicator (one of */=>@|) to entries
lines 1-23
```

19

Getting Information on Installed Packages

Another nice source for information that is often overlooked is the documentation that is isntalled automatically for many software packages in the directory /usr/share/doc/. Beneath this directory, you'll find a long list of subdirectories that all contain some usage information. In many cases, the information is really short and not very good, but in other cases, thorough and helpful information is available. Often this information is available in ASCII text format and can be viewed with less or any other utility that is capable of handling clear text.

In some cases, the information in /usr/share/doc is stored in a compressed format. You can recognize this format by the extension .gz. To read files in this format, you can use zcat and pipe the output of that to less, which allows you to browse through it page by page. For example, if you see a file with the name changelog.gz, use zcat changelog.gz | less to read it.

Note: On many distributions, **less** has been modified and can read compressed files directly. So often, there won't be a reason anymore to use **zcat** or other utilities that have a name that starts with the letter z.

In other cases, you will find the documentation in HTML format, which can only be displayed properly with a browser. If this is the case, it is good to know that you don't necessarily need to start a graphical environment to see the contents of the HTML file because many distributions come with the w3m text browser, which is designed to run from a nongraphical environment. In w3m you can use the arrow keys to browse between hyperlinks. To quit the w3m utility, use the q command. Alternatively, the **elinks** browser can be used as a text browser.

EXERCISE 1-2: GETTING HELP

1. Type **man 3 intro**. Every section in the man pages has an intro page, describing the purpose of the section.

2. Type **man lvcreate**. Use **/examples** to look for the word examples. Many man pages have an examples section near the end of the man page. In this section you can often find useful usage information.

3. Type **man -k sander**. It will tell you "Nothing appropriate". If this happens on commands that you do expect to be available on your computer, it's a good idea to use **mandb** to generate the new man pages index file.

Working with the Shell

Linux uses the kernel to address and control the machine's hardware. The kernel can be considered the heart of the Linux operating system. On top of this kernel, as shown in Figure 1-5, Linux gives users the shell interface to tell this kernel and the services running on top of it what they should do. This interface interprets the commands that users enter and translates them to machine code.

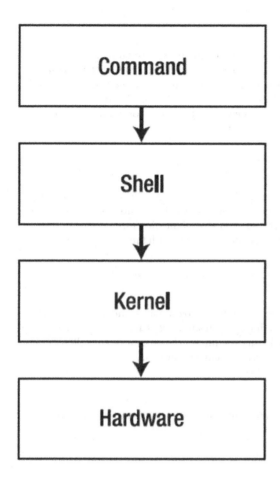

Figure 1-5. *Overview of the relation between kernel and shell*

Several shells are available for Linux, but bash is the default. The very first shell that was ever created for UNIX, back in the 1970s, was the Bourne shell. It is still available in Linux as the program file /bin/sh. Another popular shell is Bash (short for the Bourne Again Shell). The Bash shell is completely compatible with the original Bourne shell, but it has many enhancements. Bash is used as the default shell for all users on most Linux distributions. Whereas SUSE and Red Hat use Bash, Ubuntu also offers another shell, named Dash. For regular server administration tasks, there are no important differences between Bash and Dash. You should be aware that other shells are available as well. Some people prefer using these other shells, three of which I'll merely mention here:

- *tcsh*: A shell with a scripting language that works like the C programming language (and thus is fairly popular with C programmers).

- *zsh*: A shell that is compatible with Bash, but offers even more features.

- *sash*: The stand-alone shell. This is a very minimal shell that runs in almost all environments. It is thus well suited for troubleshooting systems.

Using the Shell to Best Effect

Basically, in the shell environment, an administrator is working with commands to execute the tasks he or she wants to perform. An example of such a command is ls, which can be used to display a list of files in a directory. Bash has some useful features to make working with these line commands as easy as possible.

Some shells offer the option to complete a command automatically. Bash has this feature, but it does more than just complete commands. Bash can complete almost *everything*: not just commands, but also file names and shell variables.

Working with Files and Directories

You'll find that when working in the shell, you'll often be manipulating files and directories. A directory is the folder in which files are stored that are related to one another; for instance, in the directory /bin, you will find binary files. Some directories are created by default, but you can also create directories yourself. To do this, use mkdir. For instance, the following command would create a directory with the name groups in the root of the file system:

```
mkdir /groups
```

In a directory, you'll find files. These can be text configuration files, program files, and documents; all that is stored on a Linux machine is stored in a file in some directory. In some cases, it can be useful to create a dummy text file that allows you to test functionality. To do this, use the touch command. The following command shows how to use touch to create an empty text file in the current directory:

```
touch somefile
```

This was just a very short introduction to working with files and directories. Chapter 2 of this book gives many more details on this subject.

Using automatic Command Completion

Using this feature is as simple as pressing the Tab key. For example, the cat line command is used to display the contents of an ASCII text file. The name of this file, which is in the current directory, is thisisafile. So, to open this file, the user can type **cat thi** and then press the Tab key. If the directory has only one file that starts with the letters "thi," Bash automatically completes the name of the file. If the directory has other files that start with the same letters, Bash will complete the name of the file as far as possible. For example, let's say that there is a file in the current directory with the name thisisatextfile and another with the name thisAlsoIsAFile. Because both files start with the text this, Bash will complete only up to this and no further. To display a list of possibilities, you then press the Tab key again. This allows you to manually enter more information. Of course, you can then press the Tab key again to use the completion feature once more.

Bash command line completion has developed into a very rich solution. If you want to be able to use it in the best possible way, make sure the **bash-completion** software package is installed. In this package information is available that help you using bash completion in a very rich way, against many different commands.

■ **Tip** Working with the Tab key really makes the command-line interface much easier. Imagine that you need to manage logical volumes on your server, and you remember only that the command for that starts with lv. In this case, you can type **lv** and press the Tab key twice. The result will be a nice list of all commands that start with lv, from which you'll probably recognize the command that you need.

Working with Variables

A variable is simply a common value that is used often enough by the shell that it is stored with a name. Many system variables are available from the moment your system boots, but you can set variables yourself as well. For instance, when you use the command SWEET=good on the command line, you have temporarily defined a variable that you can use later (it will disappear if you close the current shell or open a new shell). Setting variables yourself is mainly interesting when writing shell scripts; you'll read much more about this subject in Chapter 12.

Apart from the variables that you would define yourself, there are system variables as well. These system variables are stored in the user's environment and help make it easier to work from the shell. An example of such a variable is PATH, which stores a list of directories that should be searched when a user enters a command. To refer to the contents of a variable, prefix a $ sign before the name of the variable. For example, the command echo $PATH displays the content of the current search path that Bash is using.

On any Linux system, you'll get quite a few variables automatically when logging in. For an overview of all of them, you can use the env (short for *environment*) command. Listing 1-9 shows the result of this command.

Listing 1-9. The env Command Shows All Variables That Are Defined in Your Shell Environment

```
root@RNA:~# env
TERM=xterm
SHELL=/bin/bash
SSH_CLIENT=192.168.1.71 1625 22
SSH_TTY=/dev/pts/1
USER=root
MAIL=/var/mail/root
PATH=/usr/local/sbin:/usr/local/bin:/usr/sbin:/usr/bin:/sbin:/bin:/usr/games
PWD=/root
LANG=en_US.UTF-8
SHLVL=1
HOME=/root
LOGNAME=root
VISUAL=vi
```

When working from the command line, in some cases you'll need to change some variables. Several of the most relevant variables are listed here:

- MANPATH: A lists of directories where your system will look for man pages.

- PATH: A list of directories that your system will search for executable files.

- HOSTNAME: The name of your computer. When booting, your computer reads this variable from the file /etc/HOSTNAME.

- PS1: The current prompt layout that your computer uses.

- SHELL: The name of the shell the current user is using.

- TERM: The terminal type that is used. This is an important variable, because it defines how text on your console is displayed.

- USER: The name of the current user.

- LANG: The current language settings and what language is used to display items like man pages. This variable is important for international users. POSIX is the setting for US English. If, for example, you want to use the French language, change this setting to fr_FR.UTF-8.

Normally, as a user, you'll get your variables automatically when logging in to the system. The most important source of new variables is the /etc/profile file, a script that is processed for every user who logs in to the system. Want to add a new variable for all users on your system? Add it to the bottom of the /etc/profile file to make sure it is available for all users. You must, however, log in as the system administrator root if you want to do this, if you have some code you want to apply to /etc/profile. Also be aware that changes you make to /etc/profile only become active after you log out and back in to the system.

If you want to make sure that your variable experiments don't cause harm to all users on your system, use the command cd ~ to change to your home directory, and in the directory, create a file with the name .profile. All users can have such a file in their home directories, and it will be treated as an addition to /etc/profile. So if you put a new variable in this file, it will be executed only for the user in whose home directory you inserted this file.

An alternative to the /etc/profile file is /etc/bashrc. This file is processed when a user opens a new shell. That happens for instance if you open a new terminal window from a graphical console. This file also has its counterpart in user home directories, with the name .bashrc. Some Linux distributions store all variables and other shell settings just in the bashrc file, and read this file from /etc/profile as well, to make sure that the settings are executed when users are logging in to the system.

Working with Bash history

Another useful feature of the Bash shell is the history feature, which lets you reuse commands you have recently used. Many distributions will remember the last 1,000 commands that a user has used; in fact the number of commands the shell remembers is defined in a variable itself. The name of this variable is HISTSIZE. The history feature is useful for sessions beyond even the current one. A file, named .bash_ history, is created in the home directory of every user, and this file records the last 1,000 commands that the user has entered. You can see an overview of these commands by entering history at the Bash prompt. Listing 1-10 is an example of this list.

■ **Note**   In addition to the history command, you can also use the up/down arrow keys, page up/down keys, and Ctrl+P/Ctrl+N to browse the history.

Listing 1-10. The history Command Shows a List of All Commands That You Recently Used

```
sander@RNA:~$ history
....
  182   ls -l -h
  183   ls -l --human-readable
  184   clear
  185   ls -l /etc/hosts
  186   ls -R / | less
  187   ls -R
  188   ls -R /
  189   clear
  190   ls -R /
  191   clear
  192   cd /
  193   clear
  194   less /etc/hosts
  195   clear
  196   ls -R / | less
```

```
197   clear
198   mail -s hello root
199   type ls
200   type cd
201   man ls
202   clear
203   ls --help | less
204   history
```

The history feature is especially useful because you can reissue any command from this list without typing it all over again. If you want to run any of the listed (and numbered) commands again, simply type its number preceded by an exclamation mark. In this example, typing **!198** would run mail -s hello root again.

A user can also erase his or her history by using the history command. The most important option offered by this Bash internal command is -c, which clears the history list for that user. This is especially useful because everything that a user types at the command line—such as passwords—is recorded. So use history -c to make sure your history is cleared if you'd rather not have others knowing what you've been up to. Once you use this option, however, you can't use the up arrow key to access previous commands, because those are all erased.

When a user works in a current shell session, the history is kept in memory only. When the shell is normally exited, the history file gets updated. If a shell it closed in a non-regular way, the history file won't get updated. As a user you can manually force the history file to be updated, using the **history -w** command. If you want to make sure you'll never loose your history, it's a good idea to use this command.

Because everything you enter from the command line is saved in the file .bash_history in your home directory, I recommend never entering a plain-text password in the first place, even if you regularly erase the history. Never forget that the history file is also a default keylogger on your Linux system!

Managing Bash with Key Sequences

Sometimes, you'll enter a command from the Bash command line, and either nothing happens at all or something totally unexpected happens. In such an event, it's good to know that some key sequences are available to perform basic Bash management tasks. Here are some of the most useful key sequences:

- *Ctrl+C*: Use this key sequence to quit a command that is not responding (or simply takes too long to complete). This key sequence works in most scenarios where the command is operational and producing output to the screen. In general, Ctrl+C is also a good choice if you absolutely don't have a clue as to what's happening, and you just want to terminate the command that's running in your shell. If used in the shell itself, it will close the shell as well.

- *Ctrl+D*: This key sequence is used to send the "end of file" (EOF) signal to a command. Use this when the command is waiting for more input, which is indicated by the secondary prompt (>). You can also use this key sequence to close a shell session.

- *Ctrl+R*: This is the reversed search feature. It will open the "reversed I-search" prompt, which helps you locate commands that you used previously. The Ctrl+R key sequence searches the Bash history, and the feature is especially useful when working with longer commands. As before, type the first characters of the command, and you will see the last command you've used that started with the same characters.

- *Ctrl+Z*: Some people use Ctrl+Z to stop a command that is running interactively on the console (in the foreground). Although it does stop the command, it does not *terminate* it. A command that is stopped with Ctrl+Z is merely paused, so that you can easily start it in the background using the bg command or in the foreground again with the fg command. To start the command again, you need to refer to the job number that the program is using. You can see a list of these job numbers using the jobs command. You will learn more on running commands in the background in Chapter 7. For the moment, just remember *never* to use this key sequence if you want to stop a command!

EXERCISE 1-3: WORKING WITH THE SHELL

1. Log in as root.

2. Type **echo LANG**. This echoes the text LANG to the STDOUT.

3. Type **echo $LANG**. This echoes the current contents of the language variable to the STDOUT.

4. Type **LANG=fr_FR.UTF-8**. You have now set the language variable to the French language.

5. Type **ls --help**. You'll notice that the output of the command shows in French. Notice that on some distributions the language packages are not installed by default, so you won't see a change in language after doing this.

6. Create a user florence, using the command **useradd -m florence**. Use **passwd florence** to set the password for user florence. Set it to "password"

7. Log in as user florence and type **echo LANG=fr_FR.UTF-8 >> ~/.bashrc**. This appends the LANG variable with its new value to the .bashrc file in this users home directory.

8. Still as florence, type **ls --help**. You'll see the output still in English.

9. Log out, and log back in again as user Florence. Type **ls --help** again. You should now see French language output.

10. Type **echo'** and press Enter. As the command is incomplete, it will show a **>** indicating it is waiting for additional input.

11. Use **Ctrl-C** to stop the command that is waiting.

Summary

In this chapter, you have learned about the essentials you'll need to know to work with Linux. The following topics were covered:

- History of the Linux operating system

- What is open source?

- Differences between distributions

- Logging in to Linux

- Structure of a command, including options and arguments

- Piping and redirection

- Getting help with man and --help

- Working with the shell

Based on the information in this chapter, you now have the basic skills that are required to start using some commands. In the next chapter, you'll learn about some useful commands and the way they work.

CHAPTER 2

■ ■ ■

Performing Essential Command-Line tasks

At this point, you know the basics to get around. One very important topic that you've learned in Chapter 1 is how to get help. Now it's time to expand your command-line skills by exploring some essential Linux commands. In this chapter, you'll learn about the following topics:

- Changing your password

- Working with virtual consoles

- Becoming another user

- Obtaining information about other users

- Communicating with other users

- Exploring the Linux file system

- Working with files and directories

- Using some more Cool commands

Changing Your Password

As a user, you have a password that protects your account. This account includes all your personal settings and files, and therefore needs serious protection. Hence, it is a good idea to change your password regularly to minimize the risk that someone else gets to know your password and can use your credentials to authenticate. When changing a password, make sure it meets the following minimal requirements:

- A password should be long: at least six characters, though eight or more is better.

- Use complexity; mix letters, numbers, and other characters to make the password as difficult to guess as possible.

- Use upper- and lowercase letters.

- Make sure that your password doesn't look like any word in the dictionary. Attackers use "dictionary attacks" in which they feed the entire contents of a dictionary to a brute-force password cracker, and if your password is in the dictionary, they will crack it.

Changing your password is not too hard—just use the passwd command to change your own password. Then, you first have to enter your old password. This is to prevent others from changing your password. Next, enter the new password twice. Also, make sure that your password meets the complexity rules; otherwise it will not be changed. In Listing 2-1, you can see what happens when changing your password.

Listing 2-1. Changing Your Password

```
sander@nuuk:~> passwd
Changing password for sander.
Old Password:
New Password:
Reenter New Password:
Password changed.
```

If you are logged in as root, you can also change the password of other users. If you just want to change the password, that's easy: type **passwd** followed by the name of the user whose password you need to change. It won't ask you for the old password first. Since you are root, you should be able to modify users passwords without knowing the old password. There are also some options that you can use when changing a user's password. Following are the most useful of these options:

- -d: Removes the password for the specified user account.

- -l: Locks an account. Useful if you know that the account is not to be used for a given period.

- -u: Unlocks an account that has been locked with -l.

- -e: Forces the user to change his or her password at the next login.

In Exercise 2-1 you're going to change the password for a user. You'll learn how to use **passwd --stdin** to do this without being prompted, which is convenient if you'd like to change passwords automatically by using a shell script.

EXERCISE 2-1: CHANGING PASSWORDS

1. Log in as root.

2. Type **grep florence /etc/passwd**. The command should show you a line starting with the text florence from /etc/passwd, which is the database of currently existing users.

3. Type **echo secret | passwd --stdin florence**. This will change the password for user florence to secret, without prompting you to enter it twice. In a following exercise you'll test that this password modification has been successful.

Working with Virtual Consoles

On your Linux system, you work from a console. This is either a graphical or a text-based console. All distributions by default offer more than just this one console. They do this by using *virtual consoles*. You can consider a virtual console similar to the dumb terminal that was quite popular in the 1980s. This was a system where multiple screen/keyboard combinations were connected to one central computer that did all the work. Virtual consoles do more or less the same, they offer you more than one login environment, which is especially useful in a nongraphical environment. All virtual consoles are accessed from the same screen though.

Also for a modern Linux user, a virtual console can be very practical. Imagine a system administrator who wants to test a new setting and verify that it works for the user accounts. He or she can use one virtual console to change the setting as system administrator, while testing the setting by logging in as a normal user at another virtual console. Or imagine a developer tweaking the source code of a new program on one virtual console, while debugging the same program at another virtual console. Note that virtual consoles are particularly useful when working on a text-only environment. If your server shows a full graphical environment, you can just open a new terminal window instead.

Most Linux distributions offer six virtual consoles by default. The names of these consoles are tty1 through tty6. You can activate them using Ctrl+Alt+*function key*. So, to access virtual console number tty4, you need to press Ctrl+Alt+F4. If your system has started a graphical environment as well, you can use Ctrl+Alt+F7 or Ctrl-Alt-F1 to get back to the graphical environment. It is up to the descretion of the Linux distribution to decide which key sequence is used for switching back to the graphical environment.

■ **Note**   In a nongraphical environment, you can skip the Ctrl key. So, to switch between tty1 and tty2, pressing Alt+F2 also works. In a graphical environment these keys typically are assigned to other functions.

You may notice that some distributions also use some of the higher-numbered virtual consoles (such as Ctrl+Alt+F10) for logging. Therefore, you should always at least check what happens at the higher-numbered virtual consoles. For instance, SUSE Linux writes kernel log messages to tty10, which can be useful when troubleshooting a problem.

Becoming Another User

There are basically two ways to authenticate to your Linux system: as the root or as a nonroot user. It is good habit not to use root by default. Since root can do anything, a small mistake may have big consequences. As root, you can accidentally destroy everything on your system, and Linux won't ask whether you are sure about this action before wiping out everything on your hard drive (or whatever mistake you are about to make). Therefore, it is a good idea to log in as a normal user and get root permissions only when you really need them. To write a text document, you don't need root permissions (unless it's a configuration file). To change your IP address, however, you do need root permissions.

On Ubuntu, the root account by default cannot log in. Upon installation of Ubuntu, you will have created a user that is a member of the administrators group. All root tasks have to be executed by that user, and they start with **sudo**. So an Ubuntu user would type **sudo passwd florence** for instance, to reset the password of user florence.

To temporary change your identity, you can use the su (substitute user) command. (Ubuntu users: read the upcoming tip!) Its use is not hard; just issue su followed by the name of the user through whose identity you want to work. For instance:

```
su linda
```

would switch your current user account to the user account linda. If you are a normal user, you next have to enter a password. If you are root, this is not necessary (root is almighty, remember?). If you omit the name of the user you want to su to, the command assumes you want to become root. It will next prompt you to enter a password, which in this case is the password of the user root.

■ **Tip**   If you're on Ubuntu, you can't use su just like that. Ubuntu uses the sudo mechanism instead, which is covered in Chapter 6 of this book. Here's a quick-and-dirty method that helps you in using su, even on Ubuntu. It will enable you to execute privileged commands from now on. First, use the command sudo su. When asked for a password, enter the password assigned to your user account. Next, use the command passwd to give the user root a password. From this moment on, you can also log in as root on Ubuntu. If for security reasons you don't like the fact that you can do so, read Chapter 6 for information on how to disable this feature. Until then, the goal is to help you work on the command line, and to do that, you will need root permissions from time to time.

When using su, it is a good idea to use the option - at all times. This option will give you a login shell instead of a subshell. That means that using the - as an option will ensure that the /etc/profile settings are applied. If you don't use a -, this file is not processed, which might mess up your variables. If you don't use the option -, you may still work with some settings that belong to the old user account. To prevent this, use su - at all times. This ensures that you work in the complete environment of the user you are switching to. In Listing 2-2, you can see what happens when a normal user uses su - to take the identity of user root.

Listing 2-2. Switching Identity with su -

```
sander@nuuk:~> su -
Password:
nuuk:~ #
```

When done working as the other user, you can issue exit. This brings you back to your original user environment.

■ **Tip!**   Linux admins typically work on a graphical desktop on top of Linux. To do their work, they would log in to the graphical desktop as a regular user, and open a root shell using the **su -** command. That makes them root in the terminal where they need to do their work, while still being a normal regular user in their default working environment.

Obtaining Information About Other Users

If you are using Linux on your personal computer at home, you are probably the only user who is logged in to it. However, if you are a Linux user at the Linux server in your company, there can be other users as well. In the latter case, it is good to know that several commands are available to help you in getting information about users who are currently connected to the same machine. To start, there is the users command. This command shows a short list of all users currently authenticated with no further details:

```
nuuk:~ # users
linda root root sander
```

If you want more information about the users who are logged in, who is a better option. By default, it shows you not only what users are logged in currently, but also where they are logged in from and at what time they logged in. Listing 2-3 shows the output of who when used without additional options.

Listing 2-3. who Gives More Detailed Information About What Users Are Doing

```
nuuk:~ # who
root      tty1    Dec 10 09:11
sander    pts/0   Dec 10 09:31 (192.168.139.1)
root      pts/1   Dec 10 12:20 (192.168.139.1)
linda     pts/2   Dec 10 12:21 (192.168.139.1)
```

The fact that who shows the IP address of remote users is particularly useful. If, for example, a user is misbehaving himself or herself, the administrator knows from which IP address that user is working, which makes it easier to take corrective measures.

If you want to see what a user is doing, the w command is helpful. This command shows you the names of users, where they are logged in from and at what time, current usage statistics, and what program they currently are using (or have used as the last program). Listing 2-4 gives an overview of w output.

Listing 2-4. Use w If You Want to See What a User Is Doing

```
nuuk:~ # w
 13:17:23 up 4:31,  4 users,   load average: 0.00, 0.00, 0.00
USER    TTY   LOGIN@  IDLE   JCPU   PCPU  WHAT
root    tty1  09:11   4:05m  0.07s  0.07s -bash
sander  pts/0 09:31   1:41m  0.13s  0.05s sshd: sander [priv]
root    pts/1 12:20   0.00s  0.08s  0.00s w
linda   pts/2 12:21   55:43  0.04s  0.04s -bash
```

If you want to get to know as much as possible about other users, try finger (notice that not all distributions install this tool by default). This command gives a summary of the current state of a user account. This includes a lot, including information about the amount of unread mail messages the user has! By default, finger works for local systems only. For a root user it is a useful command to find out about recent activity of users. Listing 2-5 shows an example of its output.

Listing 2-5. The finger command can be used to show more details about users

```
sander@nuuk:~> finger linda
Login: linda                       Name:
Directory: /home/linda        Shell: /bin/bash
On since Wed Dec 10 12:21 (CET) on pts/2, idle 1:00, from 192.168.139.1
Mail last read Wed Dec 10 13:21 2015 (CET)
No Plan.
```

EXERCISE 3-2: VIRTUAL CONSOLES AND USER INFORMATION

1. Use the Ctrl+Alt+F2 key sequence to open a virtual console.

2. Log in a user florence, using the password "secret".

3. Type **w** to see who else is currently logged in on this system.

4. Compare the output of this command with the output of the **who** command.

5. Type **lastlog**. Notice that even if you're not the root user, you'll see information about the last login time for all users on this system.

6. Still as florence, type **finger root** to get information about the root account. You'll see why many administrators don't like this command too much on their servers.

7. Type **su -** to open a root.

8. Type **exit** to close the root shell again.

Communicating with Other Users

From the Linux command line, you have some communication options as well. Some commands allow you to communicate in real time, providing chat functionality, while others are provided to allow you to send e-mail.

Real-Time Communication

On Linux, there are two options to communicate with other users in real time. You can use `write` to talk to an individual user. If you want to send a message to all users, you can use `wall`. If you don't want to receive messages from other users, use the `mesg` command to switch message reception off or on.

Individual Chat Sessions with `write`

If you want to chat in real time with another user on the system, you can use `write`. This command is provided for communication between two users. Its use is fairly simple: initiate a `write` session to another by using the `write` command followed by the name of the user you want to talk to. For instance, the following command would initiate a session from the current user to user linda:

```
write linda
```

Next, `write` opens a prompt after which the user can type text. This text is displayed line by line on the terminal of the other user. No matter what the user is doing, the text will be displayed, as long as the user has a terminal session that is open. If a user receives a `write` message from another user, he or she can reply to that by opening his or her own `write` session. As an illustration, the following procedure demonstrates how root and linda initiate and terminate a `write` session:

1. User linda opens the `write` session to root, using the command `write root`. This opens the `write` prompt, from which linda can type her text:

   ```
   linda@nuuk:~> write root
   write: root is logged in more than once; writing to pts/1
   hi root, I'm having a problem.
   ```

2. At this moment, root receives linda's message at his console. To reply, he has to press Enter to put away linda's message first, and then enter the command `write linda`. Next, he can type his message, thereby establishing an active chat session with linda:

   ```
   nuuk:~ #
   Message from linda@nuuk on pts/2 at 13:35 ...
   hi root, I'm having a problem.
   ```

```
nuuk:~ # write linda
hi linda, how can I help you
We'll, my mouse doesn't react anymore
```

3. At the end of the session, both parties that are involved have to use the Ctrl+C key sequence to terminate the session. This will bring them back to their prompts, where they can continue their normal work.

Writing to all Users

Another tool for real-time communication is wall. This stands for write all, and you can probably guess that this tool is used to write a message to all users. It works in more or less the same way as write: after entering wall, the user who invokes wall writes a message, which is terminated by using the Ctrl+D key sequence. This message will show on the console of all users who are currently logged in. It needs no explanation that you should use this tool with care, as it is very annoying for users to receive wall messages frequently. In Listing 2-6, you can see an example of a wall session.

Listing 2-6. Writing a Message to All Users with wall

```
nuuk:~ # wall
I'll shut down the system in 5 minutes

Broadcast Message from root@nuuk
        (/dev/pts/1) at 15:27 ...

I'll shut down the system in 5 minutes
```

With wall, you can also send the contents of a text file to other users. For instance, wall /tmp/mymessage.txt would send the contents of mymessage.txt to all users who are currently connected. This function is useful for a system administrator who wants to send a longer message to all users.

Disabling Real-Time Messages

If you don't want to receive any messages from other users, use the mesg command. This command works with two arguments only. mesg n makes sure that no one can write messages to your console. If you want to open your console again for messages from other users, use mesg y.

Sending Mail from the Command Line

You may think that in order to send mail, you need a full-scale mail client, such as Thunderbird, Evolution, or Windows Mail. The Linux command line, however, also has a mail client, which you can invoke from the command line by using the mail command. I wouldn't recommend replacing your normal mail client by mail, but if you want to send a message to an Internet or local user, or if you want to read system mail, the mail command offers an excellent solution to do that.

▓ **Note**　You can use the mail command to send mail to Internet users, but this requires DNS to be set up properly on your Linux machine and an SMTP process running. Notice that Ubuntu does not install smtp by default, if you want to use **mail** on Ubuntu, install it first using **apt-get install dhcpclient**.

To send a mail message to another user, you invoke the command as `mail` *user*, where *user* is the name of a local user (e.g., `mail root`) or a user on the Internet (e.g., `mail someone@example.com`). Next, the `mail` program opens an interface where you first enter the subject, followed by the body of the mail message. When finished writing the mail body, you type a dot on a separate line and press Enter. This will tell the mail client that you're done and offer the mail message to the SMTP process on your machine, which will take care of delivering it to the correct user. In Listing 2-7, you can see what happens when using the `mail` command from the command line.

Listing 2-7. Sending Messages with the `mail` Utility

```
nuuk:~ # mail linda
Subject: 4 PM meeting
Hi Linda, can we meet at 4 PM?

Thanks,
root
.
EOT
```

You can also run the `mail` utility completely from the command line, without it opening an interface that has you input text. This, for example, is very useful if you want shell scripts or scheduled jobs to send a message automatically if a certain error condition occurs. In these cases, the body of the mail message is not very important; you probably just want to deliver a mail message with a certain subject to the user. The next command shows you how to do this: it sends a message with the text "something is wrong" to the user root. Also, take notice of the `< .` construction. Normally, the `mail` command would expect a dot on a line on its own to indicate that the message is complete. By using input redirection with `< .`, the dot is provided on the command line.

```
mail -s "something is wrong" root < .
```

The `mail` command has some other useful options as well for sending mail:

- *-a filename*: Allows you to add a file as an attachment to your message.

- *-c cc-addr*: Specifies the name of a user you want to send a copy of the message to.

- *-b bcc-addr*: Sends a blind copy to a user. The recipient of the mail cannot see that you've sent a copy to this user also.

- *-R reply-addr*: Allows you to specify the reply address. A reply to this mail message is automatically sent to this reply address.

Apart from sending mail, you can read mail messages also with the `mail` utility. The utility, however, is meant to read system mail and is not a good choice to read your POP or IMAP mail from the mail server of your Internet provider. When invoking mail to read your system messages, you should just type **mail**. In reply, the mail client shows a list of mail messages that are waiting for you (see Listing 2-8).

Listing 2-8. Just Type mail to Display a List of All Mail Messages That Are Waiting for You

```
nuuk:~ # mail
mailx version nail 11.25 7/29/05.  Type ? for help.
"/var/mail/root": 5 messages 5 unread
>U  1 root@nuuk.sander.g   Wed  Nov 19 15:13   20/661   Meeting at 10 AM
 U  2 root@nuuk.sander.g   Fri  Nov 21 09:48   20/661   10 AM meeting   cancelled
```

CHAPTER 2 ■ PERFORMING ESSENTIAL COMMAND-LINE TASKS

```
U  3  root@nuuk.sander.g   Fri  Dec  5 10:44   20/661   Nice day for Dutch users
U  4  root@nuuk.sander.g   Fri  Dec  5 12:28   19/568   hello
U  5  root@nuuk.sander.g   Wed  Dec 10 08:48   20/661   Wanna go for coffee?
?
```

To read a message, just enter the message number, and you will see its text. When finished reading the message, press q to quit. After closing a message that you've read, you can type the reply command from within the mail interface to send a reply to the user who sent the message, or type delete, followed by the message number to delete the message from your system. Next, type quit to exit the mail interface.

Finding Your Way in the File System

Now that you know how to log in to your server, it is time to get more familiar with the way a Linux file system is organized with default files and directories. Even nowadays, it is still very important that you know your way around the file system; this is because Linux is still a file system–centric operating system. Even if you want to work only from the graphical environment, you must know where you can find all important files on your server. Knowing where to find files and directories will absolutely make working on the Linux command line easier.

Default Directories

All Linux distributions use more or less the same approach in organizing the directory structure on a system. This means that certain directories will always be present, no matter what distribution you are using. You may encounter small differences between distributions though. In this section, you'll learn what default directories exist and what kinds of files you'll find in these directories.

■ **Tip!**   All the default directories are documented in **man hier**. Read this man page for a full and actual description of the default directories and their use.

On most Linux systems, you'll find the following default directories (notice that minor differences may exist between distributions):

- /: The root directory is the starting point of your Linux file system. All other directories on your system exist in the root directory.

- /bin: This is the location where you find program files (binaries) accessible to all users. These are essential binaries that must be available at all times, even if there is a problem with other parts of your system. For that reason, the directory /bin is always on the root partition. In it you will find essential utilities and commands like /bin/bash (the shell), cp (used to copy files), and many more.

- /sbin: In this directory you will find binaries for the system administrator. These are critical binaries that must be available at all times in case you need to repair your system. In this directory, you will find commands and utilities you'd rather not see in the hands of your users, like the general system management tool yast2, or the partitioning tool fdisk.

- /boot: This directory contains everything you need to boot your server. One of the most important things that you'll find in this directory is the kernel; this is the file with the name vmlinuz. (On some distributions, the version number is appended to the file name.) Other vital components are present as well, and the thing all of these have in common is that your server needs them to start.

- /dev: On a Linux system, all hardware you work with corresponds with a file on your system. If you want to address the hardware, you have to address the corresponding file. Notice that you'll need root permissions to do so though. You can find all these device files in the directory /dev. You will find, for example, a device called /dev/cdrom that refers to the optical drive that might be present in your system. Other important device files are /dev/sda, which typically refers to your hard disk, or /dev/null, which you can use to redirect error messages to.

- /etc: Most services running on Linux use an ASCII text file to store all necessary configuration. These text files are kept in the directory /etc. In this directory, you will find some important configuration files like /etc/passwd, which contains the database of local Linux users.

- /home: The personal files of a user are stored in his or her home directory, no matter if you are working on a Linux server or a personal desktop. The directory /home is used to store each user's home directory. When installing a Linux system, it may be wise to put this directory on a partition on its own to separate user data files from operating system components. That minimizes the risk that you'll lose all your personal files if something happens to the installation of your operating system.

- /lib: Many programs that are used in a Linux environment share some of their code. This shared code is stored in different library files. All the libraries needed by binaries that are in a subdirectory of your file system root are in the directory /lib. You will also find some other important modules in this directory, like the driver modules that are used by the kernel of your server. For 64 bits library files, a directory with the name /lib64 exists.

- /media: On a Linux system, to access files that are not on the hard disk of your computer, you need to make the medium accessible. You do this by mounting it (mounting devices is explained in more detail in Chapter 3). When you mount a CD-ROM, for example, you connect it to a directory on your file system. This must be a directory that exists before you start mounting anything. The default directory that is used for regular mounts on most distributions is /media. In this directory, a subdirectory is created automatically when a new removable device is detected. CDs as well as USB sticks will appear here (and on the graphical desktop as well) once they are mounted with the label of the device used as the name of the directory where the device is mounted.

- /mnt: On older Linux systems, /mnt was the default directory for mounting devices. On more recent systems, this has been replaced by the /media directory. However, /mnt still has a purpose: it is used for mounts that don't occur very often and which are created manually, such as a mount to a server that has to be accessed only once. The /mnt directory is ideal for testing purposes.

- /usr: This directory is probably the largest directory on your system. Here you can find almost all user-accessible files. Some people like to compare it to the Program Files directory on a Windows system. Because there are so many files in this directory, inside it you will find an entire structure of subdirectories, including /usr/bin, in which most programs are stored and /usr/src, where you can put the source files of the open source programs and kernel you use. Because there are so many files in the /usr directory, it is quite usual to put it on its own partition.

■ **Tip**   Have you always wanted to find out how much space a directory occupies on your hard disk? Use du -hs from a console environment. It will show you the disk usage of a specified directory. The normal output of this command is in blocks; the parameter -h presents the output in a human-readable form. The option -s makes sure that you see the summary for the selected directory only, and not how much disk space every individual file uses. For example, use du -hs /usr to find out exactly how much space is occupied by /usr. In Listing 2-9, you can see the result of the du -h /usr command.

Listing 2-9. Use du -hs to Find Out How Much Disk Space a Directory and Its Contents Occupy

```
nuuk:/ # du -hs /usr
1.8G    /usr
```

- /opt: In /usr you will find a lot of binaries. Many of these are small software packages. Normally, large software installations, such as office suites and other large programs, are stored in /opt. For example, the Gnome graphical interface, the OpenOffice suite, or the Oracle database (if installed) could be subdirectories of this directory. There seems to be no good concensus about the use of this directory, so you may find some of these packages in /usr as well.

- /proc: This is a strange directory, because it doesn't really exist on the hard disk of your computer. /proc is an interface to the memory of your computer. An advanced administrator can use it to tune the workings of the computer and get information about its current status. You can find a lot of information about your computer in the files in this directory. For example, try the command cat /proc/cpuinfo to show the contents of the text file /proc/cpuinfo (you must be root to do this). This command will show you a lot of information about the processor(s) in your computer, as you can see in Listing 2-10.

Listing 2-10. Use cat /proc/cpuinfo to Get Information About Features Your Computer's CPU Is Using

```
nuuk:/ # cat /proc/cpuinfo
processor       : 0
vendor_id       : GenuineIntel
cpu family      : 6
model           : 15
model name      : Intel(R) Core(TM)2 Duo CPU T7500 @ 2.20GHz
stepping        : 8
cpu MHz         : 2201.481
cache size      : 4096 KB
fdiv_bug        : no
```

```
hlt_bug          : no
f00f_bug         : no
coma_bug         : no
fpu              : yes
fpu_exception    : yes
cpuid level      : 10
wp               : yes
flags            : fpu vme de pse tsc msr pae mce cx8 apic sep mtrr pge mca
                   cmov pat pse36 clflush dts acpi mmx fxsr sse sse2 ss nx
                   constant_tsc pni ds_cpl ida
bogomips         : 4417.91
```

- /root: Ordinary users have their home directories in /home. A system administrator is not a normal user; in a UNIX environment, the system administrator is therefore respectfully called "superuser." Since this user may have some important tools in his or her home directory, this directory is not in /home with those of the other users. Instead, the user root uses /root as his or her home directory. There is a good reason for this: on many servers the directory /home is on a separate partition. If for any reason you cannot access this partition anymore, user root at least still has access to his or her home directory, in which he or she has probably stored some important files.

- /run: This directory is used for run-time configuration. Within this directory, separate subdirectories can be created for different users and processes and each of these can create files in these subdirectories. Files in /run are typically removed automatically when they are no longer needed.

- /srv: On some distributions, you will find all files from some important services in this directory. For example, it is used to store your entire web server and FTP server file structures on SUSE Linux. Some distributions, such as Red Hat and derivatives, don't use /srv but store this type of information in /var.

- /sys: This directory can be used to store information about the state of your system. Its use is like the use of /proc, with the difference that the information in /sys is kept on the hard disk of your server, so it is still available after you have rebooted it. The information in /sys is more directly related to the hardware you are using on your server, whereas /proc is used to store information about the current state of the kernel.

- /tmp: As the name suggests, /tmp is used for temporary files. This is the only directory on the entire system where every user can write to. This is, however, a bad idea, because the content of this directory can be wiped out automatically by any process or user without any warning being issued before that happens. It is common to use a RAM file system for the /tmp directory, to make sure it is fast and cleaned automatically upon reboot.

- /var: This last directory you will find on any Linux computer. This directory contains mostly files that are created by your system whose content can grow very fast. For example, think of spooling of print jobs—these are found in this directory. Also very common is /var/log, the directory that is used by rsyslog to write log files about events that have occurred on a Linux computer.

Working with the Linux File System

On a Linux system, everything is treated as a file. Even a device like your hard disk is addressed by pointing to a file (which, for your information, has the name /dev/sda in most cases). Therefore, to handle Linux well, it is important that you can find your way in the Linux file system. In this section, you'll learn the basics of working with the file system (more details are in Chapter 3). The following subjects are covered:

- Working with directories
- Working with files

Working with Directories

On Linux, directories are used as is the case with folders on Windows. Because files are normally organized in directories, it is important that you know how to handle them. This involves a few commands:

- pwd: Use this to show your current directory. It will display the complete directory path reference, which always starts at the root directory:

    ```
    nuuk:~ # pwd
    /root
    ```

- cd: Once you know what your current directory is, you can change to another directory using the cd command. When using cd, you should be aware of some features in the Linux file system:

    - Linux file and directory names are case sensitive. Hence, bin and BIN are not the same!

    - If you want to go to a directory that is directly under the root directory, make sure to put a / in front of the directory name. Without the slash, this command will try to find the directory as a subdirectory in the current directory.

- The cd command has one argument only: the name of the directory you want to go to. For instance, the following command brings you to the directory /usr/bin, which is directly under the root directory of the file system:

    ```
    cd /usr/bin
    ```

■ **Tip**   Switching between directories? Use cd - to return to the last directory you were in. Also good to know: if you just type **cd**, the cd command brings you to your home directory.

- mkdir: If you need to create a new directory, use mkdir. For instance, the following would create a directory named files in the directory /tmp:

    ```
    mkdir /tmp/files
    ```

- With mkdir you can create a complete directory structure in one command as well, which is something you can't do on other operating systems. For example, the command mkdir /some/directory will fail if /some does not already exist. In that case, you can force mkdir to create /some as well: do this by using the mkdir -p /some/directory command.

- rmdir: The rmdir command is used to remove directories. However, this isn't the most useful command, because it works only on directories that are already empty. If the directory still has files and/or subdirectories in it, use rm -r, or better, rm -rf, which makes sure that you'll never get a prompt for confirmation. It's best to be sure what you're doing when using this option

Working with Files

An important task from the command line is managing the files in the directories. Four important commands are used for this purpose:

- ls lists files.

- rm removes files.

- cp copies files.

- mv moves files.

Listing Files with ls

The generic syntax of ls is not too hard:

ls [*options*] *filename*

For instance, the following would show all files in the directory /usr, displaying their properties as well:

ls -l /usr

See Listing 2-11 for an example. In this example you can see that different columns are used to show the attributes of the files:

- *File type*: The very first letter shows the file type. If a - is displayed, it is a regular file. In this example, you can see one file that has the d type. This is not a regular file, but a directory.

- *Permissions*: Directly after the file type, you can see the permissions assigned to the file. There are nine positions that show you the file permissions. In Chapter 7, you'll learn much more about them.

- *Ownership*: On Linux, every file has a user owner and a group owner. In the following example, they are set to user root and group root for all files.

- *File size*: Next to the group owner, the size of the file is displayed.

- *Creation date and time*: For every file, creation date and time are shown as well.

- *File name*: In the last column of ls -l output, you can see the name of the file.

Listing 2-11. *Example Output of* ls -l

```
root@RNA:/boot# ls -l
total 10032
-rw-r--r-- 1       root root      414210 2007-04-15 02:19 abi-2.6.20-15-server
-rw-r--r-- 1       root root       83298 2007-04-15 00:33 config-2.6.20-15-server
drwxr-xr-x 2       root root        4096 2007-07-29 02:51 grub
-rw-r--r-- 1       root root     6805645 2007-06-05 04:15 initrd.img-2.6.20-15-server
-rw-r--r-- 1       root root       94600 2006-10-20 05:44 memtest86+.bin
-rw-r--r-- 1       root root      812139 2007-04-15 02:20 System.map-2.6.20-15-server
-rw-r--r-- 1       root root     1763308 2007-04-15 02:19 vmlinuz-2.6.20-15-server
-rw-r--r-- 1       root root      240567 2007-03-24 10:03 xen-3.0-i386.gz
```

Apart from the option -l, ls has many other options as well. An especially useful one is the -d option, and the following example shows why. When working with the ls command, wildcards can be used. So, ls * will show a list of all files in the current directory, ls /etc/*a.* will show a list of all files in the directory /etc that have an "a" followed by a dot somewhere in the file name, and ls [abc]* will show a list of all files whose names start with either an "a," "b," or "c" in the current directory. But something strange happens without the option -d. If a directory matches the wildcard pattern, the entire contents of that directory are displayed as well. This doesn't really have any useful application, so you should always use the -d option with ls when using wildcards. Some of the most useful options that you can use with ls are listed here:

- -a: Also show files whose name starts with a dot. Normal users will not see these by default, as files whose names start with a dot are hidden files.

- -l: Provide a long listing. This shows properties of files as well, not just file names.

- -d: Shows the names of directories and not their contents.

- -R: Shows the contents of subdirectories as well.

- -t: Sort files by access time.

- -h: Indicates human readable. This mentions file sizes in kilobytes, megabytes, or gigabytes, instead of just bytes, which is the default setting. Use this option with the -l option only.

- -S: Sorts files by file size. This option is useful only when used together with the option -l.

■ **Note**   A hidden file is a file whose name starts with a period. Most configuration files that are stored in user home directories are created as hidden files to prevent the user from deleting the file by accident.

Removing Files with rm

Cleaning up the file system is another task that needs to be performed regularly, and for this you'll use the rm command. For example, rm /tmp/somefile removes somefile from the /tmp directory. If you are root or if you have all the proper permissions on the file, you will succeed without any problem. (See Chapter 7 for more on permissions.) Removing files can be a delicate operation (imagine removing the wrong files), so it may be necessary to push the rm command a little to convince it that it really has to remove everything. You can do this by using the -f (force) switch (but only if you really are *quite* sure you want to do so). For example, use rm -f somefile if the command complains that somefile cannot be removed for some reason. Conversely, to stay on the safe side, you can also use the -i option to rm, which makes the command interactive. When using this option, rm will ask for every file that it is about to remove if you really want to remove it.

The rm command can be used to wipe entire directory structures as well; in this case the -r option has to be used. If this option is combined with the -f option, the command will become very powerful and even dangerous. For example, use rm -rf /somedir to clear out the entire content of /somedir, including the directory /somedir itself.

Obviously, you should be very careful when using rm this way, especially because a small typing mistake can have serious consequences. Imagine, for example, that you type rm -rf / somedir (with a space between / and somedir) instead of rm -rf /somedir. The rm command will first remove everything in the root of the file system, represented by the directory / and, when it is finished with that, it will remove somedir as well. Hopefully, you understand that the second part of the command is no longer required once the first part of the command has completed.

The rm command also has some useful options:

- -r: Recursive, removes files from all subdirectories as well

- -f: Force, doesn't ask anything, just removes what the user asks to remove

- -i: Interactive, asks before removing a file

- -v: Verbose, shows what is happening

In Listing 2-12, you can see what happens when removing the contents of a directory with all its subdirectories with the options -ivR. As you can see, it is not a very practical way of removing all files, but at least you'll be sure not to remove anything by accident.

Listing 2-12. Removing Files with rm -ivR *

```
nuuk:/test # rm -ivR *
rm: descend into directory `etc'? y
rm: remove regular file `etc/fstab'? y
removed `etc/fstab'
rm: descend into directory `etc/udev'? y
rm: descend into directory `etc/udev/rules.d'? y
rm: remove regular file `etc/udev/rules.d/65-cdrom.rules'? y
removed `etc/udev/rules.d/65-cdrom.rules'
rm: remove regular file `etc/udev/rules.d/31-network.rules'? y
removed `etc/udev/rules.d/31-network.rules'
rm: remove regular file `etc/udev/rules.d/56-idedma.rules'?
```

■ **Caution**   Be *very* careful using potentially destructive commands like rm. There is no good undelete mechanism for the Linux command line, and, if you ask Linux to do something, it doesn't ask whether you to confirm (unless you use the -i option).

Copying Files with `cp`

If you need to copy files from one location in the file system to another, use the `cp` command. This command is straightforward and easy to use; the basic structure of this command is as follows:

`cp source destination`

As *source*, you typically specify the name of a directory, files, or a file pattern (like * to refer to all files). For example, use `cp ~/* /tmp` to copy all files from your home directory to the /tmp directory. As you can see, in this example I introduced a new item: the tilde (~). The shell interprets this symbol as a way to refer to the current user's home directory (normally /home/*username* for ordinary users and /root for the user root). If subdirectories and their contents need to be included in the `cp` command as well, use the option -r.

The `cp` command has some useful options, some of which are listed here:

- -a: Archive; use this option to make sure that all properties of the files you copy are copied as well. Use this if you want to make sure that permissions and other file properties are copied correctly.

- -b: Backup; if your `cp` command will overwrite an existing destination file, this option makes sure that a backup is created of this destination file first.

- -f: Force; if a file at the destination prohibits you from copying your file, this option will force the copy. This means that the destination file is overwritten and `cp` tries again.

- -i: Interactive; when using this option, `cp` asks before overwriting an existing file at the destination location.

- -p: Preserve; when using this option, `cp` makes sure that attributes of the file, such as owners and permissions, are copied as well.

- -r: Recursive; this option makes sure that directories are copied recursively.

- -u: Update; this very useful option only copies if the destination file is older than the source file, or if the destination file does not exist.

You should be aware that by default the **cp** command does not copy hidden files. It just copies regular files. To copy hidden files, you need to refer to the hidden files specifically. The command **cp .*** ~ for instance would copy all hidden files, as the first argument refers to all files that have a name starting with a dot. In exercise 2.3 you'll also learn a convenient way to copy hidden files.

Moving Files with `mv`

Sometimes you need to copy your files, at other times you need to move them to a new location. This means that the file is removed from its source location and placed in the target location. The syntax of the `mv` command that you use for this purpose is comparable to the syntax of `cp`:

`mv source destination`

For example, use `mv ~/somefile /tmp/otherfile` to move the `somefile` file to /tmp. If a subdirectory with the name `otherfile` already exists in the /tmp directory, `somefile` will be created in this subdirectory. If /tmp has no directory with this name, the command will save the contents of the original `somefile` under its new name `otherfile` in the /tmp directory.

The mv command also does more than just move files. You can use it to rename files, as well as directories, regardless of whether there are any files in those directories. If, for example, you need to rename the directory /somedir to /somethingelse, use mv /somedir /somethingelse.

EXERCISE 2-3: WORKING WITH FILES

1. Open a root shell.

2. Type **mkdir /data/files**. It will give you an error message, as the /data directory doesn't exist yet.

3. To create the entire path that is specified as an argument to **mkdir**, use **mkdir -p /data/files**. This will create the directory /data as well as its subdirectory /files.

4. Type **pwd**. This shows your current directory, which should be **/root**.

5. Type **ls** and compare its output to **ls -a**. The latter command also shows all hidden files.

6. Type **cp /root /data/files**.

7. Use **ls -al /data/files/*.** (don't include the dot in your command) You'll see that nothing has been copied.

8. Use **cp -R /root /data/files** and check the contents of /data/files again. You'll see that only files that are not hidden files have been copied.

9. Remove the contents of /data/files, using **rm -f /data/files/***

10, Type **cp -R /root/. /data/files** and check the contents of /data/files again. You'll now see that also the hidden files have been copied.

Cool Commands

Some commands don't really fit into a certain theme, but are just cool and useful. In this final section, you'll learn about these commands. I'll give a short description of the following commands:

- `cal`
- `clear`
- `uname`
- `wc`
- `date`

Displaying a Calendar with `cal`

Want to know if Christmas 2018 is in a weekend? Linux has a cool utility to help you with that: `cal`. If you just type **cal**, this utility will show you the calendar of the current month. You can, however, also include a year or a month and a year as its arguments to display the calendar for a given month or a specific year. For example, the command `cal 12 2018` shows you the calendar for December 2018 (see Listing 2-13).

Listing 2-13. With cal You Can Show the Calendar for a Specific Month or Year

```
nuuk:/test # cal 12 2018
    December 2018
Su  Mo  Tu  We  Th  Fr  Sa
                         1
 2   3   4   5   6   7   8
 9  10  11  12  13  14  15
16  17  18  19  20  21  22
23  24  25  26  27  28  29
30  31
```

Clearing Your Screen with clear

Want to clear your screen so that you can see in a better way what you are doing? Use clear to do that. This command takes no argument—just typing **clear** will do the job. You may also prefer to use the key sequence Ctrl+L, which does exactly the same.

Displaying System Information with uname and hostname

In some cases you need to know more about your system. For this purpose, you can use the uname command. When using it without any arguments, it will just show you what kind of kernel you are using. This will normally be a Linux kernel, and that information might not be too useful as you probably already were aware of using Linux. However, you can also use uname to display what kernel version you are using (uname -r), or what type of CPU you are using (uname -p). And if you just want to see all there is to show about your computer, use uname -a. An example of this command is shown in Listing 2-14.

Listing 2-14. Showing System Information with uname -a

```
[root@server1 files]# uname -a
Linux server1.example.com 3.10.0-123.el7.x86_64 #1 SMP Mon Jun 30 12:09:22 UTC 2014 x86_64
x86_64 x86_64 GNU/Linux
```

You may have noticed that uname shows a lot of information, but it doesn't tell you what the name of your computer is. For this purpose, better use the hostname command. If you use it without arguments, it just shows the short host name, which is probably the same as what you already see at your computer's shell prompt. If you also want to see the name of the DNS domain that your computer is in, use hostname -f.

Counting Words, Lines, and Characters with wc

In some situations, it is useful to know how many words there are in a file. For this purpose, Linux has the wc (wordcount) command. It will not only show you words, but also characters and lines that are in the target file. Its use is easy:

```
wc filename
```

The result looks like what you see in Listing 2-15. It first shows you lines, followed by the number of words and the number of characters in the file. The **wc** command is also useful in a pipe. Some Linux commands generate a lot of output. Before starting to scroll up, you might want to check how much output really is produced. You can find out by piping the output of the command to **wc**, and you'll see exactly how many lines, words and characters this command has produced.

Listing 2-15. Counting Lines, Words, and Characters in a File with wc

```
nuuk:/ # wc /etc/hosts
 23 77 683 /etc/hosts
```

Changing and Showing Date and Time with date

At the end of the working day, you probably want to know when it is time to go home. The date command helps you with this. When used without arguments, this command shows you the current date and time, but you can also use arguments to change the time or date. For instance, date -s 14:48 sets the time to 2:48 p.m. You can also work with an mmddhhmm argument to change month, date, hour, and minute. For instance, the command date 12111449 sets the current date and time to 2:49 on December 11.

Summary

In this chapter, you've acquired some important basic skills to work with Linux on the command line. You have first learned all there is to know about your session on the Linux computer. This includes logging in and out, working with virtual consoles, and working as another user. Next, you've learned how to work together with other users. You've read how you can find out which users are connected to the system and how you can communicate with those users. Following that, you've read how to work with files and directories. Finally, at the end of this chapter, you've learned about some other useful commands. The following commands were covered in this chapter:

- passwd: Change passwords.
- su: Become another user.
- users: See who is connected.
- who: See who is connected.
- w: See who is connected.
- finger: Get information about a user.
- write: Send a real-time message to one user.
- wall: Send a real-time message to all users.
- mesg: Disable or enable reception of real-time messages.
- mail: Send e-mail to other users.
- du: See how much disk space a directory occupies.
- cat: Show contents of a text file.
- pwd: Print working directory.
- cd: Change to another directory.
- mkdir: Make a directory.
- rmdir: Remove a directory.
- ls: List files.
- rm: Remove files.

- cp: Copy files.

- mv: Move files.

- cal: Show a calendar.

- clear: Clear screen.

- uname: Show system information.

- wc: Count words, lines, and characters in a text file.

- date: Show and change current date and time.

In the next chapter, you'll get some more details about working with the Linux file system.

CHAPTER 3

■ ■ ■

Administering the Linux File System

In Chapter 2, you've read about some of the basic tasks that you may want to accomplish when working with a Linux system. In this chapter, you'll read about some of the more advanced tasks. Typically, these are tasks that you would use to administer and tune your Linux computer. First, you'll learn how to mount devices on your computer and how to make sure that devices are mounted automatically when booting. Next, you'll read how to create backups of files and directories with the tar utility, and of complete devices using dd. At the end of this chapter, you'll discover the benefits of working with links.

Mounting Disks

On a Linux computer, devices are not always mounted automatically. Therefore, you must know how to mount a device manually. Especially if you are a server administrator who needs to connect his or her computer to external storage, knowledge about the mount procedure is very important. This also holds true for more common situations, for instance, when you have to connect a USB key and it doesn't mount automatically.

Using the mount Command

To mount devices manually, you use the mount command. The basic syntax of this command is easy to understand:

```
mount /what /where
```

For the *what* part, you specify a device name, and, for the *where* part, you provide a directory. In principle, any directory can be used, but it doesn't make sense to mount a device just anywhere (for example, on /usr) because doing so will temporarily make all other files in that directory unavailable.

Therefore, on Linux, two directories are created as default mount points. These are the directories that you would typically use to mount devices. The first of these is the directory /mnt. This is typically the directory that you would use for a mount that happens only occasionally, such as if you want to test whether some device is really mountable. The second of these directories is /media, where you would mount devices that are connected on a more regular basis. You would mount a CD or DVD in that directory with the following command:

```
mount /dev/cdrom /media/
```

If a graphical user interface is used, mounts are created automatically when devices are inserted. If for instance you're inserting an optical drive on a computer that has a GNOME graphical interface that is currently running, it will be mounted under /media, in a directory that corresponds with the name of the label on the optical drive. On newer distributions, these mounts are created in /run/$USER/media/$LABEL, which makes it easier to distnguish between mounts created by different users.

The mount command lets you mount devices like CDs or DVDs, but network shares can also be mounted with this command. You just have to be more specific. If, for example, you want to mount a share named myshare that is offered by a Windows computer named lor, you would use the following command:

```
mount -t cifs -o username=yourname //lor/myshare /mnt
```

■ **Note**   The syntax in the preceding command can be used to access a share that is offered by a Windows computer, but you can also use it to access a share that is offered by a Samba file server. Samba is a service that you can run on top of any Linux computer to offer Windows-like file services.

You'll notice in this last example that some extra options were used:

- First, the file system to be used is mentioned. The mount command is perfectly capable of determining the file system for local devices by just looking at the administration that exists in the beginning of every file system. But, if you're trying to mount a share that is offered by a computer on the network, you really need to specify the file system. This is because the mount command needs to know what type of file system it is before being able to access it. In the example of the share on a Windows machine, because you want to mount on a Windows file system, the cifs file system type is used. You can use this file system type also to access shares on a Samba server.

- The next option you need to access a share on a Samba file computer is the name of the user who performs the mount. This must be the name of a valid user account on the other system.

- Third, the name of the share is given. In the prior example, a computer name (lor) is used, but, if your system has problems working with computer names, an IP address can be used just as well. The computer name is followed by the name of the share.

- Finally, the name of the directory where the mount has to be created is given. In this example, I've mounted it on /mnt, because this is a mount that you would perform only occasionally. If it were a mount you used on a more regular basis, you would create a mount point anywhere in the file system. The directory /srv is often used for this purpose. In this case, it would make sense to use the directory /srv/lor.

In Table 3-1, you can see a list of some of the most popular devices that you typically want to mount on a regular basis.

Table 3-1. *Mounting Popular Devices*

Device	Address As	Remarks
Floppy disk	/dev/fd0	Because modern computers rarely have more than one floppy device drive, the floppy drive (if present) will be fd0. If more than one drive is available, use fd1, and so on.
Hard drives	/dev/sdX	Depending on the bus the hard drive is installed on, you will see it as /dev/hdX (legacy IDE) or /dev/sdX (SCSI and SATA). X is replaced by "a" for the first drive, "b" for the second drive, and so on. Notice that normally you don't mount a complete hard drive, but a file system on a partition on the hard drive. The partition on the drive is referred to by a number, /dev/sda1 for the first partition on an SCSI hard drive, and so on. In Chapter 5, you'll find more information about partitions and ways to lay out your hard drive.
USB drives	/dev/sdX	USB drives (including USB keys) appear on the SCSI bus. Typically, you'll see them as "the next" SCSI disk. So, if you already have an sda, the USB device will appear as sdb. The USB drive normally has a partition on it. To mount it, you must mount this partition. The numbering of partitions on USB drives works like the numbering of partitions on normal hard drives (from the Linux kernel perspective, there isn't really a difference between these two different device types). So to mount the partition on a USB drive that has become available as /dev/sdb, you would typically use mount /dev/sdb1 /somewhere (don't forget to replace somewhere with the name of an existing directory).
Optical drives	/dev/sr0	On modern computers, you'll find the optical drive as /dev/sr0. To make it easier for you, your distribution will create a symbolic link (you can compare this to a shortcut) with the name /dev/cdrom or /dev/dvd. By addressing this symbolic link, you can address the real name of the device.
Tape drives	/dev/st0	Typically, a tape drive is installed at the SCSI bus and can be mounted as /dev/st0.
Hard disks in virtual machines	/dev/vdX	In Linux KVM virtual machines, the hard drive is presented by the /dev/vdX device. Naming conventions follow those of /dev/sdX.
Windows shares	//computer/share	Use // followed by the computer name, followed by the share. Additional options are required, such as -t cifs to indicate the type of file system to be used and -o username=yourusername to specify the name of the user account that you want to use.
NFS shares	computer:/share	Add -t nfs to indicate that it is an NFS (Network File System) server.

Options for the mount Command

The mount command offers many options, and some of these are rather advanced. One of the most important options for mount is the -t option, which specifies the file system type you want to use. Your computer normally would detect what file system to use by itself, but sometimes you need to help it because this file system self-check isn't working properly. Table 3-2 lists some file systems that you may encounter on your computer (or other Linux systems).

Table 3-2. *Linux File System Types*

Type	Description
minix	This is the mother of all Linux file systems. It was used in the earliest Linux version. Because it has some serious limitations, like the inability to work with partitions greater than 32MB, it isn't used much anymore. Occasionally, it can still be seen on very small media, like boot diskettes or devices that are using embedded Linux.
ext2	This has been the default Linux file system for a very long time, and it was first developed in the early 1990s. The Ext2 file system is a completely POSIX-compliant file system, which means it supports all the properties of a typical UNIX environment. However, it has one serious drawback: it doesn't support journaling, and therefore had been replaced a long time ago.
ext3	Basically, Ext3 is Ext2 with a journal added to it. The major advantage of Ext3 is that it is completely backward-compatible with Ext2. Its major disadvantage is that it is based on Ext2, an elderly file system that was never designed for a world in which partitions of several hundreds of gigabytes are used.
btrfs	btrfs (to be pronounced as butterfs) is the next generation Linux file system. It offers many new features such as multiple devices file systems, versioning and subvolumes, but at the time this book was written, wasn't considered a stable file system yet by many distributions. Chances are that by the time you're reading this, btrfs is the default file system though.
Reiser	ReiserFS is another journaling file system. It was developed by Hans Reiser as a completely new file system in the late 1990s. ReiserFS was only used as the default file system on SUSE Linux, but even SUSE has changed to Ext3 as its default because there just isn't enough community support for ReiserFS.
ext4	Ext4 is the successor to Ext3, and it fixes some of the most important shortcomings of Ext3. For example, Ext4 will use a strong indexing system that helps you work with lots of files in one single directory. At the time of writing, Ext4 is still experimental, so I will not discuss it in this book.
Xfs	The XFS file system was created as an open source file system by supercomputer manufacturer SGI. It has some excellent tuning options, which makes it a very good file system for storing your data. You'll read some more about this file system and its options later in this chapter. As the btrfs file system isn[t stable yet, xfs is used as the default file system by enterprise Linux distributions such as SUSE and Red Hat.
Msdos	If, for example, you need to read a floppy disk with files on it that were created on a computer using MS-DOS, you can mount it with the msdos file system type. This is, however, something of a legacy file system that has been replaced with vfat.
Vfat	The vfat file system is used for all Windows and DOS file systems that use a FAT file system. Use it for accessing files from a Windows-formatted diskette or optical media.

(*continued*)

Table 3-2. (*continued*)

Type	Description
ntfs	On Windows systems, NTFS is now the default file system. Not so long ago, Linux didn't have a stable open source solution for writing to NTFS. On older distributions, write support for NTFS is still missing. Modern distributions, however, offer complete read/ write support. You'll also find some excellent NTFS tools on live cds like Knoppix. On enterprise Linux distributions such as Red Hat Enterprise Linux, you won't find support for NTFS though.
iso9660	This is the file system that is used to mount CDs. Normally, you don't need to specify that you want to use this file system, as it will be detected automatically when you insert a CD.
Cifs	When working on a network, the cifs file system is very important. This file system allows you to make a connection over the network to a share that is offered by a Windows computer, as in the previous example. Linux computers also can offer shares that use this protocol, by using the Samba service (see Chapter 12 for more details). In the past, the smbfs file system type was used to address these shares, but, because cifs offers a better solution, it has replaced smbfs on modern Linux distributions. In case mounting a Samba share doesn't work with cifs, try smbfs.
Nfs	NFS is used to make connections between UNIX computers. See Chapter 12 for more information about NFS and Samba.

Apart from -t, the mount command has many other options as well, which can be prefixed by using the -o option. Most of these options are file-system dependent, so no generic list of these options is provided here. You'll find information that is specific for your file system in the man page of the mount command.

Getting an Overview of Mounted Devices

Every device that is mounted is recorded in the configuration file /etc/mtab. You can browse the content of this file with a utility like cat or less. You can also use the mount command to get an overview of file systems that are currently mounted. If this command is used without any other parameters, it reads the contents of /etc/mtab and displays a list of all mounted file systems that it can find, as shown in Listing 3-1.

Listing 3-1. The mount Command Gives an Overview of All Devices Currently Mounted

```
nuuk:/ # mount
/dev/sda2 on / type ext3 (rw,acl,user_xattr)
proc on /proc type proc (rw)
sysfs on /sys type sysfs (rw)
debugfs on /sys/kernel/debug type debugfs (rw)
udev on /dev type tmpfs (rw)
devpts on /dev/pts type devpts (rw,mode=0620,gid=5)
/dev/sda1 on /boot type ext2 (rw,acl,user_xattr)
securityfs on /sys/kernel/security type securityfs (rw)
nfsd on /proc/fs/nfsd type nfsd (rw)
/dev/sr0 on /media/VMware_Tools type iso9660 (ro,nosuid,nodev,utf8,uid=0)
/dev/sdc1 on /media/disk type vfat
      rw,noexec,nosuid,nodev,flush,fmask=0133,shortname=lower,utf8,uid=0)
```

As you can see in Listing 3-1, mount gives you information not only about mounted partitions, but also about system devices. On modern Linux distributions, this list of mounted system devices can be long.

For now, I'll ignore all lines about these system devices and just focus on the two lines where /dev/sda1 and /dev/sda2 are mounted. In these lines, you can see the name of the device first. Next, they show the name of the directory on which they are mounted. Following that, the file system type is mentioned, and lastly, the options that were used when mounting the device are listed. You can see that both sda1 and sda2 are mounted with the rw option, which means they are accessible for reads and writes. Also, these two file systems have the acl and user_xattr options. These options, which are on by default on most distributions, allow you to use some advanced security on the file system. You'll learn more about these options in Chapter 7, which discusses working with permissions.

In Listing 3-1 you can also see a /dev/sr0, which is mounted. If you see this device, chances are that it refers to your optical disk device, which is also the case here. You can also see that by the file system type that is used, iso9660, which typically is the file system used on CD devices.

The last two lines (they read as one line, but due to printing limitations are displayed as two lines) show the /dev/sdc1 device that is mounted. This is a USB key that was inserted into the system. The Linux kernel has recognized it automatically at the moment it was connected and mounted it, using all the options needed to do so. Don't worry about the specific meaning of these options; the Linux kernel has detected automatically what exactly was needed to mount this device.

Apart from the /etc/mtab file, Linux offers more options to see which file systems currently are mounted. The /proc/mounts file offers direct information provided by the kernel about currently existing mounts. In fact, the contents of /etc/mtab comes directly from this file. For an overview of real file systems that are mounted, you can use the df -h command. Listing 3-2 shows how this command displays real file systems only, and doesn't provide any information about mounted kernel interfaces.

Listing 3-2. The **df -h** command gives information about mounted file systems

```
[root@server1 ~]# df -h
Filesystem               Size  Used Avail Use% Mounted on
/dev/mapper/centos-root  6.7G  1.4G  5.4G  20% /
devtmpfs                 237M     0  237M   0% /dev
tmpfs                    245M   54M  191M  22% /dev/shm
tmpfs                    245M   25M  221M  10% /run
tmpfs                    245M     0  245M   0% /sys/fs/cgroup
/dev/vda1                497M  138M  360M  28% /boot
/dev/sdb1               1020M   33M  988M   4% /srv/gluster
/dev/drbd0              1021M   34M  988M   4% /var/lib/mysql
```

Unmounting Devices

On a Linux system, when you want to disconnect a device from your computer, you have to unmount it first. Unmounting devices ensures that all of the data that is still in cache and has not yet been written to the device is written to the file system before it is disconnected. You'll use the umount command to do this. The command can take two arguments: either the name of the device or the name of the directory where the device is mounted. So umount /dev/cdrom and umount /mnt will both work for a CD device that is mounted on the directory /mnt.

When using the umount command, you may get the message "Device is busy," and the dismount fails. This is likely because a file on the device is open, and the reason you're not allowed to disconnect the device is probably obvious: disconnecting a mounted device may lead to data loss. So first make sure that the device has no open files. The solution is sometimes simple: if you want to dismount a CD, but you are currently in the directory /media/cdrom, it is not possible to disconnect the device. Browse to another directory and try again. Sometimes, however, the situation can be more complex, and you'll need to first find out which processes are currently using the device.

To do this, you can use the `fuser` command. This command displays the IDs of processes (PIDs) using specified files or file systems. For example, `fuser -m /media` displays a list of all processes that currently have open files in /media. Based on these PIDs, you can now manually terminate the processes using the `kill` command. Listing 3-3 shows you how you can use `fuser` to list the PIDs of processes that have files open in /media, and how you can use the `kill` command next to terminate these processes. For much more information about process management, read Chapter 9.

Listing 3-3. With `fuser` and `kill`, You Can Trace and Terminate Processes That Prevent Dismounting a Device

```
nuuk:~ # fuser /media
/media:              13061c
nuuk:~ # kill 13061
```

The `fuser` command also allows you to kill these open files automatically. For open files on /media/cdrom, use fuser -km /media/cdrom. Be careful when using the option: if you are root, it may blindly kill important processes and make your computer unreadable.

As an alternative to the `fuser` command, you can use `lsof` as well. This also provides a list of all processes that currently are using files on a given file system, but it provides more information about these processes. Whereas `fuser` just gives the PID of a process, `lsof` also gives information like the name of the process and the user who owns the process. Listing 3-4 shows what the result of `lsof` looks like.

Listing 3-4. If You Need More Details About Processes Preventing You from Performing a Dismount, Use `lsof`

```
nuuk:/media # lsof /media
COMMAND    PID USER    FD    TYPE DEVICE SIZE NODE NAME
Lsof    10230 root    cwd    DIR   22,0 4096 1856 /media
Lsof    10231 root    cwd    DIR   22,0 4096 1856 /media
Bash    13061 root    cwd    DIR   22,0 4096 1856 /media
```

The example from Listing 3-4 was taken on a computer where a Bash shell was open and had its current prompt set to the /media directory. As you can see, this starts different processes, of which the PID number is in the second column. You'll need this PID to manage the process; more on that is in Chapter 9.

After using `fuser` with the -k switch on the /media directory to kill active processes, you should always make sure that the processes are really terminated by using `fuser -m /media` again, as this will show you whether there are still processes with open files.

Another way of forcing the umount command to do its work is to use the -f option as follows: umount -f /somemount. This option is especially intended for use on an NFS network mount that has become unreachable and does not work on other file systems, so you will not have much success if you try it on a local file system.

If you want to minimize the impact of unmounting a device, you can use umount with the -l option, which performs a "lazy unmount" by detaching the file system from the file system hierarchy and cleaning up all references to the file system as soon as it is no longer busy. Using this option lets you do an unmount right away, even if the file system is busy. But it may take some time to complete. This option allows you to unmount a busy file system in a very safe way, as it won't shut down any processes immediately.

■ **Tip** The `eject` command is a very easy way to dismount and eject optical media. This command will open the CD or DVD drive and eject the optical media that is currently in the drive. All you have to do is remove it. And then you can use `eject -t` to close the optical drive drawer.

EXERCISE 3-1: MOUNTING FILE SYSTEMS

To perform this exercise, you'll need to connect a USB thumb drive to your computer system.

1. Type **cat /proc/partitions**. This provides an overview of all devices that are currently known on your system.

2. Insert a USB thum drive to your computer. Type **cat /proc/partitions** again. You'll notice a new device that has appeared. For the remainder of this exercise, I'll assume the name of the device is /dev/sdb1. Change this device name if a different name shows on your computer.

3. Type **mount /dev/sdb1 /mnt** to mount the device on the /mnt directory.

4. Type **mount**. You'll see the /dev/sdb1 device in the last line of the command output.

5. Type **df -h**. This also shows the mounted device, as well as available disk space on the device.

6. Type **cd /mnt**.

7. Type **umount /mnt**. You'll see a "device busy" error message.

8. Type **lsof /mnt** and read the output of the command.

9. Type **cd** without any arguments. This will bring you to your home directory.

10. Type **umount /mnt**. You'll now be able to unmount the device.

11. You can now safely remove the USB thumb drive from your computer.

Automating Mounts with /etc/fstab

When starting your computer, some mounts need to be issued automatically. For this purpose, Linux uses the /etc/fstab file to specify how and where these file systems must be mounted. This file contains a list of all mounts that have to occur on a regular basis. In /etc/fstab, you can state per mount whether it has to happen automatically when your system starts. Listing 3-4 shows the contents of a sample /etc/fstab file.

Listing 3-4. The /etc/fstab File Makes Sure That File Systems Are Mounted During System Boot

```
nuuk:/media  # cat /etc/fstab
/dev/sda2    /                    ext4     acl,user_xattr    1 1
LABEL=boot   /boot                ext4     acl,user_xattr    1 2
/dev/sda3    swap                 swap     defaults          0 0
proc         /proc                proc     defaults          0 0
sysfs        /sys                 sysfs    noauto            0 0
debugfs      /sys/kernel/debug    debugfs  noauto            0 0
usbfs        /proc/bus/usb        usbfs    noauto            0 0
devpts       /dev/pts             devpts   mode=0620,gid=5   0 0
```

■ **Note** Some distributions use advanced features like a universal unique ID (UUID) or LVM logical volumes to mount devices from `fstab`. In this section, I explain `fstab` based on regular partitions. You can find more information about these advanced features in Chapter 6 of this book.

In the listing, you can see that not only real file systems are specified in /etc/fstab. Some system file systems are listed as well. You don't have to include these file systems as an administrator, they'll be added automatically when you're installing your server.

■ **Note** The /etc/fstab file is used at system boot, but you can also use it from the command line: enter the `mount -a` command to mount all file systems in /etc/fstab that are currently not mounted and have the option set to mount them automatically. Also, if a device is defined in /etc/fstab with its most common mount options, you don't need to specify all mount options on the command line. For example, if the /dev/cdrom device is in /etc/fstab, you can mount it by using a shortened `mount /dev/cdrom` command instead of the complete `mount /dev/cdrom ./media/cdrom` command.

In `fstab`, each file system is described on a separate line, and the fields in these lines are separated by tabs or spaces. The following fields are always present:

- *File system*: This first field describes the device or the remote file system to be mounted. Typically, you will see names like `/dev/sda1 or computer:/mount` on this line. The former is used to refer to a local partition, whereas the latter is used to refer to a network share that is offered by another computer.

- *Mount point*: The second field is used to describe the mount point for the file system. This is normally a directory where the file system must be mounted. Some file systems (such as the swap file system) don't work with a specific directory as their mount point. In the case of swap partitions, just `swap` is used as the mount point instead.

■ **Tip** On most file systems, the device name can be replaced with a label, like "ROOT". On an Ext4 file system, these labels can be created with the `tune2fs -L` command, or with `xfs_admin` on an XFS system. Using labels makes the system more robust and avoids the situation in which adding a SCSI disk adds all the device names. Labels are static and are not changed automatically when a disk is added. Nowadays, an alternative system, using UUIDs, allows you to use unique device naming. In Chapter 5 you can read more about UUIDs. They have one disadvantage though, UUID are long and hard to read. The benefit of using labels, is that as an administrator, they allow you to assign a human readble device name.

- *File system type*: The third field is used to specify the file system type you can use. As you learned earlier, many file systems are available for use on Linux. No specific kernel configuration is needed to use them, as most file systems can be activated as a kernel module that is loaded automatically when needed. Instead of the name of a file system, you can also use `ignore` in this field. This is useful to show a disk partition that is currently not in use. To determine the file system type automatically, use the option `auto`. This is what you want to use on removable media like CDs and diskettes. Don't use it, however, on fixed media like partitions and logical volumes because it may lead to a failure in mounting the file system when booting your computer.

- *Mount options*: The fourth field is used to specify the options that should be used when mounting the file system. Many options are available, and of these, many are filesystem specific. For most file systems, the option default is used, which makes sure the file system is mounted automatically when the computer boots and prohibits normal users from disconnecting the mount. Also, the options rw, suid, dev, exec, and async are used. The following list describes some of the most used options. Note that you can also use these options as arguments when using the mount command:

  - async: Does not write to the file system synchronously but through the write cache mechanism. This ensures that file writes are performed in the most efficient way, but you risk losing data if contact with the file system is suddenly lost.

  - dev: Treats block and character devices on the file system as devices and not as regular files. For security reasons, it's a good idea to avoid using this option on devices that can be mounted by ordinary users.

  - exec: Permits execution of binary files.

  - hotplug: Does not report errors for this device if it does not currently exist. This makes sense for hot-pluggable devices like USB media.

  - noatime: Does not update the access times on this file system every time a file is opened. This option makes your file system somewhat faster if many reads are performed on it. It is a good idea to switch this option on as a default for all file systems your computer is mounting, unless you want to use an accounting system to keep track of which files are accessed by which user at which specific moment.

  - noauto: Does not mount the file system automatically when the system boots or if a user uses the mount -a command to mount everything in /etc/fstab automatically.

  - mode: Sets a permission mode (see Chapter 7) for new files that are created on the file system.

  - remount: Remounts a file system that is already mounted. It only makes sense to use this option from the command line.

  - user: Allows a user to mount the file system. This option is normally used only for removable devices like diskettes and CDs.

  - sync: Makes sure the content of the file system is synchronized with the medium before the device is dismounted.

- *Dump status*: This field is for use of the dump command, which is a way of making backups of your file system. The field determines which file systems need to be dumped when the dump command is called. If the value of this field is set to 0, it will not be dumped; if set to 1, it will be dumped when dump is invoked. Make sure that the value is set to 1 on all file systems that contain important data that should always be included when making backups with dump.

■ **Note**   You may never use the `dump` command yourself to create backups, but some backup utilities do. So if you want to make sure that your backup utilities are successful, give all file systems that contain important data the value 1 in this column.

- *Fsck status*: This last field in `fstab` determines how a file system needs to be checked with the `fsck` command. At boot time, the boot loader will always check whether a file system has to be checked with `fsck` or not. If this is the case, the root file system must always be checked first and therefore has the value 1. Other file systems should have the number 2. If the file systems have the same `fsck` number, they will be checked sequentially. If the files are on different drives, they can be checked in parallel. If the value is set to 0, no automatic check will occur.

Warning! When a file system is configured for an automatic file system check upon boot, the automatic file system check may fail. If it does, your system will start booting and display the message "Enter root password for maintenance mode". If this happens to you, you should start checking the integrity of the file system. Alternatively, you can change the last column in /etc/fstab to a 0 to switch off the automatic file system check (which may lead to file system corruption at some point in time).

Checking File System Integrity

When a system crashes unexpectedly, any file systems that are open can be damaged, which may prevent you from using these file systems in a normal way. If this happens, the consistency of these file systems needs to be checked, and you'd do this with the `fsck` command. While booting, Linux always will perform a quick check of your file systems automatically. In some cases, this will fail, and you will need to do a manual check of your computer file systems. If this happens, the boot procedure will stop, and you will see a text-based login shell. This section assumes that you work from such a text-based login shell to repair your file systems.

■ **Caution**   Never use `fsck` on a mounted file system, as it may severely damage the file system! If a file system has no open files, you can remount it as read-only using the `-o remount,ro` option with `mount`. For instance, to remount the file system on /usr as read-only, use `mount -o remount, ro /usr`.

You can start the `fsck` command with the name of the device you want to check as its argument: for example, use `fsck /dev/sda1` to check files on /dev/sda1. If you run the command without any options, `fsck` will check all file systems in /etc/fstab one by one, according to the setting in the `fsck status` field in /etc/fstab. Normally, this will always happen when booting your system.

Nowadays, a system administrator does not have to regularly use `fsck` because most modern file systems are journaling file systems. The journal is used to write transactions on files to a specific log file. Having such a journal makes it possible to recover a damaged file system very fast. If a journaling file system gets damaged, the journal is checked, and all incomplete transactions can easily be rolled back. To offer some protection, an Ext or Ext file system is checked automatically every once in a while.

■ **Tip** On a nonjournaling file system, the fsck command can take a very long time to complete. In this case, the -C option can be used when performing a manual check. This option displays a progress bar— which doesn't, of course, make it go any faster, but it at least lets you know how long you still have to wait for the process to complete. Currently, the -C option is supported only on Ext file systems.

Creating Backups

One thing always seems to be true about computers: one day they'll fail. If the computer in question is an important server, the failure can cause huge problems. Companies have gone bankrupt because their vital data was lost. Therefore, making decent backups of your data is essential. In this section, I'll cover two different methods of creating backups, both of which are native Linux solutions: making file backups with tar and making device backups using dd.

Making File Backups with tar

The command-line utility tar is probably the most popular Linux backup utility. It functions as a stand-alone utility for writing backups to an archive. This archive can be tape (hence the name "tar" which stands for *tape archiver*), but it can also be anything else. For instance, tar-based backups are often written to a file instead of a tape, and, if this file is compressed with a compression utility like bzip2 or gzip, you'll get the famous tarball, which is a common method of delivering software installation archives. In this section, you'll learn how to create tar archives and how to extract files from them. I'll also provide some tips and tricks to help you get the most out of the tar utility.

■ **Note** The tar command is not used for backup and restore only; on the Internet you'll find tar packaged software archives as well. Even when working in an environment where a package manager such as yum or apt is used, you'll find that occasionally you need to unpack tar archives as well.

Creating an Archive File

In its most basic form, tar is used to create an archive file. The following command would help you do this for the directory /home:

```
tar -cvf /tmp/home.tar /home
```

This command will create a backup of /home and put that in the file /tmp/home.tar. This archive contains relative path names, which means that while restoring it, it will always restore files in the directory where you're running the tar command. This method is useful if you want to create a backup of important system files and directories. For instance, the following command would create a backup of the directories /home, /srv, /root, and /var and write that to the file /tmp/system-backup:

```
tar -cvf /tmp/system-backup.tar /home /srv /root /var
```

■ **Note** When using the `tar` command, you *can* put a - before the options, but you don't have to. You will encounter both syntax styles, and to help you getting used to that, I will use both in this book.

This `tar` command has a few arguments. First, you need to indicate what you want to do with the `tar` command. In this case, you want to create an archive. (That's why the option `c` is used; the "c" stands for *create*.)

After that, I've used the option `v` (*verbose*). Although it's not required, it often comes in handy because verbose output lets you see what the `tar` command is actually doing. I recommend always using this option because sometimes a `tar` job can take a really long time. (For instance, imagine creating a complete archive of everything that's on your hard drive.) In cases such as these, it's nice to be able to monitor what exactly happens, and that's what the option `v` is meant to do.

Next, you need to specify where you want the `tar` command to send its output. If you don't specify anything here, `tar` defaults to the standard output. In other words, it simply dumps all the data to your computer's console. This doesn't accomplish much, so you should use the option `f` (file) to specify what file or device the output should be written to.

In this example, I've written the output to a regular file, but, alternatively, you can write output to a device file as well. For example, the following command makes a backup of /home and writes that to the /dev/mt0 device, which typically refers to a tape drive:

```
tar -cvf /dev/mt0 /home
```

The last part of the `tar` command specifies exactly what you want to put into your `tar` archive. In the example, the directory /home is archived. It's easy to forget this option, but, if you do, `tar` will complain that it is "cowardly refusing to create an empty archive."

You should know a couple of other things about `tar`. First, the order of arguments *does* matter. So, for example, there is a difference between `tar -cvf /somefile /somedir` and `tar -f /somefile -vc /somedir`. The order is wrong in the last part, and `tar` won't know what you want it to do. So, in all cases, first specify what you want `tar` to do. In most cases, it's either `c` (to create an archive), `x` (to extract an archive), or `t` (to list the contents of the archive). Then specify how you want `tar` to do that; for example, you can use `v` to tell `tar` that it should be verbose. Next, use the `f` option to indicate where you want `tar` to write the backup, and then specify what exactly you want to back up. The following example line demonstrates this `tar` syntax:

```
tar { create | extract} [options] <destination file> <source files or directories>
```

Creating an archive with `tar` is useful, but you should be aware that `tar` doesn't compress one single bit of your archive. This is because `tar` was originally conceived as a tape streaming utility. It streams data to a file or (typically) a tape device. If you want `tar` to compress the contents of an archive as well, you must tell it to do so. `tar` has two options to compress the archive file:

- `z`: Use this option to compress the `tar` file with the `gzip` utility. This is the most popular compression utility, because it has a pretty decent compression ratio. This means it would gain quite a lot of disk space when compressing files. Also, it doesn't take too long to create a compressed file.

- `j`: Use this option to compress the tar file with the `bzip2` utility. This utility compresses 10 to 20% better than `gzip`, but at a cost: it takes as twice as long.

So, if you want to create a compressed archive of the directory /home and write that backup to a file with the name home.tar.gz, you would use the following command:

```
tar -czvf home.tar.gz /home
```

■ **Note**   Of course, you can use the `bzip2` and `gzip` utilities from the command line as well. Use `gzip file.tar` to compress `file.tar`. This command produces `file.tar.gz` as its result. To decompress that file, use `gunzip file.tar.gz`, which gives you the original `file.tar` back. If you want to do the same with `bzip2`, use `bzip2 file.tar` to create the compressed file. This creates a file with the name `file.tar.bz2`, which you can decompress using the command `bunzip2 file.tar.bz2`.

Path Names in tar

When creating an archive with tar, you should be careful about the directory from which you're creating the archive. To start with, do realize that all path names in a tar archive are stored as relative pathnames - this shows in code listing 3-5, where the command mentions that the leading / is removed from file names.

Apart from the leading / in the file name, the complete path name will stay in the tar archive. That means that if you're using **tar -cvf /tmp/all.tar /. file names are stored as etc/hosts, not as /etc/hosts.**

Listing 3-5. Using tar to Create an Archive That Contains Absolute File Names

```
nuuk:/ # tar cvf /tmp/old.tar /old
tar: Removing leading `/' from member names
/old/
/old/hosts
/old/shadow
/old/passwd
```

If you create the tar archive with the purpose of extracting it later at any location you like, it is not the best idea to use complete file names in the archive. This would, for example, be the case if you are a developer who wants to distribute his or her new program to users. In such a case, it is good if the user can extract the archive anywhere he or she wants. To do this, you have two options:

- Use `cd` to go to the target directory before creating the backup.

- Use the `tar` option `-C` to tell `tar` that it should create an archive file containing relative file names.

Of these two, I recommend using the latter, as it is more clear and makes it possible to create an archive that contains files from more than one directory as well. When you create a backup that has relative file names, you should always put a dot at the end of the `tar` command. This dot tells `tar` to make a backup of the contents of the current directory. Without the dot, `tar` tells you that it doesn't want to create an empty archive. In Listing 3-6, you can see how an archive is created in this way of the same directory (`/old`) that was used in the example command from Listing 3-5.

Listing 3-6. Creating an Archive Containing Relative File Names

```
nuuk:/ # tar cvf /tmp/old.tar -C /old .
./
./hosts
./shadow
./passwd
```

Extracting an Archive File

Now that you know how to create an archive file, it's rather easy to extract it. Basically, the command-line options that you use to extract an archive file look a lot like the ones you needed to create it in the first place. The important difference is that, to extract a file, you need the option x (extract), instead of c (create). Here are some examples:

- `tar -xvf /file.tar`: Extracts the contents of `file.tar` to the current directory

- `tar -zxvf /file.tar.gz`: Extracts the contents of the compressed `file.tar` to the current directory

- `tar -xvf /file.tar C /somedir`: Extracts the contents of `/file.tar` to a directory with the name `/somedir`

Moving a Complete Directory

Most of the time, `tar` is used to write a backup of one or more directories to a file. Because of its excellent handling of special files (such as stale files that are used quite often in databases), `tar` is also quite often used to move the contents of one directory to another. Let's assume that you want to move the contents of the directory `/old` to the directory `/new`. Some people perform this task by first creating a temporary file and then extracting the temporary file into the new directory. This would involve the following commands:

```
tar cvf /tmp/old.tar -C /old .
tar xvf /tmp/old.tar -C /new
```

This is not the easiest way because you need twice the disk space taken by the directory whose contents you want to move: the size of the original directory plus the space needed for the temporary file. The good news is that you don't have to do it this way. Use a pipe, and you can directly copy the contents of one directory to another directory.

To understand how this works, first try the command `tar -cC /old ..` In this command, the option c is used to tell `tar` that it should create an archive. The option C is used to archive the contents of the directory `/old` using relative path names. Now, as you may have noticed, in the `tar -cC /var` example, the option `f /tmp/old.tar` isn't used to specify where the output goes, and so all the output is sent to STDOUT, which is your console. This means that if you press Enter now, you will see the contents of all files scrolling through the console of your computer, which is not very useful.

So that's the first half of the command, and you ended up with a lot of output dumped on the console. Now, in the second part of the command, you'll use a pipe to redirect all that output to another command, which is `tar -xC /new`. This command will capture the `tar` archive from STDOUT and extract it to the directory `/new` (make sure that new exists before you run this command). You'll see that this method allows you to create a perfect copy of one directory to another. So the complete command that you need in this case looks like this:

```
tar -cC /old . | tar -xC /new
```

Creating Incremental Backups

Based on the information in the previous section, you can probably see how to create a backup of one or more directories. For instance, the tar -cvf /backup.tar /var /home /srv command creates a backup of three directories: /home, /var, and /srv. Depending on the size of these directories, this command may take some time. Because such large backups can take so long, it's often useful to make incremental backups; in an incremental backup, the only files that get written to the backup are those that have changed since the last backup. To do this, you need the option g to create a snapshot file.

An incremental backup always follows a full backup, and so you have to create the full backup first. In this full backup, you should create a snapshot file, which contains a list of all files that have been written to the backup. The following command does this for you (make sure that the directory /backup exists before running the command):

```
tar -czvg /backup/snapshot-file -f /backup/full-backup.tar.gz /home
```

The interesting thing about the snapshot file is that it contains a list of all files that have been written to the backup. If, two days after the full backup, you want to make a backup of only the files that have been changed in those two days, you can repeat essentially the same command. This time, the command will check the snapshot file to find out what files have changed since the last full backup, and it'll back up only those changed files. So your Monday backup would be created by the following command:

```
tar -czvg /backup/snapshot-file -f /backup/monday-backup.tar.gz /home
```

These two commands created two files: a small file that contains the incremental backup and a large file that contains the full backup. In an incremental backup scheme, you'll need to make sure that at some point in time a full backup is created. To do this, just remove the snapshot file that was used in the preceding example. Since tar doesn't find a snapshot file, it will assume that you need to make a full backup and create the new snapshot file for you.

If you want to restore all files from an incremental backup, you need to restore every single file, starting with the first file that was created (typically the full backup) and ending with the last incremental backup. So, in this example, the following two commands would restore the file system back to the status at the time that the last incremental backup was created:

```
tar -xzvf /backup/full-backup.tar.gz
tar -xzvf /backup/monday-backup.tar.gz
```

In this section you've read about different options that you can use with tar. For your convenience, the most relevant options are listed here:

- -c: Use this option to create an archive.

- -v: Use this option to let tar display output verbosely. Useful for longer tar commands so that you show what they are doing.

- -f: Use this option to specify the name of the output file that tar should write to.

- -C: Use this option followed by a directory name to change to this directory before starting the tar job.

- -x: Use this option to extract files from an archive.

- -g: Use this option to make an incremental or a differential backup.

- -z: Use this option to compress the tar file using gzip compression.

- -j: Use this option to compress the tar file using bzip2 compression.

In exercise 3.2 you'll learn how to work with the tar command.

EXERCISE 3-2: WORKING WITH TAR

1. Open a root shell.

2. Type **tar -cvf /tmp/etc.tar /etc**

3. Type **tar -tvf /tmp/etc.tar** to show the contents of the tar archive.

4. Type **mkdir /temp** to create a temporary directory to work with.

5. Type **tar xvf /tmp/etc.tar -C /temp**. This extracts the contents of the etc.tar file relative to the /temp directory.

6. Type **rm -rf /temp** to remove the /temp directory and all of its contents.

Making Device Backups Using dd

You won't find a more versatile utility than tar to create a file system–based backup. In some cases, however, you don't need a backup based on a file system; instead, you want to create a backup of a complete device or parts of it. This is where the dd command comes in handy.

■ **Tip**   This may sound rather abstract. You can, however, do very useful things with the dd command. For example, imagine the option to clone the entire contents of your hard disk to an external USB hard disk. I do it every Friday night, just to make sure that if something happens to my hard drive, I just have to install the cloned hard drive to get my data back. That's not more than five minutes of work (and a couple of hours of waiting before all the data is copied)!

The basic use of the dd command is rather easy because it takes just two arguments: if= to specify the input file, and of= to specify the output file. The arguments to those options can be either files or block devices. So, the command dd if=/etc/hosts of=/home/somefile can be used as a complicated way to copy a file. I would, however, not recommend using dd to copy files; cp does that in a much simpler way. However, cloning a hard disk, which you would do with the command dd if=/dev/sda of=/dev/sdb bs=4096, is something that only dd can do. (The option bs=4096 specifies that dd should work on 4K blocks, which offers a much better performance.)

■ **Note**   dd is, strangely enough, short for "convert and copy." Unfortunately, the cc command was already being used by something else, so the developers choose to use dd instead.

Or what would you think, for example, of the command dd if=/dev/cdrom of=/mycd.iso? It helps you create an ISO file of the CD that's in the drive at that moment. You may wonder why not just copy the contents of your CD to a file with the name /mycd.iso? Well, the reason is, a CD, like most other devices, typically contains information that cannot be copied by a mere file copy. For example, how would you handle the boot sector of a CD? You can't find that as a file on the device because it's just the first sector. Because dd copies sector by sector, on the other hand, it will copy that information as well.

■ **Tip**   Did you know that it's not hard to mount an ISO file that you created with dd? The only thing that you need to know is that you have to use the -o loop option, which allows you to mount a file like any normal device. So, to mount /mycd.iso on the /mnt directory, you would need mount -o loop /mycd.iso /mnt.

Working with Links

A very useful Linux feature—although one that is often misunderstood—is the *link*. A link can be compared to a shortcut: it's basically a pointer to another file. On Linux (as on any UNIX system), two different kinds of links are supported: the hard link and the symbolic link.

Why Use Links?

Basically, a link makes it easier to find files you need. You can create links for the operating system and program files that you use on that operating system, and you can use them to make life easier for users as well. Imagine that some users belong to the group account and you want the group members to create files that are readable by all other group members in the directory /home/groups/account. To do this, you can ask the users to change to the proper directory every time they want to save a file. Or you can create a link for each user in his or her home directory. Such a link can have the name account and can be placed in the home directory of all users who need to save work in the shared directory for the group account, and it's easy to see how this link makes it a lot easier for the users to save their files to the proper location.

Another example of why links can be useful comes from the world of FHS, the Filesystem Hierarchy Standard. This standard prescribes in which directory a Linux system should store files of a particular kind. In the old days, the X Windowing System had all its binaries installed in the /usr/X11 directory. Later, the name of the directory where the X Windowing System stored its configuration files was changed to /usr/X11R6. Now imagine what would happen if an application referred to the /usr/X11 directory after this change. It would naturally fail because that directory no longer exists. A link is the solution here as well. If the administrator just creates a link with the name /usr/X11 that points to the /usr/X11R6 directory, all applications that refer to /usr/X11 can still be used.

On a Linux system, links are everywhere. After Linux is installed, several links already exist, and, as an administrator, it's easy for you to add new ones. To do so, you should understand the difference between a symbolic link and a hard link, which is explained in the next two sections, "Working with Symbolic Links" and "Working with Hard Links."

Working with Symbolic Links

As mentioned previously, a link can refer to two different things: a symbolic link (also referred to as a soft link) and a hard link. A *symbolic link* is a link that refers to the name of a file. Its most important advantage is that it can be used to refer to a file that is anywhere, even on a computer on the other side of the world. The symbolic link will still work. However, the biggest disadvantage is that the symbolic link is naturally dependent on the original file. If the original file is removed, the symbolic link will no longer work.

To create a symbolic link, use the ln command with the option -s. When using the ln command, make sure that you first refer to the name of the original file and then to the name of the link you want to create. If, for example, you want to create a symbolic link with the name computers in your home directory that refers to the file /etc/hosts, use the following command:

```
ln -s /etc/hosts ~/computers
```

As a result, a shortcut with the name ~/computers will be created in your home directory. This shortcut refers to /etc/hosts. Therefore, any time you open the ~/computers file, you would really be working in the /etc/hosts file. Listing 3-7 shows you that in the output of ls -l, you can actually see that the resulting file is not a file by itself, but a symbolic link. This is indicated by the letter l in the first position of the ls -l output and also by the arrow at the end of the listing, which indicates the file the name is referring to.

Listing 3-7. With ls -l You Can See That the File Actually Is a Symbolic Link

```
nuuk:~ # ln -s /etc/hosts computers
nuuk:~ # ls -l computers
lrwxrwxrwx 1 root root 10 Jan 19 01:37 computers -> /etc/hosts
```

Understanding Inodes

To understand the difference between a hard link and a symbolic link, you should understand the role of inodes on a Linux file system. Every Linux file or directory (from a technical point of view, there's no real difference between them) has an inode, and this inode contains all of the file's metadata (that is, all the administrative data needed to read a file is stored in its inode). For example, the inode contains a list of all the blocks in which a file is stored, the owner information for that file, permissions, and all other attributes that are set for the file. In a sense, you could say that a file really *is* the inode, and names are attached to these inodes to make it easier for humans to work with them.

If you want to have a look at inodes, on an Ext file system you can use the (potentially dangerous!) command debugfs. This opens a low-level file system debugger from which you can issue advanced repair commands. You can also just check the properties of the file system and files that are used in it (which is not dangerous at all). The following procedure shows how to display the inode for a given file using this file system debugger on Ext4. Notice that this procedure only works on Ext file systems.

■ **Note**   Only the Ext2/Ext3 command debugfs offers you the possibility to show inodes. The fact that this file system has powerful utilities like this one helps in making it a very popular file system.

---

1. Use the command ls -il to find the inode number of the file /etc/hosts. As you can see in Listing 3-8, the inode number is the first item mentioned in the output of this command.

Listing 3-8. The Command ls -il Shows the Inode Number of a File

```
sander@ubuntu:/$ ls -il /etc/hosts
15024138 -rw-r--r-- 1 root root 253 2007-06-05 00:20 /etc/hosts
```

2. As root, open the file system debugger. While starting it, use as an argument the name of the Ext4 file system on which your file resides. For example, our example file /etc/hosts is on a partition with the name /dev/sda3, so the command would be sudo debugfs /dev/sda3. This opens the debugfs interactive prompt.

3. Now use the debugfs command stat to display the contents of the inode that you want to examine. For example, in this case you would type **stat <15024138>**. The result of this command is similar to what you see in Listing 3-9.

Listing 3-9. Showing the Contents of an Inode

```
Inode: 13    Type:   regular    Mode:    0644    Flags: 0x0    Generation:    5
84821287
User:    0   Group:    0   Size:    1763308
File ACL: 0    Directory ACL: 0
Links:  1   Blockcount:   3460
Fragment:   Address:  0 Number:   0 Size:   0
ctime:   0x4664e51e -- Tue Jun 5 00:22:54 2007
atime: 0x4664e51e -- Tue Jun 5 00:22:54 2007
mtime: 0x4621e007 -- Sun Apr 15 04:19:19 2007
BLOCKS:
(0-11):5716-5727,  (IND):5728,  (12-267):5729-5984,  (DIND):5985,  (IND):
5986,  (268-523):5987-6242,  (IND):6243,  (524-779):6244-6499,  (IND):650
0,  (780-1035):6501-6756,  (IND):6757,  (1036-1291):6758-7013,  (IND):701
4, (1292-1547):7015-7270, (IND):7271, (1548-1721):7272-7445
TOTAL: 1730
(END)
```

4. Use the quit command to close the debugfs interface.

Understanding the Differences Between hard and Symbolic Links

When comparing the symbolic link and the original file, you will notice a clear difference between them. First, the symbolic link and the original file have different inodes: the original file is just a name that is connected directly to the inode, and the symbolic link refers to the name. The latter can be seen from the output of ls -il (-i displays the inode number): after the name of the symbolic link, an arrow is used to indicate what file you are really working on. Also, you can see that the size of the symbolic link is significantly different from the size of the real file. The size of the symbolic link is the number of bytes in the name of the file it refers to, because no other information is available in the symbolic link. As well, you can see that the permissions on the symbolic link are completely open. This is because the permissions are not managed here, but on the original file instead. Finally, you can see that the file type of the symbolic link is set to l, which indicates that it is a symbolic link (see Listing 3-10).

Listing 3-10. Showing the Differences Between Symbolic and Hard Links

```
root@ubuntu:~# ln -s /etc/hosts symhosts
root@ubuntu:~# ln /etc/hosts hardhosts
root@ubuntu:~# ls -il /etc/hosts hardhosts symhosts
15024138 -rw-r--r--    2 root root 253 2007-06-05 00:20 /etc/hosts
15024138 -rw-r--r--    2 root root 253 2007-06-05 00:20 hardhosts
13500422 lrwxrwxrwx 1 root root   10 2007-07-02 05:45 symhosts -> /etc/hosts
```

You may ask what happens to the symbolic link when the original file is removed. Well, that isn't hard to predict! The symbolic link fails. Linux will show this when displaying file properties with the ls command; you'll get a "File not found" error message when you try to open it.

Working with Hard Links

Every file on a Linux file system has an inode. As explained earlier, all of a file's administrative data is kept in its inode. Your computer actually works entirely with inodes, and the file names are only a convenience for people who are not too good at remembering numbers. Every name that is connected to an inode can be considered a *hard link*. So, when you create a hard link for a file, all you really do is add a new name to an inode. To do this, use the ln command. The interesting thing about hard links is that there is no difference between the original file and the link: they are just two names connected to the same inode. The disadvantage of using them is that hard links must exist on the same device, which is rather limiting. But, if possible, you should always create a hard link instead of a symbolic link because they are faster.

Figure 3-1 depicts the relationship between inodes, hard links, and symbolic links.

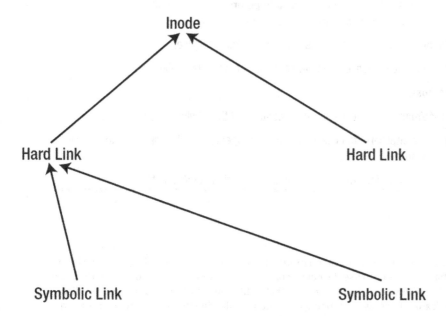

Figure 3-1. *Relationship between inodes, hard links, and symbolic links*

Links Recap

If you really want to understand what a link is all about, you do need to know about the role of the inodes. If you just want a basic knowledge of links, remember the following:

- A symbolic link is like a shortcut. It points to the original file and helps you find it easily. However, it breaks if you remove the original file.

- A hard link is like a copy of the file that is synchronized continuously. There is no difference between the original file and the hard link; they both refer to the same blocks.

Now that you've learned about hard and symbolic links, it's time to do an exercise with them.

```
                EXERCISE 3-3: WORKING WITH LINKS
```

1. Open a root shell.

2. Type **ln -s /etc/hosts ~/computers**. This creates a symbolic link with the name computers in your home directory.

3. Type **ls -il /etc/hosts ~/computers**. This shows properties of both files. Notice that the inode number on both files is different.

4. Type **ln /etc/hosts /root/machines**.

5. Type **ls -il /etc/hosts /root/machines /root/computers**. You'll notice that /etc/hosts and /root/machines have the same properties.

6. Type **echo hello > /etc/hosts**. This adds a line to the /etc/hosts file.

7. Repeat command 5. You'll notice that both hard links show updated file size.

8. Type **rm /etc/hosts**.

9. Type **echo /root/machines**. You'll still see the contents of the previous /etc/hosts file.

10. Type **echo /root/computers**. You'll see an error message: the file the link refers to doesn't exist anymore.

11. Type **ln /root/machines /etc/hosts**. This repairs the original /etc/hosts file.

Summary

In this chapter, you have learned about some of the more advanced features and maintenance tasks on the Linux file systems. You have read how to use the mount command to access devices. You've also learned how to automate mounting of devices by using the /etc/fstab file. Next, the fsck command was discussed to teach you how to check and, if necessary, repair a file system. Following that, you've read how to create backups of files and complete devices, using tar and dd. In the last part of this chapter, you've seen how to work with links to make your Linux file system more versatile. The following commands and configuration files were discussed in this chapter:

- mount: Mounts a device to a directory. Mounting devices is mandatory in Linux; without mounting a device, you can't use it.

- fstab: Indicates a configuration file in /etc that is used to automate mounting of devices on system startup.

- mtab: Indicates a configuration file in /etc that keeps track of the current mount status of devices.

- umount: Disconnects a mounted device.

- fuser: Shows you what files are currently open in a directory.

- lsof: Like fuser, but shows more detail.

- fsck: Checks the integrity of the file system.

- `tar`: Archives files. This means that it puts together multiple files into one big file.

- `gzip`: Compresses files. Often used in conjunction with `tar`.

- `gunzip`: Decompresses files that were compressed with `gzip`. Often used in conjunction with `tar`.

- `bzip2`: Alternative for `gzip`.

- `bunzip2`: Alternative for `gunzip`.

- `dd`: Utility that helps you in cloning devices.

- `ln`: Creates links.

In the next chapter, you'll learn how to work with text files.

CHAPTER 4

■ ■ ■

Working with Text Files

An important part of working on the Linux command line consists of working with text files. If you need to configure services, they'll store their configuration in text files. If you need to write program code, you'll do that in a text file as well. Linux text files are all over your computer, and to be good at the Linux command line, you'll have to know how to handle them. In this chapter, you'll learn how to work with text files. Different methods are discussed for manipulating the contents of them. First, you'll learn about the only editor that matters on Linux, Vi. Next, I'll explain different ways of displaying the contents of text files. After that, we'll talk about some useful utilities that help you in sorting and comparing the contents of different text files—and more. You'll then learn how regular expressions can help you in finding text patterns in a file in a clever way. You'll also read how the programmable filters sed and awk can help you batch-manipulate text files. At the end of this chapter, you'll also get familiar with some of the most useful commands in command-line printing.

Working with Vi

For your day-to-day management tasks from the command line, you'll often need a text editor to change ASCII text files. Although many editors are available for Linux, Vi is still the most popular and probably the most used editor as well. It is a rather complicated editor, however, and most Linux distributions fortunately include Vim, which stands for Vi Improved, the user- friendly version of Vi. When talking about Vi in this book, I'll assume that you are using Vim.

■ **Note** Most distributions use Vim, not Vi, and will start Vim when you enter the command `vi`. Clear, huh? If the commands that I describe in this chapter don't work for you, you're probably working with Vi, not Vim. In that case, use the following command as root: `echo alias vi=vim >> /etc/profile`. This makes sure that after the next time you log in to your computer, Vim is started, not Vi.

Even if Vi looks quite difficult to first time users, seen in its historical context, it was quite an improvement in the year 1976 when it was invented. In those days, only line editors such as ex were available. These editors didn't give a complete overview of a text file a user was working with, but just the current line the user was at, like an old typewriter. Vi, which stands for visual, was the first editor that worked in a mode where the complete text file was displayed which made it possible to move back and forward between lines. To do this, different commands were introduced to make it possible to address individual lines, commands that are still used in modern vi.

Everyone who wants to work from the Linux command line should be capable of working with Vi. Why? You'll find it on every Linux distribution and every version of UNIX. Another important reason why you should get used to working with Vi is that some other commands, especially commands that are important for a Linux administrator, are based on it. For example, to edit quota (which limits available disk space) for the users on your server, you would use edquota, which is just a macro built on Vi. If you want to set permissions for the sudo command, use visudo which, as you likely guessed, is another macro that is built on top of Vi. Or if you want to schedule a task to run at a given moment in time, use crontab -e, which is based on Vi as well.

■ **Note** Well, to tell you the truth, there is a variable setting. The name of the variable is VISUAL. Only when this variable is set to vi (VISUAL=vi) will commands like edquota and visudo use Vi. If it is set to something else, they will use that something else instead. This is how on Ubuntu for instance nano is used as the default editor to accomplish many tasks.

In this section, I'll provide a minimal amount of information that you need to work with Vi. The goal here is just to get you started. You'll learn more about Vi if you really start working with it on a daily basis. Some people walk around with vi cheat sheets, containing long lists of commands that can be used with vi. I don't want to scare you away immediately, which is why I rather focus on the essential commands that help you doing what needs to be done.

Vi Modes

Vi uses two modes: *command mode*, which is used to enter new commands, and *insert mode* (also referred to as the *input mode*), which is used to enter text. Before being able to enter text, you need to enter insert mode, because, as its name suggests, command mode will just allow you to enter commands. Notice that these commands also include cursor movement. As mentioned before, Vi has some pretty useful commands to address specific lines of text. While working with Vi, there often are several options for doing what needs to be done. This adds to the perception of Vi as being difficult, there's just too much to remember. The best way to work with all those different options, is by focussing on one option only. It makes no sense knowing five different commands that help you doing the exact same thing. For example, you can use many methods to enter insert mode. I'll list just four of them:

- Press i to insert text at the current position of the cursor.

- Use a to append text after the current position of the cursor.

- Use o to open a new line under the current position of the cursor (my favorite option).

- Use 0 to open a new line above the current position of the cursor.

After entering insert mode, you can enter text, and Vi will work just like any other editor. Now if you want to save your work, you should next get back to command mode and use the appropriate commands. Pressing the Esc key returns you to command mode from insert mode, and command mode is where you want to be to save text files.

■ **Tip** When starting Vi, always give as an argument the name of the file you want to create with it or the name of an existing file you would like to modify. If you don't do that, Vi will display help text, and you will have the problem of finding out how to get out of this help text. Of course, you can always just read the entire help text to find out how that works (or just type **:q** to get out there).

Saving and Quitting

After activating command mode, you can use commands to save your work. The most common method is to use the :wq! command, which performs several tasks at once. First, a colon is used just because it is part of the command. Then, w is used to save the text you have typed so far. Because no file name is specified after the w, the text will be saved under the same file name that was used when opening the file. If you want to save it under a new file name, just enter the new name after the :w command (not that you have to start the command with a colon also); for instance, the following would save your file with the name newfile:

:w newfile

Next in the :wq! command is q, which makes sure that the editor is quit as well. Last, the exclamation mark tells Vi that it shouldn't complain, but just do its work. Vi has a tendency to get smart with remarks like "A file with this name already exists" (see Listing 4-1), so you are probably going to like the exclamation mark. After all, this is Linux, and you want your Linux system to do as you tell it, not to second-guess you all the time. If you rather want to see warnings like this, just omit typing the ! and just use :wq to wite your file to disk.

Listing 4-1. Vi Will Tell You If It Doesn't Understand What You Want It to Do

```
#
# hosts         This file describes a number of hostname-to-address
#               mappings for the TCP/IP subsystem. It is mostly
#               used at boot time, when no name servers are running.
#               On small systems, this file can be used instead of a
#               "named" name server.
# Syntax:
#
# IP-Address   Full-Qualified-Hostname Short-Hostname
#

127.0.0.1      localhost

# special IPv6 addresses
::1            localhost ipv6-localhost ipv6-loopback

fe00::0        ipv6-localnet

ff00::0        ipv6-mcastprefix
ff02::1        ipv6-allnodes
ff02::2        ipv6-allrouters
ff02::3        ipv6-allhosts
127.0.0.2      nuuk.sander.gl nuuk
E13: File exists (add ! to override)              1,1          All
```

As you have just learned, you can use :wq! to write and quit Vi. You can also use the parts of this command separately. For example, use :w if you just want to write changes while working on a file without quitting it, or use :q! to quit the file without writing changes. The latter option is a nice panic key if something has happened that you absolutely don't want to store on your system. This is useful because Vi will sometimes work magic with the content of your file when you hit the wrong keys. Alternatively, you can recover by using the u command to undo the most recent changes you made to the file.

Cutting, Copying, and Pasting

You don't need a graphical interface to use cut, copy, and paste features; Vi could do this back in the '70s. But you have two ways of using cut, copy, and paste: the easy way and the hard way. If you want to do it the easy way, you can use the v command to enter visual mode, from which you can select a block of text by using the arrow keys. After selecting the block, you can cut, copy, and paste it.

- Use d to cut (in fact, delete) the selection. This will remove the selection and place it in a buffer.

- Use y to copy the selection to the area designated for that purpose in your server's memory.

- Use p to paste the selection. This will copy the selection you have just placed in the reserved area of your server's memory back into your document. It will always paste the selection at the cursor's current position.

Deleting Text

Deleting text is another thing you'll have to do often when working with Vi, and you can use many different methods to delete text. The easiest, however, is from insert mode: just use the Delete key to delete any text. This works in the exact same way as in a word processor. As usual, you have some options from Vi command mode as well:

- Use x to delete a single character. This has the same effect as using the Delete key while in insert mode.

- Use dw to delete the rest of the word. That is, dw will delete everything from the cursor's current position of the end of the word.

- Use **d$** to delete from the current cursor position until the end of the line.

- Use **d** to delete the current selection.

- Use dd to delete a complete line. This is a very useful option that you will probably like a lot.

Moving Through Text Files

Vi also offers some possibilities to move through text files. The following commands are used to search for text and to manipulate your cursor through a text file:

- Use the g key twice to go to the beginning of a text file.

- By using the G key twice, you can go directly to the end of a text file.

- To search text, you can use /, followed by the text you are searching. For instance, the command /root would find the first occurrence of the text root in the current file. This command would search from the current position down in the text file. To repeat this search action, use n (for next). To repeat the search in the opposite direction, use N.

- Use ?, followed by text you are using to search text from the current position in the text upward in the text file. For example, the command ?root would search for the text "root" from the current position in the text upward. To repeat this search action, use n for next. To repeat the search in the opposite direction, use N.

- Use: 5 to go directly to line number 5.

- Use ^ to go to the first position in the current line

- Use $ to go to the last position in the current line

■ **Tip**   To work with advanced search patterns, Vi supports regular expressions as well. Read the section "Working with Basic Regular Expressions" later in this chapter to find out all about these.

Changing All Occurrences of a String in a Text File

When working with Vi, it may happen that you need to change all occurrences of a given word in a text file. Vi has a useful option for this, which is referred to as the *global substitute*. The basic syntax of a global substitution is as follows:

```
:%s/old/new/g
```

This command starts with :%s, which tells Vi that it should make a substitution. Next, it mentions the old text string, in this case old, which in turn is followed by the new text string, new. At the end of the command, the g tells Vi that this is a global action; it will make sure that the substitution is used all over the text file.

I recommend that you analyze your text file carefully after applying a global substitution. Did it work out well? Then save the changes to your text file. If it didn't work out so well, use the u command to undo the global substitution and restore the original situation. In case you've typed one u too many, it's good to know that Ctrl-R will redo the last undo.

EXERCISE 4-1: MANIPULATING TEXT WITH VI

1. Open a root shell.

2. Type **cat /etc/passwd > ~/myfile**.

3. Open ~/myfile in Vi, using **vi ~/myfile**.

4. From within the file, type **GG** to go to the last line.

5. Now type **O** to open a new line and type **some random text**.

6. Press **Esc** to go to command mode, and Type **ZZ** to write and quit your document. This is an alternative to using **:wq!**

7. Repeat step 3 of this exercise.

8. Type **/home** to search the first occurance of the text home in your document.

9. Type **v** to enter visual mode.

10. Type **:13** to select up to line 13.

11. Press **y** to copy the current selection.

12. Type :20 to go to line 20.

13. From here, type **p** to paste the selection that you've copied to the buffer in step 11.

14. Type **u** to undo this last modification.

15. Type **Ctrl-r** to redo.

16. Type **gg** to go to the first line of the text file.

17. Type **:%s/home/HOME/g** to replace all occurances of "home" with "HOME".

18. Type **:wq!** to write and quit the document.

Vi Summarized

In this section you've learned how to work with Vi. Although there are many more commands that you can use when working with Vi, the commands that I've covered in this section will help you perform all basic tasks with Vi. Table 4-1 summarizes all commands that were treated in this section.

Table 4-1. *Summary of Vi Commands*

Command	Explanation
I	Opens insert mode for editing. Inserts text after the current cursor position.
Esc	Returns to command mode.
A	Opens insert mode for editing. Inserts text at the current cursor position.
O	Opens insert mode for editing. Opens a new line after the current line where the cursor is.
O	Opens insert mode for editing. Opens a new line before the current line where the cursor is.
:wq!	Writes and quits the current document. Suppresses any warnings.
:w	Writes the current file using the same name. Appends a file name to write the file with another name.
:q!	Quits without saving. Ignores any warnings.
u	Undoes the last command.
Ctrl-r	Undo an undo (redo)
V	Enters visual mode to mark a block on which you can use commands.

(*continued*)

Table 4-1. (*continued*)

Command	Explanation
D	Deletes the current selection.
Y	Yanks (copies) the current selection.
P	Pastes.
G	Goes to the top of the current text file.
G	Goes to the bottom of the current text file.
/text	Searches *text* from the current position of the cursor downward.
?text	Searches *text* from the current position of the cursor upward.
^	Go to the first position in the current line
$	Go to the last position in the current line
:nn	Go directly to line number nn

Displaying Contents of Text Files

When working on the command line, you will find that you often need to modify configuration files, which take the form of ASCII text files. Therefore, it's very important to be able to browse the content of these files. You have several ways of doing this:

- cat: Displays the contents of a file

- tac: Does the same as cat, but displays the contents in reverse order

- tail: Shows just the last lines of a text file

- head: Displays the first lines of a file

- less: Opens an advanced file viewer

- more: Like less, but not as advanced

Showing File Contents with cat and tac

First is the cat command. This command just dumps the contents of a file on the screen (see Listing 4-2). This can be useful, but, if the contents of the file do not fit on the screen, you'll see some text scrolling by, and when it stops, you'll only see the last lines of the file displayed on the screen. As an alternative to cat, you can use tac as well. Not only is its name the opposite of cat, its result is too. This command will dump the contents of a file to the screen, but it reverses the file contents.

Listing 4-2. The cat Command Is Used to Display the Contents of a Text File

```
root@RNA:/boot# cat /etc/hosts
127.0.0.1       localhost
127.0.1.1       RNA.lan RNA

# The following lines are desirable for IPv6 capable hosts
::1     ip6-localhost ip6-loopback
fe00::0 ip6-localnet
ff00::0 ip6-mcastprefix
ff02::1 ip6-allnodes
ff02::2 ip6-allrouters
ff02::3 ip6-allhosts
```

Showing a File's Last Lines with `tail`

Another very useful command is `tail`. If no options are used, this command will show the last ten lines of a text file. You can also modify the command to show any number of lines on the bottom of a file; for example, `tail -2 /etc/passwd` will display the last two lines of the configuration file in which usernames are stored.

Also very useful for monitoring what happens on your system in real time is the option -f, which keeps `tail` open and refreshes the output as soon as new lines are added. For example, if you use `tail -f /var/log/messages`, the most generic log file on your system is opened, and, when a new line is written to the bottom of that file, you will see it immediately. Use Ctrl+C to get out of a file that you've opened using `tail` -f. Listing 4-3 shows you what the result of `tail -f /var/log/messages` may look like. In particular, the last two lines here are of interest; you can see that user sander has tried to work as root using the su command, but failed in doing so.

Listing 4-3. Monitoring System Events in Real Time with `tail -f`

```
BTN:~ # tail -f /var/log/messages
Nov 11 08:57:27 BTN sshd[11993]: Accepted keyboard-interactive/pam for root from
 192.168.1.53 port 62992 ssh2
Nov 11 09:00:01 BTN su: (to beagleindex) root on none
Nov 11 09:00:01 BTN su: (to beagleindex) root on none
Nov 11 09:02:53 BTN su: (to nobody) root on none
Nov 11 09:02:58 BTN syslog-ng[2407]: last message repeated 3 times
Nov 11 09:02:58 BTN su: (to cyrus) root on none
Nov 11 09:02:58 BTN ctl_mboxlist[12745]: DBERROR: reading /var/lib/imap/db/skipstamp
, assuming the worst: No such file or directory
Nov 11 09:02:59 BTN ctl_mboxlist[12745]: skiplist: recovered /var/lib/imap/mailboxes
.db (0 records, 144 bytes) in 0 secondsListing 4-3: Use tail -f to monitor log files in real time
Nov 11 09:03:59 BTN sux: FAILED SU (to root) sander on /dev/pts/1
Nov 11 09:03:08 BTN sux: (to root) sander on /dev/pts/1
```

Displaying the First Lines in a File with head

The opposite of tail is the head command, which displays the top lines of a text file. As with tail, this command is useful in a shell script, if you want to display only the first line of a file, for instance. You can even combine head and tail to specify exactly which line in a file you want to display. Consider the example file that you see in Listing 4-4.

Listing 4-4. Example Text File

```
Username      Current status
Linda         enabled
Lori          disabled
Lisa          enabled
Laura         enabled
```

Imagine that, for some reason, you need to see the name of the first user only. You wouldn't get that by just using tail or by just using head. If, however, you first take the head of the first two lines, and next the tail of the result of that, you would get the required result:

```
head -n 2 textfile | tail -n 1
```

As you can see in this example, once again, by using a pipe you get a command that has some powerful additional options.

Browsing File Contents with less and more

The last two commands used to view the contents of text files are less and more. The most important thing you need to remember about them is that you can do more with less. Contrary to common sense, the less command is actually the improved version of more. Both commands will open your ASCII text file in a viewer as you can see in Listing 4-5, which shows the contents of the /etc/hosts file (which contains mappings between node names and IP addresses). In this viewer, you can browse down in the file by using the Page Down key or the spacebar. Only less offers the option to browse up as well. Also, both commands have a search facility. If the less utility is open and displays the contents of your file, use /sometext from within the less viewer to locate sometext in the file. Useful to remember: both utilities are based on the Vi editor; therefore, many key strokes that you can use in Vi will work in less and more as well. To quit both utilities, use the q command.

Listing 4-5. You Can Use the less Command As a Viewer to View File Contents

```
BTN:~ # less /etc/hosts
127.0.0.1        localhost
127.0.1.1        RNA.lan RNA
192.168.1.100    RNA.lan RNA
192.168.1.101    ZNA.lan ZNA
192.168.1.102    BTN.lan BTN
192.168.1.103    XTN.lan XTN
/etc/hosts (END)
```

Cool Text File Manipulation Tools

To change the contents of text files, you can use an editor. Apart from editors that oblige you to make changes word by word, you can also use some automated tools to do batch changes. The tools mentioned in the following text are all classical tools from the UNIX era, and you can use them to apply batch changes. You will notice though that these tools don't make their changes in the files you're working on but show the modifications on the standard output. This means that in all cases, you'll have to work with redirection to write the changes to a new file. You will see some examples explaining how this works.

Changing Contents in a Batch with tr

The tr utility is used to translate or delete characters from a file. Since it doesn't have any options to work with input or output files, you have to using piping and redirection to apply changes to files when using tr. A classical use of tr is to translate lowercase into uppercase. In the example in Listing 4-6, you can see the contents of the ~/users file before and after it is translated with tr.

Listing 4-6. Changing Lowercase into Uppercase with tr

```
BTN:~ # cat users
linda
sanne
anja
sylvia
zeina
BTN:~ # cat users | tr a-z A-Z
LINDA
SANNE
ANJA
SYLVIA
ZEINA
```

As you can see, in this example the cat command is used first to display the contents of the file user, and the result of the cat command is piped to the tr command, which translates a–z into A–Z. The result, however, is written to the standard output only, and not to a file. To write the result of the command from Listing 4-6 to a text file with the name users2, you can apply redirection to do the following:

```
cat users | tr a-z A-Z > users2
```

Instead of working with cat and a pipe that has tr process the results of the cat command, you can also work with the input redirector, <. The next command shows an alternative for the preceding command that translates and next writes the results to a new text file:

```
tr a-z A-Z < users > users2
```

Sorting Text Files with sort

Imagine that you have a list of users, and you want to sort that list. In this case, you can use the sort command. For instance, if applied to the users file from Listing 4-6, sort users would give you the result that you see in Listing 4-7.

Listing 4-7. Sorting File Contents with sort

```
BTN:~ # sort users

anja
linda
sanne
sylvia
zeina
```

At first sight, sort appears to be a simple utility that is pretty straightforward. You may be surprised, though. For instance, consider the example in Listing 4-8, in which another users file is sorted.

Listing 4-8. Sorting in Alphabetical Order?

```
BTN:~ # sort users

Angy
Caroline
Susan
anja
linda
sanne
sylvia
zeina
```

As you can see, in the example from Listing 4-8, sort first gives names that start in uppercase, and next it gives all lowercase names. This is because by default it doesn't respect alphabetical order, but it takes the order as defined in the ASCII table. Fortunately, sort has the -f option, which allows you to apply real alphabetical order and ignore case. Also useful is the option -n, which makes sure that numbers are sorted correctly. Without the -n option, sort would consider 8, 88, 9 the correct order. With this option applied, you can make sure that the numbers are sorted as 8, 9, 88.

Finding Differences Between Text Files with diff

If you want to find out differences between files, the diff utility is very useful. Typically, you would use diff to compare an old version with a newer version of a file. For instance, if you make a copy of the user database in /etc/passwd to /etc/passwd.old, you can compare these files later by using the diff utility to see whether any differences have occurred. Listing 4-9 gives an easy-to-understand example of the diff utility.

Listing 4-9. Comparing Files with diff

```
BTN:~ # diff users users2
7d6
< pleuni
```

In the example in Listing 4-9, there is only one difference between the two files that are compared: one file contains a line that reads pleuni, whereas the other line doesn't. The diff utility uses the coordinates 7d6 to indicate where it has found differences. In these coordinates, it uses a d to indicate that a line was deleted from the first file. The following indicators can be used in the coordinates:

- d: Line was deleted from the first file

- a: Line was added to the first file

- c: Line was changed in the first file

The number to the left of the letter corresponds to the line number found in the first file. The number to the right of the letter corresponds to the line in the second file used during comparison. Since diff finds the longest common sequence in both files, 7d6 means that the line pleuni was deleted from the first file to make it the same as the second file.

< and > are also clear indications of where the differences can be found. < refers to the first file, while > refers to the second file.

Another way of presenting the output given by diff is to use the --side-by-side option as well, to show the contents of both files and where exactly the differences are. You can see an example of this in Listing 4-10.

Listing 4-10. Use the --side-by-side Option to Clearly See Differences

```
BTN:~ # diff --side-by-side users users2
linda                           linda
Angy                            Angy
Susan                           Susan
sanne                           sanne
anja                            anja
Caroline                        Caroline
pleuni                          <
sylvia                          sylvia
zeina                           zeina
```

Checking Whether a Line Exists Twice with uniq

When working on a text configuration file, it is a rather common error to have a given configuration parameter twice. The risk of getting this is very real, especially if you have a configuration file that contains hundreds of lines of configuration parameters. By using the uniq utility, you'll find these lines easily. Let's consider the input file users, which is displayed in Listing 4-11.

Listing 4-11. Test Input File

```
BTN:~ # cat users
linda
Angy
Susan
sanne
anja
Caroline
pleuni
linda
sylvia
zeina
sylvia
```

As you can see, some of the lines in this input file occur twice. If, however, you use the uniq users command, the command shows you unique lines only. That is, if a given line occurs twice, you will only see the first occurrence of that line as you can see in Listing 4-12.

Listing 4-12. Displaying Unique Lines Only

```
BTN:~ # uniq users
linda
Angy
Susan
sanne
anja
Caroline
pleuni
sylvia
zeina
```

Like most other commands, uniq has some specific switches as well that allow you to tell it exactly what you need it to do. For instance, use uniq --repeated yourfile to find out which lines occur repeatedly in yourfile.

Getting Specific Information with cut

Another very useful command is cut. This command allows you to get fields from structured files. To do this, it helps if you tell cut what the field delimiter is. In Listing 4-13, you see an example. First, I've displayed the last seven lines of the /etc/passwd file in which user accounts are stored, and next, I've piped this to the cut command to filter out the third column.

Listing 4-13. Filtering a Specific Column from the passwd User Database

```
nuuk:~ # tail -n 7 /etc/passwd
lori:x:1006:100::/home/lori:/bin/bash
laura:x:1007:100::/home/laura:/bin/bash
lucy:x:1008:100::/home/lucy:/bin/bash
lisa:x:1009:100::/home/lisa:/bin/bash
lea:x:1010:100::/home/lea:/bin/bash
leona:x:1011:100::/home/leona:/bin/bash
lilly:x:1012:100::/home/lilly:/bin/bash
nuuk:~ # tail -n 7 /etc/passwd | cut -d : -f 3
1006
1007
1008
1009
1010
1011
1012
```

In this example command, the option -d : is used with cut to specify the field delimiter, which is a : in the /etc/passwd file. Next, with the option -f 3, cut learns that it should filter out the third field. You can really benefit from the options that cut has to offer, if you combine it with other commands in a pipe. Listing 4-13 already shows an example of this, but you can go beyond this example. For instance, the command cut -d : -f 3 /etc/passwd | sort -n would display a sorted list of user IDs from the /etc/passwd file.

EXERCISE 4-2: WORKING WITH TEXT PROCESSING TOOLS

1. Open a shell.

2. Type **tr [:lower:] [:upper:] < /etc/passwd > ~/myfile** to create myfile

3. Type **less ~/myfile** to open the contents of the file in the **less** viewer. Type q to quit it.

4. Type **sort ~/myfile** and observe the results. Notice that the contents of the file is sorted on the first character.

5. Type **sort -t: -k3 -n ~/myfile**. This sorts the contents of the file based on the numeric order in the third column. Notice the part -t: which defines the trailing character as a :

6. Type head **-n 5 ~/myfile**. It shows the first 5 lines of the file.

7. Type **tail -f /var/log/messages**. You'll see the last lines of /var/log/messages, with new lines scrolling by as they are added.

8. Press Ctrl-c to interrupt the tail -f command.

Advanced Text File Filtering and Processing

Up to now, we've talked about the simple text-processing tools only. There are some advanced tools as well, among which are the old and versatile sed and awk. Although these are complicated tools, you may benefit from some basic knowledge about these tools. In the next sections, you'll learn about their basics. Before diving into sed and awk details, you'll read about an advanced way to work with text patterns by using regular expressions. Each of these three subjects merits a book on its own; consider what I give here just a very basic introduction to these complex matters.

Working with Basic Regular Expressions

Many programs discussed in this chapter are used to search for and work with text patterns in files. Because working with text patterns is so important in Linux, a method is needed to refer to text patterns in a flexible way that goes beyond just quoting the text pattern literally. For instance, try a command like grep -r host /; it will give you a huge result because every word that contains the text "host" (think, for example, about words like ghostscript) would give a match. By using a regular expression, you can be much more specific about what you are looking for. For instance, you can tell grep that it should look only for lines that start with the word host.

Regular expressions are not available for all commands; the command that you use must be programmed to work with regular expressions. The most common examples of such commands are the grep and vi utilities. Other utilities, like sed and awk, which are covered later in this section, can also work with regular expressions.

An example of the use of a regular expression is in the following command:

```
grep 'lin.x' *
```

In this example, the dot in the regular expression 'lin.x' has a special meaning; it means every character at that particular position in the text string is seen as a match. To prevent interpretation problems, I advise you to always put regular expressions between single quotes. By doing this, you'll prevent the shell from interpreting the regular expression.

As mentioned in the introduction of this section, you can do many things with regular expressions. In the following list, I give examples of some of the most common and useful regular expressions:

- ^: Indicates that the text string has to be at the beginning of a line. For instance, to find only lines that have the text hosts at the beginning of a line, use the following command:

```
grep -ls '^hosts' *
```

- $: Refers to the end of a line. For instance, to find only lines that have the text hosts at the end of the line, use the following command:

```
grep -ls 'hosts$' *
```

■ **Tip**   You can combine ^ and $ in a regular expression. For instance, to find lines that contain only the word "yes," you would use grep -ls '^yes$' *.

- .: Serves as a wildcard to refer to any character, with the exception of a newline character. To find lines that contain the text tex, tux, tox, or tix, for instance, use the following command:

```
grep -ls 't.x' *
```

- [ ]: Indicates characters in the regular expression that should be interpreted as alternatives. For instance, you would use the following command to find users who have the name pinda or linda:

```
grep -ls '[pl]inda' *
```

- [^]: Ignores all characters that you put between square brackets after the ^ sign. For instance, the following command would find all lines that have the text inda in them, but not lines that contain the text linda or pinda:

```
grep -ls '[^pl]inda' *
```

- -: Refers to a class or a range of characters. You have already seen an example of this in the tr command where the following was used to translate all lowercase letters into uppercase letters:

```
tr a-z A-Z < mytext
```

Likewise, you could use a regular expression to find all files that have lines that start with a number, using the following command:

```
grep -ls '^0-9' *
```

- \< and \>: Search for patterns at the beginning of a word or at the end of a word. For instance, the following would show lines that have text beginning with san:

  grep \<san *

  These regular expressions have two disadvantages though. First is that they don't find lines that start with the provided regular expression. The other disadvantage is that they are not supported by all utilities, though Vi and grep do work with them.

- \: Makes sure that a character that has a special meaning in a regular expression is not interpreted. For instance, the following command will search a text string that starts with any character, followed by the text host:

  grep -ls '.host' *

  If, however, you need to find a text string that has a dot at the first position, which is followed by the text host, you need the following regular expression:

  grep -ls '\.host' *

The regular expressions just discussed help you find words that contain certain text strings. You can also use regular expressions to specify how often a given string should occur in a word by using regular expression *repetition operators*. For instance, you can use a regular expression to search for files containing the username linda exactly three times. When working with repetition operators, you must make sure that the entire regular expression is in quotes; otherwise, you may end up with the shell interpreting your repetition operator. Next is a list of the most important repetition operators:

- *: The asterisk is used to indicate that the preceding regular expression may occur once, more than once, or not at all. It is not the most useful character in a regular expression, but I mainly mention it so that you don't try to use it as a * in the shell. In a shell environment, * stands for any character; in regular expressions, it just indicates that the preceding regular expression may exist.

- ?: The question mark is used to indicate that there may be a character at this position, but there doesn't have to be a character. Consider the following example, where both the words "color" and "colour" will be found:

  grep -ls 'colo.r' *

- +: The preceding character or regular expression has to be present at least once.

- \{n\}: The preceding character or regular expression occurs at least n times. This is useful in a regular expression where you are looking for a number, say, between 100 and 999, as in the following command:

  grep -ls '0-9\{3\}' *

Working with Programmable Filters

In the first part of this chapter, you've read about utilities that you can use to manipulate text files. Most of the utilities discussed so far are in some way limited in use. If they just don't do what you need them to do, you may need more powerful utilities. In that case, programmable filters such as sed and awk may offer what you need.

Once you start working with power tools like sed and awk, you may end up using programming languages such as Perl and Python. You could consider languages like these as a further extension to the powerful sed and awk, with more options and more possibilities that allow you to process text files in real time, something that is quite important if, for instance, you want to offer dynamic web pages to end users. In this chapter, we won't go that far. You'll just get a basic introduction to working with sed and awk, with the purpose of making text file processing easier for you.

Working with sed

In fact sed, which stands for Stream EDitor, is just a further development of the old editor ed. With sed, you can automate commands on text files. To do this, sed processes the text file line by line to see whether a command has to be executed on these lines. By default, sed will write its result to standard output. This means you must redirect it somewhere else if you also really need to do something with this standard output.

The basic sed syntax is as follows:

```
sed 'list of commands' file ...
```

Normally, sed will walk through the files it has to work on line by line, apply its commands to each line, and then write the output to the standard output. Let's have a look at an example involving a file with the name users, shown in Listing 4-14.

Listing 4-14. Example Text File

```
nuuk:~ # cat users
lori:x:1006:100::/home/lori:/bin/bash
laura:x:1007:100::/home/laura:/bin/bash
lucy:x:1008:100::/home/lucy:/bin/bash
lisa:x:1009:100::/home/lisa:/bin/bash
lea:x:1010:100::/home/lea:/bin/bash
leona:x:1011:100::/home/leona:/bin/bash
lilly:x:1012:100::/home/lilly:/bin/bash
```

If you just want to display, say, the first two lines from this file, you can use the sed command 2q. With this command, you tell sed to show two lines, and then quit (q). Listing 4-15 shows the results of this command.

Listing 4-15. Showing the First Two Lines with sed and Quitting

```
nuuk:~ # sed 2q users
lori:x:1006:100::/home/lori:/bin/bash
laura:x:1007:100::/home/laura:/bin/bash
```

Basically, to edit lines with sed automatically, you need to find the proper way to address lines. To do this, you can just refer to the line number you want to display, but far more useful is to have sed search for lines that contain a certain string and execute an operation on that line. To refer to a string in a certain line, you can use regular expressions, which have to be between slashes. An example of this is in the following sed command, where only lines containing the string or are displayed:

```
sed -n /or/p users
```

In this example, the option -n is used to suppress automatic printing of pattern space. Without this option, you would see every matching line twice. Next, /or/ specifies the text you are looking for, and the command p is used on this text to print it. As the last part, the name of the file on which sed should do its work is mentioned. Following is a list of examples where regular expressions are used in combination with sed on the example text file from Listing 4-14:

- sed -n /or/p users: Gives the line that contains the text lori; only those lines that contain the literal string or are displayed.

- sed -n /^or/p users: Doesn't give any result, as there are no lines starting with the text or.

- sed -n /./p users: Gives all lines; the dot refers to any character, so all lines give a match.

- sed -n /\./p users: Still gives all lines. Since no quotes are used in the regular expression, the shell interprets the \ sign before sed can treat it as part of the regular expression. Therefore, the dot refers to any character, and all lines from the example file are displayed.

- sed -n /\./p users: Shows only lines that contain a dot. Since these don't exist in the example file, no result is given.

- sed -n /me\/le/p users: Shows the lines containing the text lea and leona. The regular expression in this example uses me\/le, which means that in this case sed searches for the literal string 'me/le'. Note that this command would also fail without the quotes.

Up to now, you have read about line addressing only, and just one command was displayed, which is the command p for print. sed has many other commands as well, of which the s (substitute) command is without a doubt the single most popular. By using the s command, you can substitute a string with another string. In the next example you can see how the s command is used to replace /home with /users in the example file from Listing 4-14. See also Listing 4-16 for the complete results of this command:

```
sed s/home/users/g users
```

Note that in this command, the first element that is used is the s command itself. Then follow two addresses: the name of the string to search for and the name of the string this should be replaced with. Next, the g command tells sed this is a global command, meaning that it will perform the replace action all over the file. Last, the name of the file on which sed should work is given.

The result of this command is written to STDOUT by default, and therefore is not saved in any file. If you want to save it, make sure to use redirection to write the result to a file (e.g., sed s/home/users/g users > newusers). Alternatively, you can write the results to the source file, using the -i option. But you should be sure about what you're doing, as the modifications will be applied immediately.

Listing 4-16. Using the sed Substitute Command to Replace Text

```
nuuk:~ # sed s/home/users/g users
lori:x:1006:100::/users/lori:/bin/bash
laura:x:1007:100::/users/laura:/bin/bash
lucy:x:1008:100::/users/lucy:/bin/bash
lisa:x:1009:100::/users/lisa:/bin/bash
lea:x:1010:100::/users/lea:/bin/bash
leona:x:1011:100::/users/leona:/bin/bash
lilly:x:1012:100::/users/lilly:/bin/bash
```

Manipulating text Files with awk

Another powerful tool to manipulate text files is awk. Like sed, awk is also a programming language by itself, with many possibilities. Personally I like it a lot, because it is a very versatile utility that helps you to get the information you need fast and easy.

As is the case with sed, each awk command also works with a pattern that specifies what to look for. Next, you'll use a command to specify what to do with it. Typically, the patterns are put between slashes, and the actions that you want to perform are put in braces. Since awk also works with regular expressions, it is wise to put awk patterns between single quotes as well, to avoid the shell from interpreting them by accident. The global structure of an awk command is as follows:

```
awk '/pattern/{action}' file
```

In case you don't specify a pattern, the action is performed on every line in the file. You can interpret this as "every line that matches the pattern null." If no action is specified, awk just shows you the lines that match the pattern; hence, there is no big difference with a tool such as grep. An example of this is shown in Listing 4-17, where awk displays lines containing the text lori.

Listing 4-17. Displaying Lines That Contain a Given Text Pattern with awk

```
nuuk:~ # awk '/lori/' users
lori:x:1006:100::/home/lori:/bin/bash
```

The awk utility becomes really interesting combined with its abilities to filter columns or fields out of a text file. The default field separator is a space, but you can tell awk to use something else instead by using the option -F followed by the character you want to use as a separator. In the next example line, the awk print command and the colon field separator are used to find the user ID of user lori from the users file:

```
awk -F : '/lori/{print $3}' users
```

In the preceding example, you see that $3 is used to refer to the third field in the file. You can also use $0 to refer to the entire record. Because awk is able to refer to specific fields, it's possible as well to compare fields with one another. The following operators are available for this purpose:

- ==: Equals (searches for a field that has the same value)

- !=: Not equals

- <: Smaller than

- <=: Smaller than or equal to

- >: Bigger than

- >=: Bigger than or equal to

With these operators, you can make some useful calculations on text files. For instance, the following example would search the /etc/passwd file and show all lines where the third field contains a value bigger than 999:

```
awk '$3 > 999 { print $1 }' /etc/passwd
```

■ **Tip** The preceding example allows you to find all names of user accounts that have a UID bigger than 999 (you'll learn more about commands like this in Chapter 6, which discusses user management). Typically, this gives you real usernames, and not the names of system accounts.

EXERCISE 4-3: USING SED

1. Type **awk '/root/' ~/myfile** to show all lines that contain the text root.

2. Type **awk -F : '/root/{ print $3 } ' ~/myfile**. This prints the third field of all lines that contain the text root.

3. Type **sed -n '2p' ~/myfile**. This prints the second line in the ~/myfile file.

4. Type **sed -i -e '2d' ~/myfile**. This command deletes the second line in the file and writes the contents to the file immediately.

Printing Files

On Linux, the CUPS print system is used to print files. Typically, you would set up a CUPS printing environment with the management tools that are provided with your distribution, so I won't cover that here. Once installed, you can use several command-line tools to send jobs to CUPS printers. You can find examples of some of these in the following text.

Managing CUPS Print Queues

CUPS offers a lot of tools from the command line that you can use to manage print jobs and queues. The flow of a print job is easy: a print job is placed in the printer queue, where it waits for the printer process to get it out of there and have it served by a printer. If you have worked with older UNIX print systems, I have good news for you: CUPS works with tools from thBerkeley UNIX dialect as well as the System V UNIX dialect. Since the Berkeley UNIX dialect is more common, in this subsection I will focus on the Berkeley tools.

Creating Print Jobs

To create a print job from the command line, you need the lpr tool. With this tool, you can send a file directly to a printer. In its most basic configuration, you can issue the command lpr somefile; this command will send somefile to the default printer. If you want to specify the printer where the file is sent to, you can use the -P option followed by the name of the print queue. For example, use lpr -P hplj41 somefile to send somefile to the queue for hplj41. Want to print to a remote printer? That's also possible using lpr; use lpr -P hplj41@someserver somefile to send somefile to the queue named hplj41 at someserver.

Tuning Print Jobs

From time to time, as an administrator it is useful to display print job information. For this purpose, you can use the lpq command. To get a list of all print jobs in the default queue, just issue lpq. Want to show print jobs in another queue? Specify the name of the queue you want to monitor, like lpq -P somequeue. This will get you a fairly high-level overview of the jobs and their properties. Want to see more detail? Use lpr -l -P somequeue. The option -a lets you check print jobs in all queues—just issue lpq -a.

Removing Print Jobs

Have you ever sent a print job to a queue that wasn't supposed to be sent after all? Good news: if you are fast enough, you can remove that job using the lprm command. This command can be used in many different ways. The most brute-force way of using it is with the - option and nothing else. This will remove all jobs that you have submitted to the queue, and if you are the root user, it will remove all jobs from the queue. You can be more specific as well; for example, lprm -P hplj41 3 would remove job number 3 from the queue hplj4. To find out what job number your queue is using, you can use the lpq command.

■ **Tip** When hacking CUPS from the command line, it can happen that changes are not automatically activated. If you've made a change, but you don't see any result, use the rccups restart command to restart CUPS.

Finding Files

Since Linux is a very file-oriented operating system, it is important that you know how to find files. The utility used for this purpose, find, allows you to find files based on any of the file properties that were used when storing the file on disk. Let's start with an example: the following find command helps you find all files with names that start with host on the entire hard drive of the computer:

```
find / -name "hosts*"
```

One cool thing about find is that it allows you to do a lot more than just find files based on their file names. For instance, you can find files based on their size, owner, permissions, and much more. Following is a short list of file properties that you can use to find files:

- -amin *n*: Finds all files that were last accessed less than *n* minutes ago. For instance, find -amin 5 would give all files that were accessed less than five minutes ago.

- -executable: Finds all files that are executable.

- -group *gname*: Shows all files that have *gname* as their group owner. (Read Chapter 7 for more information about ownership.)

- -mmin *n*: Shows all files that were last modified less than *n* minutes ago.

- -newer *file*: Shows all files that are newer than *file*.

- -nogroup, -nouser: Show all files that do not have a group or a user owner.

- -perm [+|-]*mode*: Finds all files that have a specific permission mode set. (See Chapter 7 for more details about permissions.)

- -size *n*: Finds all files of a specific size. With this parameter, you can also find files bigger than or smaller than a specific size. For instance, find / -size +2G would find all files larger than 2 gigabytes. When using this parameter, use K, M, and G for kilobytes, megabytes, and gigabytes, respectively. Use the + sign to indicate that you want to see files greater than a specific size.

- -type *t*: Finds files of a specific type. The most interesting file types that you can search for using this option are d for directory or f for a regular file (which is any file that is not a directory).

The interesting part of find is that you can combine different options as well. For example, you can run a find command that finds all files owned by user linda that are larger than 100MB using the following command:

```
find / -user linda -size +100M
```

Even more interesting is that you can issue any other command on the result of your find command using the -exec statement. Let's have a look at an example where find is used to find all files owned by jerry and next moves these files to the directory /root:

```
find / -user jerry -exec mv {} /root \;
```

Here you can see some specific items are used with the command you start with -exec. For instance, normally the mv command would refer to the name of some files, as in mv * /root. In this specific case, mv has to work on the result of the previous find command. You refer to this result by using {}. Next, you have to close the exec statement. To do this, use \; at the end each time you open -exec.

Let's have a look at one more example. This file first looks up all files that are owned by user linda and next executes grep to look in these files to see whether any of them contains the text blah:

```
find / -user linda -exec grep -l blah {} \;
```

As you can see, find is a useful tool that helps you in finding files, no matter what properties the file may have.

```
EXERCISE 4-3: FINDING FILES
```

1. Type **which passwd**. This command searches the $PATH for the presence of a binary with the name passwd. Notice that it does not show the /etc/passwd file.

2. Type **find / -name "passwd"**. This command searches the entire file system for files that have the string passwd in the name.

3. Type **find / -user "root"**. This searches the file system for files that are owned by user root.

4. Type **find / -user "root" -size +500M**. This searches the file system for files that are bigger than 500MB and owned by user root.

Summary

In this chapter, you've learned about commands that help you in manipulating text files. Apart from these commands, you have learned how to work with regular expressions that help you in finding text patterns in a clever way. Following is a short list in which all commands that are covered in this chapter are summarized:

- vi: Brings up a text editor that allows you to create and modify text files
- cat: Displays the contents of a text file
- tac: Displays the contents of a text file, but inversed
- tail: Shows the last n lines of a text file
- head: Shows the first n lines of a text file
- less: Allows you to walk page by page through a text file
- tr: Substitutes characters, for instance, changing all lowercase letters to uppercase
- diff: Finds differences between files
- sort: Sorts files into alphabetical or any other order
- uniq: Finds a line that has multiple occurrences in a file
- cut: Filters fields from a structured file with clearly marked field separators
- sed: Brings up a stream editor, especially useful for finding and replacing text
- awk: Applies a programmable filter, especially useful for displaying specific fields from files that contain specific text
- lpr: Allows you to send files to a printer
- lpq: Helps you in monitoring files that are waiting to be printed
- lprm: Removes jobs from the print queue

In the next chapter, you'll learn how to manage a Linux file system.

CHAPTER 5

■ ■ ■

Managing Partitions and Logical Volumes

To work with files, you need to store them. In most situations, you'll need to create a logical storage unit before you do so. Creating such a storage unit makes it easier to configure your hard drive in a flexible way. In Linux, you can choose between two of those logical storage units: partitions and logical volumes. Choose partitions if you want to work easily and you don't have very specific needs for what you do with your hard drive. If, however, you need maximal flexibility and easy resizing, working with logical volumes is a better solution. In this chapter, you'll read how to create partitions as well as logical volumes, how to make a file system on them, and how to manage that file system.

Addressing Storage Devices

Up to now, you've read how to address devices based on device names such as /dev/sda and /dev/vda. There is a problem though with these device names: they are not guaranteed to be unique. This is because normally the device name is determined at the moment the kernel finds out that a new device has been attached to the system. The following example explains the problem.

Imagine that your computer currently has a local hard disk as the only storage device. The name of this hard disk will most likely be /dev/sda. Imagine that you have two USB drives, a 1GB USB key and an 80GB USB hard disk. Say you attach the 1GB USB key first to your computer. The computer will give it the device name /dev/sdb, as the devices are named in sequential order. If after that you attach the 80GB USB hard disk, it becomes /dev/sdc. Now imagine you do the opposite and first attach the 80GB hard disk. You can probably guess what happens—it becomes /dev/sdb instead of /dev/sdc, which it was before. So you cannot be sure that these device names are always unique.

To guarantee uniqueness of device names, there are two solutions. When creating the file system with mkfs, you can put a label in the file system. You can also work with the unique device names that are created automatically in the /dev/disk directory. The next two sections give more details about both.

File System Labels

The oldest method to refer to devices in always the same way is by adding a *file system label*. This label is stored in the file system and not in the metadata. Using file system labels is useful for mounting devices, as the mount command will check for a label. However, you cannot depend on it in situations where you need to address the device itself and not the file system that is in it.

Typically, you will add a label to a file system when formatting it. For instance, to add a label to an Ext4 file system, you would use the following command:

```
mkfs.ext4 -L mylabel /dev/sda2
```

On most file systems, you can also set a label to an existing file system. On Ext file systems, you would do this using the tune2fs utility:

```
tune2fs -L mylabel /dev/sda2
```

There is more information on the use of these commands later in this chapter.

Once the file system label is set, you can use it when mounting the device. Just replace the name of the device by LABEL=*labelname* to do this. For instance, the following command would mount the file system that has the label mylabel:

```
mount LABEL=mylabel /mnt
```

udev Device Names

File system labels are useful, but only in situations where you need to address the file system that is on the device. If you need to address the device itself, they will not do. Modern Linux distributions have an alternative. This alternative is created by the udev process, which is started on all modern Linux distributions automatically. udev is the process that detects device changes on the hardware bus and is responsible for creating device names. Not only does it create the device names /dev/sdb and so on, but for each storage device it also creates a unique device name in the directory /dev/disk. In Listing 5-1, you can see an example of these device names.

Listing 5-1. udev Creates Unique Device Names for All Storage Devices

```
xen:~ # ls -Rl /dev/disk
/dev/disk:
total 0
drwxr-xr-x 2 root root 280 Jan 13 10:36 by-id
drwxr-xr-x 2 root root 140 Jan 13 10:36 by-path
drwxr-xr-x 2 root root 80 Jan 13 12:16 by-uuid

/dev/disk/by-id:
total 0
lrwxrwxrwx 1 root root 10 Jan 13 10:36 ata--part1 -> ../../sda1
lrwxrwxrwx 1 root root 10 Jan 13 10:36 ata--part2 -> ../../sda2
lrwxrwxrwx 1 root root 10 Jan 13 10:36 ata--part3 -> ../../sda3
lrwxrwxrwx 1 root root 9 Jan 13 10:36 ata-WDC_WD5002ABYS-18B1B0_WD-WMASY5022406
-> ../../sda
lrwxrwxrwx 1 root root 9 Jan 13 10:36 edd-int13_dev80 -> ../../sda
lrwxrwxrwx 1 root root 10 Jan 13 10:36 edd-int13_dev80-part1 -> ../../sda1
lrwxrwxrwx 1 root root 10 Jan 13 10:36 edd-int13_dev80-part2 -> ../../sda2
lrwxrwxrwx 1 root root 10 Jan 13 10:36 edd-int13_dev80-part3 -> ../../sda3
lrwxrwxrwx 1 root root 9 Jan 13 10:36 scsi-SATA_WDC_WD5002ABYS-_WD-WMASY5022406
-> ../../sda
```

```
lrwxrwxrwx 1 root root 10 Jan 13 10:36 scsi-SATA_WDC_WD5002ABYS-_WD-WMASY5022406
-part1 -> ../../sda1
lrwxrwxrwx 1 root root 10 Jan 13 10:36 scsi-SATA_WDC_WD5002ABYS-_WD-WMASY5022406
-part2 -> ../../sda2
lrwxrwxrwx 1 root root 10 Jan 13 10:36 scsi-SATA_WDC_WD5002ABYS-_WD-WMASY5022406
-part3 -> ../../sda3

/dev/disk/by-path:
total 0
lrwxrwxrwx 1 root root 9 Jan 13 10:36 pci-0000:00:1f.2-scsi-0:0:0:0 -> ../../sda
lrwxrwxrwx 1 root root 10 Jan 13 10:36 pci-0000:00:1f.2-scsi-0:0:0:0-part1
-> ../../sda1
lrwxrwxrwx 1 root root 10 Jan 13 10:36 pci-0000:00:1f.2-scsi-0:0:0:0-part2
-> ../../sda2
lrwxrwxrwx 1 root root 10 Jan 13 10:36 pci-0000:00:1f.2-scsi-0:0:0:0-part3
-> ../../sda3
lrwxrwxrwx 1 root root 9 Jan 13 10:36 pci-0000:00:1f.2-scsi-0:0:1:0 -> ../../sr0

/dev/disk/by-uuid:
total 0
lrwxrwxrwx 1 root root 10 Jan 13 10:36 4e77311a-ce39-473c-80c4-caf6e53ef0c5
-> ../../dm-0
lrwxrwxrwx 1 root root 10 Jan 13 10:36 cd200dac-4466-4a1f-a713-64e6208b5d6d
-> ../../sda2
```

As you can see in Listing 5-1, under /dev/disk are three subdirectories; there could be more, depending on the hardware you are using, and depending on what exactly you have done so far with the disks. These subdirectories are by-path, by-id, and by-uuid, and each of them provides a unique way of addressing the device. The by-path devices refer to the hardware path the device is using. The devices in the subdirectory by-id use the unique hardware ID of the device, and the devices in by-uuid use the universal unique ID that is assigned to the device. If you want to use a file system–independent way to refer to a device, a way that also will never change, pick one of these device names. In case of doubt, to find out which device is which, you can use ls -l; the udev device names are all symbolic links, and ls -l shows you what device these links are referring to, as you can see in Listing 5-1.

Working with UUID

When creating a file system on a disk device, a Universal Unique ID (UUID) is assigned as well. This UUID provides another method that allows you to refer to disk devices and that will survive changes in the storage topology. The UUID is unique, but it has the disadvantage that it is hard to read. To get an overview of UUIDs that are currently assigned, you can use the **blkid** command. Listing 5-2 shows the output of this command.

Listing 5-2. Displaying UUIDs with blkid

```
[root@server1 ~]# blkid
/dev/block/252:2: UUID="SZ4HOM-LSMe-liOR-Nq2d-fgtS-n7rn-zq3trw" TYPE="LVM2_member"
/dev/block/253:1: UUID="55031bda-353a-4151-9851-4bf34d00ce7c" TYPE="xfs"
/dev/block/252:1: UUID="d806f86e-8475-498c-abb8-b5140a5424ee" TYPE="xfs"
/dev/block/253:0: UUID="ff356bed-7a9a-4cae-b5fa-08d0b9e09cbe" TYPE="swap"
/dev/sda: UUID="c4abbe88289c3531" TYPE="drbd"
/dev/sdb1: UUID="7ac0d799-5cca-47c2-ab99-fed34787eaf2" TYPE="xfs"
/dev/drbd0: UUID="1be88a0a-6177-438f-b2bc-4bd2eefce41f" TYPE="xfs"
```

To mount a file system using UUID, you can use UUID="nnnn-nnnn" instead of the device name while using the mount command. For instance, the /dev/sdb1 device that is displayed in Listing 5-2, can be mounted using **mount UUID**="7ac0d799-5cca-47c2-ab99-fed34787eaf2" /mnt.

Even if a UUID is not easy to read and reproduce, you'll see them as the default solution for mounting devices on most current Linux distributions.

Creating Partitions

The partition is the basic building block on a computer hard drive. As an alternative to using partitions, you could use logical volumes as well to create your computer's file systems. But, even when using logical volumes, you should create partitions on the disk device first. In this section, you'll learn everything you need to know about partitions. First, you'll see how partitions are used on the computer's hard drive. Following that, you'll learn how to create them using fdisk, the most important partition management utility. As the last part in this section, you'll learn how to recover lost partitions.

Understanding Partitions

Compare the hard disk in your computer to a pizza. To do something with it, you'll need a file system on the hard drive. You can put the file system directly on the hard drive, which is like cooking a pepperoni pizza: the ingredients are the same throughout. On Linux, different file systems have to be used on the same hard drive, which is basically like cooking a *pizza quattro stagioni*, four different pizzas in one—you don't want everything mixed together. To make it easier to make such a pizza, you could consider cutting the pizza into slices. The same goes for computer hard drives, but rather than slices, you divide a drive into *partitions*. In this section, you'll learn how your computer works with partitions from the moment it boots.

If you were to put just one file system on your computer hard drive, there would be no need to create partitions. You can do this, for instance, with a USB key. If there is just one hard drive in your computer, however, you normally need to create different file systems on it. The least you would need is a swap file system and a "normal" file system. Therefore, you will need to create partitions on your hard drive.

Note: From a technical perspective, it is possible to create a file system directly on a disk device, without creating partitions first. This is very bad habit though. Other operating systems - such as Windows - won't see that a file system is used if it hasn't been created on top of a partition. They will just report a disk device that is not initialized and tell you that it needs to be initialized - after which you'll loose all data on it.

Understanding MBR and GPT Disks

For a very long time, hard disks have been using Master Boot Record (MBR) to initialize the boot procedure. In the MBR, 64 bytes disk space are reserved to store partitions. This allows for the creation of a total of 4 partitions, on disks with a maximum size of 2 Terabytes.

For a couple of years, disks with sizes beyond 2TB have become common. These disks cannot be adressed with MBR anymore. For that reason, a new partition table type has been introduced: GUID Partition Table (GPT). Using GTP, the address space to create paritions has been increased, which allows for the creation of a maximum amount of 256 partitions. Also, the 2 TB disk size limitation has been eliminated. You'll read how to work with GPT partitions later in this chapter.

Creating MBR Partitions

When a computer boots, it reads the Master Boot Record (MBR) from the hard drive that is marked as primary in the BIOS. From the MBR, it starts the boot loader, which is typically GRUB2. Next, it checks the partition table, which is also in the MBR, to find out about the file systems that it can use. In the MBR,

64 bytes are reserved for partitions. This is 16 bytes per partition, just enough to store the begin and end cylinders, the partition type, and info indicating whether the partition is active. You can also display this information by issuing the command fdisk -l on your hard drive; for instance, fdisk -l /dev/sda shows a list of all partitions that have been created on hard drive /dev/sda. Listing 5-3 shows what the result of this command looks like.

Listing 5-3. With fdisk -l, You Can Show Basic Properties of Your Partitions

```
[root@localhost ~]# fdisk -l /dev/sda

Disk /dev/sda: 8589 MB, 8589934592 bytes, 16777216 sectors
Units = sectors of 1 * 512 = 512 bytes
Sector size (logical/physical): 512 bytes / 512 bytes
I/O size (minimum/optimal): 512 bytes / 512 bytes
Disk label type: dos
Disk identifier: 0x000a9dbd

Device Boot      Start        End      Blocks   Id  System
/dev/sda1   *     2048    1026047      512000   83  Linux
/dev/sda2       1026048   10283007    4628480   8e  Linux LVM
```

A special role is played by the active partition. The boot loader will check the 512-byte boot sector that it finds at the beginning of this partition to find out whether a boot loader is stored in it. For the rest, all you need to access a partition is the start and end cylinders. This tells the kernel of the operating system where exactly it has to look to find the file system within the partition.

In the 64 bytes that are allocated in the MBR to create partitions, you can create four partitions only. As this may not be enough, you can create one of these partitions as an extended partition. In an extended partition, you can create logical partitions. These have the same role as normal partitions, with one exception only: they are not stored in the MBR, but in the boot sectors of the four primary partitions. You can create a maximum of 56 logical partitions.

Every partition has a specific partition type. This partition type is used to indicate what type of data is found in it. As an administrator, you should make sure that the partition types are correct, because some utilities depend on the correct partition type being set and will refuse services if this is not the case. Four partition types are of particular interest in a Linux environment:

- *83 (Linux)*: This is the native Linux partition type. You can use it for any Linux file system.

- *82 (Linux swap)*: Use this partition type for Linux swap partitions.

- *8e (Linux LVM)*: Use this partition type for working with LVM logical volumes (see the section "Creating Logical Volumes" later in this chapter).

- *5 (Extended)*: Use this for extended partitions.

Managing Partitions with fdisk

Still the most common, though rather old, utility for creating partitions on Linux is fdisk. fdisk offers a command-line interface that allows you to perform all partition manipulations that you can think of. In the following procedure description, you'll read how to work with fdisk.

While working with fdisk, you'll create primary as well as extended partitions. This is because the Master Boot Record has only 64 bytes to store partitions, which is enough to create 4 partitions. If you need to go beyond a total of 4 partitions, one of these partitions is created as an extended partition. Within the extended partition, you'll create logical partitions.

Creating Partitions

In this procedure, you'll see how to create partitions with fdisk. This procedure assumes that you are working on a hard drive that is completely available and contains no important data. If you want to test the steps as described in this procedure, I recommend using an empty USB key. After attaching it to your computer, it will show up as /dev/sdb in most cases.

Since making a mistake about the hard drive on which you create partitions would be fatal, let's have a look first at how to recognize which drive is which on your computer. If you've just attached an external medium like a USB drive to your computer and want to find out the device name of this medium, use the dmesg utility. In Listing 5-4, you can see the last part of its output, right after I've attached a USB key to my computer. As you can see, the kernel recognizes the USB key and initializes it as /dev/sdc.

Listing 5-4. Using dmesg, It Is Easy to Find Out How the Kernel Recognizes Your USB Key

```
usb 1-1: new device found, idVendor=0951, idProduct=1603
usb 1-1: new device strings: Mfr=1, Product=2, SerialNumber=3 usb 1-1:
        Product: DataTraveler 2.0
usb 1-1: Manufacturer: Kingston
usb 1-1: SerialNumber: 899000000000000000000049
usb 1-1: configuration #1 chosen from 1 choice
scsi2 : SCSI emulation for USB Mass Storage devices
usb-storage: device found at 3
usb-storage: waiting for device to settle before scanning
  Vendor: Kingston Model: DataTraveler 2.0 Rev: 1.00
  Type:    Direct-Access                    ANSI SCSI revision: 02
SCSI device sdc: 15769600 512-byte hdwr sectors (8074 MB)
sdc: Write Protect is off sdc: Mode Sense: 23 00 00 00
sdc: assuming drive cache: write through
SCSI device sdc: 15769600 512-byte hdwr sectors (8074 MB)
sdc: Write Protect is off
sdc: Mode Sense: 23 00 00 00
sdc: assuming drive cache: write through
  sdc: sdc1
sd 2:0:0:0: Attached scsi removable disk sdc
sd 2:0:0:0: Attached scsi generic sg2 type 0
usb-storage: device scan complete
```

After connecting the USB key to your system, it will have multiple drives attached. There are multiple ways of getting an overview of all of them. If you are using a modern system that has sd devices only and no hd devices (which refer to old parallel ATA IDE drives), you can use lsscsi. This command lists all drives that are using the SCSI driver. This includes not only SCSI drives (which are pretty rare in end-user computers), but also SATA drives and USB drives. Listing 5-5 gives an overview of what the result of this command could look like.

Listing 5-5. Use lsscsi to Get an Overview of All SCSI, SATA, and USB Disks on Your Computer

```
nuuk:~ # lsscsi
[0:0:0:0]    disk    VMware,  VMware Virtual S 1.0     /dev/sda
[0:0:1:0]    disk    VMware,  VMware Virtual S 1.0     /dev/sdb
[2:0:0:0]    disk    Kingston DataTraveler 2.0 1.00    /dev/sdc
```

Another way to display the block devices on your computer, is by using the **lsblk** command. This command gives a convenient overview of all storage devices that are available on your computer. Listing 5-6 gives an overview of the output of this command.

Listing 5-6. Use lsblk for an overview of available block devices

```
[root@server1 ~]# lsblk
NAME            MAJ:MIN RM  SIZE RO TYPE MOUNTPOINT
sda               8:0  0    1G  0 disk
└─drbd0         147:0  0 1024M  0 disk /var/lib/mysql
sdb               8:16 0    1G  0 disk
└─sdb1            8:17 0 1023M  0 part /srv/gluster
sr0              11:0  1 1024M  0 rom
vda             252:0  0    8G  0 disk
├─vda1          252:1  0  500M  0 part /boot
└─vda2          252:2  0  7.5G  0 part
  ├─centos-swap 253:0  0  820M  0 lvm  [SWAP]
  └─centos-root 253:1  0  6.7G  0 lvm  /
```

At this point you should be able to find out which is which on your computer hard drives. Time to start configuring partitions. The next procedure describes how to do this with fdisk. In this procedure, I'll assume that you are working on a USB disk that is attached as /dev/sdb. If needed, replace /dev/sdb with the actual name of the disk you are working on.

1. Before you start creating partitions, check whether your disk already contains some partitions. To do this, open fdisk on the disk by using the fdisk /dev/sdb command. Next, type p to print the current partition table. This gives you a result such as the one in Listing 5-7. The error messages are returned because this is a completely empty disk device, on which not even a partition table exists.

Listing 5-7. Displaying Partition Information with fdisk

```
[root@localhost ~]# fdisk /dev/sdb
Welcome to fdisk (util-linux 2.23.2).

Changes will remain in memory only, until you decide to write them.
Be careful before using the write command.

Device does not contain a recognized partition table
Building a new DOS disklabel with disk identifier 0x68b876f1.

Command (m for help): p

Disk /dev/sdb: 1073 MB, 1073741824 bytes, 2097152 sectors
Units = sectors of 1 * 512 = 512 bytes
Sector size (logical/physical): 512 bytes / 512 bytes
I/O size (minimum/optimal): 512 bytes / 512 bytes
Disk label type: dos
Disk identifier: 0x68b876f1

   Device Boot      Start         End      Blocks   Id  System
```

2.   As you can see in Listing 5-7, no partitions exist yet. To create a new partition, press n now. fdisk will first ask you what type of partition you want to create. As no partitions exist yet, you can type p to create a primary partition. Next, provide the partition number that you want to create. Since nothing exists yet, type 1 to create the first partition. Now fdisk asks for the start sector. By default, the first partition on a new device starts at sector 2048, this leaves place for the first MB on the device to be used for metadata Next, it asks what you want to use as the last sector. You can enter a sector number here, but it is more convenient to enter the size of the partition that you want to create. Start this size with a + sign, next specify the amount, and following that use M or G for megabytes or gigabytes; for instance, entering +1G would create a 1GB partition. In Listing 5-8, you can see the code for this procedure.

Listing 5-8. Creating a New Partition in fdisk

```
Command (m for help): n
Partition type:
   p   primary (0 primary, 0 extended, 4 free)
   e   extended
Select (default p): p
Partition number (1-4, default 1): 1
First sector (2048-2097151, default 2048):
Using default value 2048
Last sector, +sectors or +size{K,M,G} (2048-2097151, default 2097151): +500M
Partition 1 of type Linux and of size 500 MiB is set:
```

3.   As fdisk doesn't show you the result, it is a good idea to use the p command now; this will give you an overview of currently existing partitions.

4.   When you have finished creating partitions, you would normally write the partitions to the partition table. Before doing so, I will first show you how to create an extended partition with a logical partition inside, and how to change the partition type. So with the fdisk interface still open, type n now to create another new partition. Next, type e to create an extended partition. You would normally use an extended partition to fill up the rest of the available disk space with logical partitions; therefore, you can press Enter twice now to use all remaining disk space for the extended partition.

5.   After creating the extended partition, you can now create logical partitions inside it. To do this, type n again to start creating a new partition. fdisk now asks whether you want to create a logical or a primary partition. Type l now for logical partition. Next, as when creating a normal partition, you need to specify the start sector and size of the partition. When you have done that, type p again for the partition overview. You'll now see that the first logical partition is created as /dev/sdb5, and it has the Linux partition type.

6.   In some cases, you have to change the default partition type. Every partition that you create is automatically defined as type 83 (Linux). For instance, if you need to create a swap partition, you have to change this partition type. In most cases, however, the default Linux partition type works well, as you can format any Linux file system on it.

Let's have a look now at how to change the default partition type. To do this, from within fdisk, enter the l command to display a list of all supported partition types. This shows you that for a Linux swap, you have to use partition type 82. To apply this partition type, use the t command now. Next, enter the partition number and the partition type you want to use on that partition to change it. fdisk will now tell you that it has sucessfully changed the partition type (see Listing 5-9).

Listing 5-9. In Some Situations, You Need to Change the Partition Type

```
Command (m for help): t
Partition number (1-5): 5
Hex code (type L to list codes): 82
Changed system type of partition 5 to 82 (Linux swap / Solaris)

Command (m for help):
```

7. Once you have made all changes that you want to apply to your partitions, it's time to write the changes if you are happy with them, or just quit if you are not sure about the parameters you have changed. Before doing anything, use the p command again.
This shows you the current changes in the partition table. Are they what you wanted? Use w to write the changes to disk. If you've made an error and don't want to mess up the current partitioning on your hard drive, use q to bail out safely. When using q, nothing is changed, and the drive remains as it existed before you started working with fdisk.

Telling the Kernel about the New Partitions

You have now written the new partition table to the MBR. If you changed partitions on a device that was in use at the moment you changed the partition parameters, you will have seen an error message indicating the device was busy and that you have to reboot to apply the changes you've made to the partition table. This is because fdisk has updated the partition table, but by default it doesn't tell the kernel about the updated partition table. You can check this in the file /proc/partitions, which contains a list of all the partitions that the kernel knows about (see Listing 5-10).

Listing 5-10. The File /proc/partitions Contains a List of All Partitions That the Kernel Knows About

```
nuuk:~ # cat /proc/partitions
major minor #blocks name
   8     0   8388608   sda
   8     1    104391   sda1
   8     2   7534485   sda2
   8     3    747022   sda3
   8    16   8388608   sdb
   8    17    987966   sdb1
   8    18         1   sdb2
   8    21   1959898   sdb5
 253     0   4194304   dm-0
 253     1    131072   dm-1
```

If the device on which you have changed partitions has mounted partitions on it, the /proc/partitions file doesn't get updated automatically. Fortunately, there is a command that you can use to force an update: partprobe. Issuing this command tells the kernel about updated partitions, even for devices that were in use when you were manipulating the partition table.

■ **Caution** The partprobe utility works very well for adding new partitions. It doesn't work so well if you've also removed partitions. To make sure that your computer knows that some partitions have disappeared, you better reboot your computer after removing partitions.

Deleting Partitions

If you know how to create a partition, deleting a partition is not hard. You use the same fdisk interface, only with a different command. There is only one thing that you should be aware of: when deleting a logical partition, you risk changing the order of the remaining logical partitions. Assume that you have partitions /dev/sdb5 and /dev/sdb6. After deleting /dev/sdb5, the partition /dev/sdb6 will be renumbered to /dev/sdb5, and all partitions after /dev/sdb6 will also get renumbered. This will cause problems accessing the remaining partitions, so be very careful when removing logical partitions! Fortunately, this problem only exists for logical partitions; the number that is assigned to a primary or an extended partition will never change.

The next procedure shows you how to delete a partition.

1. Open fdisk on the device where you want to delete a partition; for instance, use /dev/sdb if you want to delete a partition from the sdb device. Next, use p to display a list of all partitions that exist on the device.

2. Determine the number of the partition that you want to delete, and enter that number to delete it from your hard disk.

3. Use the p command again to verify that you have deleted the right partition. If so, use w to write the changes to disk. If not, use q to quit without saving changes.

■ **Tip** If you have deleted the wrong partition, it doesn't necessarily mean that all your data is lost. As long as you haven't created another file system at this partition, just re-create it with the same parameters—this allows you to access the data in that partition again without any problems.

Fixing the Partition Order

In some cases, you will need to use some of the advanced partition options to change partition parameters. You might, for instance, have to change the order of partitions. By deleting and recreating logical partitions, you may accidentally change the partition order. In Listing 5-11, you can see an example in which this has happened.

Listing 5-11. Occasionally, You Will See Problems Like a Wrong Partition Order

```
Command (m for help): p

Disk /dev/sdb: 1073 MB, 1073741824 bytes, 2097152 sectors
Units = sectors of 1 * 512 = 512 bytes
Sector size (logical/physical): 512 bytes / 512 bytes
I/O size (minimum/optimal): 512 bytes / 512 bytes
Disk label type: dos
Disk identifier: 0x68b876f1

Device Boot      Start        End     Blocks   Id  System
/dev/sdb1         2048    1026047     512000   83  Linux
/dev/sdb2      1026048    2097151     535552    5  Extended
/dev/sdb5      1234944    1439743     102400   83  Linux
/dev/sdb6      1028096    1234943     103424   83  Linux

Partition table entries are not in disk order
```

The fact that the partitions are out of order will severely disturb some utilities. Therefore, this is a problem that you should fix. fdisk makes this possible through some of its advanced options. The following procedure describes how to fix this problem:

1. Start fdisk on the hard disk where you want to modify the partition table.

2. Type **x** to enter fdisk expert mode. In this mode, you'll have access to some advanced options. Listing 5-12 gives an overview of the options in expert mode.

Listing 5-12. In fdisk Expert Mode, You Will Get Access to Advanced Options

```
v    verify the partition table
w    write table to disk and exit
x    extra functionality (experts only)

Command (m for help): x

Expert command (m for help): m
Command action

   b    move beginning of data in a partition
   c    change number of cylinders
   d    print the raw data in the partition table
   e    list extended partitions
   f    fix partition order
   g    create an IRIX (SGI) partition table
   h    change number of heads
   m    print this menu
   p    print the partition table
   q    quit without saving changes
   r    return to main menu
   s    change number of sectors/track
   v    verify the partition table
   w    write table to disk and exit

Expert command (m for help):
```

3.   From the expert interface, use f to fix the partition order. fdisk replies with a simple "done" to tell you that it has finished doing so. You can now use r to return to the main menu, and from there, use p to print the current partition layout. If you are happy with the changes, use w to write them to disk and exit fdisk.

Creating GPT Partitions with gdisk

On modern hard disks, you'll need to use GPT partitions instead of MBR partitions. Using GPT partitions helps you overcome some limitations that exist for MBR environments.

- In GPT, a total of 128 partitions can be created

- In GTP, a backup partition table is stored on disk as well

- All partitions can be created as primary partitions

- GTP allows you to work with disk that have a size beyond 2TB

To create GPT partitions, you'll need the **gdisk** utility. If you know how to work with fdisk, working with gdisk is easy, as the interface it offers is very similar to the fdisk interface, and similar commands are used. The **gdisk** utility offers one important item though: it allows you to convert MBR partition tables to GPT partition tables. Don't ever use this option, because it is likely to make all data that are stored on the MBR partition inaccessible. Listing 5-13 shows the message that gdisk shows when it is used on a disk that currently contains an MBR partition table.

Listing 5-13. Using gdisk on MBR disks is a very bad idea

```
[root@localhost ~]# gdisk /dev/sda
GPT fdisk (gdisk) version 0.8.6

Partition table scan:
  MBR: MBR only
  BSD: not present
  APM: not present
  GPT: not present

***************************************************************
Found invalid GPT and valid MBR; converting MBR to GPT format.
THIS OPERATION IS POTENTIALLY DESTRUCTIVE! Exit by typing 'q' if
you don't want to convert your MBR partitions to GPT format!
***************************************************************

Command (? for help):
```

Working with cfdisk

If you don't like the fdisk interface, another partitioning utility is available for you to try as well: cfdisk. This utility is not as advanced as fdisk and lacks several options, but if you just want to perform basic partition operations, you may like it, particularly as it is using a menu-driven interface that makes creating partitions a bit easier. Listing 5-14 shows the cfdisk interface.

Listing 5-14. cfdisk Offers an Easier Interface to Perform Basic Partitioning Actions

```
                        cfdisk (util-linux 2.23.2)

                        Disk Drive: /dev/sda
                   Size: 8589934592 bytes, 8589 MB
             Heads: 255    Sectors per Track: 63    Cylinders: 1044

   Name          Flags       Part Type  FS Type          [Label]        Size (MB)
  --------------------------------------------------------------------------------
                             Pri/Log    Free Space                         1.05*
   sda1          Boot        Primary    xfs                              524.29*
   sda2                      Primary    LVM2_member                     4739.57*
                             Pri/Log    Free Space                      3325.04*

     [   Help    ] [   New    ] [  Print   ] [  Quit   ] [  Units   ]
     [  Write    ]

                   Create new partition from free space
```

cfdisk offers a menu interface that gives you different options that are context sensitive. That is, based on the current partition type that you have selected by manipulating the arrow keys, you'll see different options. To navigate between the different options, use the Tab key. Following are short descriptions of these options:

- Bootable: Use this option to mark a partition as bootable. This is equivalent to the fdisk option to mark the active partition.

- New: Use this option to create a new partition in unallocated disk space.

- Delete: Use this option to remove a partition.

- Help: This option shows usage information about cfdisk.

- Maximize: With this option, you can increase the size of a partition on a disk where unallocated cylinders are still available. Note that after using this option, you should increase the file system in that partition also.

- Print: This option gives you three different choices for printing partition information; you can print the raw partition information, information about partitions sectors, and the contents of the partition table.

- Quit: Use this option to close the cfdisk interface.

- Type: With this option, you can change the partition type.

- Units: This option changes the units in which the partition sizes are displayed.

- Write: Use this option to write changes to the partition table to disk and exit.

Recovering Lost Partitions with gpart

Occasionally, something may go terribly wrong, and you may lose all partitions on your hard disk. The good news is that a partition is just a marker for the start and end of a file system that exists within the partition. If you lose the information in the partition table, it doesn't necessarily mean that you also lose the file system that exists in it. Therefore, in many cases, if you re-create the lost partition with the same partition boundaries, you will be able to access the file systems that existed in the partition as well. So if you have good documentation of how the partition table once was structured, you can just re-create it accordingly.

On the other hand, if you have no documentation that shows you how the partitioning on your hard disk once was, you can use the gpart utility. This utility analyzes the entire hard disk to see whether it can recognize the start of a file system. By finding the start of a file system, it automatically also finds the partition in which the file system was created. However, gpart doesn't always succeed in its work, especially on extended partitions, where it may fail to detect the original partitioning. Let's have a look at how well it does its work based on the partition table in Listing 5-15.

Listing 5-15. The Original Partition Table for This Example

```
nuuk:~ # fdisk -l /dev/sdb

Disk /dev/sdb: 8589 MB, 8589934592 bytes
255 heads, 63 sectors/track, 1044 cylinders
Units = cylinders of 16065 * 512 = 8225280 bytes

Device Boot      Start         End      Blocks   Id  System
/dev/sdb1            1         123      987966   83  Linux
/dev/sdb2          124         367     1959930   83  Linux
/dev/sdb3          368        1044     5438002+   5  Extended
/dev/sdb5          368         490      987966   83  Linux
/dev/sdb6          491         856     2939863+  83  Linux
```

gpart does have some options, but you may find that those options don't really add much to its functionality. It just tries to read what it finds on your hard drive, and that's it. In Listing 5-16, you can see how well it did in trying to find the partition table from Listing 5-15.

Listing 5-16. gpart Results

```
nuuk:~ # gpart /dev/sdb

Begin scan...
Possible partition(Linux ext2), size(964mb), offset(0mb)
Possible partition(Linux ext2), size(1913mb), offset(964mb)
Possible extended partition at offset(2878mb)
   Possible partition(Linux ext2), size(964mb), offset(2878mb)
   Possible partition(Linux ext2), size(2870mb), offset(3843mb)
End scan.

Checking partitions...
Partition(Linux ext2 filesystem): primary
Partition(Linux ext2 filesystem): primary
   Partition(Linux ext2 filesystem): logical
   Partition(Linux ext2 filesystem): logical
Ok.

Guessed primary partition table:
Primary partition(1)
   type: 131(0x83)(Linux ext2 filesystem)
   size: 964mb #s(1975928) s(63-1975990)
   chs: (0/1/1)-(122/254/59)d (0/1/1)-(122/254/59)r
```

```
Primary partition(2)
   type: 131(0x83)(Linux ext2 filesystem)
   size: 1913mb #s(3919856) s(1975995-5895850)
   chs: (123/0/1)-(366/254/59)d (123/0/1)-(366/254/59)r

Primary partition(3)
   type: 015(0x0F)(Extended DOS, LBA)
   size: 3835mb #s(7855785) s(5895855-13751639)
   chs: (367/0/1)-(855/254/63)d (367/0/1)-(855/254/63)r

Primary partition(4)
   type: 000(0x00)(unused)
   size: 0mb #s(0) s(0-0)
   chs: (0/0/0)-(0/0/0)d (0/0/0)-(0/0/0)r
```

As you can see, gpart did a pretty good job in this case, but you can't just take the information as is when re-creating the partitions. When using gpart, you should start by analyzing the first part of the gpart output. This part gives you a list of all partitions that it has found, including their sizes. As fdisk works primarily on cylinders, you may find the end of the gpart output more usable. The four Primary partition indicators refer to either primary or extended partitions that are normally stored in the MBR. Also very useful: it gives you chs (cylinder/ head/sector) information, telling you exactly the first cylinder and the last cylinder used by the partition. By using the chs information, gpart tells you exactly on which cylinder, head, and sector the partition started, which helps you in re-creating the partition. Be aware, however, that fdisk calls the first cylinder on a disk cylinder 1, whereas gpart calls it cylinder 0. Therefore, when re-creating the partitions, add 1 to the list of cylinders as displayed by gpart to re-create the right partition sizes.

EXERCISE 5-1: CREATING PARTITIONS WITH FDISK

To apply the steps in this exercise, you'll need a dedicated disk device. Don't perform these steps on an existing disk device! If you're working on a physical computer, you can use a USB thumb drive as external disk device - make sure it does not contain any important data though. If you're using a virtual machine, you can add an additional disk device through the virtualization software. I'll use /dev/sdb as the name for this new additional disk device throughout the exercise, make sure to replace /dev/sdb with the name of the disk device that applies to your environment.

1. Type **cat /proc/partitions** to get a list of devices and partitions that the kernel currently is aware of.

2. If you haven't attached the additional disk device yet, you can do it now. After attaching it to your computer, type **dmesg** to show kernel messages which show that the device has been detected and added. Also type **cat /proc/partitions** again and compare the results with the results of step 1. Use the disk device name that has just been added in the rest of this exercise. I'm using /dev/sdb as the name of this device, your device name might be different! If that is the case, make sure to use your device name and not /dev/sdb.

3. Type **fdisk /dev/sdb**. Next, type **p** to show the current partitioning on the device. It will most likely show some partitions.

4. Type **d** to delete all partitions that currently are existing on the device. Enter the partition number, and proceed until you have removed all partitions.

5. If you are sure that you're okay with removing all partitions, type **w** to write the changes to disk and close **fdisk**. If you are not sure you really want to destroy all partitions, type **q** to quit and write nothing to disk.

6. Type **fdisk /dev/sdb** again. Now, type **n** to create a new partition.

7. When asked if you want to create a primary or an extended partition, type **p** to create a primary partition.

8. Press Enter when fdisk asks for the start sector of the new partition. Type +200M to make this a 200MB partition.

9. Type **w** to write the changes to disk and quit **fdisk**.

10. Type **proc /cat/partitions** to see the contents of the kernel partition table. If you do not see the newly created partition, type **partprobe** to have the kernel probe for the new partitions and update the kernel partition table.

Creating Logical Volumes

In the first part of this chapter, you have read about using partitions to allocate disk space. Working with partitions is fine if you have a simple setup without any special requirements. However, if you need more flexibility, you may need another solution. Such a solution is offered by the Logical Volume Manager (LVM) system. Some distributions, such as Red Hat and derived distributions, even use LVM as their default hard disk layout. Working with LVM offers some benefits, of which the most important are listed here:

- You can resize logical volumes easily.

- Using logical volumes allows multiple physical disk devices to be combined into one logical entity.

- By using the snapshot feature, it is easy to freeze the state of a logical volume, which makes it possible to make a stable backup of a versatile file system.

- Logical volumes offer support for use in a cluster environment, where multiple nodes may access the same volumes.

- The number of logical volumes that you can create is much higher than the number of traditional partitions.

In the next sections, you'll read about the way logical volumes are organized and the management of logical volumes.

Understanding Logical Volumes

The Linux LVM uses a three-layer architecture. At the bottom layer are the storage devices. In LVM terminology, these are referred to as *physical volumes*. These can be hard disks, RAID arrays, and partitions, and you can even use sparse files (these are files that are completely filled with zeroes to have them occupy disk space) as the storage back end. In order to use the storage back end in an LVM setup, you need to run the pvcreate command, which tells the LVM subsystem that it can use this device to create logical volumes.

If you want to put a partition in an LVM setup, you need to create that partition is type 8e as well. The section "Understanding Partitions" earlier in the chapter described how to do so with fdisk.

Based on the physical volumes, you can create the second level, which consists of *volume groups*. These are just collections of storage devices. You can use a one-on-one solution in which one physical volume represents one volume group. You can also use a multiple-on-one solution, which means you can put multiple storage devices in one volume group and create multiple volume groups on one storage device. However, the former solution is not such a good idea. If you have multiple storage devices in one volume group, the volume group will break if one of the devices in it fails. So better not to do it that way, and make sure that you have some redundancy at this level.

The third level consists of the *logical volumes*. These are the flexible storage units that you are going to create and on which you are going to put a file system. A logical volume is always created on top of a volume group, and you can create multiple logical volumes from one volume group or just one logical volume on each volume group—whichever you prefer. In the next section, you'll learn how to set up an LVM environment.

Setting Up a Disk with Logical Volume Manager

Setting up an environment that uses logical volumes is a three-step procedure. First you need to set up the physical volumes. Next, you have to create the volume group. Finally, you need to create the logical volumes themselves.

Creating Physical Volumes

Creating the physical volume is not too hard—you just need to run the pvcreate command on the storage device that you want to use. If this storage device is a partition, don't forget to change its partition type to 8e before you start. Next, use the pvcreate command, followed by the name of the storage device. The following line creates a physical volume for the partition /dev/sdb2:

```
pvcreate /dev/sdb2
```

After creating it, you can use pvdisplay /dev/sdb2 to show the properties of the physical volume that you've just created. Listing 5-17 shows the results of both commands.

Listing 5-17. Creating a Physical Volume and Showing Its Properties

```
nuuk:~ # pvcreate /dev/sdb2
   Physical volume "/dev/sdb2" successfully created
nuuk:~ # pvdisplay /dev/sdb2
   --- NEW Physical volume ---
   PV Name                /dev/sdb2
   VG Name
   PV Size                7.06 GB
   Allocatable            NO
   PE Size (KByte)        0
   Total PE               0
   Free PE                0
   Allocated PE           0
   PV UUID                MH3Nlh-TR27-tPmk-5lWi-jZrH-NKwb-rBN3WY
```

The pvdisplay command shows information about the different properties of the physical volume:

- PV Name: The name of the physical volume.

- VG Name: The name of the volume group, if any, that is already using this physical volume.

- PV Size: The size of the physical volume.

- Allocatable: Indicator of whether this physical volume is usable or not.

- PE Size: The size of the physical extents. *Physical extents* are the building blocks of physical volumes, as blocks are the building blocks on a computer hard drive.

- Total PE: The total number of physical extents that is available.

- Free PE: The number of physical extents that is still unused.

- Allocated PE: The number of physical extents that is already in use.

- PV UUID: A random generated unique ID for the physical volume.

Instead of using **pvdisplay**, you can also use the **pvs** command. This command just gives a brief summary of the physical volumes that exist on a computer without too much details.

Creating Volume Groups

Now that you have created the physical volume, you can use it in a volume group. To do this, you need the vgcreate command. This command does have some options that you will normally never use; to create the volume group, it's usually enough to specify the name of the volume group and the name of the physical volume(s) that you want to use for them. If you're using **vgcreate** against a partition that hasn't been marked as a logical volume yet, the **vgcreat** command will take care of that automatically for you.

Also, you can specify the size of the physical extents that are used in building the volume. Physical extents are the building blocks for logical volumes, and you set the size of these building blocks when creating the volume group. The default size of the physical extent is 4MB, which allows you to create LVM volumes with a maximal size of 256GB. If you need bigger volumes, you need bigger physical extents. For example, to create an LVM volume with a size of 1TB, you would need a physical extent size of 16MB. In the following example, you can see how to create a volume group that uses a physical extent size of 16MB:
vgcreate -s 16M volgroup /dev/sdb2

After creating your volume group, you may want to verify its properties. You can do this by using the vgdisplay command. Listing 5-18 shows the result of this command. Alternatively, you can use the **vgs** command to show just a brief summary og volume groups that are currently existing on your system.

Listing 5-18. Showing Properties of a Volume Group with vgdisplay

```
nuuk:~ # vgdisplay /dev/volgroup
  --- Volume group ---
  VG Name               volgroup
  System ID
  Format                lvm2
  Metadata Areas        2
  Metadata Sequence No  1

VG Access             read/write
VG Status             resizable
MAX LV                0
```

```
Cur LV                       0
Open LV                      0
Max PV                       0
Cur PV                       2
Act PV                       2
VG Size                      7.05 GB
PE Size                      4.00 MB
Total PE                     1805
Alloc PE / Size              0 / 0
Free PE / Size               1805 / 7.05 GB
VG UUID                      011soU-FKOu-oafC-3KxU-HuLH-cBpf-VoK9eO
```

As you can see, the vgdisplay command shows you what size is allocated currently to the volume group. Since it is a new volume group, this size is set to 0 (Alloc PE / Size). It also shows you how many physical volumes are assigned to this volume group (Cur PV). To get more details about which physical volumes these are, use the pvdisplay command again with- out arguments. This will show all available physical volumes, and also to which volume group they currently are assigned.

Creating Logical Volumes

Now that you have created the physical volumes as well as the volume group, it's time to create the logical volumes. As shown when issuing lvcreate --help (see Listing 5-19), there are many options that you can use with lvcreate.

Listing 5-19. When Creating Logical Volumes, There Are Many Options You Can Use

```
nuuk:~ # lvcreate --help
  lvcreate: Create a logical volume

lvcreate
        [-A|--autobackup {y|n}]
        [--addtag Tag]
        [--alloc AllocationPolicy]
        [-C|--contiguous {y|n}]
        [-d|--debug]
        [-h|-?|--help]
        [-i|--stripes Stripes
        [-I|--stripesize StripeSize]]
        {-l|--extents LogicalExtentsNumber |
         -L|--size LogicalVolumeSize[kKmMgGtTpPeE]}
        [-M|--persistent {y|n}] [--major major] [--minor minor]
        [-m|--mirrors Mirrors [--nosync] [--corelog]]
        [-n|--name LogicalVolumeName]
        [-p|--permission {r|rw}]
        [-r|--readahead ReadAheadSectors]
        [-R|--regionsize MirrorLogRegionSize]
        [-t|--test]
        [--type VolumeType]
        [-v|--verbose]
        [-Z|--zero {y|n}]
        [--version]
        VolumeGroupName [PhysicalVolumePath...]
```

For example, you can use the --readahead parameter to configure read-ahead, an option that will enhance the performance of file reads on the logical volume. There are, however, only a few options that are really useful:

- -L: Use this option to specify the size that you want to assign to the logical volume. You can do this in kilobytes, megabytes, gigabytes, terabytes, petabytes, or exabytes, as well as bits. Alternatively, you can use -l to specify the volume size in extents, the building blocks for logical volumes. Typically, these extents have a size of 4MB, which is set when creating the volume group. It is mandatory to use either -L or -l.

- -n: The optional option -n allows you to specify a name for the logical volume. If you don't specify a name, the volume will get its name automatically, and typically, this name will be lv1 for the first volume you create, lv2 for the second volume, and so on. To use a name that has more meaning, use -n *name*.

- VolumeGroupName: This is a mandatory parameter that has you specify in which volume group you want to create the logical volume.

- PhysicalVolumePath: This optional parameter allows you to specify exactly on which physical volume you want to create the logical volume. This option is useful if your volume group has more than one physical volume. By using this option, you can ensure that the logical volume still works if the physical volume that doesn't contain the logical volume goes down.

Based on this information, you can create a logical volume. For example, if you want to create a logical volume that has the name data, uses the physical volume /dev/sdb2, and is created in the volume group volgroup with a size of 500MB, you would use the following command:

```
lvcreate -n data -L 500M volgroup /dev/sdb2
```

After creating a logical volume, you can display its properties using lvdisplay. or **lvs** if you just want to see a short summary.To do this, you need to use the complete device name of the logical volume. In this device name, you'll first use the name of the device directory /dev, followed by the name of the volume group, which in turn is followed by the name of the logical volume. For instance, the logical volume data in volume group volgroup would use the device name /dev/volgroup/data. In Listing 5-20, you can see an example of the output of this command.

Listing 5-20. Showing the Properties of a Logical Volume with lvdisplay

```
nuuk:~ # lvcreate -n data -L 500M volgroup /dev/sdb2 Logical volume "data" created
  nuuk:~ # lvdisplay /dev/volgroup/data
  --- Logical volume ---
  LV Name                /dev/volgroup/data
  VG Name                volgroup
  LV UUID                PvZLFz-W6fX-Vrma-BLYM-rCN1-YnTn-ZUTpTf
  LV Write Access        read/write
  LV Status              available
  # open                 0
  LV Size                500.00 MB
  Current LE             125
  Segments               1
  Allocation             inherit
  Read ahead sectors     0
  Block device           253:2
```

In Listing 5-20, the following information is provided:

- `LV Name`: The name of the logical volume.

- `VG Name`: The name of the volume group.

- `LV UUID`: A unique ID that is given to the volume.

- `LV Write Access`: The read/write status of the volume. As you can see, users who have enough file system permissions can write to this volume.

- `LV Status`: The current status of the volume. This should read `available`; otherwise, the volume cannot be used.

- `open`: The number of files that are open on the volume.

- `LV Size`: The size of the volume.

- `Current LE`: The number of logical extents. A *logical extent* is the logical representation of the physical extent in the volume.

- `Segments`: The number of physical devices on which this volume is contained.

- `Allocation`: The current allocation status. This parameter should be set to `inherit`.

- `Read Ahead Sectors`: The number of sectors the operating system should read ahead on a volume. For performance optimization, you can set this number. That is, if the operating system asks for the information in section 13 and the `Read Ahead Sectors` parameter is set to 4, it would read sectors 13 to 17. Although this sounds like something you would want to do, on modern hardware the controller of the storage device takes care of this, so there is no need to set this parameter.

- `Block Device`: The address that the kernel uses to find this volume.

At this point, you have logical volumes. As the next step, you need to create file systems on them. Read the section "Working with File Systems" later in this chapter for information how to do that.

Working with Snapshots

Among the many things you can do with logical volumes is the option to work with snapshots. For instance, snapshots can be useful when creating a backup of a volume that has many open files. Normally, backup software will fail to back up a file that is open. Working with snapshots allows the backup software to back up the snapshot instead of the actual files, and by doing this it will never fail on open files.

A snapshot freezes the current status of a volume. It does so by initially copying the metadata of the volume into the snapshot volume. This metadata tells the file system driver where it can find the blocks in which the files are stored. When the snapshot is initially created, the metadata redirects the file system to the original blocks that the file system uses. This means that by reading the snapshot, you follow pointers to the original volume to read the blocks of this volume. Only when a file gets changed do the original blocks get copied to the snapshot volume, which at that moment grows. This also means that the longer the snapshot volume exists, the bigger it will grow. Therefore, you should make sure to use snapshots as a temporary measure only; otherwise they may trash your original volume as well.

■ **Caution**   A snapshot is meant to be a temporary solution, not a permanent solution. Make sure that you remove it after some time, or it may trash the associated volume.

Before creating a snapshot, you have to determine the approximate size that it's going to have. Ultimately, this depends on the time you think the snapshot is going to be around and the amount of data that you expect will change within that time frame. A good starting point is to create it with a size that is 10% larger than the original volume. However, if you think it's going to be around longer, make sure that it is bigger so that it can keep all data that changes on the original volume from the moment that you have created the snapshot.

Creating a snapshot volume works basically the same as creating a normal volume. There are two differences though: you need to use the option -s to indicate that it is a snapshot volume, and you need to indicate the original volume that you want to make the snapshot for.

The next line shows how you can create a snapshot with the name data_snap for the volume

```
/dev/volgroup/data:
```

```
lvcreate -s -L 50M -n data_snap /dev/volgroup/data
```

After creating the snapshot, you can access it like any other volume device. This means you can mount it or have your backup software take a copy of it. Don't forget that when you are done with it and don't need it anymore, you have to remove it. To do that for a snapshot with the name data_snap, use the following command:

```
lvremove /dev/volgroup/data_snap
```

■ **Caution**   Failing to remove your snapshot volume may make the original volume inaccessible. So never forget to remove your snapshot after usage!

EXERCISE 5-2: CREATING AN LVM LOGICAL VOLUME

This exercise assumes that you've completed exercise 5-2. It continues on the partitioning layout that you have created on the /dev/sdb device in exercise 5-2.

1. From a root shell, type **fdisk /dev/sdb**.

2. Type **n** to create a new parition. Type **p** to make it a primary partition.

3. When asked for the starting sector, press Enter to accept the default suggestion. Next, type **+200M** to make this a 200MB partition.

4. Type **t** to change the partition type. Next, type **8e** to set it to the LVM partition type.

5. Press **w** to write the changes to disk and type **partprobe** to update the kernel partition table.

6. Type **cat /proc/partitions** to verify that the new /dev/sdb2 partition has been added.

7. Now use **pvcreate /dev/sdb2** to mark the newly created partition as an LVM physical volume.

8. Use **vgcreate vgdata /dev/sdb2** to create a volume group with the name vgdata, that is using the /dev/sdb2 partition.

9. Type **lvcreate -n lvdata -l 100%FREE vgdata**. This command creates a logical volume with the name lvdata, that uses all available disk space in the vgdata volume group.

10. Type **lvs** to verify the succesfull creation of the logical volume.

Basic LVM Troubleshooting

Occasionally, you may run into trouble when working with LVM. The first problem arises when the computer fails to initialize the logical volumes when booting. This may occur when the service that scans for logical volumes comes up when your devices are not all connected yet. If that happens, you need to initialize the logical volumes manually. In the following procedure, to show you how to fix this problem, I have attached a device containing logical volumes after booting the computer. First, I will show you that the device is not activated as a physical volume automatically, and following that, you'll read how you can activate it manually.

1. If you have just attached the device that contains logical volumes, use the dmesg command. This command shows you kernel messages and will display which device was connected last. Listing 5-21 shows you the last part of its output.

Listing 5-21. Use dmesg to Show the Name of the Device That You've Just Connected

```
usb 2-1: Manufacturer: Kingston
usb 2-1: SerialNumber: 5B7A12860AFC
usb 2-1: configuration #1 chosen from 1 choice
Initializing USB Mass Storage driver...
scsi1 : SCSI emulation for USB Mass Storage devices
usb-storage: device found at 2
usb-storage: waiting for device to settle before scanning
usbcore: registered new driver usb-storage
USB Mass Storage support registered.
  Vendor: Kingston Model: DataTraveler 2.0 Rev: PMAP
  Type:   Direct-Access                    ANSI SCSI revision: 00
SCSI device sdc: 8060928 512-byte hdwr sectors (4127 MB)
sdc: Write Protect is off
sdc: Mode Sense: 23 00 00 00
sdc: assuming drive cache: write through
SCSI device sdc: 8060928 512-byte hdwr sectors (4127 MB)
sdc: Write Protect is off
sdc: Mode Sense: 23 00 00 00
sdc: assuming drive cache: write through
 sdc: sdc1 < sdc5 sdc6 > sdc2
sd 1:0:0:0: Attached scsi removable disk sdc
sd 1:0:0:0: Attached scsi generic sg2 type 0
susb-storage: device scan complete
```

As you can see from the dmesg output, I have connected a 4GB USB key to the system that has obtained the device name /dev/sdc.

2. Use the pvs command to show a list of all physical volumes that the system knows about at the moment. This gives a result like the one in Listing 5-22.

Listing 5-22. Use pvs to Show a List of All Known Physical Volumes

```
nuuk:~ # pvs
  PV            VG        Fmt  Attr   PSize      PFree
  /dev/sda2     system    lvm2 a-      7.18G      3.06G
  /dev/sda3     vm1       lvm2 a-    728.00M    728.00M
  /dev/sdb2     volgroup  lvm2 a-      2.77G      2.28G
  /dev/sdb3     volgroup  lvm2 a-      4.28G      4.28G
```

As you can see, some physical volumes are known to the system, but /dev/sdc is not among them.

3. At this point, you should tell the LVM subsystem to scan for physical volumes. To do this, use the pvscan command. This command will check all currently connected storage devices and show you all physical volumes that it has found on them. As a result, it will now also see the /dev/sdc device. Listing 5-23 shows you what the result looks like.

Listing 5-23. With pvscan You Scan All Storage Devices for the Occurence of Physical Volumes

```
nuuk:~ # pvscan
  PV /dev/sdc2     VG group      lvm2 [956.00 MB / 156.00 MB free]
  PV /dev/sdb2     VG volgroup   lvm2 [2.77 GB / 2.28 GB free]
  PV /dev/sdb3     VG volgroup   lvm2 [4.28 GB / 4.28 GB free]
  PV /dev/sda3     VG vm1        lvm2 [728.00 MB / 728.00 MB free]
  PV /dev/sda2     VG system     lvm2 [7.18 GB / 3.06 GB free]
  Total: 5 [15.88 GB] / in use: 5 [15.88 GB] / in no VG: 0 [0    ]
```

4. Now that the physical volumes have been initialized, it's time to go up in the stack and see what volume groups your computer knows about. For this purpose, use the vgs command (see Listing 5-24).

Listing 5-24. The vgs Command Gives a List of All Available Volume Groups

```
nuuk:~ # vgs
  VG         #PV #LV #SN Attr       VSize      VFree
  group        1   2   1 wz--n-   956.00M    156.00M
  system       1   2   0 wz--n-     7.18G      3.06G
  vm1          1   0   0 wz--n-   728.00M    728.00M
```

5. At this point, if you don't see all the volume groups that you've expected, use the vgscan command to tell your computer to scan all physical volumes for volume groups. Listing 5-24 shows you what the result of this command looks like. For instance, the volume volgroup is not listed. Running vgscan will fix this problem, as you can see in Listing 5-25.

Listing 5-25. *The vgscan Command Scans All Physical Devices for Volume Groups*

```
nuuk:~ # vgscan
  Reading all physical volumes. This may take a while...
  Found volume group "group" using metadata type lvm2
  Found volume group "volgroup" using metadata type lvm2
  Found volume group "vm1" using metadata type lvm2
  Found volume group "system" using metadata type lvm2
```

6.   Now that all volume groups are available, it's time for the last task: to see whether you can access the logical volumes that exist in them. To do this, first use the lvs command (see Listing 5-26).

Listing 5-26. *Use the lvs Command for a List of All Logical Volumes*

```
nuuk:~ # lvs
  LV           VG         Attr        LSize   Origin Snap% Move Log Copy%
  one          group      owi---      300.00M
  one_snap     group      swi---      100.00M    one
  two          group      -wi---      400.00M
  root         system     -wi-ao        4.00G
  swap         system     -wi-ao      128.00M
  data         volgroup   -wi-a-      500.00M
```

7.   In case there are missing logical volumes, use lvscan to scan all devices for logical volumes. This should now activate all volumes that you've got.

8.   At this point, all logical volumes are available, but they probably are not activated yet. To confirm if this is the case, use the lvdisplay command on the volume group that you've just activated. For instance, if the name of the volume group is group, lvdisplay group shows you the current status of the volumes in it. As you can see in Listing 5-27, all logical volumes have the status inactive.

Listing 5-27. *After Scanning for Volumes Manually, They Still Are in an Inactive State*

```
nuuk:~ # lvdisplay group
  --- Logical volume ---
  LV Name                   /dev/group/one
  VG Name                   group
  LV UUID                   bYvwJU-8e3O-lUmW-xWCK-v8nE-pIqT-CUYkO9
  LV Write Access           read/write
  LV snapshot status        source of
                            /dev/group/one_snap [INACTIVE]
  LV Status                 NOT available
  LV Size                   300.00 MB
  Current LE                75
  Segments                  1
  Allocation                inherit
  Read ahead sectors        0
```

```
--- Logical volume ---
LV Name                   /dev/group/two
VG Name                   group
LV UUID                   yBxTuU-mHvh-3HCb-MIoU-D2ic-6257-hVH9xI
LV Write Access           read/write
LV Status                 NOT available
LV Size                   400.00 MB
Current LE                100
Segments                  2
Allocation                inherit
Read ahead sectors        0

--- Logical volume ---
LV Name                   /dev/group/one_snap
VG Name                   group
LV UUID                   DCBU5O-w4SD-HPEu-J32S-pnVH-inen-YOMcoU
LV Write Access           read/write
LV snapshot status        INACTIVE destination for /dev/group/one
LV Status                 NOT available
LV Size                   300.00 MB
Current LE                75
COW-table size            100.00 MB
COW-table LE              25
Snapshot chunk size       8.00 KB
Segments                  1
Allocation                inherit
Read ahead sectors        0
```

9. At this point, you need to activate the logical volumes. You can do that by using the vgchange command to change the status of the volume group the volumes are in. So if the name of the volume group is group, use vgchange -a y group to change the group status to active (see Listing 5-28).

Listing 5-28. Use vgchange to Change the Group Status to Active

```
nuuk:~ # vgchange -a y group
  2 logical volume(s) in volume group "group" now active
```

10. Using vgchange has activated all logical volumes. At this point, you can mount them and use the file systems that are on them.

Working with File Systems

Working with file systems is a very important task for the Linux administrator. Different file systems are available; you have to choose the best file system for the tasks that you want to perform, and make sure that it is available and performing well. In this section, you'll learn about the different file systems and how to format them. Next, you will find information on maintaining, tuning, and resizing them. At the end of this section, you will also find information on how to work with Windows file systems.

Understanding File Systems

A file system is the structure that is used to access logical blocks on a storage device. For Linux, different file systems are available, of which Ext4, XFS and the relatively new Btrfs are the most important ones. What they have in common is that all organize logical blocks on the storage device in a certain way. All also have in common that inodes and directories play a key role in allocating files. Other distinguishing features play a role as well. In the following sections, you'll learn about common elements and distinguishing features that file systems are using.

About Inodes and Directories

The basic building block of a file system is the block. This is a storage allocation unit on disk your file system is using. Typically, it exists on a logical volume or a traditional partition. To access these data blocks, the file system collects information on where the blocks of any given file are stored. This information is written to the inode. Every file on a Linux file system has an inode, and the inode almost contains the complete administration of your files. To give you an impression, in Listing 5-29 you can see the contents of an inode as it exists on an Ext4 file system, as shown with the debugfs utility. Use the following procedure to display this information:

1. Locate an Ext4 file system on your machine. Make sure files on the file system cannot be accessed while working in debugfs. You should consider remounting the file system using mount -o remount /yourfilesystem.

2. Open a directory on the device that you want to monitor and use the ls -i command to display a list of all file names and their inode numbers. Every file has one inode that contains its complete administration. Make sure that you'll remember the inode number later, as you will need it in step 4 of this procedure.

3. Use the debugfs command to access the file system on your device in debug mode. For example, if your file system is /dev/sda1, you would use debugfs /dev/sda1.

4. Use the stat command that is available in the file system debugger to show the contents of the inode. When done, use exit to close the debugfs environment.

Listing 5-29. The Ext debugfs Tool Allows You to Show the Contents of an Inode

```
root@mel:/boot# debugfs /dev/sda1
debugfs 1.40.8 (13-Mar-2015)
debugfs: stat <19>
Inode: 19  Type: regular    Mode: 0644  Flags: 0x0    Generation: 2632480000
User:  0  Group:  0  Size: 8211957
File ACL: 0  Directory ACL: 0
Links: 1  Blockcount: 16106
Fragment: Address: 0  Number: 0 Size: 0
ctime: 0x48176267 -- Tue Apr 29 14:01:11 2008
atime: 0x485ea3e9 -- Sun Jun 22 15:11:37 2008
mtime: 0x48176267 -- Tue Apr 29 14:01:11 2008
BLOCKS:
(0-11):22749-22760, (IND):22761, (12-267):22762-23017, (DIND):23018, (IND):23019,
 (268-523):23020-23275, (IND):23276, (524-779):23277-23532, (IND):23533, (780-1035
):23534-23789, (IND):23790, (1036-1291):23791-24046, (IND):24047, (1292-1547):
24048-24303,(IND):24304, (1548-1803):24305-24560, (IND):24561, (1804-1818):24562
```

```
-24576, (1819-2059):25097-25337, (IND):25338, (2060-2315):25339-25594, (IND):
25595, (2316-2571):25596-25851, (IND):25852, (2572-2827):25853-26108, (IND):
26109, (2828-3083):26110-26365,(IND):26366, (3084-3339):26367-26622, (IND):26623,
(3340-3595):26624-26879, (IND):26880,(3596-3851):26881-27136, (IND):27137, (3852
-4107):27138-27393, (IND):27394, (4108-4363):27395-27650, (IND):27651, (4364-4619)
:27652-27907, (IND):27908, (4620-4875):27909-28164, (IND):28165, (4876-5131):28166
-28421, (IND):28422, (5132-5387):28423-28678,(IND):28679, (5388-5643):28680-28935,
(IND):28936, (5644-5899):28937-29192, (IND):29193,(5900-6155):29194-29449, (IND)
:29450, (6156-6411):29451-29706, (IND):29707, (6412-6667):29708-29963, (IND):
29964, (6668-6923):29965-30220, (IND):30221, (6924-7179):30222-30477, (IND):
```

If you look hard enough at the information that is displayed by using the stat command in debugfs, you'll recognize some of the information that is displayed when using ls -l on a give file. For instance, the mode parameter tells you what permissions are set, and the user and group parameters give information about the user and group that are owners of the file. The debugfs utility adds some information to that. For instance, in its output you can see the blocks that are in use by your file as well, and that may come handy when restoring a file that has been deleted by accident.

The interesting thing about the inode is that within the inode, there is no information about the name of the file. This is because from the perspective of the operating system, the name is not important. Names are for users who normally can't handle inodes too well. To store names, Linux uses a directory tree.

A directory is a special kind of file, containing a list of files that are in the directory, plus the inode that is needed to access these files. Directories themselves have an inode number as well; the only directory that has a fixed location is /. This guarantees that your file system can always start locating files.

If, for example, a user wants to read the file /etc/hosts, the operating system will first look in the root directory (which always is found at the same location) for the inode of the directory /etc. Once it has the inode for /etc, it can check what blocks are used by this inode. Once the blocks of the directory are found, the file system can see what files are in the directory. Next, it checks what inode it needs to open the /etc/hosts file and will present the data to the user. This procedure works the same for every file system that can be used.

In a very basic file system such as Ext2, it works exactly in the way just described. Advanced file systems may offer options to make the process of allocating files somewhat easier. For instance, the file system can work with extents which is a default part of the Ext4 file system. An extent is a large number of contiguous blocks that are allocated by the file system as one unit. This makes handling large files a lot easier. Using extents makes file system management a lot more efficient. Listing 5-30 shows how block allocation is organized in an extent based file system.

Listing 5-30. A File System That Supports Extents Has Fewer Individual Blocks to Manage and Therefore Is Faster

```
root@mel:/# debugfs /dev/system/root
debugfs 1.40.8 (13-Mar-2008)
debugfs: stat <24580>

Inode: 24580    Type: regular    Mode: 0644    Flags: 0x0    Generation: 2026345315
User:     0    Group:     0    Size: 8211957
File ACL: 0     Directory ACL: 0
Links: 1    Blockcount: 16064
Fragment: Address: 0     Number: 0     Size: 0
ctime: 0x487238ee -- Mon Jul 7 11:40:30 2008
atime: 0x487238ee -- Mon Jul 7 11:40:30 2008
mtime: 0x487238ee -- Mon Jul 7 11:40:30 2008 BLOCKS:
(0-11):106496-106507, (IND):106508, (12-1035):106509-107532, (DIND):107533,
(IND):107534, (1036-2004):107535-108503
TOTAL: 2008 (END)
```

A file system may use other techniques to work faster as well, such as allocation groups. By using allocation groups, a file system divides the available space into chunks and manages each chunk of disk space individually. By doing this, the file system can achieve a much higher I/O performance. All Linux file systems use this technique; some even use the allocation group to store backups of vital file system administration data.

About Superblocks, Inode Bitmaps, and Block Bitmaps

To mount a file system, you need a file system superblock. Typically, this is the first block on a file system, and it contains generic information about the file system. You can make it visible using the stats command from a debugfs environment. In Listing 5-31, the logical volume /dev/system/root is first opened with debugfs, and next the stats utility is used to display information from the file system superblock.

Listing 5-31. Example of an Ext3 Superblock

```
root@mel:~# debugfs /dev/system/root
debugfs 1.40.8 (13-Mar-2008)
debugfs: stats
Filesystem volume name:   <none>
Last mounted on:          <not available>
Filesystem UUID:          d40645e2-412e-485e-9225-8e7f87b9f568
Filesystem magic number:  0xEF53
Filesystem revision #:    1 (dynamic)
Filesystem features:      has_journal ext_attr resize_inode dir_index filetype needs
_recovery sparse_super large_file
Filesystem flags:         signed_directory_hash
Default mount options:    (none)
Filesystem state:         clean
Errors behavior:          Continue
Filesystem OS type:       Linux
Inode count:              6553600
Block count:              26214400
Reserved block count:     1310720
Free blocks:              23856347
Free inodes:              6478467
First block:             0
Block size:              4096
Fragment size:           4096
Reserved GDT blocks:      1017
Blocks per group:        32768
Fragments per group:     32768
```

Without the superblock, you cannot mount the file system, and therefore most file systems keep backup superblocks at different locations in the file system. If the real file system gets broken, you can mount using the backup superblock and still access the file system anyway.

Apart from the superblocks, the file system contains an inode bitmap and a block bitmap.

By using these bitmaps, the file system driver can determine easily whether a given block or inode is available. When creating a file, the inode and blocks used by the file are marked as in use; when deleting a file, they will be marked as available and can be overwritten by new files.

After the inode and block bitmaps, the inode table is stored. This contains the administration of all files on your file system. Since it normally is big (an inode is at least 128 bytes), there is no backup of the inode table.

Journaling

For modern computers, *journaling* is an important feature. With the exception of Ext2, all current Linux file systems support journaling. The journal is used to track changes. This concerns changes to files and changes to metadata as well. The goal of using a journal is to make sure that transactions are processed properly. This is especially the case for situations involving a power outage. In those cases, the file system will check the journal when it comes back up again, and depending on the journaling style that is configured, do a rollback of the original data or a check on the data that was open while the computer crashed. Using a journal is essential on large file systems where lots of files get written to. Only if a file system is very small or writes hardly ever occur on the file system can you configure the file system without a journal.

When using journaling, you can specify three different journaling modes for the file system. All of these are specified as options while mounting the file system, which allows you to use different journaling modes on different file systems.

First, there is the data=ordered option, which you can use by adding the -o option to mount. To activate it, use a command like the following:

```
mount -o data=ordered /dev/sda3 /data
```

When using this option, only metadata is journaled, and barriers are enabled by default. This way, data is forced to be written to hard disk as fast as possible, which reduces chances of things going wrong. This journaling mode uses the optimal balance between performance and data security.

In case you want the best possible performance, use the data=writeback option. This option only journals metadata, but does not guarantee data integrity. This means that based on the information in the journal, when your computer crashes, the file system can try to repair the data but may fail, in which case you will end up with the old data after a system crash. At least it guarantees fast recovery after a system crash, and for many environments, that is good enough.

If you want the best guarantees for your data, use the data=journal option. When using this option, data and metadata are journaled. This ensures the best data integrity, but gives bad performance because all data has to be written twice—first to the journal, and then to the disk when it is committed to disk. If you need this journaling option, you should always make sure that the journal is written to a dedicated disk. Every file system has options to accomplish that.

Indexing

When file systems were still small, no indexing was used. You don't need an index to get a file from a list of a couple of hundreds of files. Nowadays, directories can contain many thousands, sometimes even millions of files, and to manage these amounts of files, you can't do without an index.

Basically, there are two approaches to indexing. The easiest approach, *directory indexing*, is used by the Ext3 file system; it adds an index to all directories and thus makes the file system faster when many files exist in a directory. This, however, is not the best way of performing indexing, because it doesn't offer any significant increase of performance if your file system uses many directories and subdirectories.

For optimal performance, it is better to work with a *balanced tree* (also referred to as *b-tree*), which is integrated in the heart of the file system itself. In such a balanced tree, every file is a node in the tree, and every node can have child nodes. Because of this method where every file is represented in the indexing tree, the file system is capable of finding files in a very fast way, no matter how many files there are in a directory. Using a b-tree for indexing makes the file system also a lot more complicated. If things go wrong, the risk exists that you have to rebuild the entire file system, and that can take a lot of time. In this process, you even risk losing all data on your file system. Therefore, when choosing a file system that is built on top of a b-tree index, make sure it is a stable file systemModern Linux file systems are using b-tree indexing to make the file system faster. Only all file systems from the Ext family are based on the older h-tree index, which is the reason why on modern Linux systems Ext4 isn't used as the default file system anymore.

Btrfs

Since 2008 developer Chris Mason is working on the next generation Linux file system: Btrfs. This file system is developed as a Copy on Write (CoW) file system, which means that old versions of files can be maintained while working on them. When writing block, the old block is copied to a new location, so that two different versions of the data block exist, which helps preventing issues on the file system. In 2009 Btrfs was accepted in the Linux kernel and since then it is available in several Linux distributions.

Apart from being a CoW file system, Btrfs has many other useful features. Amongst these features are the subvolumes. A subvolume can be seen as something that sits between a volume or logical partition and a directory. It is not a different device, but subvolumes can be mounted with their own specific mount options. This makes working with file systems completely different: where on old Linux file systems you needed a dedicated device if you needed to mount a file system with specific options, in Btrfs you can just keep it all on the same subvolume.

Another important feature of Btrfs, are snapshots. A snapshot freezes the state of the file system at a specific moment, which can be useful if you need to be able to revert to an old state of the file system, or if you need to make a backup of the file system.

Because Btrfs is a CoW file system, snapshots are very easy to create. While modifying files a copy is made of the old file. That means that the state of the old file is still available, and only new data blocks have to be added to that. From the metadata perspective it is very easy to deal with both of these, which is why it is easy to create snapshots and revert files to an earlier version.

Snapshots are useful if you want to revert to a previous version of a file, but they also come in handy for making backups. Files in a snapshot will never have a status of open. That means that files in a snapshot always have a stable state that can be used to create a backup.

Btrfs Tools and Features

As mentioned before, the Btrfs file system introduces many new features. Some of the Btrfs features make working with LVM unnecessary and some new features have also been introduced. The key new features in Btrfs is that it is a copy on write file system. Because of that, it supports snapshots by itself, allowing users and administrators an easy rollback to a previous situation.

Also, Btrfs has support for multiple volumes. That means that when running out of disk space on a particular Btrfs volume, another volume can be added. Also, after adding or removing a volume from a Btrfs file system, online shrinking and growth of the file system is supported. The Btrfs file system also supports meta data balancing. That means that depending on the amount of volumes that is used, the file system metadata can be spread in the most efficient way. Apart from that, there are Btrfs subvolumes.

Understanding Subvolumes

A Btrfs subvolume is a namespace that can be mounted independently with specific mount options. Multiple subvolumes can reside on the same file system and allow administrators from creating different mount points for specific needs. By default, all file systems have at least one subvolume, which is the file system device root but additional subvolumes can also be created. Apart from the support of per-subvolume mount options, snapshots are created on subvolumes. After unmounting a subvolume, a roll-back of the snapshot can be effected.

Listing 5-32. Btrfs subvolumes

```
UUID=c7997ed8-2568-49c3-bb84-3d231978707c / btrfs defaults 0 0
UUID=c7997ed8-2568-49c3-bb84-3d231978707c /boot/grub2/i386-pc btrfs subvol=@/boot/grub2/
i386-pc 0 0
UUID=c7997ed8-2568-49c3-bb84-3d231978707c /boot/grub2/x86_64-efi btrfs subvol=@/boot/grub2/
x86_64-efi 0 0
UUID=c7997ed8-2568-49c3-bb84-3d231978707c /home btrfs subvol=@/home 0 0
UUID=c7997ed8-2568-49c3-bb84-3d231978707c /opt btrfs subvol=@/opt 0 0
UUID=c7997ed8-2568-49c3-bb84-3d231978707c /srv btrfs subvol=@/srv 0 0
UUID=c7997ed8-2568-49c3-bb84-3d231978707c /tmp btrfs subvol=@/tmp 0 0
UUID=c7997ed8-2568-49c3-bb84-3d231978707c /usr/local btrfs subvol=@/usr/local 0 0
UUID=c7997ed8-2568-49c3-bb84-3d231978707c /var/crash btrfs subvol=@/var/crash 0 0
UUID=c7997ed8-2568-49c3-bb84-3d231978707c /var/lib/mailman btrfs subvol=@/var/lib/mailman 0 0
UUID=c7997ed8-2568-49c3-bb84-3d231978707c /var/lib/named btrfs subvol=@/var/lib/named 0 0
UUID=c7997ed8-2568-49c3-bb84-3d231978707c /var/lib/pgsql btrfs subvol=@/var/lib/pgsql 0 0
UUID=c7997ed8-2568-49c3-bb84-3d231978707c /var/log btrfs subvol=@/var/log 0 0
UUID=c7997ed8-2568-49c3-bb84-3d231978707c /var/opt btrfs subvol=@/var/opt 0 0
UUID=c7997ed8-2568-49c3-bb84-3d231978707c /var/spool btrfs subvol=@/var/spool 0 0
UUID=c7997ed8-2568-49c3-bb84-3d231978707c /var/tmp btrfs subvol=@/var/tmp 0 0
UUID=c7997ed8-2568-49c3-bb84-3d231978707c /.snapshots btrfs subvol=@/.snapshots
```

Using subvolumes allows administrators to treat the most common directories that have been created with their own mount options, and create snapshots for them as well if so required. The subvolumes are created on mount by including the btrfs specific subvol=@/some/name option. Subvolumes can only be created if the parent volume is mounted first. You can see that in the first list of output in Listing 5-32, where the /dev/sda2 device is mounted as a Btrfs device. For each subvolume after creation, specific mount options can be added to the mount options column in /etc/fstab.

From a shell prompt, you can request a list of subvolumes that are currently being used. Use the command **btrfs subvolume list** / to do so, this will give you a result like in Listing 5-33.

Listing 5-33. Requesting a list of current subvolumes

```
linux-ia9r:~ # btrfs subvolume list /
ID 257 gen 48 top level 5 path @
ID 258 gen 39 top level 257 path boot/grub2/i386-pc
ID 259 gen 39 top level 257 path boot/grub2/x86_64-efi
ID 260 gen 42 top level 257 path home
ID 261 gen 28 top level 257 path opt
ID 262 gen 39 top level 257 path srv
ID 263 gen 45 top level 257 path tmp
ID 264 gen 39 top level 257 path usr/local
ID 265 gen 39 top level 257 path var/crash
ID 266 gen 39 top level 257 path var/lib/mailman
ID 267 gen 39 top level 257 path var/lib/named
ID 268 gen 39 top level 257 path var/lib/pgsql
ID 269 gen 48 top level 257 path var/log
ID 270 gen 39 top level 257 path var/opt
ID 271 gen 48 top level 257 path var/spool
ID 272 gen 41 top level 257 path var/tmp
ID 276 gen 39 top level 257 path .snapshots
```

Apart from the subvolumes that are created by default, an administrator can add new subvolumes manually. To do this, the command **btrfs subvolume create** is used, followed by the path of the desired subvolume. Use for instance the command **btrfs subvolume create /root** to create a subvolume for the home directory of the user root.

After creating a subvolume, snapshots can be created. To do this, use the command **btrfs subvolume snapshot** followed by the name of the subvolume and the name of the snapshot. Notice that it is good practice, but not mandatory to create snapshots within the same name space as the subvolume. In exercise 3-2 you'll apply these commands to work with snapshots yourself.

EXERCISE 5-3: WORKING WITH BTRFS SUBVOLUMES

In this exercise you'll create a subvolume. You'll next put some files in the subvolume and create a snapshot in it. After that, you'll learn how to perform a roll-back to the original state, using the snapshot you've just created.

1. On an existing Btrfs file system, type **btrfs subvolume create /test**.

2. Type **btrfs subvolume list /**, this will show all currently existing snapshots including the snapshot you have just created.

3. Copy some files to /test, using the command **cp /etc/[abc]* /test**.

4. At this point, it's time to create a snapshot, using **btrfs subvolume snapshot /test /test/snap**.

5. Remove all files from /test.

6. To get back to the original state of the /test subvolume, use **mv /test/snap/* /test**.

Working with multiple devices in Btrfs

Another benefit of the Btrfs file system is that it allows you to work with multiple devices. By doing this, Btrfs offers a new approach to creating RAID volumes. To create a Btrfs volume that consists of multiple devices, type a command like **mkfs.btrfs /dev/sda1 /dev/sda2 /dev/sda3**. To mount a composed device through /etc/fstab, you'll need to take a special approach. You'll have to refer to the first device in the composed device, and specify the names of the other devices as a btrfs mount option, as in the following example line:

```
/dev/sda1      /somewhere      btrfs     device=/dev/sda1,device=/dev/sda2,device=/dev/sda3 0 0
```

Btrfs also allows you to add devices to a file system that is already created. Use **btrfs device add /dev/sda4 /somewhere** to do so. Notice that the device add command works on the name of the mount point and not the name of the volume. After adding a device to a Btrfs file system, you should rebalance the device metadata, using **btrfs filesystem balance /somewhere**. You can request the current status of a multi-device Btrfs volume by using the **btrfs device stats /somewhere** command.

A multi-volume device as just described, is just a device that consists of multiple volumes. If one of the devices in the volume gets damaged, there's no easy option to repair. If you do want an easy option to repair, you should create a Btrfs RAID volume. The command **mkfs.btrfs -m raid1 /dev/sdb /dev/sdc /dev/sdd /dev/sde** will do that for you. If one of the devices in the RAID setup gets missing, you'll first need to mount it in degraded state. That's for metadata consistency and it allows you to remove the failing device.

If for instance /dev/sdb is showing errors, you would use the command mount -o degraded /dev/sdb /mnt. Notice that it must be mounted on a temporary mount and not on the mount point of the Btrfs RAID device. After mounting it, you can use **btrfs device delete missing /mnt** to remove it.

Formatting File Systems

Now that you know more about the different file systems and their properties, you can make a choice for the file system that best addresses your needs. After making that choice, you can format the file system. In the next sections, you will read how to do this for the different file systems.

The basic utility to create a file system is mkfs. This utility works with modules to address different file systems. You can choose the module that you want to employ by using the -t option, followed by the file system type that you want to create. Alternatively, you can use mkfs, followed by a dot and the name of the file system that you want to create. In this way, you can create every file system that is supported; for instance, mkfs.ext4 is used to create an Ext4 file system, and mkfs.xfs is used to create an XFS file system.

Maintaining File Systems

Normally, your file systems will work just fine. Occasionally, you may run into problems, and instead of mounting the file system properly, you'll get a message indicating that there is a problem that you have to fix. If this happens, different tools are at your disposal, depending on the file system that you are using. Ext offers the most extensive tools, but there are options for XFS and Btrfs as well.

Analyzing and Repairing Ext

In some situations, problems will occur on your Ext2/Ext3 file system. If that happens, the file system offers some commands that can help you in analyzing and repairing the file system. The first command is e2fsck, the file system check utility that works on all Ext4 file systems.

If you think that anything may be wrong with your file system, run e2fsck. You should make sure though that the file system on which you run it is not currently mounted. Since this is hard to accomplish if you want to run it on your root file system, it is not a bad idea to use the automatic check that occurs every once in a while when mounting an Ext file system. This check is on by default, so don't switch it off!

When running e2fsck on an Ext3 or Ext4 file system, the utility will check the journal and repair any inconsistencies. Only if the superblock indicates that there is a problem with the file system will the utility check data as well. On Ext2 it will always check data, since this is the only option. Normally, it will automatically repair all errors it finds, unless a certain error requires human intervention. In that case, e2fsck will notify you, and you can use one of the advanced options. Table 5-1 gives an overview of the most useful options that e2fsck has to offer.

Table 5-1. *Most Useful e2fsck Options*

Option	Description
-b *superblock*	Use this option to read one of the backup superblocks. Contrary to the mount command, you can refer to the normal block position where the file system can find the backup superblock, which will be block 32768 in most cases.
-c	This option lets e2fsck check for bad blocks. If it finds them, it will write them to a specific inode reserved for this purpose. In the future, the file system will avoid using any of these blocks. Be aware though that bad blocks are often an indication of real problems on your hard drive. Use the -c option with e2fsck as a temporary solution until you replace your hard drive.
-f	This option forces checking, even if the file system seems to be without problems.
-j *external_journal*	Use this option to specify where the external journal can be found. You'll need this option if your file system uses an external journal.
-p	This option automatically repairs everything that can be repaired without human intervention.
-y	Use this to have e2fsck assume an answer of yes to all questions. This goes further than default -p behavior and will also automatically enter yes on questions that normally require human intervention.

In some situations, e2fsck may not do its work properly. If that is the case, there are two useful utilities to analyze a little bit further what is happening. The first of them is dumpe2fs. This utility dumps the contents of the superblock and also the information about all block group descriptors. The latter is information that you will hardly ever find useful at all; therefore I recommend you use dumpe2fs with the -h option, which makes it more readable. In Listing 5-34, you can see what the output of this command looks like.

Listing 5-34. The dumpe2fs Utility Shows the Contents of the Superblock and All Group Descriptors

```
Filesystem volume name:   <none>
Last mounted on:          <not available>
Filesystem UUID:          3babfd35-de36-4c81-9fb9-1a988d548927
Filesystem magic number:  0xEF53
Filesystem revision #:    1 (dynamic)
Filesystem features:      filetype sparse_super
Default mount options:    (none)
Filesystem state:         not clean
Errors behavior:          Continue
Filesystem OS type:       Linux
Inode count:              490560
Block count:              979933
Reserved block count:     48996
Free blocks:              898773
Free inodes:              490529
First block:              1
Block size:               1024
Fragment size:            1024
Blocks per group:         8192
Fragments per group:      8192
Inodes per group:         4088
```

```
Inode blocks per group:    511
Last mount time:           Tue Jul 8 02:58:33 2008
Last write time:           Tue Jul 8 02:58:33 2008
Mount count:               1
Maximum mount count:       30
Last checked:              Tue Jul 8 02:58:16 2008
Check interval:            0 (<none>)
Reserved blocks uid:       0 (user root)
Reserved blocks gid:       0 (group root)
First inode:               11
Inode size:                128

Group 0: (Blocks 1-8192)
  Primary superblock at 1, Group descriptors at 2-5
  Block bitmap at 6 (+5), Inode bitmap at 7 (+6)
  Inode table at 8-518 (+7)
  2029 free blocks, 4070 free inodes, 2 directories
  Free blocks: 532-2560
  Free inodes: 17, 20-4088
Group 1: (Blocks 8193-16384)
  Backup superblock at 8193, Group descriptors at 8194-8197
  Block bitmap at 8198 (+5), Inode bitmap at 8199 (+6)
  Inode table at 8200-8710 (+7)
  2095 free blocks, 4088 free inodes, 0 directories
  Free blocks: 14290-16384
  Free inodes: 4089-8176
Group 2: (Blocks 16385-24576)
  Block bitmap at 16385 (+0), Inode bitmap at 16386 (+1)
  Inode table at 16392-16902 (+7)
  5749 free blocks, 4088 free inodes, 0 directories
  Free blocks: 16387-16391, 16903-22646
  Free inodes: 8177-12264
```

If you see a parameter that you don't like when using dumpe2fs, you can use tune2fs to change it. Basically, tune2fs works on the same options as mkfs.ext3, so you won't have a hard time understanding its options. For instance, in the preceding listing, the maximum mount count is set to 30. That means that after being mounted 30 times, on the next mount the file system will be checked automatically, which may take a lot of time. To change this, use the -C option with tune2fs. For instance, the following command would set the maximum mount count to 60 on /dev/sda1:

```
tune2fs -C 60 /dev/sda1
```

If you really are ready for a deep dive into your file system, debugfs is the utility you need.

Before starting with it, make sure that you use it on an unmounted file system. The debugfs tool is working at a very deep level and may severely interfere with other processes that try to access files while you are debugging them. So if necessary, take your live CD and use debugfs from there.

After starting debugfs, you'll find yourself in the debugfs interface. In this environment, some specific commands are available for you. You will also recognize some generic Linux commands that you know from a Bash environment, but as you will find out, they work a bit differently in a debugfs environment. For example, the ls command in debugfs will not only show you file names, but also the number in blocks in use by this item and the inode of this item, which is very useful information if you really need to start troubleshooting. In Listing 5-35, you can see what happens when using the ls command from the debugfs interface.

Listing 5-35. The ls Command in debugfs Gives Information Other Than What You Are Used to from It

```
root@mel:/# debugfs /dev/system/root
debugfs 1.40.8 (13-Mar-2008)
debugfs: ls

2 (12) . 2 (12) ..      11 (20) lost+found     6135809 (12) var
4202497 (12) boot 5095425 (12) srv              335873 (12) etc
2924545 (16) media  24577 (16) cdrom             24578 (20) initrd.img
5808129 (12) lib  1073153 (12) usr             1417217 (12) bin
5865473 (12) dev  1966081 (12) home            1572865 (12) mnt
6168577 (12) proc 6086657 (12) root            2277377 (12) sbin
4947969 (12) tmp    360449 (12) sys            5586945 (12) opt
1302529 (16) initrd 24579 (16) vmlinuz         4808705 (16) tftpboot
2949121 (20) clonezilla  1785857 (12) isos
24580 (36) initrd.img-2.6.24-16-server  24581 (3692) 335873
(END)
```

In case you wonder how this information may be useful to you, imagine a situation where you can't access one of the directories in the root file system anymore. This information gives you the inode that contains the administration of the item. Next, you can dump the inode from the debugfs interface to a normal file. For instance, the command dump <24580> /24580 would create a file with the name 24580 in the root of your file system and fill that with the contents of inode 24580. That allows you to access the data that file occupies again and may help in troubleshooting.

This information may also help when recovering deleted files. Imagine that a user comes to see you and tells you that he or she has created a few files, of which one has been lost. Say the names of these files are /home/user/file1, /home/user/file2, and /home/user/file3.

Imagine that file2 was deleted by accident and no matter what, the user needs to get it back. The first thing you can do is use the lsdel command from the debugfs interface. Chances are it gives you a list of deleted inodes, including their original size and deletion time; see Listing 5-36 for an example.

Listing 5-36. debugfs' lsdel Can Give You an Overview of Deleted Files

```
root@mel:/# debugfs /dev/sda1
debugfs 1.40.8 (13-Mar-2015)
debugfs: lsdel

 Inode   Owner Mode    Size    Blocks    Time deleted
 233029      0 100644  16384    17/     17 Sun Jul 6 11:27:49 2008
 233030      0 100644  16384    17/     17 Sun Jul 6 15:41:01 2008
     17      0 100644    814     1/      1 Tue Jul 8 06:33:45 2008
3 deleted inodes found.
(END)
```

As you can see, the information that lsdel gives you includes the inode number, original owner, size in blocks and—most important—the time the file was deleted. Based on that, it's easy to recover the original file. If it was the file in inode 233030, from the debugfs interface, use dump <233030> /originalfile to recover it. Unfortunately, due to some differences between Ext2 and Ext3/4, lsdel works well on Ext2 and rarely on Ext3/4.

Given the fact that the user in our example has created some files, it may be interesting to see what inodes were used. Let's say file1 still uses inode 123, file2 uses 127, and file3 is removed, so you can't find that information anymore. Chances are, however, that the inode that file3 has used was not too far away from inode 127, so you can try and dump all inodes between inode 128 and 140. This likely allows you to recover the original file, thanks to dumpe2fs.

There are many other commands available from debugfs as well. I recommend you at least take a look at these commands. The help command from within the debugfs interface will give you a complete list. Have a look at these commands, and try to get an impression of the possibilities they offer—you may need them some day.

Analyzing and Repairing XFS File Systems

Since it is a completely different file system, the XFS file system offers options that are totally different from the Ext options. There are four commands that are useful when getting into trouble with XFS. The first and most important of them is xfs_check. As its name suggests, this command will check you XFS file system and report whether it has found any errors. Before running xfs_check, you must unmount the file system on which you want to run it.

Next, just run the command without additional arguments; it will tell you whether some serious errors were found. For instance, the following command would check the XFS file system that has been created in /dev/sdb1:

```
xfs_check /dev/sdb1
```

If no problems were found, xfs_check will report nothing. If problems were found, it will indicate what problems these are and try to give an indication of what you can do about them as well. The next step would then be to run the xfs_repair utility. Again, you can run this utility on an unmounted file system only. This utility does have some advanced options, which you would use in specific situations only. Normally, by just running xfs_repair on the device that you want to check, you should be able to fix most issues. For instance, the following example command would try to repair all issues on the XFS file system in /dev/sdb1:

```
xfs_repair /dev/sdb1
```

Basically, if with these commands you can't fix the issue, you are lost. But XFS also has an advanced option to dump the file system metadata to a file, which you can send over for support. However, this is not an option that you are very likely to use, as it requires extensive knowledge of the file system that normally only one of the file system developers would have.

Resizing File Systems

When resizing file systems, you should be aware that the procedure always involves two steps. You have to resize the storage device on which you have created the file system as well as the file system itself. It is possible to resize logical volumes. If you want to resize a partition, you have to use a special utility with the name GParted. I will first explain how to resize a file system that is in a logical volume. All file systems can be resized without problems.

Resizing a File System in a Logical Volume

The following procedure details how the volume is first brought offline and then the file system that sits on the volume is resized. It is presumed that the volume you want to shrink is called data, and it is using an Ext4 file system. It is mounted on the directory /data.

■ **Caution**   Online resizing of a file system is possible in some cases. For example, the command `ext2online` makes it possible to resize a live file system. However, because resizing file systems is very labor intensive, I wouldn't recommend doing it this way. There's always a risk that it won't work out simply because of all of the work that has to be done. So, to stay on the safe side, `umount` your volume before resizing it.

Several utilities exist to resize file systems. You could consider resizing the file system and the underlying logical volume apart. This is not a very smart procedure though. If you want to resize filesystems in an efficient way, you better use the **lvresize** tool with the **-r** option. This option resizes the logical volume, and at the same time resizes the file system that resides on the logical volume. Use for instance **lvresize -L +1G -r /dev/vgdata/lvdata** to add 1GB of disk space to the /dev/vgdata/lvdata file system. This will work provided that the disk space you want to add it available in the LVM volume group.

Resizing Partitions with GParted

This book is about command-line administration. GParted is not a command-line administration tool, and therefore I will not cover it in a step-by-step description. It does need to be mentioned though, as it offers an easy-to-use interface that helps you in resizing partitions. You can install it locally on your Linux computer, but to unleash its full power, it's better to download the GParted live CD at `http://gparted.sourceforge.net`. Reboot your computer from this live CD and start GParted to resize any partition on your computer, Windows as well as Linux partitions. As you can see in Figure 5-1, GParted shows a graphical representation of all partitions on your computer. To resize a partition, click the partition border, and drag it to the new intended size.

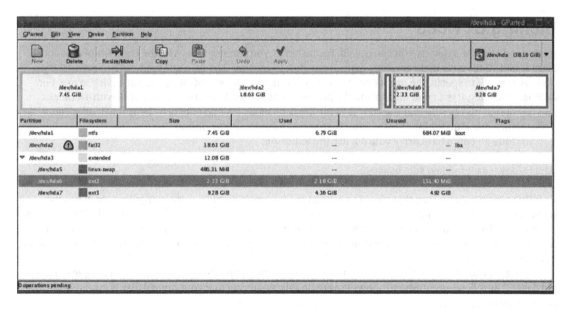

Figure 5-1. *GParted helps you to resize partitions from an easy-to-use graphical interface*

Working with Windows File Systems

On Linux, you can work with Windows file systems as well. For all FAT-based needs, the vfat file system is the best option. Almost all Linux distributions have support for this file system built in by default. This means that if you connect a USB key that is formatted with FAT32 to your system, for instance, it will mount automatically, and you will be able to read and write files on it.

The support for NTFS is a different story. Until recently, most Linux distributions did include only the read-only ntfs driver, because stable write support for NTFS is a recent development. Therefore, if you can't write to an NTFS device, make sure to upgrade to the latest driver that is available. Also, with the new version of NTFS, some cool utilities have become available. Following is a short list of the most important of these utilities:

- mkntfs: This is the utility you need to create an NTFS file system.

- ntfsresize: Use this utility to resize an NTFS file system. Using this, you can resize an NTFS partition on Windows as well.

- ntfsclone: Use this to clone an NTFS partition. This utility makes sure that the cloned partition has a unique ID, which is required for all NTFS file systems.

- ntfsfix: Use this tool to fix issues on an NTFS file system. This also works to repair Windows file systems that have errors.

- ntfsundelete: Use this to recover files that you have deleted by accident from an NTFS file system.

- ntfswipe: This utility cleans out all data from an NTFS file system. Use it if you want to make sure that recovery of your NTFS data is never possible.

Cloning Devices

If you need to clone a device, you can use dd. For instance, you can use it to write the contents of an optical drive to an ISO file or to make an exact copy of one disk to another. The dd command has two mandatory options. Use if= to specify the input device. Next, by using of=, you specify what output device to use. For optimal efficiency, it is a good idea to add the parameter bs=4096. Most file systems work with 4K blocks, and this option makes sure that the copy is made block by block instead of byte by byte. It will offer you a performance that is about four times better than without using the bs= option.

To clone an entire hard drive with dd, use the following:

```
dd if=/dev/sda of=/dev/sdb bs=4096
```

This command assumes that there is a second hard drive available in your computer, which has the name /dev/sdb. It will completely overwrite all data on this /dev/sdb with data from /dev/sda. Because this command will make an exact copy of /dev/sda, you must make sure that the drive you are writing to is as least as big as the original drive. If the destination drive is bigger, you'll later have to resize the file systems on that drive.

Using dd, you can also write the contents of an optical disk to an ISO file (or make boot floppies in the old days). The following command shows how to do this, assuming that your optical disk is available via the /dev/cdrom device:

```
dd if=/dev/cdrom of=/mycd.iso bs=4096
```

Summary

In this chapter, you have read all about management of the information on your hard disk. You have read how to manage partitions, volumes, and file systems. Based on this information, you will be able to use the best possible configuration on your disk. The following commands have been covered:

- fdisk: Creates partitions.

- cfdisk: Creates partitions. This is not as easy to use as fdisk, but it does have an interface that is easier to use.

- pvcreate: Creates LVM physical volumes.

- pvdisplay: Displays properties of LVM physical volumes.

- vgcreate: Creates LVM volume groups.

- vgdisplay: Displays properties of LVM volume groups.

- lvcreate: Creates LVM logical volumes.

- lvdisplay: Displays the properties of an LVM logical volume.

- pvs: Shows a short list of all present LVM physical volumes.

- pvscan: Scans storage devices for the presence of LVM physical volumes.

- vgscan: Scans storage devices for the presence of LVM volume groups.

- vgs: Shows a list of LVM volume groups.

- lvscan: Scans storage devices for the presence of LVM logical volumes.

- lvs: Shows a list of LVM logical volumes.

- vgchange: Changes the status from LVM volume groups and the volumes in it from active to inactive and vice versa.

- debugfs: Serves as an advanced debugger for the Ext2/Ext3 file systems.

- e2fsck: Checks the integrity of the Ext2/Ext3 file systems.

- tune2fs: Changes the properties of the Ext2/Ext3 file systems.

- dumpe2fs: Shows the properties of the Ext2/Ext3 file systems.

- reiserfsck: Checks the integrity of a ReiserFS file system.

- reiserfstune: Changes the properties of a ReiserFS file system.

- resize_reiserfs: Resizes a ReiserFS file system.

- debugreiserfs: Shows the properties of the ReiserFS file system.

- mkfs: Creates file systems.

- xfs_check: Checks the integrity of an XFS file system.

- xfs_repair: Repairs an XFS file system that has errors.

- ext2online: Resizes an Ext2/Ext3 file system without taking it offline.

- resize2fs: Serves as an offline Ext2/Ext3 resizing utility.

- `lvextend`: Extends the size of an LVM logical volume.

- `mkntfs`: Creates an NTFS file system.

- `ntfsresize`: Resizes an NTFS file system.

- `ntfsclone`: Clones an NTFS file system.

- `ntfsfix`: Fixes the integrity of a damaged NTFS file system.

- `ntfsundelete`: Undeletes a file in an NTFS file system.

- `ntfswipe`: Wipes all data in an NTFS file system, without the possibility to undelete the data.

In the next chapter, you'll learn how to manage users and groups.

CHAPTER 6

■ ■ ■

Managing Users and Groups

This chapter is about the user environment. You will learn how to set up a user account, which is an important task, even if you are not a computer administrator. You will also learn about the way authentication is handled using the PAM (pluggable authentication module) and nsswitch systems, as well as explore the configuration files that contain the definition of the working environment for your users. For instance, you will see how to provide a user with default settings by using the /etc/profile file and all related files. Also, you will get a look at the sudo mechanism, which allows you to perform administration tasks without needing to log in as root.

Setting Up User Accounts

Before starting to discuss how to create user accounts, it is important to understand what a user is. On Linux a user is not always exclusively bound to a person that logs in to a computer. A user account is an entity that is created on a Linux system to grant permissions that allow the user to perform specific tasks. User accounts exist for people that need access to a computer, but also for services that need access to specific files and other system resources.

There are different ways to create a user. You can use one of the commands that are available, like useradd or adduser. (useradd is the default utility; some distributions have a utility named adduser, which in most cases is just a symbolic link to useradd. On Ubuntu, **adduser** is an interactive script that walks the person that invokes it through the different steps that are needed to create user account.)

It is also possible to create a user by editing the user database directly. This database is stored in the two configuration files, /etc/passwd en /etc/shadow, and you can modify it using the vipw command, or just plain vi. If you decide to change the configuration files directly, it's a good idea to use vipw, not plain The vipw command does a check on the consistency of the configuration files once you are done, which is not the case for vi. Also, **vipw** writes to a temporary file, which prevents locking problems caused by other users accessing the file simultaneously.

Before taking your first steps in user management, you need to understand a little bit more about users and their properties. In the following sections, you'll first learn which properties a user has. Following that, you'll read how to manage users using commands like useradd and usermod, and how to modify the user database directly.

Understanding Users and Their Properties

Before starting to create users, it makes sense to know about the different properties that Linux users typically have. These properties are stored in the /etc/passwd and /etc/shadow files. Based on this knowledge, you'll be better able to create the user according to your specific needs. When creating a user, you need to provide a value for the following properties, which you can read more about in the next sections:

- Username
- Password
- User ID (UID)
- ID of the primary group of the user
- Comment field
- Home directory
- Default shell

Username

Every user has a unique username. This name is used when the user authenticates to the system. In most cases, it will be a real name, like lori, but you can use a numeric name as well, such as an employee number. I recommend using letters and numbers only in the username. After installation, your computer will already have some usernames. One of them is the user name root, which is used for system administration purposes.

You'll also find that some other system accounts are created by default. These are needed for system tasks and services, and you should never change or remove them. The names of these accounts depend on the services that are installed on your computer. In general, you can recognize them because they have a User IDentification number (UID) that is lower than 500 or 1000.

Password

Every user should have a password. This is required for authentication to the Linux system. When choosing a password, make sure that it is strong. A *strong password* is a password that can't be found in any dictionary and is a combination of upper and lowercase letters as well as numbers. User passwords should be difficult to guess, and in general it is a good idea not to use passwords shorter than six characters. When setting a password, the administrator can set some properties for the password as well, such as the expiration date of the password. The user root can also disable the password if he or she doesn't want the user to log in anymore. As an administrator, you can determine how long it takes before the user password expires.

The password and related settings are stored in the /etc/shadow file, which is covered later in this chapter.

UID

The UID is another major piece of information when creating a user. For your computer, this is the only way to identify a user; usernames are just a convenience for humans (who can't quite handle numbers as well as a computer does). In general, all users need a unique UID. Most Linux distributions start generating UIDs for local users at 1000. In the default Linux configuration, a total of 16 bits was available for creating UIDs. This means that the highest available UID is 65535. On modern Linux distributions, UIDs beyond 65535 can be used. If you exceed this limit, you'll need a directory server such as OpenLDAP. Typically, UIDs below 500 are reserved for system accounts that your computer needs to start services such as a web server or the printing process. The UID 0 is also a special one: the user with it has complete administrative permissions to the computer. UID 0 is typically reserved for the user root.

Group Membership

On Linux, all users must be a member of at least one group. This is referred to as the *primary group assignment*. Apart from the primary group, users can be a member of additional groups as well. The primary group setting is stored in the /etc/passwd file, and secondary groups are in the /etc/group file, which is discussed later in this chapter.

Gecos Field

The official name for the next field in the documentation is the General Electric Comprehensive Operating System (Gecos) field, and it is used to include some comment to make it easier to identify the user. It is a good habit to put a description of the user account in this field, although you can do without it as well. The finger utility (see Chapter 2) displays the content of the Gecos field if someone requests information about a user. You can put in any description you like.

Home Directory

Most users have a home directory. This directory, which typically resides in /home, is where users can store files. You will also find that some default configuration files often exist in the user's home directory. These configuration files make the user's default environment. Also, some subdirectories are created that allow users to store different types of files. Apart from the home directory, the only directory where users are allowed to write files is /tmp. You are free to change this at will, of course; you'll read how to do so in Chapter 7, which is about permissions. In Listing 6-1, you can see an example of the contents of the home directory of user linda, which is /home/linda, with all of the default files that were copied into that directory. These default files are stored in the /etc/skel directory. When a user account is created, the contents of the /etc/skel directory is copied to the users home directory.

Listing 6-1. Example of a Home Directory and Its Contents

```
nuuk:/home/linda # ls
.bash_history  .fonts      .muttrc    .xim.template public_html
.bashrc        .gnu-emacs  .profile   .xinitrc.template
.dvipsrc       .inputrc    .urlview   .xtalkrc
.emacs         .kermrc     .xcoralrc  Documents
.exrc          .mozilla    .xemacs    bin
```

Shell

Any user who needs to log in to your computer needs a shell (not all users need to log in though). This is the environment where the user types commands that need to be executed on the computer. SUSE and Red Hat use /bin/bash as the default shell, where Ubuntu uses the /bin/dash shell. Most users won't notice the difference; after all, the shell is just a command interpreter.

You should know that not every user needs a shell. A user with a shell is allowed to log in locally to your system and access any files and directories stored on that system. If you'reusing your system as a Samba file server, for example, the user will typically never need to log in to your system directly. In this case, it is a good idea to use /bin/false or **/sbin/**nologin as the default shell; this will prohibit users from ever logging in to your system.

Commands for User Management

For user management, your distribution provides some commands. If you want to add users from the command line, useradd is just the ticket. You can use this command to add a user and all of the properties mentioned previously. The other commands for user management are just as convenient. Following is an overview of all commands available to manage user accounts:

- useradd: Adds users to the local authentication system

- usermod: Modifies properties for users

- userdel: Deletes users from a system

- passwd: Modifies passwords for users

Using useradd is simple. In its easiest form, it just takes the name of a user as its argument; thus useradd zeina creates a user called zeina to the system. Most Linux distributions will create a home directory for the user in /home. If you're using SUSE Linux (or any other distribution where you notice that a home directory hasn't been created), use the option -m with **useradd** to ensure the creation of the home directory.

If a user has been added without a home directory, unfortunately, there is no easy way to create that home directory later. (There is a hard way though. You'll understand all about that after reading Chapter 7, which is about file system permissions.) This hard way consists of copying over all files in the /etc/skel directory to the user home directory, and applying correct permissions to these files after they have been copied. Following is a list of the most important options that you can use with useradd:

- -c *comment*: Allows you to enter a comment field to the user account. If this comment has white spaces or other special characters, make sure that they are in quotations. Information set this way can be requested with the finger command, and this comment field typically is used for the user's name. You will notice that for some of the system processes, this field gives a short description of the process that is responsible for the user account.

- -e *date*: Sets the expiration date for the user. Use this option to automatically disable the user's account on the specified date. This can be entered in the YYYY-MM-DD format or as the number of days since January 1, 1970. You'll probably prefer to specify the date.

- -G *groups*: Makes the user a member of some additional groups. By default, the user becomes a member of only those groups listed in /etc/default/useradd.

- -g *gid*: Sets the primary group of a user (see the section "Group Membership" later in this chapter for more details).

- -m: Creates a home directory automatically. For instance, if you use this option when creating a user named linda, the home directory that is created is /home/linda.

■ **Note**   The useradd command also has the option -p. If you read the man page, you'll notice that this option can be used to change the password of a user. There is a catch though; the -p option can only be used to specify a password that is already encrypted by a program that uses the crypt (3) function. This is not typically the way you want to change a password, so use the passwd command instead.

If you understand the useradd command, it's not hard to understand usermod as well. This command works on the same user properties as useradd. However, you will notice that some options are not available with usermod. For instance, you can't use usermod to create a home directory for a user who doesn't have a home directory yet.

If you want to change password related properties for a user, use **chage** instead of usermod. This command offers all you need to define validity settings for user passwords. In exercise 6-1 you'll learn how to work with this command.

If a user account is no longer needed, you can use userdel as follows: to remove a user with the name chris, issue userdel chris. By default, userdel does not remove the home directory and mail spool for the user. If you want these to be removed as well, use the option -r. So, userdel -r chris removes chris and his home directory as well. You will notice that this does not work if in chris's home directory files exist that are not owned by this user. If you are sure that you want to remove these as well, add the -f option.

■ **Tip** Before removing a user and his or her home directory, it might be a good idea to make a backup of that home directory and all other files that the user has created first. The following command shows how to do this. It uses find to locate all files that are owned by user chris and copies them to the directory /root/chris. This location ensures that no one else but root has permissions to read and, if needed, recover these files:

```
find / -user chris -exec cp {} /root/chris \;
```

Chapter 4 has more details on the find command.

EXERCISE 6-1: CREATING USERS

1. Open a root shell and type **useradd lara**.

2. Still as root, type **su - lara** to log in as user lara. Verify that the user has a home directory. To do this, type **pwd**, you should see /home/lara as the result. If this is not the case, as root type **userdel lara** and **useradd -m lara**, to create the user again but this time with a home directory as well.

3. Still from the lara shell, type **id**. This should show that currently you're logging in as user lara.

4. Use the Ctrl+Alt+F2 key sequence to open a virtual console. At the login prompt, type the user name lara, and when asked for a password press Enter. You'll get an access denied error message because no password has been set for the new user.

5. Open a root shell and type **echo password I passwd --stdin lara**. This command sets the password for user lara. Repeat step 4 of this exercise, you should now be able to log in as user lara.

6. From a root shell, type **chage lara**. You'll be prompted for a series of password related settings. Enter the settings you want to use to restrict access to the account of user lara.

Working with Default Values for User Management

When managing users, two configuration files are involved that allow you to specify default settings for users. First is /etc/defaults/useradd, which specifies default values for the useradd command. Next is /etc/login.defs, which is used to specify the default user environment.

Setting Default Values Using /etc/default/useradd

As you have seen, a few options come with the useradd command. If an option isn't specified, useradd will read its configuration file in /etc/default/useradd, where it finds some default values such as what groups the user should become a member of and where to create the user's home directory. When using an option with useradd, you will always overwrite the default values. Listing 6-2 shows the contents of this file as it is used on a Fedora system.

Listing 6-2. Default Options for Creating Users in the Configuration File /etc/default/useradd

```
[root@fedora ~]# cat /etc/default/useradd
# useradd defaults file
GROUP=100
HOME=/home
INACTIVE=-1
EXPIRE=
SHELL=/bin/bash
SKEL=/etc/skel
CREATE_MAIL_SPOOL=yes
```

In this example /etc/default/useradd file, the following options are used:

- GROUP=100: Ensures that new users will get the group with group ID (GID) 100 as their default primary group.

- HOME=/home: Specifies that user home directories must be created in /home.

- INACTIVE=-1: Makes sure that the user account is set to inactive, until the moment that someone sets a password for the user.

- EXPIRE=: Makes sure that the user password expires after a given number of days.

- SHELL=/bin/bash: Specifies what to use as the default shell for new users.

- SKEL=/etc/skel: Specifies the name of the skeleton directory that has some default configuration files for new users. When creating a user who has a home directory with useradd -m, the contents of this skeleton directory are copied to the user's home directory.

- CREATE_MAIL_SPOOL=yes: Ensures that new users will have a directory in /var/mail where the mail process can store mail messages. If your users don't need to work with the internal Linux mail facility (for more about this, see the section "Sending Mail from the Command Line" in Chapter 2), you can give this variable the value no.

Creating a Default environment Using /etc/login.defs

The /etc/login.defs file defines some generic settings that determine all kinds of things relating to user login. Some of the settings in /etc/login.defs can be conflicting with settings in /etc/default/useradd. If this is the case, the /etc/login.defs settings take precedence. The login.defs file is a readable configuration file that contains variables. Each line in this file corresponds to one variable and its value. The variable relates to logging in or to the way in which certain commands are used.. The following list contains some of the more interesting variables that you can use in the login.defs file:

- DEFAULT_HOME: By default, a user will be allowed to log in, even if his or her home directory does not exist. If you don't want that, change this parameter's default value of 1 to the value 0.

- ENV_PATH: This variable contains the default search path that's applied for all users who do not have UID 0.

- ENV_ROOTPATH: This variable works in the same manner as ENV_PATH, but for root.

- FAIL_DELAY: After a login failure, it will take a few seconds before a new login prompt is generated. This variable, set to 3 by default, specifies how many seconds it takes.

- GID_MAX and GID_MIN: This lets you specify the minimum and maximum GID used by the groupadd command (see "Commands for Group Management" later in this chapter).

- LASTLOG_ENAB: If enabled by setting the Boolean value to 1, LASTLOG_ENAB specifies that all successful logins must be logged to the file /var/log/lastlog. This only works if the lastlog file also exists. (If it doesn't, create it by using touch /var/log/lastlog.)

- PASS_MIN_LEN: This is the minimum number of characters that must be used for new passwords.

- UID_MAX and UID_MIN: These are the minimum and maximum UIDs to be used when adding users with the useradd command.

- USERGROUPS_ENAB: This parameter, if set to yes, ensures that if a user is created, a group with the same name of the user is created as well. This group is set as the primary group of the user.

Managing Passwords

If your user really needs to do anything on your system, he or she needs a password. By default, login for a user you create is denied, and no password is supplied. Basically, your newly created user can't do anything on your computer because the password is disabled. As root you'll need to use **passwd <username>** to set a password for the user so that the user can log in. Once login has been enabled, users can use **passwd** themselves as well.

If the user uses the command to change his or her password, he or she will be prompted for the old password and then the new one. Only the user root can change passwords for other users. To do this, root can specify the name of the user he or she wants to change the password for as the argument of the passwd command. For example, root can use the command passwd linda to change the password for user linda, which is always useful in case of forgotten user passwords.

The passwd command can be used in three ways. First, you can use it for password maintenance (such as changing a password, as you have just seen). Second, it can also be used to set an expiration date for the password. Third, the passwd command can be used for account maintenance. For example, an administrator can use it to lock a user's account so that login is temporarily disabled. In the next section, you'll learn more about password management.

Performing Account Maintenance with passwd

In an environment in which many users use the same computer, it's crucial that you perform some basic account maintenance. These tasks include locking accounts when they are unneeded for a longer time, unlocking an account, and reporting password status. Also, an administrator can force a user to change his or her password after logging in for the first time. To perform these tasks, the passwd command has the following options:

- -l: Enables an administrator to lock an account. For example, passwd -l jeroen locks the account for user jeroen.

- -u: Unlocks a previously locked account. For instance, the account for user jeroen, which was locked in the previous example, would be unlocked with the command passwd -u jeroen.

- -S: Reports the status of the password for a given account:

  ```
  nuuk:/home/linda # passwd -S linda
  linda PS 12/10/2018 0 99999 7 -1
  ```

This status line contains the following information:

- Name of the user

- Date on which the password was set

- Days before a password may be changed

- Days after which the password must be changed

- Days before the password is to expire that the user is warned

- Days after which the password expires that the account is locked

- -e: Forces the user to change his or her password upon next login.

Managing Password Expiration

Although not many people are aware of the password expiration feature, it allows you to manage the maximum number of days that a user can use the same password. As an alternative to using the chage command which has been discussed earlier in this chapter, the passwd command has four options to manage expirations:

- -n min: This option is applied to set the minimum number of days that a user must use his or her password. If this option is not used, the user can change his or her password anytime.

- -x max: With this option, you can set the maximum number of days that the user can use his or her password without changing it.

- -c warn: Use this option to send a warning to the user when his or her password is about to expire. The argument of this option specifies how many days the user is warned before his or her password expires.

- -i *inact*: Use this option to make an account expire automatically if it hasn't been used for a given period. The argument of this option specifies the exact duration in days of this period.

■ **Caution**   By default, a password can be used for 99,999 days. So, if you do nothing, a user may use his or her password for 273 years without changing it. If you don't want that, make sure you use the -x option.

Behind the Commands: Configuration Files

In the previous section, you learned about the commands to manage users from a console environment. All of these commands put user-related information into the user database, which is stored in the configuration files /etc/passwd, /etc/shadow, and /etc/group. The aim of this section is to give you some insight into these configuration files.

/etc/passwd

The first and probably most important of all user-related configuration files is /etc/passwd, which is the primary database for user information: everything except the user password is stored in this file. Listing 6-3 gives you an impression of what the fields in this file look like.

Listing 6-3. Contents of the User Database File /etc/passwd

```
root@RNA:~# cat /etc/passwd
root:x:0:0:root:/root:/bin/bash
daemon:x:1:1:daemon:/usr/sbin:/bin/sh
bin:x:2:2:bin:/bin:/bin/sh
dhcp:x:100:101::/nonexistent:/bin/false
syslog:x:101:102::/home/syslog:/bin/false
klog:x:102:103::/home/klog:/bin/false
mysql:x:103:106:MySQL Server,,,:/var/lib/mysql:/bin/false
bind:x:104:109::/var/cache/bind:/bin/false
sander:x:1000:1000:sander,,,:/home/sander:/bin/bash
messagebus:x:105:112::/var/run/dbus:/bin/false
haldaemon:x:106:113:Hardware abstraction layer,,,:/home/haldaemon:/bin/false
gdm:x:107:115:Gnome Display Manager:/var/lib/gdm:/bin/false
sshd:x:108:65534::/var/run/sshd:/usr/sbin/nologin
linda:x:1001:1001::/home/linda:/bin/sh
zeina:x:1002:1002::/home/zeina:/bin/sh
```

You can see that /etc/passwd uses different fields to store user properties. These fields are separated with a colon. The following list gives the order of fields from left to right; see the section "Understanding Users and Their Properties" earlier in this chapter for more details:

- Username
- Password
- UID
- GID
- GECOS
- Home directory
- Shell

As an administrator, you can manually edit /etc/passwd and the related /etc/shadow. If you intend to do this, however, don't use any editor. Use vipw instead. This tailored version of the Vi editor is specifically designed for editing these critical files. Any error can have serious consequences, such as no one being able to log in. Therefore, if you make manual changes to any of these files, you should check their integrity. Besides vipw, another way to do this is to use the pwck command, which you can run without any options to see whether there are any problems you need to fix. Listing 6-4 shows you the results of pwck on a healthy user environment. As you can see, it notifies you about nonexisting directories, and if it finds a line that contains a serious error, it proposes to remove that line.

Listing 6-4. To Check the Integrity of the User Database, Use the pwck Command

```
[root@fedora ~]# pwck
user adm: directory /var/adm does not exist
user uucp: directory /var/spool/uucp does not exist
user gopher: directory /var/gopher does not exist
user ftp: directory /var/ftp does not exist
user avahi-autoipd: directory /var/lib/avahi-autoipd does not exist
user pulse: directory /var/run/pulse does not exist
invalid password file entry
delete line 'linda:x:501:::/home/linda:/bin/bash'? y
no matching password file entry in /etc/passwd
delete line 'linda:!!:14224:0:99999:7:::'? y
pwck: the files have been updated
```

/etc/shadow

Encrypted user passwords are stored in the /etc/shadow file. The file also stores information about password expiration. Listing 6-5 shows an example of its contents.

Listing 6-5. Example Contents of the /etc/shadow File

```
root:$1$15CyWuRM$g72U2o58j67LUW1oPtDS7/:13669:0:99999:7:::
daemon:*:13669:0:99999:7:::
bin:*:13669:0:99999:7:::
sys:*:13669:0:99999:7:::
dhcp:!:13669:0:99999:7:::
syslog:!:13669:0:99999:7:::
klog:!:13669:0:99999:7:::
```

```
mysql:!:13669:0:99999:7:::
bind:!:13669:0:99999:7:::
sander:$1$QqnOp2NN$L7W9uL3mweqBa2ggrBhTBO:13669:0:99999:7:::
messagebus:!:13669:0:99999:7:::
haldaemon:!:13669:0:99999:7:::
gdm:!:13669:0:99999:7:::
sshd:!:13669:0:99999:7:::
linda:!:13671:0:99999:7:::
zeina:!:13722:0:99999:7:::
```

Just as in /etc/passwd, the lines in /etc/shadow are divided into several fields as well. The first two fields matter especially for the typical administrator. The first field stores the name of the user, and the second field stores the encrypted password. Note that in the encrypted password field, the ! and * characters can be used as well. The ! denotes the login is currently disabled, and the * denotes a system account that can be used to start services but that is not allowed for interactive shell login (so basically it has the same effect as the !). Following is a short list of all the fields in /etc/shadow. Use the passwd command to change these fields:

- Login name.

- Encrypted password.

- Days between January 1, 1970, and the date when the password was last changed.

- Minimum: Days before password may be changed. (This is the minimum amount of time that a user must use the same password.)

- Maximum: Days after which password must be changed. (This is the maximum amount of time that a user may use the same password.)

- Warn: Days before password expiration that user is warned.

- Inactive: Days after password expiration that account is disabled. (If this happens, administrator intervention is required to unlock the password.)

- Expire: Days between January 1, 1970, and the date when the account was disabled.

- Reserved field (this field is currently not used).

EXERCISE 6-2: MANAGING USER PROPERTIES

This exercise continues where Exercise 6-1 has stopped and allows you to set some parameters for user lara.

1. Open a root shell, and type **passwd -l lara**. This will lock access to the account of user lara.

2. Use Ctrl+Alt+F2 to open a virtual console and try logging in as user lara. You'll get access denied.

3. As root, type **grep lara /etc/shadow** and notice the exclamation mark at the start of the password field. If the password file in /etc/shadow starts with an exclamation mark, login is denied.

4. Type **passwd -u lara** to unlock the account of user lara and try logging in again. You should now be able to do so.

Group Membership

In any Linux environment, a user can be a member of two different kinds of groups. First, there's the primary group, which every user has. (If a user doesn't have a primary group, he or she won't be able to log in.) The primary group is the group that is specified in the fourth field of /etc/passwd.

There are two approaches to handling primary groups. On Ubuntu and Red Hat, all users get their own private groups as their primary groups, and this private group has the same name as the user. On SUSE, a group with the name users is created, and all users are added as members to that group.

A user can be a member of more than just the primary group and will automatically inherit the permissions granted to these other groups (more about permissions in Chapter 7). The most important difference between a primary group and other groups is that the primary group will automatically become group owner of any new file that a user creates - you'll read more about this in chapter 7. If a user has his or her own private group, this won't be a great challenge for your computer's security settings (as the user is the only member). If, however, a scheme is used where all users are member of the same group, this means that everyone has access to all files this user creates by default.

Creating Groups

As you've already learned, all users require group membership. You've read about the differences between the primary group and the other groups, so let's have a look at how to create these groups. We'll discuss the commands that you can run from the shell and the related configuration files.

Commands for Group Management

Basically, you manage the groups in your environment with three commands: groupadd, groupdel, and groupmod. So, as you can see, group management follows the same patterns as user management. And, there's some overlap between the two as well. For example, usermod as well as groupmod can be used to make a user a member of some group. The basic structure for the groupadd command is simple: groupadd *somegroup*, where *somegroup* of course is the name of the group you want to create. Also, the options are largely self-explanatory: it probably doesn't surprise you that the option -g gid can be used to specify the unique GID number you want to use for this group. Because groups don't have many properties, there are no other important options.

Behind the Commands: /etc/group

When a group is created with groupadd, the information entered needs to be stored somewhere, and that's the /etc/group file. As shown in Listing 6-6, this is a rather simple file that has just a few fields for each group definition.

Listing 6-6. Content of /etc/group

```
plugdev:x:46:sander,haldaemon
staff:x:50:
games:x:60:
users:x:100:
nogroup:x:65534:
dhcp:x:101:
syslog:x:102:
klog:x:103:
scanner:x:104:sander
```

```
nvram:x:105:
mysql:x:106:
crontab:x:107:
ssh:x:108:
bind:x:109:
sander:x:1000:
lpadmin:x:110:sander
admin:x:111:sander
messagebus:x:112:
haldaemon:x:113:
powerdev:x:114:haldaemon
gdm:x:115:
linda:x:1001:
zeina:x:1002:
```

The first field in /etc/group is reserved for the name of the group. The second field stores the password for the group (an ! signifies that no password is allowed for this group). You can see that most groups have an x in the password field, and this refers to the /etc/gshadow file where you can store encrypted group passwords. However, this feature isn't used often because it is very uncommon to work with group passwords. You'll notice that many Linux distributions don't even have an /etc/gshadow file anymore.

The third field of /etc/group provides a unique group ID, and, finally, the last field lists the names of the members of the group. These names are only required for users for whom this is not the primary group; primary group membership itself is managed from the /etc/passwd configuration file. However, if you want to make sure that a user is added to an additional group, you have to do it here or use usermod -G.

The Use of Group Passwords

As mentioned, group passwords are used so rarely, you probably won't ever need them. But what can they be used for anyway? In all cases, a user has a primary group. When the user creates a file, this group is assigned as the group owner for that file automatically. This means that all members of the same group can normally access the file. If a user wants to create files that have a group owner different from their primary group, the user can use the newgrp command. This opens a subshell, in which the user has another primary group that is set on a temporary basis.

For example, newgrp sales would set the primary group of a user to the group sales. Using this command would work without any question if the user is a member of the group sales. However, if the user is not a member of that group, the shell will prompt the user to enter a password. This password is the password that needs to be assigned to that group. To set a group password, you need the passwd -g command. Because this feature is hardly ever used, you'll find that this feature is not available on all Linux distributions.

To make users a member of other than their primary group, you can use different commands. A very common command, is **usermod**. You should however notice that this command shows different behavior on the different Linux distributions, so by all means, read the man page or help before using it. On Red Hat, you'll use **usermod -aG groupname username** to add a user to additional secondary groups. Make sure you'll use the **-a** option as without this option you'll overwrite all current secondary group assignments.

A more universal way to add users to secondary groups, is by using the **vigr** or **vi /etc/group** command. These commands open an editor directly on the /etc/group file, which allows you to add the user name in the last field of the line where the group is defined. If you want to use this approach, make sure to use **vigr** and not **vi /etc/group**, because the **vigr** command makes sure that you won't have any locking issues that can occur when the file is accessed by multiple users simultaneously. In exercise 6-3 you'll work with some of these commands.

EXERCISE 6-3: MANAGING GROUPS

1. Open a root shell.

2. Type **for i in daphne marcha isabella; do useradd $i; done**. This executes a small shell scripting structure to add three users while using only one command.

3. Type **groupadd sales** and **groupadd account** to add the groups sales and account.

4. Type **id daphne**. You'll see that currently this user only is a member of the primary group.

5. Type **grep sales /etc/group**. You'll notice that no users are listed in the fourth field of this file, so currently, the group sales has no members.

6. Type **usermod -aG sales daphne**. This adds user daphne to the group sales.

7. Type **id daphne**. You'll now see that she is a member of the sales group.

8. Type **usermod -G account daphne** and use **id daphne** again to verify current group membership. You'll notice that daphne is indeed a member of the group account, but no longer a member of the group sales.

9. Use **usermod -aG sales isabella** and **usermod -aG sales,account marcha** to add the other users to a secondary group as well.

10. Verify that you have succeeded, using **id marcha; id daphne; id sales** as root. Notice the use of the semicolon, which allows you to rune several commands on one line.

Managing the User's Shell Environment

To make sure that a user account can do its work properly, the user needs a decent shell environment as well. When creating a user, a shell environment is created as well, and this environment will do in most situations. Sometimes, however, a user has specific needs, and you need to create a specific environment for him or her. Without going into detail about specific shell commands, this section provides an overview of how you create a shell environment. I'll first explain about the files that can be used as login scripts for the user, and next you'll learn about files that are used to display messages for users logging in to your system.

■ **Note**   The tasks described next are typically ones that you would perform on a file server that is accessed by users directly. However, if a user never logs in to the computer, there is no need to perform these tasks.

Creating Shell Login Scripts

When a user logs in to a system, the /etc/profile configuration file is used. This generic shell script (which can be considered a login script) defines environment settings for all users upon login. Think of settings like variables, that define the working environment for users. Also, commands can be included that need to be issued when the user first logs in to a computer. The /etc/profile file is a generic file processed by all users logging in to the system. It also has a user-specific version (.profile) that can be created in the home directory of the user. The user-specific .profile of the shell login script is executed last, so if there is a conflict in settings between the two files, the settings that are user specific will always be used. In general, it isn't a good idea to give a login file to too many individual users; instead, work it all out in /etc/profile. This makes configuring settings for your users as easy as possible.

■ **Note** If you are working on SUSE Linux, you shouldn't modify the /etc/profile file. When updating the computer, the update process may overwrite your current /etc/profile. Instead, make your modifications to /etc/profile.local, which is included when logging in.

Now /etc/profile and the user-specific .profile are not the only files that can be processed when starting a shell. If a user starts a subshell from a current environment, such as by executing a command or by using the command /bin/sh again, the administrator may choose to define additional settings for that. The name of this configuration file is /etc/bashrc, and it also has a user-specific version, ~/.bashrc. On some distributions the most important part of the default shell settings is in profile and .profile; other distributions use bashrc and .bashrc to store these settings.

Note: It can be confusing to understand if you need to use /etc/profile or /etc/bashrc to include settings for execution upon login. On many distributions, the /etc/profile command includes the line **source /etc/bashrc**. This allows administrators to put all relevant commands in the /etc/bashrc file, and have that executed upon start of a subshell, as well as upon login.

After making changes to these configuration files, you can source them to activate the new settings. To do this, you can use the source command or its equivalent, the . (dot) command. The advantage of this technique is that you don't have to log out and in again to activate the changes. The following two example lines show how to do this:

```
source ~/.bashrc
. ~/.bashrc
```

Showing Messages to Users Logging In

It may be useful to display messages to users logging in to your computer. However, this only works if a user logs in to a nongraphical desktop. On a graphical desktop, the user is not able to see messages that are in these files. You can use two files for this: /etc/issue and /etc/motd. The first, /etc/issue, is a text file whose content is displayed to users before they log in. You may, for example, use the file to display a message instructing users how to log in to your system, or include a message if login has been disabled on a temporary basis.

Another way to show messages to users logging in is by using /etc/motd. This file shows messages to users after they complete the login procedure. Typically, this file can be used to display messages related to day-to-day system maintenance.

Applying Quota to Allow a Maximum Amount of Files

As a part of maintaining the user environment, you should know about user quota. This can be used to limit the amount of disk space available to a user. Configuring user quota is a five-step procedure:

1. Install the quota software.

2. Prepare the file system where you want to use quota.

3. Initialize the quota system.

4. Apply quota to users and groups.

5. Start the quota service.

Quotas are always user or group related and apply to a complete volume or partition. That is, if you have one disk in your computer, with one partition on it that holds your complete root file system, and you apply a quota of 100MB for user zeina, this user can create no more than 100MB of files, no matter where on the file system. The Linux quota system does not allow you to limit the maximal amount of data that a directory can contain. If you want to accomplish that, put the directory on a separate partition or volume and limit the size of the volume.

The quota system works with a *hard limit*, a *soft limit*, and a *grace period*:

- The soft limit is a limit that cannot be surpassed on a permanent basis, but the user can create more data than the quota allows on a temporary basis. That means that the soft limit is a limit that you shouldn't surpass, but if you do, the quota system tolerates it on a temporary basis.

- The grace period relates to the soft limit. It is the length of time that the user can temporarily exceed the soft limit.

- The hard limit is an absolute limit, and after it's reached (or when the grace period elapses, whichever is sooner), the user will not be permitted to create new files. So users can never create more files than specified in the hard limit.

Working with soft and hard limits is confusing at first glance, but it has some advantages: if a user has more data than the soft limit allows, he or she still can create new files and isn't stopped in his or her work immediately. The user will, however, get a warning to create some space before the hard limit is reached.

Installing the Quota Software

Most distributions don't install the quota software by default. It's easy to find out whether the quota software is installed on your system: if you try to use one of the quota management utilities (such as edquota) when the quota software has yet not been installed, you'll see a message that it has to be installed first. Use the software management solution for your distribution to install the quota software, which typically is in the quota package in that case. In Chapter 8, you can read more about software installation.

Preparing the File System for Quota

Before you can use the quota software to limit the amount of disk space that a user can use on a given file system, you must add an option to /etc/fstab for all file systems that must support quota.

■ **Tip** If it's not possible to restart your server at this moment so that the file system can be mounted with the newly added options, you can use mount -o remount,usrquota,grpquota instead. For example, if you need to apply the quota options to your root file system and can't reboot now, just use mount -o remount, usrquota,grpquota /. At the same time, change your fstab as well to make sure that the new settings will also be applied when your server reboots.

Here's the procedure to modify fstab:

1. Open /etc/fstab with an editor.

2. Select the column with options. Add the option usrquota if you want to apply quota to users and grpquota for groups. Repeat this procedure for all file systems where you want to use quota.

3. Remount all partitions in which quota has been applied (or restart your computer).

Initializing Quota

Now that you've finished the preliminary steps, you need to initialize the quota system. This is necessary because all file systems have to be searched for files that have already been created, and for a reason that's probably obvious: existing files count toward each user's quota, and so a report must be created in which the quota system can see which user owns which files. The report generated by this quota initialization is saved in two files that should be in the root of the mount point where you want to apply the quota: aquota.user is created to register user quotas, and aquota.group is created for group quotas.

To initialize a file system for the use of quotas (which will also create the quota files for you), you need to use the quotacheck command. This command can be used with some options, and I'll list only the most important ones here:

- -a: This option ensures that all file systems are searched when initializing the quota system.

- -u: This option ensures that user information is searched. This information will be written to the aquota.user file.

- -g: This option ensures that group information is searched as well. This information is written to the aquota.group file.

- -m: Use this option to make sure that no problems will occur on file systems that are currently mounted.

- -v: This option ensures that the command will work in verbose mode to show exactly what it is doing.

So, the best way to initialize the quota system is to use the quotacheck -augmv command, which (after a while) creates the files aquota.user and aquota.group to list all quota information for current users. This can take a few minutes on a large file system, as the quota system has to calculate current file usage on the file system where you want to create the quota. So if you want to apply quota to /home where /home is on the dedicated partition /dev/sda3, which uses Ext3, make sure to do the following:

1. Include the following line in /etc/fstab:

   ```
   /dev/sda3    /home    ext3    usrquota,grpquota    0 0
   ```

2. Activate the new setting using the following command:

   ```
   mount -o remount,rw,usrquota,grpquota /home
   ```

3. Run the quotacheck -a command to generate the quota files automatically.

4. Make sure that the quota files are in /home/aquota.user and /home/aquota.group.

Setting Quota for Users and Groups

Now that the quota databases have been created, it's time for the real work because you're ready to apply quota to all users and groups on your system. You'll do this with the edquota command, which uses the vi editor to create a temporary file. This temporary file is where you'll enter the soft and hard limits you've decided upon for your users and groups. If, for example, you want to apply a soft limit of 100,000 blocks and a hard limit of 110,000 blocks for user florence, follow these steps:

1. The edquota command works only with blocks and not bytes, kilobytes, or anything else. So, to set quota properly, you need to know the block size that's currently used. To find that, use the dumpe2fs | less command. You'll find the block size in the second screen.

2. Issue the command edquota -u florence. This opens the user's quota file in the quota editor as you can see in Listing 6-7.

Listing 6-7. Example User Quota File

```
Disk quotas for user florence (uid 1014):
  Filesystem                 blocks   soft   hard   inodes   soft   hard
  /dev/mapper/system-root  116      0      0      25       0      0
~
~
~
~
~
~
~
~
~
~
~
~
~
"/tmp//EdP.af6tIky" 3L, 220C                                  1,1      All
```

3. In the editor screen, represented by Listing 6-7, six numbers specify the quota for all file systems on your computer. The first of these numbers is the number of blocks that are currently being used by the user you're creating the quota file for. The second and third numbers are important as well: the second number is the soft limit for the number of blocks, and the third number is the hard limit on blocks in kilobytes. The fifth and sixth numbers do the same for inodes, which roughly equal the number of files you can create on your file system. The first and fourth numbers are used to record the number of blocks and inodes that are currently being used for this user.

4. Close the editor and write the changes in the quota files to disk.

In this procedure, you learned that quota can be applied to the number of inodes and blocks. If quotas are used on inodes, they specify the maximum number of files that can be created. Most administrators think it doesn't make sense to work this way, so they set the values for these to 0. A value of 0 indicates that this item currently has no limitation.

After setting the quota, if the soft limit and hard limit are not set to the same value, you need to use the edquota -t command to set the grace time. This command opens another temporary file in which you can specify the grace time you want to use, either in hours or in days. The grace time is set per file system, so there's no option to specify different grace time settings for different users.

Once you have set quotas for one user, you may want to apply them to other users. Instead of following the same procedure for all users on your system, you can use the edquota -p command. For example, edquota -p florence alex copies the quotas currently applied for user florence to user alex.

■ **Caution** To set quotas, the user you are setting quotas for must be known to the quota system. This is not done automatically. To make sure that new users are known to the quota system, you must initialize the quota system again after creating the new users. I recommend setting up a cron job (see Chapter 9) to do this automatically.

When all the quotas have been set the way you want, you can use the repquota command to monitor the current quota settings for your users. For example, the repquota -aug command shows current quota settings for all users and groups on all volumes. You can see an example of this in Listing 6-8. Now that you've set all the quotas you want to work with, you just have to start the quota service, and you'll do this with the /etc/init.d/quota start command.

Listing 6-8. Use repquota -aug to Show a List of Current Quota Usage

```
nuuk:~ # repquota -aug
*** Report for user quotas on device /dev/mapper/system-root
Block grace time: 7days; Inode grace time: 7days
                        Block limits            File limits
User            used    soft    hard  grace   used  soft  hard  grace
--------------------------------------------------------------------
root        --  2856680    0      0           134133    0     0
uucp        --        8    0      0                2    0     0
wwwrun      --        4    0      0                1    0     0
sander      --      108    0      0               25    0     0
linda       --      140    0      0               29    0     0
sanne       --      120    0      0               25    0     0
stephanie   --      116    0      0               25    0     0
alex        --      120    0      0               25    0     0
caroline    --      116    0      0               25    0     0
lori        --      116    0      0               25    0     0
laura       --      116    0      0               25    0     0
lucy        --      116    0      0               25    0     0
lisa        --      116    0      0               25    0     0
lea         --      116    0      0               25    0     0
leona       --      116    0      0               25    0     0
lilly       --      116    0      0               25    0     0
florence    --      116 110000 100000           25    0     0
```

Techniques Behind Authentication

When a user authenticates, a lot of settings have to be applied. For instance, the system needs to know where to get the login information from and what restrictions apply to the user. To do this, your system uses a pluggable authentication module, or PAM. PAM modules make authentication modular; by using PAM modules, you can enable functionality for specific situations. Also, your system needs to know where it has to read information about users. For this purpose, it uses the /etc/nsswitch.conf file. In this file, it reads—among other things—what files to consult to get user information. On the following pages, you can read how to configure both of these systems for viable user authentication.

Understanding Pluggable Authentication Modules

Normally, the local user database in the Linux files /etc/passwd and /etc/shadow is checked at login to a Linux workstation. In a network environment, however, the login program must fetch the required information from somewhere else (for example, an LDAP directory service such as OpenLDAP). But how does the login program know where it has to search for authentication information? That's where PAM modules come in.

PAM modules are what make the login procedure on your workstation flexible. With a PAM, you can redirect any application that has anything to do with authentication to any service that handles authentication. A PAM is used, for example, if you want to authenticate with a private key stored on a USB stick, to enable password requirements, to prevent the root user from establishing a telnet session, and in many other situations. The cool thing about a PAM is that it defines not only how to handle the login procedure, but also authentication for all services that have something to do with authentication. The only requirement is a PAM that supports your authentication method.

The main advantage of a PAM is its modularity. In a PAM infrastructure, anything can be used for authentication, provided there's a PAM module for it. So, if you want to implement some kind of strong authentication, ask your supplier for a PAM module, and it will work. PAM modules are stored in the directory /lib/security, and the configuration files specifying how these modules must be used (and by which procedures) are in /etc/pam.d. Listing 6-9 is an example of just such a configuration file, in which the login procedure learns that it first has to contact an LDAP server before trying any local login.

Listing 6-9. Sample PAM Configuration File

```
auth        sufficient     /lib/security/pam_ldap.so
account     sufficient     /lib/security/pam_ldap.so
password    sufficient     /lib/security/pam_ldap.so
session     optional       /lib/security/pam_ldap.so
auth        requisite      pam_unix2.so
auth        required       pam_securetty.so
auth        required       pam_nologin.so
#auth       required       pam_homecheck.so
auth        required       pam_env.so
auth        required       pam_mail.so
account     required       pam_unix2.so
password    required       pam_pwcheck.so      nullok
password    required       pam_unix2.so        nullok use_first_pass use_authok
session     required       pam_unix2.so
session     required       pam_limits.so
```

The authentication process features four different instances, and these are reflected in Listing 6-9. Authentication is handled in the first instance; these are the lines that start with the keyword auth. During the authentication phase, the user login name and password are first checked, followed by the validity of the account and other account-related parameters (such as login time restrictions). This happens in the lines that start with account. Then, all settings relating to the password are verified (the lines that start with password). Last, the settings relating to the establishment of a session with resources are defined, and this happens in the lines that start with session.

The procedure that will be followed upon completion of these four instances is defined by calling the different PAM modules. This occurs in the last column of the example configuration file in Listing 6-9. For example, the module pam_securetty can be used to verify that the user root is not logging in to a Linux computer via an insecure terminal. Think of a remote connection where user root tries to log in with telnet, which by default uses unencrypted passwords.

The keywords sufficient, optional, required, and requisite are used to qualify the degree of importance that the conditions in a certain module are met. Except for the first four lines (which refer to the connection a PAM has to make to a server that provides LDAP authentication services and work with the option sufficient), conditions defined in all modules must be met; they are all required. Without going into detail, this means that authentication will fail if one of the conditions implied by the specified module is not met.

By default, many services on Linux work with PAM, and you can see this from a simple ls command in the directory /etc/pam.d, which will show you that there is a PAM file for login, su, sudo, and many other programs.

The true flexibility of PAM is in its modules, which you can find in /lib/security. Each of these modules has a specific function. The next section provides a short description of some of the more interesting modules.

Discovering PAM Modules

The usefulness of a system like PAM is entirely determined by its modules. Some of these modules are still experimental, and others are pretty mature and can be used to configure a Linux system. I'll discuss some of the most important modules.

pam_deny

The pam_deny module can be used to deny all access. It's very useful if used as a default policy to deny access to the system. If you ever think there is a security hole in one of the PAM enabled services, use this module to deny all access.

pam_env

The module pam_env is used to create a default environment for users when logging in. In this default environment, several system variables are set to determine what the environment a user is working in looks like. For example, there is a definition of a PATH variable in which some directories are included that must be in the search path of the user. To create these variables, pam_env uses a configuration file in /etc/security/pam_env.conf. In this file, several variables are defined, each with its own value to define essential items like the PATH environment variable.

pam_limits

Some situations require an environment in which limits are set to the system resources that a user can access. Think, for example, of an environment in which a user can use no more than a given number of files at the same time. To configure these limitations, you would modify the /etc/security/limits.conf file. To make sure that the limitations you set in /etc/security/ limits.conf are applied, use the pam_limits module.

In /etc/security/limits.conf, limits can be set for individual users as well as groups. The limits can be applied to different items, some of which are listed here:

- fsize: Maximum file size
- nofile: Maximum number of open files
- cpu: Maximum CPU time in minutes
- nproc: Maximum number of processes
- maxlogins: Maximum number of times this user can log in simultaneously

The following code presents two examples of how these limitations can be applied. In the first line, the user ftp is limited to start a maximum of one process simultaneously. Next, everyone who is a member of the group student is allowed to log in four times simultaneously.

```
ftp             hard      nproc          1
@student        -         maxlogins      4
```

When applying these limitations, you should remind yourself of the difference between hard and soft limits: a hard limit is absolute, and a user cannot exceed it. A soft limit can be exceeded, but only within the settings that the administrator has applied for these soft limits. If you want to set the hard limit to the same as the soft limit, use a character as shown in the previous code example for the group student.

pam_mail

The useful pam_mail module looks at the user's mail directory and indicates whether there is any new mail. It is typically applied when a user logs in to the system with the following line in the relevant PAM configuration file:

```
Login     session    optional    pam_mail.conf
```

pam_mkhomedir

If a user authenticates to a machine for the first time and doesn't have a home directory yet, pam_mkhomedir can be applied to create this home directory automatically. This module will also make sure that the files in /etc/skel are copied to the new home directory. This module is especially useful in a network environment in which users authenticate through an authentication server and do not always work on the same machine.

pam_nologin

If an administrator needs to conduct system maintenance like installing new hardware, and the computer must be brought down for a few moments, the pam_nologin module may prove useful. This module makes sure that no users can log in when the file /etc/nologin exists. So, before performing any maintenance, make sure to create this file. The user root will always be allowed to log in to the system, regardless of whether this file exists or not.

pam_permit

pam_permit is by far the most insecure PAM service available. It does only one thing, and that's to grant access—*always*—no matter who tries to log in. All security mechanisms will be completely bypassed in this case, and even users who don't have a valid user account can use the services that are configured to use pam_permit. The only sensible use of pam_permit is to test the PAM awareness of a certain module or to disable account management completely and create a system that is wide open to everyone.

pam_rootok

The pam_rootok module lets user root access services without entering a password. It's used, for example, by the su utility to make sure the user root can su to any account, without having to enter a password for that user account.

pam_securetty

In the old days when telnet connections were still very common, it was important for the user root never to use a telnet session for login because telnet sends passwords in clear text over the network. For this purpose, the securetty mechanism was created: the file /etc/securetty can be created to provide a list of all TTYs from which root can log in. By default, these only include local TTYs 1 through 6. On modern distributions, this module is still used by default, which means that you can limit the TTYs where root can log in by manipulating this file. Listing 6-10 shows the default contents of this file on a computer running Fedora Linux.

Listing 6-10. The /etc/securetty File Is Used to Limit the Terminals Where Root Can Authenticate

```
nuuk:~ # cat /etc/securetty
#
# This file contains the device names of tty lines (one per line,
# without leading /dev/) on which root is allowed to login.
#
tty1
tty2
tty3
tty4
tty5
tty6
# for devfs:
vc/1
vc/2
vc/3
vc/4
vc/5
vc/6
```

pam_tally

The useful pam_tally module can be used to keep track of attempts to access the system. It also allows the administrator to deny access if too many attempts fail. pam_tally works with an application that uses the same name, pam_tally, which can be used to set the maximum number of failed logins that are allowed. All attempts are logged by default in the /var/log/faillog file. If this module is called from a configuration file, be sure to at least use the options deny=n and lock_time. The first determines the maximum number of login attempts a user can make, and the second determines how long an account will be locked after that number of login attempts has been reached. The value given to lock_time is expressed in seconds by default.

pam_time

Based upon the configuration file /etc/security/time.conf, the pam_time module is used to limit the times between which users can log in to the system. You can use this module to limit access for certain users to specific times of the day. Also, access can be further limited to services and specific TTYs that the user logs in from. The configuration file time.conf uses lines with the following form:

services;ttys;users;times

The next line is an example of a configuration line from time.conf that denies access to all users except root (the ! character in front of the times is used to deny access). This might be a perfect solution to prevent users from breaking into a system that they shouldn't be trying to log in to anyway.
login ; tty* ; !root ; !Al0000-2400

pam_unix

pam_unix is probably the most important of all modules: it is used to redirect authentication requests through the /etc/passwd and /etc/shadow files. The module can be used with several arguments, such as nullok and try_first_pass. The nullok argument allows a user with an empty password to connect to a service, and the try_first_pass argument will always try the password a user has already used (if a password is asked for again). Notice that many PAM configuration files include a line to call the common configuration file common-auth. The pam_unix file is called from here.

pam_warn

The pam_warn module is particularly useful with log errors: its primary purpose is to enable logging information about proposed authentication or password modification. For example, it can be used in conjunction with the pam_deny module to log information about users trying to connect to your system.

The role of /etc/nsswitch.conf

Whereas PAM is used to determine what exactly is allowed and what is not during the authentication process, /etc/nsswitch.conf is used to tell different Linux services where they should look for specific services. These services include authentication services, but other services as well, such as host-resolving services that tell your computer if it has to use DNS or something else, like the /etc/hosts file. The nsswitch mechanism is used not only while authenticating, but also at other moments. The only requirement is that the service in question has to be programmed to use nsswitch. You don't have to worry about that though; this is the responsibility of the person who wrote the program.

Listing 6-11 shows the default contents of the nsswitch.conf file on SUSE Linux.

Listing 6-11. nsswitch.conf Lines Related to Authentication

```
nuuk:~ # cat /etc/nsswitch.conf
#
# /etc/nsswitch.conf
#
# An example Name Service Switch config file. This file should be
# sorted with the most-used services at the beginning.
#
# The entry '[NOTFOUND=return]' means that the search for an
# entry should stop if the search in the previous entry turned
# up nothing. Note that if the search failed due to some other reason
# (like no NIS server responding), then the search continues with the
# next entry.
#
# Legal entries are:
#
#       compat              Use compatibility setup
#       nisplus             Use NIS+ (NIS version 3)
#       nis                 Use NIS (NIS version 2), also called YP
#       dns                 Use DNS (Domain Name Service)
#       files               Use the local files
#       [NOTFOUND=return] Stop searching if not found so far
#
# For more information, please read the nsswitch.conf.5 manual page.
#

# passwd: files nis
# shadow: files nis
# group: files nis

passwd: compat
group:  compat

hosts:          files dns
networks:       files dns

services:       files
protocols:      files
rpc:            files
ethers:         files
netmasks:       files
netgroup:       files nis
publickey:      files

bootparams:     files
automount:      files nis
aliases:        files
```

As you can see, for different subsystems, the nsswitch.conf file tells where to look for configuration. The following specifications are available:

- `files`: Uses the normal default configuration files (`/etc/passwd` and `/etc/shadow`), which are stored locally. Red Hat uses this as the default to handle authentication.

- `compat`: Serves as an alternative way to tell the authentication processes only that they should look in the `/etc/passwd` and `/etc/shadow` configuration files. Using this option makes it easier to hook up your system to an LDAP-based authentication service.

- `nis, nisplus`: Refer to the legacy UNIX NIS authentication services.

- `ldap`: Uses an LDAP Directory Server for authentication.

- `dns`: Specifies that host and network-specific information must be looked up in DNS.

EXERCISE 6-4: WORKING WITH PAM

1. Open a root shell. Type **cat /etc/securetty** and check the contents of this file. You should see the TTY devices tty1 up to tty12 at least. The fact that these are included in the file ensures that user root can log in from all of these virtual terminals.

2. Use the Ctrl+Alt+F3 key sequence to open the virtual console tt3. Enter the username root and the root password. You'll notice that you can log in as root.

3. Open the file /etc/securetty and remove the line that reads tty4.

4. Use Ctrl+Alt+F4 and try to log in from the virtual console that opens, using user name root and the associated password. This should not work.

5. Still from the virtual console tty4, log in using username lara and password "password". This should be possible.

6. Use **su -** to open a root shell. This also is allowed.

7. Open the file /etc/pam.d/su and make sure it includes the following line:

   login required pam_secure.tty.

8. Close the configuration file and write changes to disk. Type **exit** until you see the tty4 login prompt again.

9. Repeat steps 5 and 6 from this exercise and notice that you're no long able to log in as user root from virtual console tty4.

Configuring Administrator Tasks with `sudo`

If you want to perform administration tasks, you could just log in as the user root. However, this has some security risks, the most important of which is that you might make a mistake and thus by accident remove everything from your computer. Therefore, on some Linux distributions such as Ubuntu, the root account is disabled by default. It doesn't even have a password, so you cannot log in as root after a default installation. To perform tasks for which root privileges are required, use the `sudo` mechanism instead.

Even if the account for user root is not disabled by default, it may still be a good idea to use `sudo`. This is especially true for environments where specific users or groups of users need root permissions to accomplish a limited set of tasks. Imagine the developer who needs root permissions to compile new programs, the network administrator who just needs to be able to modify network parameters, or the help desk employee who needs to be able to reset a password for a user.

The idea of sudo is that specific administrator tasks can be defined for specific users. If one such user wants to execute one of the sudo commands that he or she has been granted access to, that user has to run it with sudo. For example, where normally the user root would enter useradd -m caroline to add the user caroline if the user would work with root permissions, a user with sudo privileges would enter sudo useradd -m caroline, thus telling sudo that he or she needs to run a sudo task. Next, the user enters his or her password, and the user is created. In Listing 6-12, you can see what happens when user alex tries to create another user in this way.

Listing 6-12. Adding a User with sudo

```
alex@nuuk:~> sudo /usr/sbin/useradd -m caroline

We trust you have received the usual lecture from the local System
Administrator. It usually boils down to these three things:

    #1) Respect the privacy of others.
    #2) Think before you type.
    #3) With great power comes great responsibility.
alex's password:
alex@nuuk:~>
```

As you can see, the user first uses the sudo command, followed by the complete path to the command he or she needs to use. That is because the user needs to run a command from the /usr/sbin directory, and this directory is not in the default user search path. Next, the user sees a message that indicates he or she should be careful and following that, the user needs to enter his or her password. This password is cached for the duration of the session, which means that if a short while later the user wants to use sudo again, he or she doesn't have to enter his or her password again.

To create a sudo configuration, you need to use the editor visudo. This editor is used to open a temporary file which is later written to the file /etc/sudoers. In this file, you can define all sudo tasks that must be available on your computer. You should never open the /etc/sudoers file for editing directly because that involves the risk of completely locking yourself out if you make an error.

■ **Tip** On Ubuntu, visudo uses the text editor ano by default. If you are a Linux veteran who is used to Vi, you'll probably won't like this. Want to use Vi instead of nano? Then use the command export VISUAL=vi. Like what you see? Put it as the last line in /etc/profile or your own .profile, and from now on, every time you use either visudo or edquota, Vi is started instead of nano. In this book, I'm using the Vi alternative because it automatically saves all files in the locations where they have to be saved.

In Listing 6-13, you can see what the default configuration in /etc/sudoers looks like.

Listing 6-13. Default Configuration in /etc/sudoers

```
root@RNA:/etc# cat sudoers
# /etc/sudoers
#
# This file MUST be edited with the 'visudo' command as root.
#
# See the man page for details on how to write a sudoers file.
# Host alias specification
# User alias specification
```

```
# Cmnd alias specification

# Defaults

Defaults        !lecture,tty_tickets,!fqdn

# User privilege specification
root      ALL=(ALL) ALL
# Members of the admin group may gain root privileges
%admin ALL=(ALL) ALL
```

It's really just two lines of configuration. The first line is root ALL=(ALL) ALL, which specifies that user root has the right to run all commands from all machines. Next, you can see that the same is true for all users who belong to the user group admin. If, for example, you would like to specify that user linda is allowed to run the command /sbin/shutdown, no matter what host she is connecting from, add the following line:

```
Linda     ALL=/sbin/shutdown
```

This line consists of three parts. In the first part, the username is entered. Instead of the name of a specific user, you can refer to groups as well, but if you do that, make sure to put a % sign before the group name. The second part—ALL in this example—refers to the name of the host where the user is logged on. Here, that host name has no limitations, but you can specify the name of a specific machine to minimize the risk of abuse by outsiders. Next, the command that this user is allowed to use (/sbin/shutdown, no options) is specified. This means that the user is allowed to run all options that can be used with this command. If you want to allow the user just one option, you need to include that option in the command line. If that's the case, all options that do not match the pattern you have specified in sudoers are specifically denied.

Now that the sudo configuration is in place, the specified user can run his or her commands. To do this, the complete command should be referred to because the directories that typically house the root commands (/sbin, /usr/sbin) are not in the search path for normal users. So, user linda should use the following command to shut down the machine:

```
sudo /sbin/shutdown -h now
```

On many Linux servers, privileges are granted to a group of administrators to execute administration tasks using the **sudo** command. The most convenient way to configure this, is by making all administrator users a member of the group wheel, using **usermod -aG wheel <username>**. After making your administrator users a member of the group wheel, type **visudo** adn make sure that the following line is included:

```
%wheel    ALL=(ALL)    ALL
```

If this line is included, all users that are member of the group wheel are allowed to run administrator tasks. Before actually executing the task, they will be prompted for their password. If you don't want a valid sudo user to be prompted for his password, make sure the following line is included:

```
%wheel    ALL=(ALL)    NOPASSWD: ALL
```

It may also be useful to define sets of specific commands that can be executed by users. For instance, a help desk agent many need to reset user properties and passwords, but may not need permissions to run all commands as user root. This can be configured by using a Cmnd_Alias that defines all commands that the users should be granted access to. This can start with the following line:

```
Cmnd_Alias    HELPDESK = /usr/bin/passwd, /usr/sbin/usermod
```

After defining the command alias, the appropriate permissions must be granted to a user or group of users. The most convenient way of doing so, would be to allow all commands in the alias to the members of a specific group. The following would allow all members of the Linux group helpdesk to run all commands that are defined in the command alias:

```
%helpdesk    ALL=HELPDESK
```

EXERCISE 6-5: CONFIGURING SUDO

1. Open a root shell.

2. Type **visudo** to open the sudo editor.

3. Include the following line:

   Cmnd_Alias HELPDESK = /usr/bin/passwd, /usr/sbin/usermod

4. Further on in the file, include the following line:

   %helpdesk ALL=HELPDESK

5. Write the changes to disk, using :wq!

6. As root, type **groupadd helpdesk**.

7. User **usermod -aG helpesk lara**.

8. Use **su - lara** to open a shell in which you are working as user lara.

9. Type **sudo passwd marcha** and verify that you can change the password of user marcha.

Summary

In this chapter, you have learned how to manage the user environment. First, you have read about management of users, passwords, and groups. You've also learned how to manage the default user environment in the shell files /etc/profile and ~/.profile. Next, you've learned how to use the quota system to limit the amount of disk space available to a user. After that, you've read how PAM and nsswitch.conf are used to determine where your Linux computer gets user-related information from. At the end of this chapter, you saw how to use sudo to allow nonroot users to perform administration tasks with root permissions. The following commands were covered in this chapter:

- useradd: Adds new users

- usermod: Modifies user properties

- userdel: Deletes users

- passwd: Sets or changes user passwords

- groupadd: Adds new groups

- groupdel: Deletes groups

- groupmod: Modifies group properties

- `quotacheck`: Enables quotas on all file systems that have the quota options
- `addquota`: Opens editor to change user quota settings
- `repquota`: Generates a report of current quota usage
- `sudo`: Allows end users to execute tasks with root permissions

In the next chapter, you'll learn how to create a secure environment, working with Linux permissions.

CHAPTER 7

Managing Permissions

On a Linux system, permissions are used to secure access. In this chapter, you'll learn how to modify ownership to accommodate permissions. To begin with, the basic read, write, and execute permissions are covered. Next, you'll learn how to apply advanced Linux permissions for some extra security. Finally, at the end of this chapter you'll learn how to create Access Control Lists to give permissions to more than one user or group and how to work with attributes to add an extra layer of protection to files.

Setting Ownership

File and directory ownership is vital for working with permissions. In this section, you'll learn how you can determine ownership, as well as how to change user and group ownership for files and directories.

Displaying Ownership

On Linux, every file and every directory has an owner. To determine whether you as a user have permissions to a file or a directory, the shell checks ownership. First, it will see whether you are the *user owner*, which is also referred to as the *user of the file*. If you are the user, you will get the permissions that are set for the user, and the shell looks no further. If you are not the user owner, the shell will check whether you are a member of the *group owner*, which is also referred to as the *group of the file*. If you are a member of the group, you will get access to the file with the permissions of the group, and the shell looks no further. If you are neither the user nor the group owner, you'll get the permissions of the others entity. This entity applies to everybody else.

From the above follows that permissions are not applied additive. That means that a user who is owner, but also is a member of the group that is owner, will only work with the user owner permissions and not with the group owner permissions.

Note   Unless specifically mentioned otherwise, in this chapter all that is true for files is true for directories as well. So if you read about a file, you can assume that it also goes for a directory.

To see current ownership assignments, you can use the ls -l command. This command shows the user as well as the group owner. In Listing 7-1, you can see the ownership settings for directories in the directory /home on a system that uses the public group approach where all users are members of the same group, users. In this output, you can see the name of the user owner in the third column, followed by the name of the group in the fourth column.

Listing 7-1. Use ls -l to Show User and Group Ownership

```
nuuk:/home # ls -l
total 24
drwxr-xr-x 8    alex          users 4096 Dec 12 12:02 alex
drwxr-xr-x 8    caroline      users 4096 Dec 12 12:02 caroline
drwxr-xr-x 8    linda         users 4096 Dec 10 11:36 linda
drwxr-xr-x 8    sander        users 4096 Dec 10 13:22 sander
drwxr-xr-x 8    sanne         users 4096 Dec 12 11:59 sanne
drwxr-xr-x 8    stephanie     users 4096 Dec 12 12:01 stephanie
```

Using the ls command, you can display ownership for files in a given directory. It may on occasion be useful to get a list of all files on the system that have a given user or group as owner. To do this, you may use find together with its -user argument. For instance, the following command would show all files that have user linda as their owner:

```
find / -user linda
```

You can also use find to search for files that have a specific group as their owner. For instance, the following command would search for all files that are owned by the group users:

```
find / -group users
```

Changing User Ownership

When working with permissions, it is important to know how to change file ownership. For this purpose, there is the chown command. The syntax of this command is not hard to understand:

```
chown who what
```

For instance, the following command would change ownership for the file account to user julie:

```
chown julie account
```

The chown command has one important option: -R. You may guess what it does, as this option is available for many other commands as well; it allows you to set ownership recursively, which allows you to set ownership of the current directory and everything below. This includes files as well as directories. The following command would change ownership for the directory /home and everything beneath it to user julie:

```
chown -R julie /home
```

Changing Group Ownership

You actually have two ways to change group ownership. You can do it with chown, but there's also a specific command with the name chgrp that does the job. If you want to use the chown command, use a . or : in front of the group name. The following would change the group owner of directory /home/account to the group account:

```
chown .account /home/account
```

To see how to use the chgrp command to change group ownership, imagine the following example in which chgrp sets group ownership for the directory /home/account to the group account:

```
chgrp account /home/account
```

As is the case for chown, you can use the option -R with chgrp to change group ownership recursively. If you need to change user ownership as well as group ownership, chown offers you that option. After specifying the options, specify the username followed by a dot or a colon, and immediately after that the name of the group you want to set as the owner. As the last part of the command, mention the name of the file or the directory you want to set ownership for. For example, the following command would set user linda and group sales as the owner in one command:

```
chown -R linda.sales /home/sales
```

Default Ownership

You may have noticed that when a user creates a file, default ownership is applied. The user who creates the file will automatically become user owner, and the primary group of that user automatically becomes group owner. Normally, this will be the group that is set in the /etc/passwd file as the user's primary group. However, if the user is a member of more groups, he or she can change the effective primary group using the **newgrp** command.

To show the current effective primary group, a user can use the groups command. The group that is effective as the primary group at that moment is listed first, followed by the names of all other groups the user is a member of. Following is an example:

```
linda@nuuk:~> groups
users dialout video
```

As an alternative, the **id** command can be used. This command shows information about a user account, in which the effective primary group is listed first.

If the current user linda wants to change the effective primary group, she can use the newgrp command, followed by the name of the group she wants to set as the new effective primary group. In Listing 7-2, you can see how user linda uses this command to make sales her effective primary group.

Listing 7-2. Using newgrp to Change the Effective Primary Group

```
linda@nuuk:~> groups
users dialout video sales
linda@nuuk:~> newgrp sales
linda@nuuk:~> groups
sales dialout video users
linda@nuuk:~>
```

After changing the effective primary group, all new files that the user creates will get this group as their group owner. To return to the original primary group setting, use exit. This closes the subshell in which another effective primary group was used and will bring you back to the previous effective primary group setting.

```
┌─────────────────────────────────────────────────────────────────────────────┐
│                    EXERCISE 7-1: CHANGING OWNERSHIP                          │
└─────────────────────────────────────────────────────────────────────────────┘
```

1. Open a root shell.

2. Type **mkdir -p /data/sales** to create the directory /data/sales. Next type **mkdir /data/account** to create the /data/account directory as well.

3. Type **chown marcha:sales /data/sales**, followed by **chown marcha:account /data/account**. This makes user marcha user owner of both directories, and ensures that the group sales is owner of the /data/sales directory, and that the group account is set as the owner of the /data/account directory.

4. Type **ls -l /data** to check the ownership settings on /data/account and /data/sales.

Basic Permissions: Read, Write, and Execute

The Linux permissions system was invented in the 1970s. Since computing needs were limited in those years, the basic permission system that was created then was rather limited as well.

This system consists of three permissions that you can apply to files and directories. In this section, you'll learn how the system works and how to modify these permissions.

Before doing this, let's have a look at how to read the current permissions. The best method to do so is by using ls -l, which will show you a list of all files and directories in the current directory. The first character indicates the type of file. For instance, it gives d if it is a directory or l if it is a symbolic link. Next are nine characters to specify the permissions that are set to the file or directory. The first set of three are the user permissions, the next set of three are the group permissions, and the last set of three refer to the permissions granted to others. So in the example command listing that follows, user linda has rwx, group owner sales has r-x, and others have no permissions at all:

```
ls -ld /home/sales
drwxr-x--- 2    linda    sales    4096    sales
```

Understanding Read, Write, and Execute Permissions

The three basic permissions allow you to read, write, and execute files. The effect of these permissions will be different when applied to files or directories. If applied to a file, the read permission gives you the right to open the file for reading. This means that you can read its contents, but it also means that your computer can open the file to do something with it. A program file that needs access to a library might require, for example, read access to that library. From this, it follows that the read permission is the most basic permission you need to work with files.

If applied to a directory, read permission allows you to list the contents of that directory. You should be aware that this permission does not allow you to read files in the directory as well. The Linux permission system does not know inheritance, and the only way to read a file is by using the read permissions on that file. To open a file for reading, however, you do need read permissions to the directory, because you wouldn't see the file otherwise. Notice that it's not enough to have only read permissions on a directory. The read permission on directories always needs to be used together with the execute permission. Without execute permissions, users won't be able to access the directory.

As you can probably guess, the write permission, if applied to a file, allows you to write in the file. Stated otherwise, write allows you to modify the contents of existing files. However, it does not allow you to create new files or delete existing files. To do that, you need write permission on the directory where you want to create the file. On directories, this permission also allows you to create and remove new subdirectories.

Note: Let me elaborate this with an example. If user root creates a file in the home directory of linda, is user linda allowed to delete that file or not? Many people give the wrong answer to this question: as root has created the file, the user linda has no write permissions on the file. This however doesn't matter at all. To be able to remove a file, you need write permissions on the directory, and the permissions on the file don't matter at all.

The execute permission is what you need to execute a file. That means that you'll need execute on any program file or script file that you have created. It will never be set by default, which makes Linux almost immune to viruses. Someone who is owner of the directory will be capable of applying the execute permission to files in that directory. Also, if you're owner of the file you cna use the **chmod** command to set the execute permission on that file.

■ **Note**   Although there are almost no viruses for Linux, it doesn't mean that you are immune from security problems when using Linux. The Linux alternative for a virus is called a *root kit.* You can compare a root kit to a trojan in the Windows world: a root kit is a back door that allows others to take control of your computer. The best security measure to protect against root kits is not to work with root permissions unless it is really necessary.

Whereas the execute permission on files allows the user to run a program file, if applied to a directory, the user is allowed to use the cd command to go to that directory. This means that execute is an important permission for directories, and you will see that it is normally applied as the default permission to directories. Without it, there is no way to get into that directory! So if you want to have read permission on a directory, you must have execute permission as well. It makes no sense just to give a user read permission on a directory. Table 7-1 summarizes the use of the basic permissions.

Table 7-1. *Use of Read, Write, and Execute Permissions*

Permission	Applied to Files	Applied to Directories
Read	Open a file	List contents of a directory
Write	Change contents of a file	Create and delete files
Execute	Run a program file	Change to the directory

Applying Read, Write, and Execute Permissions

To apply permissions, you use the chmod command. When using chmod, you can set permissions for user, group, and others. You can use this command in two modes: relative mode and absolute mode. In absolute mode, three digits are used to set the basic permissions. Table 7-2 gives an overview of the permissions and their numerical representation.

Table 7-2. *Numerical Representation of Permissions*

Permission	Numerical Representation
Read	4
Write	2
Execute	1

When setting permissions, you should calculate the value that you need. For example, if you want to set read, write, and execute permissions for the user, read and execute permissions for the group, and read and execute permissions for others on the file /somefile, you would use the following chmod command:

```
chmod 755 /somefile
```

When using chmod in this way, all current permissions are replaced by the permissions you set. If you want to modify permissions relative to the current permissions, you can use chmod in relative mode. When using chmod in relative mode, you work with three indicators to specify what you want to do. First, you'll specify for whom you want to change permissions. To do this, you can choose between user (u), group (g), and others (o). Next, you use an operator to add or subtract permissions from the current mode, or set them in an absolute way. At the end, you use r, w, and x to specify what permissions you want to set.

■ **Note**   You will set read and write permissions quite often. This is not the case for the execute permission. Though you will set it on directories all the time, you will rarely apply execute permission to files, unless they are files that should be run as program files.

When changing permissions in relative mode, you may omit the "to whom" part to add or remove a permission for all entities. For instance, the following would add the execute permission for all users:

```
chmod +x somefile
```

When working in relative mode, you may use more complex commands as well. For instance, the following would add the write permission to the group and remove read for others:

```
chmod g+w,o-r somefile
```

Before moving over to the advanced permissions, let's practice applying basic permissions first.

EXERCISE 7-2: APPLYING BASIC PERMISSIONS

This exercise continues on the tasks that have been performed in exercise 7-1. Make sure that you have completed this exercise before going through the tasks in this exercise.

1.   Open a root shell.

2.   To make sure that the owner and group have all permissions on the directory and its contents, use **chmod -R 770 /data/sales** on the /data/sales director.

3.   Let's do the same using relative permissions on /data/account: type **chmod -R u=rwx,g=rwx,o=- /data/account**.

4.   Type **ls -l /data/** to verify that the permissions have been applied correctly.

Advanced Permissions

Apart from the basic permissions that you've just read about, Linux has a set of advanced permissions as well. These are special purpose permissions that have been added to the spectre of available Linux permissions later, to meet the demand for more advanced security settings.

Understanding Advanced Permissions

There are three advanced permissions. The first is the *Set User ID* (SUID) permission. On some specific occasions, you may want to apply this permission to executable files.

By default, a user who runs an executable file runs this file with his or her own permissions (provided that user has all permissions needed to run this file). For normal users, this normally means the use of the program is restricted. In some cases, however, the user needs to be able to run a command with root permissions. Consider, for example, the situation where a user needs to change his or her password. To do this, the user needs to write the new password to the /etc/shadow file. This file, however, is not writable for users with nonroot permissions:

```
nuuk:/home # ls -l /etc/shadow
-rw-r----- 1 root shadow 853 Dec 12 12:02 /etc/shadow
```

The SUID permission offers a solution for this problem. On the /usr/bin/passwd file, this permission is applied by default. So when changing his or her password, the user temporarily has root permissions, which allow the user to write to the /etc/passwd file. You can see the SUID permission with ls -l as an s at the position where normally you would expect to see the x for the user permissions:

```
nuuk:/ # ls -l /usr/bin/passwd
-rwsr-xr-x 1 root shadow 73300 May  4  2007 /usr/bin/passwd
```

The SUID permission may look useful—and it is—but at the same time, it is potentially dangerous. If applied wrongly, you may give away root permissions by . accident. I therefore recommend you use it with greatest care only. Let me explain why.

Imagine a shell script with the name gone that has the following contents:

```
#!/bin/bash
rm -rf /
```

Now imagine that user linda finds this shell script and tries to execute it. What will happen? She will remove her own files only. That is because for all the other files, she doesn't have enough permissions to remove them. Now imagine that this shell script has root as its owner and the SUID permission set. So ls -l on this script would give the following:

```
ls -l gone
-rwsr-xr-x 1     root root     19     gone
```

But what happens if linda tries to run this script in this scenario? Can you imagine what would happen? It would actually remove all files on the hard drive of this computer, as the script is executed in a subshell where linda has root permissions. This is because user root is owner of the script, and the SUID permission is set. So linda would run it as root, and given this, she would have more than enough permissions to perform her destructive command. For that reason, there's mainly one thing you need to remember about applying SUID: Don't!

The second special permission is *Set Group ID* (SGID). This permission has two effects.

If applied on an executable file, it gives the user who executes the file the permissions of the group owner of that file. So SGID can accomplish more or less the same thing that SUID does. For this purpose, however, SGID is hardly used, and you should never apply it to accomplish this yourself!

When applied to a directory, SGID may be useful, as you can use it to set default group ownership on files and subdirectories created in that directory. By default, when a user creates a file, his or her effective primary group is set as the owner for that file. For example, if you have a shared group environment, this is not very useful, because no one else will be able to modify the files you're creating, even if they're member of the same group.

Imagine a situation where users linda and lori work for the accounting department and are both members of the group accounting. For security reasons, however, the administrator has decided to work with private primary groups. That means that linda is the only member of her primary group, linda, and lori is the only member of her primary group, lori. Both users, however, are members of the accounting group as well, but as a secondary group setting.

The default situation would be that when either of these users creates a file, the primary group becomes owner. However, if you create a shared group directory (say, /data/account) and make sure that the SGID permission is applied to that directory and that the group accounting is set as the group owner for the directory, all files created in this directory and all of its subdirectories would also get the group accounting as the default group owner. Notice that this is very useful behavior and for that reason, you should consider using SGID on all shared group environments.

The SGID permission shows in the output of ls -l with an s at the position where you normally find the group execute permission:

```
nuuk:/groups # ls -ld account
drwxr-sr-x 2 root account 4096 Dec 14 15:17 account
```

The third of the special permissions is *sticky bit*. This permission is useful to protect files against accidental deletion in an environment where multiple users can create files in the same directory. It is for that reason applied as a default permission to the /tmp directory.

Without the sticky bit permission, if a user can create files in a directory, he or she can also delete files from that directory. In a shared group environment, this may be annoying. Imagine users linda and lori both have write permissions to the directory /groups/account because of their membership in the group accounting. This means that linda is capable of deleting files that lori has created and vice versa. This may not be an ideal situation.

When applying the sticky bit permission, a user can delete files only if either of the following is true:

- The user is owner of the file.

- The user is owner of the directory where the file exists.

Notice that this means that sticky bit cannot be used to prevent users to remove files from their home directory. As the user is owner of the home directory, the user will always have permissions to remove files from this directory.

When using ls -l, you can see sticky bit as a t at the position where you normally see the execute permission for others:

```
nuuk:/groups # ls -ld account/
drwxr-sr-t 2 root account 4096 Dec 14 15:17 account/
```

Applying Advanced Permissions

To apply SUID, SGID, and sticky bit, you can use chmod as well. SUID has numerical value 4, SGID has numerical value 2, and sticky bit has numerical value 1. If you want to apply these permissions, you need to add a four-digit argument to chmod, of which the first digit refers to the special permissions. The following line, for example, would add the SGID permission to a directory, and set rwx for the user and rx for the group and others:

```
chmod 2755 /somedir
```

It is rather impractical if you have to look up the current permissions that are set before working with chmod in absolute mode (you would risk overwriting permissions if you didn't). Therefore, I recommend working in relative mode if you need to apply any of the special permissions. For SUID, use chmod u+s; for SGID, use chmod g+s; and for sticky bit, use chmod +t followed by the name of the file or the directory that you want to set the permissions on.

Table 7-3 presents all you need to know about these special permissions.

Table 7-3. *Working with SUID, SGID, and Sticky Bit*

Permission	Numerical Value	Relative Value	On Files	On Directories
SUID	4	u+s	User executes file with permissions of file owner.	No meaning.
SGID	2	g+s	User executes file with permissions of group owner.	File created in directory gets the same group owner.
Sticky bit	1	+t	No meaning.	Users are prevented from deleting files from other users.

When applying these permissions with chmod in absolute mode, you'll use four digits (normally you would use three only) to set the permissions. Of these four digits, the first relates to the special permissions. So in the command chmod 4755 somefile, the SUID permission is set to somefile, and in chmod 3755, SGID as well as sticky bit are applied. In exercise 7-3 you'll apply the advanced permissions to your test machine.

EXERCISE 7-3: APPLYING ADVANCED PERMISSIONS

Notice that this exercise continues on the tasks that you've permformed in Exercise 7-1 and 7-2. Make sure to work through these exercises before applying the tasks in this exercise.

1. Open a shell as user marcha. Use **id** to verify that marcha is a member of the sales as well as the account group.

2. Type the command **touch /data/sales/marcha**. This creates an empty file in the shared group environment. Use the same command to creaet some more files in this directory.

3. Type **ls -l /data/sales** and notice that the group sales is not assigned as group owner on the files.

4. Open a root shell. From the root shell, type **chmod g+s /data/***. This applies the SGID permission on the /data/sales directory as well as the /data/account directory.

5. Open a shell as user daphne. Check that she is a member of the sales group. If this is not the case, make sure that she's assigned as a member of the sales group before moving on.

6. Type **echo daphne >> /data/sales/marcha**. Notice that this doesn't work. This is because daphne is accessing the file as a part of the "others" entity, which doesn't have write permissions on the file.

7. Use **touch /data/sales/daphne** to create a file as user daphne and repeat this command a couple of times. Use **ls -l /data/sales** to verify that these files have inherited the group owner of the directory, because of the SGID permission that has been set on the directory.

8. Still as daphne, type **rm -f /data/sales/marcha.** Notice that this works. As a member of the sales group, daphne has write permissions to the directory so she's allows to remove all files from this directory.

9. Open a root shell and type **chmod +t /data/*** to apply sticky bit to /data/sales and /data/account.

10. Open a shell as user daphne again, and try to remove the other files that marcha has created in /data/sales. Because of the Sticky bit permission that has been applied now, it is no longer allowed to do this.

Working with Access Control Lists

Even with the additional features that were added with SUID, SGID, and sticky bit, serious functionality was still missing in the Linux permission scheme. In particular, the ability to grant multiple users and groups permissions to the same file or directory For that reason, Access Control Lists (ACLs) were added. In this section, you'll learn what ACLs are and how to apply them.

Understanding ACLs

The Linux permissions system without ACLs has two serious shortcomings:

- There can only be one user owner and one group owner.

- It's not possible to work with inheritance so that the permissions that are set on a higher level (such as a directory) are inherited to the lower level (such as the files in that directory).

These shortcomings are addressed by the ACL subsystem. By adding this feature to your file system, you can make it possible to grant permissions to additional entities on your file systems and work with inheritance as well.

Although the ACL subsystem adds great functionality to your server, there is one drawback: not all utilities support it. This means that you may lose ACL settings when copying or moving files, and also that your backup software may not be capable of backing up ACL settings. This doesn't have to be a problem though. ACLs are often applied to directories to make sure that new files that are created in a directory will get the permissions you want them to have automatically. Consider ACLs as something that is applied when designing the file system lay-out, not as something that will be applied later. You will rarely set ACLs on individual files. This means you won't have lots of ACLs, just a few applied on smart places in the file system. Hence, it will be relatively easy to restore the original ACLs you were working with, even if your backup software doesn't support them.

Preparing Your File System for ACLs

Before starting to work with ACLs, you must verify that your file system supports ACLs. This isn't always the case. If ACLs are not, you need to make sure your file system is mounted with the `acl` option (which most distributions will do automatically for you). For a mounted file system, you can do that by remounting the file system with the `acl` option. The following line shows how to do that for the root file system:

```
mount -o remount,acl /
```

The more elegant solution is to put the ACL option in `fstab` so that it is activated at all times when your system reboots. Listing 7-3 shows how this is done by default on a SUSE system. Notice that in this example, the user_xattr mount option has been used as well, to offer support for user extended attributes (discussed in more detail later in this chapter).

Listing 7-3. To Work with ACLs, You Need to Mount File Systems with ACL Support

```
nuuk:/ # cat /etc/fstab
/dev/system/root      /      ext4    acl,user_xattr 1 1
/dev/sda1             /boot  ext4    acl,user_xattr 1 2
/dev/system/swap      swap   swap    defaults       0 0
...
```

Tip! It isn't always very clear whether or not ACLs can be used on a file system. The best way to find out, is just be trying to apply the setfacl command as discussed below. If this command is giving you the "operation not supported" error message, ACL support is not available and you'll need to fix this as described above.

Changing and Viewing ACL Settings with setfacl and getfacl

To work with ACLs, you need the `setfacl` command. This command has many options, some of them rather confusing. In this section, I'll just discuss the useful options, which are not too hard to understand. The basic syntax of `setfacl` is as follows:

```
setfacl [options] operation entity:entityname:permissions file
```

In this example, the following components are used:

- *Options*: Use this part for specific options to moderate the way `setfacl` does its work. A few options can be useful:

    - `-d`: Use this option to set a default ACL. This is an ACL setting that is inherited by subdirectories and files as well.

    - `-k`: Use this option to remove a default ACL.

    - `-R`: Use this option to apply the ACL setting recursively.

■ **Note**   A default ACL is for new files and does not influence existing files. All new files will get the
permission as you set them in the default ACL. Basically, by using the option -d, you enable permission
inheritance. Without the option -d, the setfacl command works on existing files only. To make sure that all new
files will get the desired ACL settings, you should use the setfacl command twice. First with the -d option so that
the default ACL is set, and next with the -R and without the -d option to take care of currently existing files.

- *Operation*: The operation tells setfacl to either add or remove an ACL setting. The
  following operations are available:

  - --set: Use this operation to set an ACL. It will replace any existing ACL, so use
    it with care.

  - -m: If you need to modify an ACL, use -m. It will not replace an existing ACL,
    instead adding to the current settings.

  - -x: Use this option to remove an existing ACL.

- *Entity and entity name*: These two define for whom you want to set the ACL. There
  are two types of entity: u for user and g for group. After specifying the type of entity,
  you need to specify the name of the entity.

- *Permissions*: These are the permissions that you want to set using ACLs. Use the
  Linux permissions as discussed previously.

- File: This is the name of the file or the directory to which you want to apply the
  ACLs.

Based on this information, it's time to have a look at some examples, starting with some easy ones.
Assume you want to add the group account as someone who has rights (this is called a trustee) to the
directory account. The setfacl command to do this would be as follows:

```
setfacl -m g:account:rwx account
```

However, it does not make sense to start working on ACLs without having a look at the current
permissions first. Therefore, in Listing 7-4, you can see the permission settings for the directory
/groups/account before and after I've changed the ACL.

Listing 7-4. Permission Settings Before and After Changing the ACL

```
nuuk:/groups # ls -l
total 4
drwxr-sr-t    2 root users 4096 Dec 14 15:17 account
nuuk:/groups # setfacl -m g:account:rwx account
nuuk:/groups # ls -l
total 8
drwxrwsr-t+ 2 root users 4096 Dec 14 15:17 account
```

As you can see, there was already a group owner, users, and this group owner was not touched by
changing the ACLs with setfacl. The only thing indicating that something is going on is the + sign that is
shown directly after the permission listing in ls -l. This + indicates that an ACL is effective.

To see the ACLs themselves, you need the getfacl command. In Listing 7-5, you can see what this
command shows for the directory account on which I've just applied an ACL.

Listing 7-5. Showing ACL Settings with getfacl

```
nuuk:/groups # getfacl account
# file: account
# owner: root
# group: users
user::rwx
group::r-x
group:account:rwx
mask::rwx
other::r-x
```

As you can see in the output of getfacl, this command shows you the names of user and group owners and the permissions that are set for them. Following that, it shows there is also a group account that has rwx permissions. Just ignore the information that is shown in the mask line; ACL masks are a complex and confusing feature that you only need to compensate for in a bad directory structure design, and therefore I will ignore it in this book. On the last line, the permissions of others are displayed as well.

In the second example, I'll show you how to modify an existing ACL so that it becomes a default ACL. Basically, you use the same command that you've seen before, but with the option -d added to it. Also, the command adds a second group in the ACL setting by using a comma to separate the names of the two groups:

```
nuuk:/groups # setfacl -d -m g:account:rwx,g:sales:rx account
```

At this moment, you have a default ACL. This means that all files and all directories created under /groups/account will get the same ACL setting. You can show this with the getfacl command, as demonstrated in Listing 7-6.

Listing 7-6. Using getfacl to Show Default ACL Settings

```
nuuk:/groups # getfacl account
# file: account
# owner: root
# group: users
user::rwx
group::r-x
group:account:rwx
mask::rwx
other::r-x
default:user::rwx
default:group::r-x
default:group:sales:r-x
default:group:account:rwx
default:mask::rwx
default:other::r-x
```

As you can see, shown are not only the user and group owner names, but also their permissions and the default settings that will be applied to new files. You should notice that at this point, however, an interesting mix exists between the normal Linux permission scheme and the ACL settings. This shows when user linda, who belongs to the group users, creates a subdirectory in the directory /groups/account. You can see the getfacl result on that directory in Listing 7-7: for the "normal" user and group owners, the normal rules of ownership are applied, and the ACL settings are added to that. This means that when you are working with default ACLs, you should always carefully plan what you want to do before applying them!

Listing 7-7. ACLs and Normal Ownership Rules Are Both Effective

```
linda@nuuk:/groups/account> getfacl subdir
# file: subdir
# owner: linda
# group: users
user::rwx
group::r-x
group:sales:r-x
group:account:rwx
mask::rwx
other::r-x
default:user::rwx
default:group::r-x
default:group:sales:r-x
default:group:account:rwx
default:mask::rwx
default:other::r-x
```

You have now learned how to work with an ACL. This is a useful feature if you need to enhance the capabilities of Linux file system permissions. I personally rely on it a lot when configuring a Linux file server, which typically is an environment where one group has requirements different from another group. I've also used it on a web server environment to grant access to a developer to all the files in the HTML document root without changing the default permissions in that environment, which could have negative impact on the working of the web server. Use this feature sparsely though, because a Linux system that has too many ACLs applied is a Linux system that is more difficult to understand.

EXERCISE 7-4: WORKING WITH ACLS

In this exercise you'll apply ACLs. Notice that this exercise continues on Exercise 7-1 through 7-3, make sure you have permformed these exercises before working your way through the steps that are described in this exercise.

1. Open a root shell.

2. Type **getfacl /data/sales/marcha** to check the current ACL assingments to this file. As no ACLs have been applied, you'll just see permission settings.

3. Type **setfacl -R -m g:account:rx /data/sales** to ensure that the account group gets permissions to all files in the /data/sales directory.

4. Type **getfacl /data/sales/marcha** again to check the newly applied ACL setting.

5. Type **touch /data/sales/newfile** and check the ACL settings on the file, using **getfacl /data/sales/newfile**. You'll notice that no ACL settings have been applied, because no default ACL has been created yet.

6. Type **setfacl -m d:g:account:rx /data/sales** to apply default ACLs to the sales directory.

7. Create another new file in /data/sales and use **getfacl** to check the ACL settings on the new file.

8. Use **setfacl -m d:g:sales:rx /data/account** followed by **setfacl -R -m g:account:rx /data/sales**

Setting Default Permissions with umask

In the discussion about ACLs, you have learned how to work with default ACLs. If you don't use ACLs, there is a shell setting that determines the default permissions that you will get: umask. In this section, you'll learn how to modify default permissions using this setting.

You have probably noticed that when creating a new file, some default permissions are set. These permissions are determined by the umask setting, a shell setting that is applied to all users when logging in to the system. In the umask setting, a numeric value is used that is subtracted from the maximum permissions that can be set automatically on a file; the maximum setting for files is 666 and for directories is 777. In other words, to derive numeric permissions from the umask, subtract the umask from 666 for files and from 777 for directories.

There are, however, some exceptions to this rule; you can find a complete overview of umask settings in Table 7-4. Of the digits used in the umask, like with the numeric arguments for the chmod command, the first digit refers to end-user permissions, the second digit refers to the group permissions, and the last refers to default permissions set for others. The default umask setting of 022 gives 644 for all new files and 755 for all new directories that are created on your server.

Table 7-4. umask Values and Their Result

Value	Applied to Files	Applied to Directories
0	Read and write	Everything
1	Read and write	Read and write
2	Read	Read and execute
3	Read	Read
4	Write	Write and execute
5	Write	Write
6	Nothing	Execute
7	Nothing	Nothing

There are two ways to change the umask setting: for all users and for individual users. If you want to set the umask for all users, you must make sure the umask setting is entered in the configuration file /etc/profile. If the umask is changed in this file, it applies to all users after logging in to your server. You can set a default umask by just adding a line like the following to /etc/profile:

umask 027

An alternative to setting the umask in /etc/profile, where it is applied to all users logging in to the system, is to change the umask settings in a file with the name .profile, which is created in the home directory of an individual user. Settings applied in this file are applied for the individual user only; therefore this is a nice method if you need more granularity. I personally like this feature to change the default umask for user root to 027, whereas normal users work with the default umask 022 on many distributions.

Working with Attributes

Permissions always relate to a trustee, which is a user or a group who has permissions to a file or directory. Attributes offer a different way to specify what can be done to a file. Attributes do their work, regardless of the user who accesses the file. Of course, there is a difference: the owner of a file can set file attributes, whereas other users (except for root who is almighty) cannot do that. Working with attributes is useful in some cases, but it's not very common.

For file attributes as well, an option must be provided in /etc/fstab before they can be used. This is the user_xattr option that can be seen in the fstab example in Listing 7-3 earlier in this chapter. Some attributes are available, but not yet implemented. Don't use them, because they bring you no benefit. Following are the most useful attributes that can be applied:

- A: This attribute ensures that the access time of the file is not modified. Normally, every time a file is opened, the file access time must be written to the file's metadata. This affects performance in a negative way; therefore, on files that are accessed on a regular basis, the A attribute can be used to disable this feature.

- a: This attribute allows a file to be added to, but not to be removed. For example, you could use it on log files as an additional layer of security that ensures that entries can be added, but the log file cannot be removed by accident.

- c: If you are using a file system where volume-level compression is supported, this file attribute makes sure the file is compressed the first time the compression engine gets active.

- D: This attribute makes sure that changes to files are written to disk immediately, and not to cache first. This is a useful attribute on important database files to make sure that they don't get lost between file cache and hard disk.

- d: This attribute makes sure the file is not backed up in backups where the dump utility is used.

- I: This attribute enables indexing for the directory where it is enabled (see Chapter 5 for more details on indexing). This allows faster file access for primitive file systems like Ext3 that don't use a b-tree database for fast access to files.

- j: This attribute ensures that on an Ext3 file system the file is first written to the journal and only after that to the data blocks on the hard disk. Use this to make sure that the journal offers maximum protection, and the chance of losing data is reduced to a minimum.

- s: This overwrites the blocks where the file was stored with zeros after the file has been deleted. This makes sure that recovery of the file is not possible after it has been deleted.

- u: This attribute saves undelete information. This allows a utility to be developed that works with that information to salvage deleted files.

■ **Note**   Although there are quite a few attributes that can be used, you should be aware that most attributes are rather experimental and only of any use if an application is employed that can work with the given attribute. For example, it doesn't make sense to apply the u attribute as long as no application has been developed that can use this attribute to recover deleted files.

If you want to apply attributes, you can use the chattr command. For example, use chattr +s somefile to apply the attribute s to somefile. Need to remove the attribute again? Then use chattr -s somefile, and it will be removed. To get an overview of all attributes that are currently applied, use the lsattr command.

EXERCISE 7-4: USING ATTRIBUTES

1. Open a root shell.

2. Type **touch /root/somefile** to create a test file.

3. Type **chattr +i /root/somefile** to apply the "immutable" attribute to the file.

4. Still as root, use **rm -f /root/somefile** to try removing the file. You'll notice that this doesn't work. Attributes apply to all users, including the user root!

5. Use **chattr -i /root/somefile**. This removes the attribute. You'll now be able to remove the file.

Summary

In this chapter, you have learned how to work with permissions. You've first discovered the role of ownership when determining your effective permissions. Next, you have learned about the three basic permissions: read, write, and execute. Following that, you have seen how to work with advanced features such as the SUID, SGID, and sticky bit permissions as well as ACLs. You've also read how to apply file attributes to add an additional layer of security to your file system. In this chapter, the following commands have been discussed:

- chown: Change ownership of files and directories.

- chgrp: Change group ownership of files and directories.

- groups: List group ownership for users.

- newgrp: Temporarily change the effective primary group for a user.

- chmod: Change permission mode on files and directories.

- setfacl: Set ACLs.

- getfacl: Read current ACLs.

- chattr: Change file attributes.

- lsattr: List file attributes.

In the next chapter, you will learn about process management.

CHAPTER 8

■ ■ ■

Managing Software

By default, your Linux distribution will come with lots of software packages. Even if lots of packages are available by default, you will encounter soon enough a situation where you need to install new packages. In this chapter, you'll learn how to do this. First, I'll tell you about the different ways that software management is handled on Linux. Next, you'll read about how to work with RPM-based packages. Then you'll learn how to install packages that are delivered in the .deb format. You'll also learn about software and package management tools such as yum, apt-get, and zypper; tracking and finding software packages; and managing updates and patches.

■ **Note**   Occasionally, software packages are delivered as tar archives. Refer to Chapter 3 for additional information about tar.

Understanding Software Management

Linux software packages are very modular. This means that everything you need is rarely in one software package. Instead, to be able to work with a program a collection of software packages needs to be installed. Because the software packages are small in general, most software packages have dependencies. These dependencies are packages that also need to be installed for your software package to function well.

Managing these software package dependencies is amongst the greatest challenges when working with software packages in Linux. If you choose a solution that doesn't know how to handle dependencies, you may see error messages indicating that in order to install package A, you also need to install packages B, C, and D. This is also referred to as *dependency hell,* and in the past it has been a very good reason for people not to use Linux.

Nowadays, all Linux distributions have some solution to manage these dependencies.

These solutions are based on software repositories. A *repository* is an installation source that contains a list of all installable packages. This means that your distribution's software management solution knows which software packages are available and installs dependencies automatically. While installing, your installation medium will be a repository; to add new software, you will find yourself adding new repositories regularly. After installation you'll typically make use of the on line repositories that are provided by your Linux distribution.

Managing RPM Packages

RPM stands for Red Hat Package Manager. It is the package management standard that was invented by Red Hat, and nowadays it is used by important distributions like Red Hat and its derivatives and SUSE. RPM is based on packages that have the extension .rpm. The names of these packages typically include name, version, and architecture of the software you are about to install. In this section, As an example, let's take the package nmap-6.40-4.el7.x86_64.rpm. In this package you can read the name and subversion of the package (nmao-6.40-4). Next, the package name states the distribution, which in this case is "Enterprise Linux", which stands for CentOS. Following that, the platform is identified as x86_64. You'll see this platform in most cases, older platform types such as i386 are becoming quite scarce nowadays. If an RPM package hasn't been written with a specific platform in mind, you'll see "noarch" as the platform identifier. Make sure that you select the package that is written for your architecture. You will see packages that are written for noarch as well. These are installable on all hardware platforms.

Working with RPM

The most basic way to handle RPM packages is by using the rpm command. Although this command provides an easy method for package management, it doesn't care about dependencies - which is why you shouldn't use it to install software packages anymore. This means that you may need to install all dependencies themselves. However, if you just want to install a simple package, this command can help you. First, you may use it to install packages. To do this, use the -i option as in the following example command:

```
rpm -i iftop-0.16-1.i386.rpm
```

If all goes well, this command just installs the package without showing any output. If some condition exists that prevents your package from installing smoothly, however, this command will complain and stop installing immediately, which you can see in the following example:

```
nuuk:~ # rpm -i iftop-0.16-1.i386.rpm
        package iftop-0.16-1 is already installed
```

A common reason why package installation may fail is that a package with the same name is already installed, which was the case in the second attempt to install the package iftop. It's easy to avoid that problem: instead of using rpm -i, better use rpm -Uvh.

If a package with the name of the package you are trying to install is already installed, it will be upgraded by using the option -U. If it's not installed yet, the rpm command will install it. Therefore, I'd recommend always using this command and not rpm -i. The other options are used to show more output to the user. The -v option adds verbosity, meaning it will show what the rpm command is actually doing. Finally, the -h option shows hashes, meaning you'll be able to see progress while installing the software. Listing 8-1 shows two examples where rpm -Uvh is used.

Listing 8-1. Using rpm -Uvh to Install Packages

```
nuuk:~ # rpm -Uvh iftop-0.16-1.i386.rpm
Preparing...                      ######################################### [100%]
        package iftop-0.16-1 is already installed
nuuk:~ # rpm -Uvh logtool-1.2.8-1.i386.rpm
Preparing...                      ######################################### [100%]
   1:logtool                       ######################################### [100%]
```

Apart from installing packages, you can also use rpm to remove packages. To do this, issue rpm with the option -e, as demonstrated in the following command:

```
rpm -e iftop-0.16-1-i386.rpm
```

Although the rpm command offers an easy solution for installing individual packages, you may not want to use it as your preferred package management solution. There are two package management interfaces that make package management really easier, yum and zypper, and you can read more about them in the next two sections.

Even if the **rpm** command isn't used much anymore for package installation, it is still being used frequently to perform queries in installed packages and packages that are about to be installed. To start with, there is the **rpm -qa** command. This command gives a list of all packages that are installed, and the results of the command can conveniently be searched with the grep utility. Also, rpm queries allow you to figure out what is inside a package. The following queries are particularly helpful:

- **rpm -ql packagename**: shows all files inside a package
- **rpm -qc packagename**: shows all configuration files in a package
- **rpm -qd packagename**: shows documentation that is included in the package
- **rpm -qi packagename**: shows generic package information.
- **rpm -qf packagename**: shows which package /file/name has been installed from

In exercise 8-1 you'll learn how to work with RPM queries.

EXERCISE 8-1: WORKING WITH RPM QUERIES

Note that this exercise will work only on RPM based distributions such as Red Hat and its derivatives and SUSE.

1. Type **rpm -qa** to see a list of all packages that are installed on your computer.

2. Type **rpm -qa | grep bash** to find out which version of the bash shell has been installed.

3. Type **rpm -ql $(rpm -qa | grep bash)**. This command uses command subsitution: the result of the command **rpm -qa | grep bash** is used by the **rpm -ql** command, to list the contents of the bash package on your system.

4. Type **rpm -qc $(rpm -qa | grep bash).** This will show a list of all configuration files that are installed from the bash package.

5. Type **rpm -qf /etc/passwd**. This shows the name of the package that the /etc/passwd file was installed from.

Working with yum

The yum system makes working with RPM packages easy. This package management interface works with repositories that contain lists of installable software. As an administrator, your first task is to make sure that you have all the software repositories you need in your configuration. Based on this repository list, the yum command is used to perform all kinds of software package management tasks.

Managing yum Repositories

Managing yum all starts with managing software repositories. For this purpose, your distribution provides the /etc/yum.conf configuration file; most distributions also include the directory /etc/yum.repos.d, which can contain configuration files for individual software repositories. In Listing 8-2, you can see what the default repository configuration for Fedora software packages looks like.

Listing 8-2. Default Software Repository Configuration for Fedora

```
[root@fedora yum.repos.d]# cat fedora.repo
[fedora]
name=Fedora $releasever - $basearch
failovermethod=priority
#baseurl=http://download.fedoraproject.org/pub/fedora/linux/releases/$releasever/
   Everything/$basearch/os/
mirrorlist=http://mirrors.fedoraproject.org/mirrorlist?repo=fedora-
   $releasever&arch=$basearch
enabled=1
gpgcheck=1
gpgkey=file:///etc/pki/rpm-gpg/RPM-GPG-KEY-fedora-$basearch

[fedora-debuginfo]
name=Fedora $releasever - $basearch - Debug
failovermethod=priority
#baseurl=http://download.fedoraproject.org/pub/fedora/linux/releases/$releasever/
   Everything/$basearch/debug/
mirrorlist=http://mirrors.fedoraproject.org/mirrorlist?repo=fedora-debug-
   $releasever&arch=$basearch
enabled=0
gpgcheck=1
gpgkey=file:///etc/pki/rpm-gpg/RPM-GPG-KEY-fedora-$basearch

[fedora-source]
name=Fedora $releasever - Source
failovermethod=priority
#baseurl=http://download.fedoraproject.org/pub/fedora/linux/releases/$releasever/
   Everything/source/SRPMS/
mirrorlist=http://mirrors.fedoraproject.org/mirrorlist?repo=fedora-source-
   $releasever&arch=$basearch
enabled=0
gpgcheck=1
gpgkey=file:///etc/pki/rpm-gpg/RPM-GPG-KEY-fedora-$basearch
```

As you can see, each of the package sources contains a few common items:

- *Name of the repository*: This is just the identification for your repository. Make sure that it is unique.

- *Failover method*: It is possible to configure repositories in a failover configuration. This means you refer to two or more different repositories that contain the same software. This is useful for creating some redundancy for repositories: if one repository fails, the other one will take over. If you choose to do that, this line indicates whether this is the repository with priority.

- *Base URL*: This is the base URL that brings you to the repository. As you can see, the URL mentioned here is commented out, which ensures that only the mirrors as specified in the mirror list are used.

- *Mirror list*: This line refers to a location where a list of mirror servers is found.

- *Enabled status*: This indicates whether this repository is on or off. You can see that on installation of the Fedora software, three repositories are listed in this file, but of these three, only one has the value of 1 and is on.

- *GPG configuration*: To check the integrity of software packages, GPG is used. The line gpgcheck=1 switches this feature on. In the line gpgkey=, there is an indication of what GPG key to use.

■ **Note**   GPG offers PGP (Pretty Good Privacy)–based integrity checking of software packages. GPG is just the GNU version of PGP, which is available for free usage.

Note that on most Linux distributions, only online package repositories are used. This ensures that you'll always get the latest version of the package you need to install, and it also makes sure that you can update your software smoothly. If you have already installed software from the online repositories, it is a bad idea to install packages from the installation media later, as you may end up with the wrong version of the package and some installation problems. If you are sure that you will never do online package management on a particular system, however, it is a good idea to configure yum to work with the local installation media only. The following procedure describes how you can do this for a Fedora system:

1. Before working with yum, make sure that the installation media is mounted at a fixed mount point. In this example, I'll assume that you have configured your system to mount the installation media on /cdrom. You need to not only configure fstab for this purpose, but also make sure that it is actually mounted at this moment.

2. Open the /etc/yum.conf file and make sure that you switch off PGP checking. The following line accomplishes this:

   ```
   gpgcheck=1
   ```

3. Open the repository files one by one and disable all online repositories. Just check for a repository that has enable=1 and change that to enable=0.

4. In any of the repository files (you can create a new file in /etc/yum.repos.d or include this information in one of the existing files), include the following lines:

```
[fedora-dvd]
name=Fedora installation DVD
baseurl=file:///cdrom
```

At this point, you have configured your system to look on the installation DVD only. Don't forget to switch the online resources back on again if you ever intend to connect this system to the Internet to install software packages. You can do so by changing the value for the enable parameter that you used in step 3 of the procedure back to 1.

It will on occasion also happen that you need to create your own repository. This is useful if you're using custom RPMs that are not in the default repositories and you want to install them using the **yum** command. To do this, you'll need to copy the RPMs to a local directory and create the repository metadata for this directory. Once this is done, you can use the repository to install software.

EXERCISE 8-2: CREATING A LOCAL REPOSITORY

Using repositories for software installation is convenient, because while doing so the installer will always try to install software dependencies as well. In this exercise you'll configure your own repository. Notice that this exercise works on Red Hat only.

1. Type **mkdir /repo** to create a directory that will be used as a repository.

2. Type **cd /repo** and next type **yumdownloader nmap http vsftpd**. If the command yumdownloader is not installed, install it by using **yum install -y yum-utils**.

3. Type **createrepo /repo**. This will generate the required indexes to make of the/repo directory a repository.

4. Type **yum repolist**. This command shows all repositories that are currently known. It will not include the newly created repository.

5. To start using the newly created repository, create the file **/repo/local.repo** and give it the following contents:

```
[localrepo]
name=local
baseurl=file:///repo
gpgcheck=0
```

6. Type **yum repolist** again. The newly created repository should now be listed.

Managing Software Packages with yum

Based on the software repositories you have installed, you can use the yum command. This command is written to be intuitive. You want to install a package? Use yum install. Need to update? yum update will help. Following are some examples of the most important arguments that you can use with yum:

- install: Use this to install a package. For instance, yum install nmap would search the software repositories for the nmap package and, if found, install it (see Listing 8-3). This installation is interactive; yum will first show you what it found and next install that for you.

Listing 8-3. Installing Software Packages with yum

```
[root@fedora etc]# yum install nmap
Loaded plugins: refresh-packagekit
fedora-dvd                                      | 2.8 kB        00:00
Setting up Install Process
Parsing package install arguments
Resolving Dependencies
--> Running transaction check
---> Package nmap.i386 2:4.68-3.fc10 set to be updated
--> Finished Dependency Resolution
Dependencies Resolved

================================================================================
 Package          Arch           Version                  Repository      Size
================================================================================
Installing:
 nmap             i386           2:4.68-3.fc10            fedora-dvd      914 k

Transaction Summary
================================================================================
Install       1 Package(s)
Update        0 Package(s)
Remove        0 Package(s)

Total download size: 914 k
Is this ok [y/N]: y
Downloading Packages:
Running rpm_check_debug
Running Transaction Test
Finished Transaction Test
Transaction Test Succeeded
Running Transaction
  Installing     : nmap                                                     1/1

Installed:
  nmap.i386 2:4.68-3.fc10

Complete!
```

- update: Use yum update if you want to update your entire system. You can also use the update command on a specific package; for instance, yum update nmap would search the software repositories to see whether a newer version of nmap is available, and if this is the case, install it.

- remove: Use this to remove a package from your system. For instance, yum remove nmap would delete the nmap package, including all dependencies that become obsolete after removing this package.

- list: This option contacts the repositories to see what packages are available and show you which are and which are not installed on your system. Just use yum list to see a complete list of all packages. This command used in combination with grep allows you to search for specific packages.

- The yum list command has some specific options itself. By default, it shows all packages, installed or not, that are available. In case you just want to see a list of packages that are installed, you can use yum list installed.

- info: If you want more information about any of the installed packages on your system, use yum info, followed by the name of the package. For instance, yum info nmap would give you all available details about the nmap package (see Listing 8-4). Based on this information, you can make the decision whether or not you need this package.

Listing 8-4. Use yum info to Get More Information About a Package

```
[root@fedora etc]# yum info nmap
Loaded plugins: refresh-packagekit
Installed Packages
Name        : nmap
Arch        : i386
Epoch       : 2
Version     : 4.68
Release     : 3.fc10
Size        : 3.2 M
Repo        : installed
Summary     : Network exploration tool and security scanner
URL         : http://www.insecure.org/nmap/
License     : GPLv2
Description: Nmap is a utility for network exploration or security auditing.
            : It
            : supports ping scanning (determine which hosts are up), many port
            : scanning techniques (determine what services the hosts are
            : offering), and TCP/IP fingerprinting (remote host operating
            : system
            : identification). Nmap also offers flexible target and port
            : specification, decoy scanning, determination of TCP sequence
            : predictability characteristics, reverse-identd scanning, and
            : more.
```

- provides: The yum provides command tells you what RPM package provides a given file. Listing 8-5 shows you the result of this command when used to find out where the file /etc/samba/smb.conf comes from.

Listing 8-5. Use yum provides to Find Out What RPM Package a Given File Comes From

```
[root@fedora ~]# yum provides /etc/samba/smb.conf
Loaded plugins: refresh-packagekit
samba-common-3.2.4-0.22.fc10.i386 : Files used by both Samba servers and
clients
Matched from:
Filename    : /etc/samba/smb.conf
```

- search: The yum search command allows you to search for a specific package, based on a search string that is composed as a regular expression. For instance, yum search nmap would give you the names of all packages whose name contains the text nmap.

- provides: The **yum provides** command will find a package based on a specific file you're looking for. For instance, type **yum provides */gedit** to find the specific RPM package that contains the gedit file. Notice that the file should always be referred to using a path reference: yum provides */gedit and not yum provides gedit.

- localinstall: In older Red hat you could use **yum localinstall** for installing RPM packages that are not in a repository. On recent Red Hat, you can do this with **yum install** also.

In exercise 8-3 you'll learn how to work with yum repositories.

EXERCISE 8-3: WORKING WITH YUM REPOSITORIES

Notice that this exercise can be done on Red Hat and its derivatives only.

1. Type **yum repolist**. This command will show a list of currently available repositories.

2. Type **yum list all**. This shows a list of all packages, also packages from repositories that haven't been installed yet.

3. Type **yum list installed**. This shows installed packages only. Notice that it also shows the name of the repository the package has been installed form.

4. Type **yum search nmap**. This will show the name of the nmap package as found in the repositories.

5. Type **yum install nmap** to install it.

6. Use **yum provides */semanage**. This will show the name of the package that contains the semanage command file.

Working with zypper

On SUSE Linux, an alternative to the RPM package manager is used, the zypper package manager. The intention of this package manager was to provide the same functionality that yum does, but in a faster way. The zypper package also works with package repositories and command-line utilities.

Managing zypper Software Repositories

In zypper, a repository is called an *installation source*. Installation sources are kept in the zypper database, which is in /var/lib/zypp. To manage zypper installation sources, you have to use the zypper command. The most important options that are related to package management are listed here:

- service-add URI: The zypper service-add command will add an installation source. This command is followed by a Universal Resource Identifier (URI), which can be a web address, but which can also refer to a local directory on your system. For instance, the command zypper service-add file:///packages would add the contents of the directory /packages to the installation sources, as shown in Listing 8-6.

Listing 8-6. Adding an Installation Source with zypper

```
nuuk:~ # zypper service-add file:///packages
3211 zmd
ZENworks Management Daemon is running.
WARNING: this command will not synchronize changes.
Use rug or yast2 for that.
Determining file:/packages source type...
.. not YUM
.. not YaST
Unknown source type for file:/packages
```

As you can see, the zypper service-add command uses URL format. In Listing 8-6, the URL that was used refers to something on the local file system. However, you can also use zypper to refer to something that is on the Internet. For instance, zypper service-add http://www.example.com/packages would add an installation source that is on a web server. zypper uses the same URL syntax that you use when working with a browser and is therefore intuitive to work with.

- service-list: As its name suggests, this command allows you to display a list of all available zypper installation sources (zypper uses services as a synonym for installation sources).

- service-remove: Use this to remove installation sources from the list of available services.

Managing RPM Packages with zypper

Once the service lists are all configured, you can use zypper at the command line to manage software packages. In its use, zypper looks a lot like the yum utility; basically, you can just replace the yum command by the zypper command in most cases. However, there are also some useful additions to the zypper command that do not have yum equivalents. Following is an overview of the most important zypper command-line options:

- install: Use zypper install to install a package. For instance, to install the package nmap, you would use the command zypper install nmap.

- remove: Use zypper remove to remove a package from your system. For instance, to remove the package nmap, type zypper remove nmap.

- update: Use this to update either your complete system or just one package. To update the entire system, use zypper update; to update one package only, add the name of the package you want to update to this command. For instance, if you want to update the package nmap, use zypper update nmap.

- search: Use this to search for a particular package. By default, zypper will search in the list of installed packages, as well as the list of packages that haven't been installed yet. If you want to modify this behavior, add the option -i to search in installed packages only or -u to search in uninstalled packages only. The argument used with zypper search is interpreted as a regular expression. For instance, the command zypper search -i samba would just look for all packages that have the string samba in their name and show a list of these. Listing 8-7 shows what the result of this command looks like.

Listing 8-7. Use zypper search to Get a List of All Packages That Contain a Given String in Their Name

```
nuuk:~ # zypper search -i samba
Restoring system sources...
Parsing metadata for SUSE Linux Enterprise Server 10 SP2-20090121-231645...
S | Catalog                        | Type    | Name               | Version      | Arch
--+--------------------------------+---------+--------------------+--------------+--------
i | SUSE Linux Enterprise Server 10
    SP2-20090121-231645             | package | samba              | 3.0.28-0.5   | i586
i | SUSE Linux Enterprise Server 10
    SP2-20090121-231645             | package |samba-client        | 3.0.28-0.5   | i586
i | SUSE Linux Enterprise Server 10
    SP2-20090121-231645             | package |yast2-samba-client  | 2.13.40-0.3  | noarch
i | SUSE Linux Enterprise Server 10
    SP2-20090121-231645             | package |yast2-samba-server  | 2.13.24-0.3  | noarch
```

- patches: This useful command will show a list of all available patches. Use this command if you not only want to update, but also would like to know what exactly an update will do to your system.

In some cases, the zypper command will give you a lot of information. To filter out only the parts you need, use the grep utility.

Managing DEB Packages

RPM is not the only way to package software for Linux. Another very popular package format is the .deb format. This format was originally developed on Debian Linux but is now also the default package format for other distributions, of which Ubuntu is the most important. In this section, you'll learn how to manage packages in this format. I've based this section on Ubuntu; you may therefore find some differences with the way other distributions handle .deb packages.

Managing .deb Software Repositories

On an Ubuntu system, a list of all these installation sources is kept in the file /etc/apt/sources.list. Although the most important software repositories are added to this file automatically, you may occasionally want to add other software repositories to this list. To understand how this works, it is useful to distinguish between the different package categories that Ubuntu uses. This will tell you more about the current status of a package, for example, if the package is considered safe or if it has licensing that doesn't comply to common open source standards.

In all repositories, you'll always find the following five package categories:

- *Main*: The main category portion of the software repository contains software that is officially supported by Canonical, the company behind Ubuntu. The software that is normally installed to your server is in this category. By working with only this software, you can make sure that your system remains as stable as possible and—very important for an enterprise environment—that you can get support for it at all times.

- *Restricted*: The restricted category is basically for supported software that uses a license that is not freely available, such as drivers for specific hardware components that use a specific license agreement, or software that you have to purchase. You'll typically find restricted software in a specific subdirectory on the installation media.

- *Universe*: The universe category contains free software that is not officially supported. You can use it, and it is likely to work without problems, but you won't be able to get support from Canonical for software components in this category.

- *Multiverse*: The multiverse component contains unsupported software that falls under license restrictions that are not considered free.

- *Backports*: In this category, you'll find bleeding-edge software. If you want to work with the latest software available, you should definitely get it here. Never use it if your goal is to install a stable server.

When installing software with the apt-get utility, it will look for installation sources in the configuration file /etc/apt/sources.list. Listing 8-8 shows a part of its contents.

Listing 8-8. Definition of Installation Sources in sources.list

```
root@ubuntu:~# cat /etc/apt/sources.list
#

# deb cdrom:[Ubuntu-Server 14.04.2 LTS _Trusty Tahr_ - Release amd64 (20150218.1)]/ trusty
main restricted

#deb cdrom:[Ubuntu-Server 14.04.2 LTS _Trusty Tahr_ - Release amd64 (20150218.1)]/ trusty
main restricted

# See http://help.ubuntu.com/community/UpgradeNotes for how to upgrade to
# newer versions of the distribution.
deb http://us.archive.ubuntu.com/ubuntu/ trusty main restricted
deb-src http://us.archive.ubuntu.com/ubuntu/ trusty main restricted

## Major bug fix updates produced after the final release of the
## distribution.
deb http://us.archive.ubuntu.com/ubuntu/ trusty-updates main restricted
deb-src http://us.archive.ubuntu.com/ubuntu/ trusty-updates main restricted

## N.B. software from this repository is ENTIRELY UNSUPPORTED by the Ubuntu
## team. Also, please note that software in universe WILL NOT receive any
## review or updates from the Ubuntu security team.
deb http://us.archive.ubuntu.com/ubuntu/ trusty universe
deb-src http://us.archive.ubuntu.com/ubuntu/ trusty universe
deb http://us.archive.ubuntu.com/ubuntu/ trusty-updates universe
deb-src http://us.archive.ubuntu.com/ubuntu/ trusty-updates universe

## N.B. software from this repository is ENTIRELY UNSUPPORTED by the Ubuntu
## team, and may not be under a free licence. Please satisfy yourself as to
## your rights to use the software. Also, please note that software in
## multiverse WILL NOT receive any review or updates from the Ubuntu
## security team.
deb http://us.archive.ubuntu.com/ubuntu/ trusty multiverse
deb-src http://us.archive.ubuntu.com/ubuntu/ trusty multiverse
deb http://us.archive.ubuntu.com/ubuntu/ trusty-updates multiverse
deb-src http://us.archive.ubuntu.com/ubuntu/ trusty-updates multiverse

## N.B. software from this repository may not have been tested as
## extensively as that contained in the main release, although it includes
## newer versions of some applications which may provide useful features.
## Also, please note that software in backports WILL NOT receive any review
## or updates from the Ubuntu security team.
deb http://us.archive.ubuntu.com/ubuntu/ trusty-backports main restricted universe multiverse
deb-src http://us.archive.ubuntu.com/ubuntu/ trusty-backports main restricted universe
multiverse
```

```
deb http://security.ubuntu.com/ubuntu trusty-security main restricted
deb-src http://security.ubuntu.com/ubuntu trusty-security main restricted
deb http://security.ubuntu.com/ubuntu trusty-security universe
deb-src http://security.ubuntu.com/ubuntu trusty-security universe
deb http://security.ubuntu.com/ubuntu trusty-security multiverse
deb-src http://security.ubuntu.com/ubuntu trusty-security multiverse
```

you can see, the same format is used in all lines of the sources.list file. The first field in these lines specifies the package format to be used. Two different package formats are used by default: .deb for binary packages (basically precompiled program files) and .deb-src for packages in source file format. Next, the URI is mentioned. This typically is an HTTP or FTP URL, but it can be something else as well. For instance, it can refer to installation files that you have on an installation CD or in a directory on your computer. After that you'll see the name of the distribution (trusty), and you'll always see the current distribution version there. Last, every line refers to the available package categories. As you can see, most package categories are in the list by default.

Now that you understand how the sources.list file is organized, it follows almost automatically what should happen if you want to add some additional installation sources to this list: make sure that all required components are specified in a line, and add any line you like referring to an additional installation source. Once an additional installation source has been added, it will be automatically checked when working on software packages. For example, if you should use the apt-get update command to update the current state of your system, the package manager will check your new installation sources as well.

■ **Tip!** In some cases you may want to add your own repository. This is useful if you have a couple of .deb files and want to make them accessible for installation to user computers. Doing so is a simple 3-step procedure. Start by creating the directory and putting the .deb files in that directory. Next, you'll run the dpkg-scanpackages command to create the repository metadata. As the last step, add the newly created repository to the sources.list files on all computers that need to use it.

A second important management component used by package managers on your computer is the package database. The most fundamental package database is the dpkg database, which is managed by the Debian utility dpkg. On Ubuntu as well as Debian, however, the Advanced Packaging Tools (apt) set is used for package management. These Ubuntu tools add functionality to package management that the traditional dpkg approach typically cannot offer. Because of this added functionality, the apt tools use their own database, which is stored in /var/lib/apt. By communicating with this database, the package manager can query the system for installed software, and this enables your server to automatically solve package-dependency problems.

■ **Tip!** To summarize it briefly: if you want to install software or manage installed software packages, use **apt** which talks to the apt database. If you want to query installed packages, use **dpkg**.

Every time a package is installed, a list of all installed files is added to the package database. By using this database, the package manager can even see whether certain configuration files have been changed, which is very important if you want to update packages at your server!

Ubuntu Package Management Utilities

You can use any of several command-line package management utilities on Ubuntu. The most important of these interact directly with the package database in /var/lib/apt. You would typically use the apt-get command for installation, updates, and removal of packages, and so you'll find yourself working with that utility most of the time. You should also know of the aptitude utility, which works in two ways. You can use aptitude as a command-line utility to query your server for installed packages, but aptitude also has a menu-driven interface that offers an intuitive way to manage packages (see Figure 8-1).

Figure 8-1. *The aptitude menu drive interface makes package management easier*

Another approach to managing packages is the Debian way. Because Ubuntu package management is based on Debian package management, you can use Debian package management tools like dpkg as well. However, these do not really add anything to what Ubuntu package management already offers, and so I will not cover the Debian tools in this book.

Understanding apt

Before you start working on packages in Ubuntu, it is a good idea to decide what tool you want to use. It's a good idea because many tools are available for Ubuntu, and each of them uses its own database to keep track of everything installed. To prevent inconsistencies in software packages, it's best to choose your favorite utility and stick to that. In this book, I'll focus on the apt-get utility, which keeps its database in the /var/lib/apt directory. This is my favorite utility because you can run apt-get as a very easy and convenient tool from the command line to perform tasks very quickly. The apt-get utility works with commands that are used as its argument, such as apt-get install *something*. In this example, install is the command you use to tell apt-get what you really want to do. Likewise, you can use some other apt-get commands. The following four commands are the most important building blocks when working with apt-get:

- update: This is the first command you want to use when working with apt-get. It updates the list of packages that are available for installation. Use it to make sure that you install the most recent version of a package.

- upgrade: Use this command to perform an upgrade of your server's software packages.

- install: This is the command you want to use every time you install software. It's rather intuitive. For example, if you want to install the nmap software package, you would just type apt-get install nmap.

- remove: You've probably guessed already, but you'll use this one to remove installed packages from your system.

Notice that you can use many package management operations using the apt-get command. You can not use it to search for specific packages though. To do this, you'll use the **apt-cache search** command. In exercise 8-4 you'll use this command.

EXERCISE 8-4: WORKING WITH APT-GET

In this exercise you'll learn how to work with apt-get. Notice that this exercise will only work on Ubuntu and related Linux distributions.

1. Open a shell on your Ubuntu system.

2. Type **sudo cat /etc/apt/sources.list.** This shows the list of repositories that currently are being used.

3. Type **sudo apt-get update**. This downloads the latest package index files from the repositories, which allows you to compare currently installed packages with the packages that are available in the repositories.

4. Type **sudo apt-cache search nmap**. The apt-cache command allows you to search the current index files for the availability of packages.

5. Type **sudo apt-get install nmap** to install the nmap package.

6. Type **sudo apt-get upgrade** to upgrade all packages to the latest version.

Showing a List of Installed Packages

Before you start managing packages on Ubuntu Server, you probably want to know what packages are already installed, and you can do this by issuing the dpkg -l command. It'll generate a long list of installed packages. Listing 8-9 shows a partial result of this command.

■ **Note** The apt-get utility is not the most appropriate way to list installed packages because it can see only those packages that are installed with apt. If you have installed a package with dpkg (which I would not recommend), you won't see it with apt-get. So, to make sure that you don't miss any packages, I recommend using dpkg -l to get a list of all installed packages.

Listing 8-9. The dpkg -l Command Shows Information About Installed Packages

```
root@ubuntu:~# dpkg -l | head
Desired=Unknown/Install/Remove/Purge/Hold
| Status=Not/Inst/Conf-files/Unpacked/halF-conf/Half-inst/trig-aWait/Trig-pend
|/ Err?=(none)/Reinst-required (Status,Err: uppercase=bad)
||/ Name               Version              Architecture Description
+++-==================-====================-============-====================================
ii  accountsservice 0.6.35-0ubuntu7.1     amd64        query and manipulate user account
                                                        information
ii  acpid           1:2.0.21-1ubuntu2     amd64        Advanced Configuration and Power
                                                        Interface event daemon
ii  adduser         3.113+nmu3ubuntu3     all          add and remove users and groups
ii  apparmor        2.8.95~2430-0ubuntu5.1 amd64       User-space parser utility for
                                                        AppArmor
ii  apport          2.14.1-0ubuntu3.7     all          automatically generate crash reports
                                                        for debugging
```

The result of the dpkg command shows information about packages and their status. The first character of the package shows the desired status for a package, and this status indicates what should happen to the package. The following status indicators are used:

- i: You'll see this option in most cases, indicating that the package should be installed.

- h: This option (for "hold") indicates that the package cannot be modified.

- p: This option indicates that the package should be purged.

- r: This option indicates that the package is supposed to be removed without removing associated configuration files.

- u: This option indicates that the current desired status is unknown.

The second character reveals the actual state of the package. You'll find the following options:

- I: The package is installed.

- c: Configuration files of the package are installed, but the package itself is not.

- f: The package is not guaranteed to be correctly installed.

- h: The package is partially installed.

- n: The package is not installed.

- u: The package did install, but the installation was not finalized because the configuration script was not successfully completed.

The third character indicates any known error state associated with the package. In most cases you'll just see a space (so, basically, you don't see anything at all) indicating that nothing is wrong. Other options are as follows:

- H: The package is put on hold by the package management system. This means that dependency problems were encountered, in which case some required packages are not installed.

- R: Reinstallation of the package is required.

- X: The package requires reinstallation and has been put on hold.

You can also use the dpkg utility to find out what package owns a certain file. This is very useful information. Imagine that a file is broken and you need to refresh the package's installation. To find out what package owns a file, use dpkg --search /your/file. The command will immediately return the name of the package that owns this file.

Using aptitude

On Ubuntu, a few solutions are available for package management. One of these is aptitude. The major benefit of this solution is that it is somewhat more user friendly because it can work with keywords, which are words that occur somewhere in the description of the package. For example, to get a list of all packages that have samba (the name of the well-known Linux file server package that you can use to provide Windows file services on your Linux computer) in their description, you would use aptitude search samba. Listing 8-10 shows the result of this command.

Listing 8-10. Showing Package Status Based on Keywords

```
sander@mel:~$ aptitude search samba
[sudo] password for sander:
p   dpsyco-samba           - Automate administration of access to samba
p   ebox-samba             - ebox - File sharing
p   egroupware-sambaadmin - eGroupWare Samba administration applicatio
p   gsambad                - GTK+ configuration tool for samba
p   samba                  - a LanManager-like file and printer server
v   samba-client           -
p   samba-common           - Samba common files used by both the server
p   samba-dbg              - Samba debugging symbols
p   samba-doc              - Samba documentation
p   samba-doc-pdf          - Samba documentation (PDF format)
p   system-config-samba    - GUI for managing samba shares and users
```

Once you have found a package using the aptitude command, you can also use it to show information about the package. To do this, you'll use the show argument. For example, aptitude show samba will show you exactly what the package samba is all about (see Listing 8-11). As you can see, in some cases very useful information is displayed, including a list of dependencies that shows all packages that need to be installed if you want to use this package.

Listing 8-11. The aptitude show Command Shows What Is Offered by a Package

```
root@ubuntu:~# aptitude show samba
Package: samba
State: not installed
Version: 2:4.1.6+dfsg-1ubuntu2.14.04.9
Priority: optional
Section: net
Maintainer: Ubuntu Developers <ubuntu-devel-discuss@lists.ubuntu.com>
Architecture: amd64
Uncompressed Size: 11.4 M
Depends: adduser, heimdal-hdb-api-8, libpam-modules, libpam-runtime
         (>=1.0.1-11), lsb-base (>= 4.1+Debian), procps, python (>= 2.7),
         python-dnspython, python-ntdb, python-samba, samba-common
         (=2:4.1.6+dfsg-1ubuntu2.14.04.9), samba-common-bin
         (=2:4.1.6+dfsg-1ubuntu2.14.04.9), samba-dsdb-modules, tdb-tools,
         update-inetd, sysv-rc (>= 2.88dsf-24) | file-rc (>= 0.8.16), python
         (<2.8), python2.7:any, libasn1-8-heimdal (>= 1.4.0+git20110226), libbsd0
         (>= 0.5.0), libc6 (>= 2.14), libcomerr2 (>= 1.01), libhdb9-heimdal
         (>=1.4.0+git20110226), libkdc2-heimdal (>= 1.4.0+git20110226),
         libkrb5-26-heimdal (>= 1.4.0+git20110226), libldb1 (>= 0.9.21),
         libpopt0 (>= 1.14), libpython2.7 (>= 2.7), libroken18-heimdal
         (>=1.4.0+git20110226), libtalloc2 (>= 2.0.4~git20101213), libtdb1
         (>=1.2.7+git20101214), libtevent0 (>= 0.9.14), samba-libs
         (=2:4.1.6+dfsg-1ubuntu2.14.04.9)
PreDepends: dpkg (>= 1.15.6~), multiarch-support
Recommends: attr, logrotate, samba-vfs-modules
Suggests: bind9 (>= 1:9.5.1), bind9utils, ldb-tools, ntp, smbldap-tools,
         winbind, ufw
Conflicts: libldb1 (< 1:1.1.15), libldb1 (< 1:1.1.15), samba (< 2:3.3.0~rc2-5),
         samba (< 2:3.3.0~rc2-5), samba-ad-dc, samba-ad-dc, samba-doc
         (<2:4.0.5~), samba-doc (< 2:4.0.5~), samba-tools, samba-tools, samba4
         (< 4.0.0~alpha6-2), samba4 (< 4.0.0~alpha6-2), samba
Replaces: libsamdb0 (< 4.0.0~alpha17~), libsamdb0 (< 4.0.0~alpha17~),
         python-samba (< 2:4.1.4+dfsg-3), python-samba (< 2:4.1.4+dfsg-3),
         samba-ad-dc, samba-ad-dc, samba-common (<= 2.0.5a-2), samba-common
         (<=2.0.5a-2), samba-doc (< 2:4.0.5~), samba-doc (< 2:4.0.5~), samba-libs
         (< 2:4.1.4+dfsg-2), samba-libs (< 2:4.1.4+dfsg-2), samba4, samba4
Enhances: bind9, ntp
Description: SMB/CIFS file, print, and login server for Unix
 Samba is an implementation of the SMB/CIFS protocol for Unix systems, providing
 support for cross-platform file and printer sharing with Microsoft Windows,
 OS X, and other Unix systems.  Samba can also function as an NT4-style domain
 controller, and can integrate with both NT4 domains and Active Directory realms
 as a member server.
```

This package provides the components necessary to use Samba as a stand-alone file and print server or as an NT4 or Active Directory domain controller. For use in an NT4 domain or Active Directory realm, you will also need the winbind package.

This package is not required for connecting to existing SMB/CIFS servers (see smbclient) or for mounting remote filesystems (see cifs-utils). Homepage: http://www.samba.org.

Adding and Removing Software with `apt-get`

The best tool for Ubuntu and Debian to perform package management from the command line is apt-get. It provides a very convenient way to install, update, or remove software packages on your machine. It requires root permissions, so you should always start the command with sudo.

Before you do anything with apt-get, you should always use the apt-get update command first. Because apt-get gets most software packages online, it should always know about the latest available versions of those packages. The apt-get update command makes sure of this, and it caches a list of the most recent version of packages that are available on your server. Once the update is performed, you can use apt-get to install and remove software. Installation is rather easy: to install the package blah, use apt-get install blah. The advantage of the apt-get command is that it really tries to understand what you are doing. This is shown in Listing 8-12, where the apt-get command is used to install the Samba server software.

Listing 8-12. The apt-get Command Tries to Understand What You Want to Do

```
root@ubuntu:~# apt-get install samba
Reading package lists... Done
Building dependency tree
Reading state information... Done
The following extra packages will be installed:
  attr libaio1 libavahi-client3 libavahi-common-data libavahi-common3 libcups2
  libfile-copy-recursive-perl libhdb9-heimdal libkdc2-heimdal libldb1 libntdb1
  libtalloc2 libtdb1 libtevent0 libwbclient0 python-crypto python-dnspython
  python-ldb python-ntdb python-samba python-talloc python-tdb samba-common
  samba-common-bin samba-dsdb-modules samba-libs samba-vfs-modules tdb-tools
  update-inetd
Suggested packages:
  cups-common python-crypto-dbg python-crypto-doc bind9 bind9utils ldb-tools
  ntp smbldap-tools winbind heimdal-clients
The following NEW packages will be installed:
  attr libaio1 libavahi-client3 libavahi-common-data libavahi-common3 libcups2
  libfile-copy-recursive-perl libhdb9-heimdal libkdc2-heimdal libldb1 libntdb1
  libtalloc2 libtdb1 libtevent0 libwbclient0 python-crypto python-dnspython
  python-ldb python-ntdb python-samba python-talloc python-tdb samba
  samba-common samba-common-bin samba-dsdb-modules samba-libs
  samba-vfs-modules tdb-tools update-inetd
0 upgraded, 30 newly installed, 0 to remove and 128 not upgraded.
Need to get 8,026 kB of archives.
After this operation, 46.0 MB of additional disk space will be used.
Do you want to continue? [Y/n]
```

In the example from Listing 8-12, everything went all right because a package with the name samba exists. In some cases, you'll see that apt-get doesn't understand what you want it to do. If that happens, it sometimes gives a hint on the package that you need to install instead. If that doesn't happen either, try to search the appropriate package first, using the aptitude search command.

You can also use apt-get to remove software, upgrade your system, and much more. The following list provides an overview of the most important functions of the apt-get command. Be aware that you should always run the command with root permissions, so use sudo to start apt-get (or set a root password and work as root directly).

- *Install software*: Use sudo apt-get install package.

- *Remove software*: Use sudo apt-get remove package. This option does not remove configuration files. If you need to remove those as well, use sudo apt-get remove --purge package.

- *Upgrade software*: To upgrade your complete operating system, use sudo apt-get update first so that you're sure that apt-get is aware of the most recent version of the packages. Then use sudo apt-get dist-upgrade.

Summary

In this chapter, you have read how to manage software packages. You have learned that software packages can be installed as individual packages, but because of dependencies, this is not a very good idea. Therefore, all distributions currently work with a package management solution where the software repository is used to list installable packages and an intelligent command is used to manage packages as well as their dependencies. You have read how to manage packages from the RPM world with the yum and zypper commands, as well as packages from the Debian world with the apt commands. The following commands and utilities were discussed in this chapter:

- rpm: Command to create and manage RPM-based packages.

- yum: Package management utility in the Red Hat world.

- yumdownloader: Allows you to download packages from a repository to your system without installing them.

- zypper: Package management utility in the SUSE works. Works more or less the same as yum.

- apt-get: Ubuntu/Debian package management utility. Does a great job in installing and updating software.

- apt-cache: Tool that allows you to search for pacakges in the locally cached index files

- dpkg: Original Debian package management utility, which has been made more or less obsolete by apt-get. Still, dpkg is useful, especially for listing where the files from a package are installed.

- dpkg-scanpackages: Tool that allows you to convert a directory containing .deb packages into a repository.

- aptitude: Alternative for apt-get. According to some, this utility is easier to use.

In the next chapter, you'll learn how to manage processes on your Linux computer.

CHAPTER 9

■ ■ ■

Process and System Management

When working with Linux, from an administrative perspective, working with processes is important. Every application or task you start on a Linux computer is started as a process. You will find that in some instances, a task may hang, or something else may happen that urges you to do some process management. In this chapter, you will learn how to monitor and manage processes. You will also learn how to schedule processes for automatic startup.

Understanding Linux Processes

When your computer boots, it will start a kernel. The *kernel* on its turn is responsible for starting the first process, which on modern distributions is the systemd process. This process is responsible for all other processes. When starting a process, systemd starts the process as a child of its own. If for instance you're working from a bash session in a GNOME graphical environment, systemd starts gnome-terminal, and from there bash is started. To gnome-terminal is the parent process for bash, adnd systemd is its grandparent.

To get an overview of the relations between parent and child processes, you can use the pstree command, of which partial output is shown in listing 9-1.

Listing 9-1. pstree Shows the Parent-Child Relation Between Processes

```
systemd-+-ModemManager---2*[{ModemManager}]
        |-NetworkManager---3*[{NetworkManager}]
        |-2*[abrt-watch-log]
        |-abrtd
        |-accounts-daemon---2*[{accounts-daemon}]
        |-alsactl
        |-at-spi-bus-laun-+-dbus-daemon---{dbus-daemon}
        |                 `-3*[{at-spi-bus-laun}]
        |-at-spi2-registr---{at-spi2-registr}
        |-atd
        |-auditd-+-audispd-+-sedispatch
        |        |         `-{audispd}
        |        `-{auditd}
        |-avahi-daemon---avahi-daemon
        |-bluetoothd
        |-chronyd
        |-colord---2*[{colord}]
        |-crond
        |-cupsd
```

```
|-2*[dbus-daemon---{dbus-daemon}]
|-dbus-launch
|-dconf-service---2*[{dconf-service}]
|-evolution-addre---4*[{evolution-addre}]T
```

o run a process, the Linux kernel works with a queue of runnable processes. In this queue, every process waits for its turn to be serviced by the scheduler. By default, Linux works with time slices for process handling. This means that every process gets a fair amount of system time before it has to make place for other processes. If a process needs more attention, you can use the nice function to increase (or decrease if necessary) the system time that is granted to the process. More on using nice on processes later in this chapter.

In some situations, you will have to stop a process yourself. This may happen if the process doesn't reply anymore, or if the process behaves in a way that harms other processes. To stop a process, the Linux kernel will tell the responsible parent process that this process needs to be stopped. Under normal circumstances, the parent process that was responsible for starting a given process will always be present until all its children are stopped.

In the abnormal situation where the child is still there, but the parent is already stopped, the child process cannot be stopped anymore, and it becomes a zombie. From the command line there is nothing that you can do to stop a zombie process; the only solution is to restart your computer.

You will find that if zombie processes occur, often the same processes are involved. That is because the occurrence of zombie processes is often due to bad programming. So you may have to update the software that creates the zombie process to get finally rid of your zombie processes. In the following sections, you will learn how to monitor and manage processes.

Apart from zombie status, processes can be in other states as well. You can see these states when using the ps aux command, which shows current process status; these are displayed in the STAT column (see Listing 9-2). Processes can be in the following states:

- *Running*: The process is active.

- *Sleeping*: The process is loaded in memory but hasn't been active recently.

- *Zombie*: The process is in defunctional state.

- *Stopped*: The process is stopped by a user that has used the Ctrl-Z command - it can be started again using the **fg** command.

Listing 9-2. Processes Can Be In Different States

```
USER     PID %CPU %MEM    VSZ   RSS TTY    STAT START    TIME COMMAND
root       1  0.0  0.4  59732  4984 ?      Ss   07:29    0:02 /usr/lib/systemd/systemd
                                                               --switched-root --system
                                                               --deserialize 24
root       2  0.0  0.0      0     0 ?      S    07:29    0:00 [kthreadd]
root       3  0.0  0.0      0     0 ?      S    07:29    0:00 [ksoftirqd/0]
root       5  0.0  0.0      0     0 ?      S<   07:29    0:00 [kworker/0:0H]
root       7  0.0  0.0      0     0 ?      S    07:29    0:00 [migration/0]
root       8  0.0  0.0      0     0 ?      S    07:29    0:00 [rcu_bh]
root       9  0.0  0.0      0     0 ?      S    07:29    0:00 [rcuob/0]
root      10  0.0  0.0      0     0 ?      S    07:29    0:00 [rcuob/1]
root      11  0.0  0.0      0     0 ?      S    07:29    0:00 [rcuob/2]

[root@workstation ~]#
```

You should know that there a different kinds of processes. Among these are the service processes, the so-called daemons. An example is the httpd process, which provides web services on your system. Daemon processes are automatically started when your server boots and systemd is entering a specific *target*. A systemd target defines the state a system should be in, and the processes and services tahat should be started to get into that state. On the flip side are the interactive processes, which typically are started by typing some command at the command line of your computer.

Finally, there are two ways in which a process can do its work to handle multiple tasks. First, it can just launch a new instance of the same process to handle the incoming request. If this is the case, you will see the same process listed multiple times in ps aux. The alternative is that the process works with one master process only, but launches a thread, which is a kind of a subprocess, for each new request that comes in. Currently, processes tend to be multithreaded, as this uses system resources more efficiently. For a Linux administrator, managing a multi-threaded process is a bit more challenging. Threads are managed from the master process itself, and not by an administrator who's trying to manipulate them from the command line.

Monitoring Processes

All work on processes that you'll need to do will start by monitoring what the process is doing. Two commands are particularly important: top and ps. The ps command allows you to display a list of all processes that are running on your computer. Because ps lists all processes (when used as root), that makes it an excellent choice if you need to find a given process to perform management tasks on it. The top command gives an overview of the most active processes.

This overview is refreshed every 5 seconds by default. As it also offers you a possibility to perform management tasks on these active processes, top is a very useful command for process management, especially for users who are taking their first steps on the Linux command line.

Monitoring Processes with top

The single most useful utility for process management is top. You can start it by typing the top command at the command line. Make sure that you have root permissions when doing this; otherwise, you can't do process management. In Listing 9-3, you can see what the top screen looks like.

Listing 9-3. top Makes Process Management Easy

```
top - 10:22:12 up  2:52,  3 users,  load average: 0.00, 0.01, 0.05
Tasks: 290 total,   2 running, 288 sleeping,   0 stopped,   0 zombie
%Cpu(s):  0.3 us,  0.0 sy,  0.0 ni, 99.7 id,  0.0 wa,  0.0 hi,  0.0 si,  0.0 st
KiB Mem :  1010336 total,   122568 free,   566424 used,   321344 buff/cache
KiB Swap:  1048572 total,  1041076 free,     7496 used.   253484 avail Mem

  PID USER      PR  NI    VIRT    RES    SHR S %CPU %MEM     TIME+ COMMAND
  772 root      20   0  268820   3160   2308 S  0.3  0.3   0:09.78 vmtoolsd
  804 root      20   0  550176  16596   4084 S  0.3  1.6   0:01.40 tuned
    1 root      20   0   59732   4988   2768 S  0.0  0.5   0:02.67 systemd
    2 root      20   0       0      0      0 S  0.0  0.0   0:00.02 kthreadd
    3 root      20   0       0      0      0 S  0.0  0.0   0:00.12 ksoftirqd/0
    5 root       0 -20       0      0      0 S  0.0  0.0   0:00.00 kworker/0:0H
    7 root      rt   0       0      0      0 S  0.0  0.0   0:00.00 migration/0
```

```
 8 root      20   0        0        0      0 S   0.0   0.0   0:00.00 rcu_bh
 9 root      20   0        0        0      0 S   0.0   0.0   0:00.00 rcuob/0
10 root      20   0        0        0      0 S   0.0   0.0   0:00.00 rcuob/1
11 root      20   0        0        0      0 S   0.0   0.0   0:00.00 rcuob/2
12 root      20   0        0        0      0 S   0.0   0.0   0:00.00 rcuob/3
13 root      20   0        0        0      0 S   0.0   0.0   0:00.00 rcuob/4
14 root      20   0        0        0      0 S   0.0   0.0   0:00.00 rcuob/5
15 root      20   0        0        0      0 S   0.0   0.0   0:00.00 rcuob/6
16 root      20   0        0        0      0 S   0.0   0.0   0:00.00 rcuob/7
17 root      20   0        0        0      0 S   0.0   0.0   0:00.00 rcuob/8
```

top basically shows you all you need to know about the current status of your system, and it refreshes its output every 5 seconds by default. Its results are divided in two parts. On the top part of the output window, you can see how busy your system is; in the lower part, you'll see a list of the busiest processes your computer currently has.

The upper five lines of the top output (see Listing 9-3) shows you what your system currently is doing. This information can be divided into a few categories:

- *Data about uptime and users*: On the first line, top shows you the current time (10.22 in this example), which is followed by the time the system has been up and the number of users connected to the system. Although useful, this is not critical information for process management.

- *Current usage statistics*: Still on the first line, there are three numbers related to current system usage. These three numbers indicate how busy your computer is relative to the amount of CPUs or CPU cores in your computer (from the perspective of top, there is no difference between a CPU and a CPU core): they give you the average for the last minute, the last 5 minutes, and the last 15 minutes.

- The numbers give an overview of the average amount of processes that has been waiting to get services in the indicated period. In general, the number that you see here shouldn't be superior to the number of CPU cores in your computer (but exceptions to this generic guideline do exist).

- *Overview of tasks*: The second line of top shows you information about the total number of tasks and their current status. On an average computer, you won't see many more than about 200 tasks here, but specific workloads may have a much higher or lower amount of processes being active. The following status information for these tasks is displayed:

  - *Running*: These are tasks that have been actively serviced during the last polling loop.

  - *Sleeping*: These are tasks that have not been active in the last polling loop.

  - *Stopped*: These are tasks that are stopped using the Ctrl-Z key stroke.

  - *Zombie*: These are tasks of which the parent no longer is available and hence cannot be stopped or managed anymore.

- *Overview of CPU usage*: If the load average of your computer is relatively high, the CPU usage line can give an indication of exactly what your computer is doing. In this line, a subdivision is made of the different kinds of demands that processes are issuing on your CPU. On a multi-CPU system, you'll see the summary for all CPUs together. If you want to see the load statistics for each of the CPUs from the top interface, press 1. The following options are listed:

  - us: The amount of load that was issued in user space. These typically are tasks that run without root privileges and cannot access kernel functions directly.

  - sy: The amount of load that was issued in system space. These typically are tasks that were started with root privileges and can access kernel functions directly. As compared to user space–level tasks, the number of tasks that you see here should be relatively low on most systems, but exceptions do exist.

  - ni: Processes of which the priority has been adjusted using nice.

  - id: The activity of the idle loop. This gives the percentage of inactivity on your system. It is no problem at all if this parameter is high.

  - wa: The amount of time that your system has spent in waiting mode. This is the time that your system has been waiting for I/O. If you see a high value here, it indicates that you have a lot of I/O-related tasks on your computer and that the storage in your computer cannot deal with it efficiently. An average that is higher than 30% may indicate that your I/O channel doesn't perform as it should.

  - hi: The amount of time that your computer has spent handling hardware interrupts. It should be low at all times. If you see a high value here, it often indicates that some badly functioning drivers are used.

  - si: The amount of time that your system has spent handling software interrupts.

  - st: This parameter applies to environments where virtualization is used. It indicates the amount of time that was stolen from the processor in this machine by other virtual machines.

- *Current memory use*: In the last part of the upper lines of top output, you can see information about the amount of memory your computer is using. These two lines give information about the usage of real memory and swap memory, which is emulated memory on the hard disk of your computer, at the same time. The following parameters are listed:

  - KiB Mem total: the total amount of memory in Kilobytes that is available as physical installed RAM

  - free: the amount of memory that currently isn't used for anything.

  - used: the amount of memory that has been allocated by programs and services running on your computer.

  - buff/cache: the amount of memory that is being used to cache read and write requests.This is memory that the Linux kernel can make available for other tasks in case this is needed.

  - KiB Swap total: The total amount of swap memory that is available

- free: The amount of swap that is not being used

- used: The amount of swap that currently has been allocated

- avail Mem: The total amount of memory that is available. This amount consist of the amount that is listed as free, with in addition the amount of memory that can be freed immediately by liberating unneccessary buffer and cache memory.

The lower part of the top output shows you process information, divided in a couple of columns that are displayed by default. You should know that more columns are available than the ones displayed by default. If you want to activate the display of other columns, you should press the F key while in the top screen. This shows you a list of all columns that are available, indicating with an * which are currently active, as you can see in Listing 9-4. To toggle the status of a column, press the letter associated with that column. For instance, pressing J will show you which CPU was last used by a process.

Listing 9-4. You Can Toggle Other Columns to Be Displayed As Well in top

```
Fields Management for window 1:Def, whose current sort field is %CPU
    Navigate with Up/Dn, Right selects for move then <Enter> or Left commits,
    'd' or <Space> toggles display, 's' sets sort.  Use 'q' or <Esc> to end!

* PID     = Process Id       PGRP    = Process Group   vMj     = Major Faults
* USER    = Effective Use    TTY     = Controlling T   vMn     = Minor Faults
* PR      = Priority         TPGID   = Tty Process G   USED    = Res+Swap Size
* NI      = Nice Value       SID     = Session Id      nsIPC   = IPC namespace
* VIRT    = Virtual Image    nTH     = Number of Thr   nsMNT   = MNT namespace
* RES     = Resident Size    P       = Last Used Cpu   nsNET   = NET namespace
* SHR     = Shared Memory    TIME    = CPU Time        nsPID   = PID namespace
* S       = Process Statu    SWAP    = Swapped Size    nsUSER  = USER namespac
* %CPU    = CPU Usage        CODE    = Code Size (Ki   nsUTS   = UTS namespace
* %MEM    = Memory Usage     DATA    = Data+Stack (K
* TIME+   = CPU Time, hun    nMaj    = Major Page Fa
* COMMAND = Command Name/    nMin    = Minor Page Fa
  PPID    = Parent Proces    nDRT    = Dirty Pages C
  UID     = Effective Use    WCHAN   = Sleeping in F
  RUID    = Real User Id     Flags   = Task Flags <s
  RUSER   = Real User Nam    CGROUPS = Control Group
  SUID    = Saved User Id    SUPGIDS = Supp Groups I
  SUSER   = Saved User Na    SUPGRPS = Supp Groups N
  GID     = Group Id         TGID    = Thread Group
  GROUP   = Group Name       ENVIRON = Environment v
```

The following list describes the columns that are listed by default:

- PID: This is the process identification (PID) number of the process. Every process has a unique PID, and you will need this PID number to manage the process.

- USER: This indicates the name of the user who started the process.

- PR: This indicates the current process priority. Processes with a higher priority (which is expressed with a lower number!) will be serviced before processes with a lower priority. If a process with a higher priority needs CPU time, it will always be handled before the process that has a lower priority. Some processes have the RT (real time) priority, which means that they can access system resources at all times.

- NI: Between processes that have the same priority, the nice value indicates which has precedence. Processes with a low nice value are not so very nice and will always go before processes with a high nice value. However, this works only for processes that have the same priority.

- VIRT: This column refers to the total amount of memory that is allocated by a process. The amount that is mentioned here is just a reservation of an address range and doesn't refer to any physically used memory. All processes on Linux can make virtual memory reservations from a total address space of 32 TB!

- RES: This column indicates the amount of resident memory, which is memory that the process has allocated and is currently also actively using. You may see differences between VIRT and RES because processes like to ask for more memory than they really need at the moment, which is referred to as memory over allocation.

- SHARE: This refers to shared memory. Typically, these are libraries the process uses that are used by other processes as well.

- S: This column gives the process status. The values that you find here are the same as the values in the second line of the top output, as discussed previously.

- %CPU: This column shows the percentage of CPU cycles that the process has been using. This is also the column that top sorts by default; the most active process is listed at the top of the list.

- %MEM: This column refers to the percentage of memory that the process is using.

- TIME: This indicates the accumulated real time that the process has used the CPU during the total period since it has started.

- COMMAND: This indicates the command that was used to start this process.

By default, top output is sorted on CPU usage. You can sort the output on any other information as well; there are over 20 different ways to do so. Some of my favorites are listed here:

- b: By process parent ID. This allows you to see in a quick overview all processes that are started by the same parent process.

- w: By process status. This allows you to group all processes that have the same status in an easy way.

- d: By UID. This allows you to see all processes that were started by the same user.

- h: By priority. This allows you to see processes with the highest priority listed on top.

- n: By memory usage. This shows the processes that have the largest amount of memory in use listed first.

When done monitoring process activity with top, you can exit the utility. To do this, issue the q command. Apart from the interactive mode that you've just read about, you can also use top in batch mode. This is useful if you want to redirect the output of top to a file or pipe it to some other command. When using top in batch mode, you can't use any of the commands discussed previously. You tell top to start in batch mode by passing some options to it when starting it:

- -b: Starts top in batch mode

- -d: Tells top what delay it should use between samples

- -n: Tells top how often it should produce its output in batch mode

For instance, the following would tell top to run in batch mode with a 5-second interval, doing its work two times:

```
top -b -d 5 -n 2
```

EXERCISE 9-1: MONITORING PROCESSES WITH TOP

In this exercise you'll start some processes and monitor behavior using top.

1. Type **dd if=/dev/zero of=/dev/null &**

2. Repeat step 1 three more times.

3. Observe system load in top. What numbers do you see in the load average indicators?

4. How much CPU load is currently happening on your servers?

5. Observe the idle loop, it should be next to 0.

6. Observe how the processes are equally using system resources.

7. From the top interface, type **r**. Next, enter the PID of one of the four dd processes, and enter the nice value -5. This should lower the amount of CPU time this processes is geting.

8. From the top interace, press **k**. Next, enter the PID of one of the four dd processes. This should remove the process from your system.

9. Repeat the procedure from step 8 to remove all other **dd** processes also.

Finding Processes with ps

If you want to manage processes from scripts in particular, the ps command is invaluable. This command shows you a list of all processes that are currently active on your computer. ps has many options, but most people use it in two ways only: ps aux and ps -ef. The value of ps is that it shows all processes in its output in a way that you can grep for the information you need. Imagine that you see in top that there is a zombie process; ps aux | grep defunc will show you which is the zombie process. Or imagine that you need the PIDs of all instances of your Apache web server; ps aux | grep httpd will give you the result.

One way of displaying all processes and their properties is by using ps aux. Listing 9-5 shows a part of the output of this command. To make it more readable I've piped the results of this command through less.

Listing 9-5. ps aux Shows All Processes and a Lot of Details About What the Processes Are Doing

```
nuuk:/ # ps aux | less
USER       PID %CPU  %MEM    VSZ    RSS TTY     STAT  START   TIME  COMMAND

Root       1    0.0   0:0    728    284  ?      S     Dec16   0:00  init [5]
Root       2    0.0   0.0    0      0    ?      SN    Dec16   0:00  [ksoftirqd/0]
Root       3    0.0   0.0    0      0    ?      S<    Dec16   0:00  [events/0]
Root       4    0.0   0.0    0      0    ?      S<    Dec16   0:00  [khelper]
root       5    0.0   0.0    0      0    ?      S<    Dec16   0:00  [kthread]
```

```
root       8    0.0    0.0    0        0    ?   S<   Dec16   0:00  [kblockd/0]
root       9    0.0    0.0    0        0    ?   S<   Dec16   0:00  [kacpid]
root      10    0.0    0.0    0        0    ?   S<   Dec16   0:00  [kacpi_notify]

root     110    0.0    0.0    0        0    ?   S    Dec16   0:00  [pdflush]
root     111    0.0    0.0    0        0    ?   S    Dec16   0:00  [pdflush]
root     112    0.0    0.0    0        0    ?   S    Dec16   0:00  [kswapd0]
root     113    0.0    0.0    0        0    ?   S<   Dec16   0:00  [aio/0]
root     320    0.0    0.0    0        0    ?   S<   Dec16   0:00  [cqueue/0]
root     321    0.0    0.0    0        0    ?   S<   Dec16   0:00  [kseriod]
root     365    0.0    0.0    0        0    ?   S<   Dec16   0:00  [kpsmoused]
root     723    0.0    0.0    0        0    ?   S<   Dec16   0:00  [scsi_eh_0]
root     833    0.0    0.0    0        0    ?   S<   Dec16   0:00  [ksnapd]
root     837    0.0    0.0    0        0    ?   S<   Dec16   0:00  [ata/0]
root     838    0.0    0.0    0        0    ?   S<   Dec16   0:00  [ata_aux]
root     895    0.0    0.0    0        0    ?   S    Dec16   0:00  [kjournald]
root     964    0.0    0.1    2408   684    ?   S<s  Dec16   0:00  /sbin/udevd --daemon
lines 1-22
```

In the command ps aux, three options are used to ask the system to show process information. First, the option a makes sure that all processes are shown. Next, the option u gives extended usage information, whereas the option x also shows from which TTY and by what user a process is started. You can see the results in Listing 9-5, in which the following columns are listed. Because many of these columns are similar to the columns in top, I will give a short description of them only.

- USER: The name of the user who started the process.

- PID: The PID of the process. The command ps aux sorts the processes by their PID.

- %CPU: The percentage of CPU time the process has used since startup.

- %MEM: The percentage of memory the process is currently using.

- VSZ: The virtual memory size, which is the total amount of memory claimed by this process.

- RSS: The resident memory size, which is the amount of memory the process currently has in use.

- TTY: The terminal (TTY) from which the process was started. A question mark indicates a daemon process that is not associated to any TTY.

- STAT: The current status of the process.

- START: The time at which the process was started.

- TIME: The total amount of system time this process has been using since it started.

- COMMAND: The command that was used to start this process. If the name of this command is between square brackets (you can see quite a few examples of this in Listing 9-5), the process is not started with a command at the command line, but is a kernel thread.

■ **Note** The ps command can be used in two ways, both of which go back to the time when there were two major styles in UNIX versions: the BSD style and the System V style. The command ps aux was used in the BSD style to give a list of all processes and their properties, and ps -ef was used in System V style to do basically the same. There are some minor differences, but basically both commands have the same result. So feel free to make your choice here!

The second way in which the ps command is often used is by issuing the ps -ef command. You can see a partial output of this command in Listing 9-6.

Listing 9-6. ps -ef Provides Just Another Way of Displaying Process Information

```
nuuk:~ # ps -ef | less
UID     PID PPID C STIME TTY     TIME CMD

root      1   0  0  Dec16    ?   00:00:00   init [5]
root      2   1  0  Dec16    ?   00:00:00   [ksoftirqd/0]
root      3   1  0  Dec16    ?   00:00:00   [events/0]
root      4   1  0  Dec16    ?   00:00:00   [khelper]
root      5   1  0  Dec16    ?   00:00:00   [kthread]
root      8   5  0  Dec16    ?   00:00:00   [kblockd/0]
root      9   5  0  Dec16    ?   00:00:00   [kacpid]
root     10   5  0  Dec16    ?   00:00:00   [kacpi_notify]
root    110   5  0  Dec16    ?   00:00:00   [pdflush]
root    111   5  0  Dec16    ?   00:00:00   [pdflush]
root    112   1  0  Dec16    ?   00:00:00   [kswapd0]
root    113   5  0  Dec16    ?   00:00:00   [aio/0]
root    320   5  0  Dec16    ?   00:00:00   [cqueue/0]
root    321   5  0  Dec16    ?   00:00:00   [kseriod]
root    365   5  0  Dec16    ?   00:00:00   [kpsmoused]
root    723   5  0  Dec16    ?   00:00:00   [scsi_eh_0]
root    833   5  0  Dec16    ?   00:00:00   [ksnapd]
root    837   5  0  Dec16    ?   00:00:00   [ata/0]
root    838   5  0  Dec16    ?   00:00:00   [ata_aux]
root    895   1  0  Dec16    ?   00:00:00   [kjournald]
root    964   1  0  Dec16    ?   00:00:00   /sbin/udevd --daemon
root   1530   5  0  Dec16    ?   00:00:00   [khubd]
lines 1-23
```

Just two columns in ps -ef are new compared to the output for ps aux. First is the PPID column. This column tells you which process was responsible for starting this process, the so-called parent process. Then there is the column with the name C, which refers to the CPU utilization of this process and hence gives the same information as the %CPU column in ps aux.

Personally, I like ps aux a lot if I need to terminate all processes that were started with the same command. On my SUSE box, it happens that the management program YaST crashes. This program basically uses two kinds of processes: processes that have yast in their command name and processes that have y2 in their command line. To get a list of PIDs for these processes, I use the following commands:

```
ps aux | grep yast | grep -v grep | awk '{ print $2 }' ps
aux | grep y2 | grep -v grep | awk '{ print $2 }'
```

Next, it is fairly easy to kill all instances of this process based on the list of PIDs that these two commands will show. You'll read more about this in the section "Killing Processes with kill, pkill, and killall" later in this chapter.

Another useful way of showing process activity with **ps**, is by using **ps fax**. The option **f** shows the process list in a forest view, which allows you to easily see relations between parent and child processes. This offers an alternative way of showing parent-child relations to the **pstree** command.

Finding PIDs with pgrep

In the preceding section, you read how you can find processes with ps and grep. There is a different option also: the pgrep command. This command is fairly easy to use: enter pgrep followed by the name of the process whose PID you are looking for, and as a result you will see all PIDs that instances of this process currently are using. For instance, if you want to know all PIDs that the Gnome processes are using, use pgrep gnome. This will display a result similar to what you see in Listing 9-7.

Listing 9-7. The pgrep Command Offers an Alternative If You Need to Find PIDs Easily

```
nuuk:~ # pgrep gnome 3781
3836
3840
3854
3860
3882
3889
3893
3921
3922
```

A useful feature of pgrep is that you can search for processes based on specific attributes as well. For instance, you can use -u to locate processes that are owned by a specific user, as in the following command:

```
pgrep -u linda
```

Also useful is that you can have it display processes if you are not sure about a property. For example, if you want to see processes that are owned by either linda or lori, use the following:

```
pgrep -u linda,lori
```

Showing Parent-Child Relations with pstree

For process management purposes, it is useful to know about parent-child relations between processes as well. You can use the pstree command without arguments to show a complete hierarchical list of all processes on your computer, or with a PID as an argument to show a process tree that starts on the selected PID only. If the output of pstree looks weird, you should use the -G option to give the result of pstree in a specific format for your terminal.

I need this to ensure proper display in a PuTTY window, for example. In Listing 9-8, you can see a partial output of this command.

Listing 9-8. Use pstree to Find Out More About the Hierarchical Relation Between Processes

```
nuuk:~ # pstree -G
ilulissat:~ # pstree -G
init---acpid
     |-application-bro
     |-auditd---{auditd}
     |-bonobo-activati
     |-cron
     |-cupsd
     |-2*[dbus-daemon]
     |-dbus-launch
     |-dhcpcd
     |-esd
     |-events/0
     |-events/1
     |-gconfd-2
     |-gdm---gdm---X
     |           |-gnome-session
     |-gnome-keyring-d
     |-gnome-panel
     |-gnome-power-man
     |-gnome-screensav
     |-gnome-settings---{gnome-settings-}
     |-gnome-terminal---bash
     |            |-gnome-pty-helpe
     |            |-{gnome-terminal}
     |-gnome-vfs-daemo---{gnome-vfs-daemo}
     |-gnome-volume-ma
     |-gpg-agent
     |-hald---hald-addon-acpi
     |           |-hald-addon-stor
     |-intlclock-apple
     |-irqbalance
     |-khelper
     |-kjournald
     |-klogd
     |-ksoftirqd/0
     |-ksoftirqd/1
     |-kswapd0
     |-kthread---aio/0
     |           |-aio/1
     |           |-ata/0
     |           |-ata/1
     |           |-ata_aux
     |           |-cqueue/0
     |           |-cqueue/1
     |           |-kacpi_notify
     |           |-kacpid
     |           |-kauditd
```

```
|         |-kblockd/0
|         |-kblockd/1
|         |-kgameportd
|         |-khubd
|         |-kpsmoused
|         |-kseriod
|         |-2*[pdflush]
|         |-scsi_eh_0
|-main-menu---{main-menu}
|-master---pickup
|         |-qmgr
|-metacity
|-migration/0
|-migration/1
|-6*[mingetty]
|-mixer_applet2
|-nautilus---3*[{nautilus}]
|-nscd---6*[{nscd}]
|-portmap
|-powersaved
|-resmgrd
|-shpchpd_event
|-slpd
|-sshd---sshd---bash---pstree
|-startpar
|-syslog-ng
|-udevd
|-zen-updater---6*[{zen-updater}]
|-zmd---13*[{zmd}]
```

In the output of pstree, you can see which process is responsible for calling which other process. For instance, in Listing 9-8, init is the first process that is started. The output of this command is generated on an older Linux distribution, where init was used as the service manager instead of the more recent systemd.

This process calls basically all the other processes such as acpid, application-bro, and so on. If a process has started other processes, you will see that with pstree as well. For instance, you can see that the pstree command used for this example listing actually is in the output listing as well, as a child of the bash process, which on its turn is started from an SSH environment.

■ **Note** Some people like to run a graphical user interface on their server; some people don't. From the process perspective, it certainly makes sense not to run a GUI on your server. If you are not sure this really is useful, you should compare the result of pstree on a server that does have a GUI up and running with the result of the same command on a server that does not have a GUI up and running. You'll see amazing differences as the result.

Managing Processes

At this point you know how to monitor the generic state of your computer. You have read how to see what processes are doing and know about monitoring process activity. In this section, you'll learn about some common process management tasks. These include killing processes that don't listen anymore and adjusting process priority with nice. In a dedicated subsection, you can read how to manage processes from the top utility.

Killing Processes with `kill`, `pkill`, and `killall`

Among the most common process management tasks is the killing of processes. Killing a process, however, goes beyond the mere termination of a process. If you use the kill command or any of its alternatives, you can send a signal to the process. Basically, by sending it a signal, you give the process a command that it simply cannot ignore. A total of 32 signals are available, but of these only four are common. Table 9-1 gives an overview of these common signals.

Table 9-1. *Common Process Management Signals*

Signal	Value	Comment
SIGHUP	1	Forces a process to reread its configuration without really stopping the process. Use it to apply changes to configuration files.
SIGKILL	9	Terminates the process using brute force. You risk losing data from open files when using this signal. Use it only if the process doesn't stop after sending it a signal 15.
SIGTERM	15	Requests the process to terminate. The process may ignore this.
SIGUSR1	30	Sends a specific user-defined signal to the process. Only works if defined within the command.

When sending a signal to the process, you normally can choose between the signal name or the signal number. In the next three sections, you will see how to do this with the kill, pkill, and killall commands.

Killing processes with `kill`

The kill command provides the most common way to send signals to processes, and you will find it quite easy to use. This command works with only two arguments: the signal number or name and the PID upon which you want to act. If you don't specify a signal number, kill by default sends signal 15, asking the process to terminate.

kill does not work with process names, just PID numbers. This means you first have to find the PIDs of the processes you want to send a signal to, which you can do with a command such as pgrep. You can specify multiple PIDs as arguments to kill. The following example shows you how to kill three PIDs with a single command:

```
kill 3019 3021 3022
```

Only some commands listen to user-defined signals. An example of these is the dd command, which you can use to clone a device. You can send this command signal USR1, which will ask dd to show its current progress. To find out whether a command listens to one of the USR signals, go to the man page for kill.

Killing processes with killall

Compared to kill, killall is a more versatile command, specifically due to its ability to work with some arguments that allow you to specify which processes you want to kill in a versatile way. For instance, you can use killall to terminate processes that have a specific file open at that time by just mentioning the file name. Some of the most useful options for killall are listed here:

- -I: This option tells killall to ignore case. Useful if you don't want to think about upperand lowercase.

- -i: This option puts killall in interactive mode. You'll have to confirm before any process is killed.

- -r: This option allows you to work with regular expressions. This is useful because you won't have to enter the exact process name.

- -u: This option kills only processes that a specific user owns. Useful if you need to terminate everything a user is doing right now.

For example, if you want to kill all processes that linda currently has opened, use the following command:

```
killall -u linda
```

Or if you need to terminate all http processes, use regular expressions as in the following command:

```
killall -r http
```

Killing processes with pkill

The third command that you can use to send signals to processes is pkill. Like killall, pkill can also look up processes based on their name or other attributes, which you can address using specific options. For instance, to kill all processes that are owned by user linda, use the following:

```
pkill -u linda
```

Another useful feature of pkill is that you can kill processes by their parent ID. For example, if you need to kill all processes that have process 1499 as their parent ID, use the following:

```
pkill -P 1499
```

Adjusting Process Priority with nice

As discussed earlier in this chapter, every process is started with a default priority. You can see the priority in the default output of the top command. By default, all processes that have the same priority are treated as equal by the operating system. If within these priorities you want to give more CPU time to a process, you can use the nice and renice commands to change their nice status. Process niceness ranges from -20 to 19. -20 means that a process is not very nice and will get the most favorable scheduling. 19 means that a process is very nice to others and gets the least favorable scheduling.

There are two ways to change the niceness of a program: use nice to start a program with the niceness that you specify, and use renice to change the niceness of a program that has already been started. The following shows how to change the niceness of top to the value of 5:

```
nice -n 5 top
```

In case you need to change the nice value for a program that is already running, you should use renice. A useful feature is the option to change the nice status of all processes that a given user has started. For instance, the following command would change the niceness of all processes linda has started to the value -5:

```
renice -5 -u linda
```

You can also just use a PID to change the nice value of a process:

```
renice -5 1499
```

Process Management from top

You have already learned how to monitor processes using top. You've also learned how to manage processes using different command-line tools. From within the top interface, you can also perform some process management tasks. Two tasks are available: you can send processes a signal using kill functionality, and you can renice a process using nice functionality. To do this, use the following options from within the top interface:

- k: Sends a signal to a process. It will first ask for the PID, and then what signal to send to that PID. You should use the numerical PID to manipulate the process.

- r: Changes the niceness of a process. When using this command, you next have to enter the PID of the process whose niceness you need to change.

EXERCISE 9-2: MANAGING PROCESSES

In this exercise you'll learn how to manage processes using **kill killall** and **nice**.

1. Create some workload: type the command **dd if=/dev/zero of=/dev/null** & four times.

2. Type **ps aux** to verify that the four processes have been started. Processes that have been started last will show in the end of the list. Notice the PID of one of the **dd** processes.

3. Type PID=nnn, where nnn is the process PID that you have found in step 2 of the previous step

4. Type **renice -5 $PID**. This adjusts the niceness of the process to -5, which leaves more place for other processes.

5. Type **pidof dd**. This shows the PIDs of all dd processes that are currently running.

6. Use **kill nnn** to kill one of the **dd** processes. Make sure to replace **nnn** with one of the PIDs that you have found in the previous step.

7. Type **killall dd**. This will kill all of the remaining **dd** processes.

Scheduling Processes

On your computer, some processes will start automatically. In particular, these are the service processes your computer needs to do its work. Other processes are started manually. This means that you have to type a command at the command line to start them. There is also a solution between these two options. If you need a certain task to start automatically at predefined intervals, you can use cron to do so.

There are two parts in cron. First is the cron daemon crond. This process starts automatically on all computers and will check its configuration every minute to see whether it has to issue a certain task. By default, cron reads its master configuration file, which is /etc/crontab. Listing 9-9 shows what this file looks like on an Ubuntu server system.

Caution! The file /etc/crontab directs all tasks that should be scheduled through cron. Notice that you should NOT modify this file directly. After the discussion of the contents of this file, you'll read how you should make changes to the configuration of scheduled tasks through cron. Modifications that have been made to /etc/crontab will work, but you might loose them as this file can be overwritten during package updates.

Listing 9-9. Example /etc/crontab File

```
root@ubuntu:~# cat /etc/crontab
# /etc/crontab: system-wide crontab
# Unlike any other crontab you don't have to run the `crontab'
# command to install the new version when you edit this file
# and files in /etc/cron.d. These files also have username fields,
# that none of the other crontabs do.

SHELL=/bin/sh
PATH=/usr/local/sbin:/usr/local/bin:/sbin:/bin:/usr/sbin:/usr/bin

# m h dom mon dow user    command
17 *  *  *  *   root    cd / && run-parts --report /etc/cron.hourly
25 6  *  *  *   root    test -x /usr/sbin/anacron || ( cd / && run-parts --report
/etc/cron.daily )
47 6  *  *  7   root    test -x /usr/sbin/anacron || ( cd / && run-parts --report
/etc/cron.weekly )
52 6  1  *  *   root    test -x /usr/sbin/anacron || ( cd / && run-parts --report
/etc/cron.monthly )
```

In all crontab configuration, you will find three different elements. First, you can see an indication of the time when a command should run. Next is the name of the user with whose permissions the job has to execute, and the last part is the name of the command that has to run.

You can use five time positions to indicate when a cron job has to run:

- Minute

- Hour

- Day of month

- Month

- Day of week

For instance, a task definition in /etc/crontab can look as follows:

```
10 5 3 12 * nobody /usr/bin/false
```

This task would start 10 minutes after 5 a.m. on December 3 only. A very common error that people make is shown in the following example:

```
* 5 * * * nobody /usr/bin/false
```

The purpose of this line is probably to run a task at 5 a.m. every morning; however, it would run every minute between 5:00 a.m. and 5:59 a.m., because the minute specification is an asterisk, which means "every." Instead, to run the task at 5 a.m. only, the following should be specified:

```
0 5 * * * nobody /usr/bin/false
```

Creating user crontabs

Apart from the system crontab, individual users can have crontabs as well. This is normally the common way to make adjustments to the scheduled tasks. Imagine that you want to make a backup every morning. To do so, you probably have a backup program, and this backup program may run automatically with the permissions of a specific user. You can, of course, make the definition in /etc/crontab, with the disadvantage that only root can schedule jobs this way. Therefore, the alterative in which users themselves specify the cron job may be more appealing. To do this, you have to use the crontab command. For instance, if user linda wants to install a cron job to send a mail message to her cell phone every morning at 6 a.m., she would use the following command:

```
crontab -e
```

This opens an editor window in which she can define the tasks that she wants cron to run automatically. Because the crontab file will be installed as her crontab file, there is no need to include a user specification there. This means just including the following line would be enough:

```
0 6 * * 1-5 mail -s "wakeup" mycellphone@example.com < .
```

Notice the use of 1-5 in the specification of the day of the week. This tells the cron process to run this job only on days 1 through 5, which is from Monday to Friday.

If you are logged in as the root user, you can also create cron jobs for other users. To do this, use crontab -u followed by the name of the user you want to create the cron job for. The command crontab -u linda, if issued as root for example, would create a cron job for user linda. This command also opens the crontab editor, which allows you to enter all the required commands. Also useful if you are root: the command crontab -l gives an overview of all the crontab jobs that are currently scheduled for a given user account.

Understanding cron.{hourly|daily|weekly|monthly}

Cron also uses four different directories to execute cron jobs at a regular interval. These are the directories /etc/cron.hourly, /etc/cron.daily, /etc/cron.weekly and /etc/cron.monthly. In these directories you can put scripts that will be executed at the indicated intervals. You can create these scripts as administrator, but many scripts will be placed here automatically when new packages are installed. The logrotate processes for instance are executed this way.

The contents of these scripts is bash shell scripting code, and they don't contain any of the time indicators that are specific to cron. This is not needed, because the cron helper process anacron is taking care of execution of these scripts. Anacron was developed to ensure that specific tasks will be executed at a guarnateed interval. That ensures that the task will also run if the system has been down for maintenance temporarily.

Using /etc/cron.d

Yet another way of running tasks through cron, is by creating files in /etc/cron.d. All files in the directory /etc/cron.d will be included when the cron process is started. Using this approach offers an alternative to making modifications to the /etc/crontab file. The advantage of this approach is that your changes won't get lost during software updates. The contents of the files in /etc/cron.d is exactly the same as the contents of the lines that are added in /etc/crontab.

Summary

In this chapter, you have learned how to tune and manage processes and memory on your computer. You have learned about the way that Linux works with processes and also about memory usage on Linux. You acquired knowledge about some of the most important commands related to process management, including top and ps. In this chapter, the following commands and utilities have been discussed:

- init: First process loaded on a Linux computer.

- mingetty: Process responsible for initializing terminal windows.

- pstree: Command that shows a hierarchical overview of parent and child processes.

- nice: Command that sets priority of a process as it starts up.

- renice: Command that resets nice value for processes that are currently active.

- ps: Command that shows a list of processes and much useful information about each of them.

- top: Command that allows you to monitor processes and perform basic process management actions.

- pgrep: grep utility that is optimized for process management.

- free: Command that shows the amount of memory that is still available.

- kill: Command for terminating processes.

- pkill: Command for terminating processes.

- killall: Command for terminating processes. Optimized to terminate multiple processes using one command.

- crond: Process that allows you to run processes at a fixed time on a regular basis.

- crontab: Command that interfaces with crond to schedule processes.

In the next chapter, you'll learn how to configure system logging.

CHAPTER 10

■ ■ ■

System Logging

Most of the time, your Linux computer will work just fine. From time to time, however, your program won't start, or system components will break. When this is the case, you'll need all the help that you can get. Assuming that you've already used the available command documentation that is on your computer, such as man and --help, you'll need to find out now what exactly is happening when you try to accomplish your task. That brings us to system logging.

Understanding Logging

One of the items that you will like on Linux—once you'll understand how it works—is the way that Linux handles system logging. Logging on Linux is extensive, and you'll be able to tell it to send log messages anywhere you want. The result is not only a bunch of files that are created in /var/log, but in many cases also more important messages that are written to the virtual consoles on your computer as well as log information that is made available through the systemctl command. Think about the virtual consoles that Linux works with; for instance, just while installing, several consoles are available through which you can monitor the output of different commands.

■ **Note**   In Chapter 2, you read how to activate a virtual console, using Ctrl+Alt+F1 up to Ctrl+Alt+F6. On most distributions, even the graphical console is a virtual console, which is available using the Ctrl+Alt+F7 keystroke.

Behind all these messages is often a process with the name syslog. This process is configured to monitor what happens on your computer. It does that by watching the messages that the commands you use are generating. syslog captures these messages and sends them to a destination, which is often a file, but as mentioned can also be a virtual console on your computer.

Syslog has different implementations. The early version of syslog is just called "syslog". This logging process has been enhanced and replaced with the more flexible rsyslog service. On occasion you'll also find syslog-ng which is taking care of logging. On current Linux distributions, rsyslog is the de facto standard though. It is completely backwards compatible with the old syslog service, but offers many new features as well, which will be discussed later in this chapter. As rsyslog is the current standard for logging system information, in this chapter I will focus on its working.

Apart from the rsyslog process that captures the messages and directs them somewhere, there is also the command or process that generates the messages. Not all of these are handled by rsyslog, the Apache web service for instance is taking care of its own logging. The reason for many services to take care of their own logging, is that even the newer rsyslog has always been bound by backwards compatibility, with the result that filtering information for specific services is rather limited.

With the release of systemd as the default service manager, a new log system has been introduced as well. It has the name systemd-journald, and often is referred to as just journald. This service grasps log information that is generated by all items that are started through systemd and provides a generic interface to get access to that information. When typing **systemctl status** on any service, you'll by default see the most recent information that has been logged by that service. Listing 10-1 shows an example, where log information for the sshd process is shown. Journald also has its own interface to get access to information, which is provided through the journalctl command.

Listing 10-1. Displaying log information using systemctl status

```
[root@localhost ~]# systemctl status sshd
sshd.service - OpenSSH server daemon
   Loaded: loaded (/usr/lib/systemd/system/sshd.service; enabled)
   Active: active (running) since Sat 2015-10-31 10:15:49 EDT; 1h 9min ago
 Main PID: 1045 (sshd)
   CGroup: /system.slice/sshd.service
           └─1045 /usr/sbin/sshd -D

Oct 31 10:15:49 localhost.localdomain systemd[1]: Started OpenSSH server daemon.
Oct 31 10:15:49 localhost.localdomain sshd[1045]: Server listening on 0.0.0.0...
Oct 31 10:15:49 localhost.localdomain sshd[1045]: Server listening on :: port...
Oct 31 10:16:31 localhost.localdomain sshd[2202]: Connection closed by 192.16...
Oct 31 10:16:59 localhost.localdomain sshd[2204]: Connection closed by 192.16...
Oct 31 10:17:26 localhost.localdomain sshd[2207]: Accepted password for root ...
Hint: Some lines were ellipsized, use -l to show in full.
```

Apart from the logging that is done for services as described above, you might on occasion want your regular commands to be more verbose as well. For this purpose, many commands support the -v option to make them more verbose.

A random example of this is the cp command, which by default does not show you what it is doing. However, if you add the -v option to it, it shows exactly what it is doing, even if it just succeeds in copying the file. Listing 10-2 gives an example of this.

Listing 10-2. Many Commands Can Work with -v to Show Exactly What They Are Doing

```
nuuk:~ # cp -v /etc/[qx]* /tmp
`/etc/xattr.conf' -> `/tmp/xattr.conf'
cp: omitting directory `/etc/xdg'
`/etc/xinetd.conf' -> `/tmp/xinetd.conf'
cp: omitting directory `/etc/xinetd.d'
cp: omitting directory `/etc/xml'
cp: omitting directory `/etc/xscreensaver'
```

Then there are also the commands that you run from a graphical interface. Normally, they don't show what they are trying to do. However, if you find out what the name and exact location of the command are, and you try running the command from a command line instead of just clicking its icon, you'll be surprised by how much output the command gives. In Listing 10-3, you can see what running the Gnome file explorer Nautilus from the command line looks like. Notice that doing so also displays any error messages about networking that you would never see when starting the command the normal way.

Listing 10-3. Starting a Graphical Command from the Command Line Often Produces a Lot of Startup Information

```
login as: root
Using keyboard-interactive authentication.
Password:
Last login: Sat Dec 20 03:50:05 2008 from 192.168.26.1
nuuk:~ # /opt/gnome/bin/nautilus
Initializing nautilus-open-terminal extension
Initializing nautilus-share extension

** (nautilus:10427): WARNING **: Cannot calculate _NET_NUMBER_OF_DESKTOPS

** (nautilus:10427): WARNING **: Cannot calculate _NET_NUMBER_OF_DESKTOPS

** (nautilus:10427): WARNING **: Cannot get _NET_WORKAREA

** (nautilus:10427): WARNING **: Cannot determine workarea, guessing at layout
Nautilus-Share-Message: REFRESHING SHARES
Nautilus-Share-Message: ----------------------------------------
Nautilus-Share-Message: spawn arg "net"
Nautilus-Share-Message: spawn arg "usershare"
Nautilus-Share-Message: spawn arg "info"
Nautilus-Share-Message: end of spawn args; SPAWNING
Nautilus-Share-Message: returned from spawn: SUCCESS:
Nautilus-Share-Message: exit code 255
Nautilus-Share-Message: ----------------------------------------
Nautilus-Share-Message: Called "net usershare info" but it failed: 'net
  usershare' returned error
 255: net usershare: usershares are currently disabled
```

Most commands, however, write to the system log to indicate that something is wrong. Before discussing the workings of this system log, the next section explains more about the log files it writes and how you can monitor them. Before getting into that, Table 10-1 provides an overview of the different ways to get log information out of commands and services.

Table 10-1. *Methods for showing log information*

Command verbosity	Use -v with many commands
Rsyslog	Generic solution that writes information to files in /var/log and other destinations
Direct logging	Some services don't use rsyslog, but write information directly to log files in /var/log
Journald	Integrated component of systemd that writes information to the journal. This information is accessed through the systemctl status and the journalctl commands.

Monitoring Files in /var/log

There is no standardization between different Linux distributions as to where information should be logged to. What is sure is that you'll find all of the log files that are written in the /var/log directory. On many distributions /var/log/messages is the most important destination for log files, but you'll find other log destinations as well, such as /var/log/system. Log files are just text files, so you can read them as you would any other text file—open it with less, for instance, or watch the last couple of lines with the tail command. A particularly useful way of monitoring the content of these files, however, is through tail -f, in which -f stands for follow. When invoked in this way, tail opens the last ten lines of the log file and automatically shows new lines as they are created. This technique is particularly useful when trying to understand what exactly a command or service is doing. As it shows you real-time information, you'll see immediately whether something doesn't work out, which allows you also to take action straight away.

When watching log files, many people tend to forget that there are more than just /var/log/messages. Have a look at the log files that exist on your computer and try to understand what they are used for. For instance, did you know that most computers write a log entry not only for every single mail message they receive, but also for every failed attempt to send an e-mail? This information, which is useful when trying to understand why sending an e-mail doesn't work, is not written to /var/log/messages. Hence, have a look at the contents of /var/log and see what other files you need to know about to find all log information that commands on your computer are generating. Later in this chapter you'll learn how rsyslog is configured to specify which destination log information should be written to. Listing 10-4 gives an impression of what the contents of /var/log looks like on my computer.

Listing 10-4. The Messages File Is Not the Only File in /var/log

```
[root@localhost log]# ls -l
total 1388
drwxr-xr-x. 2 root root   4096 Oct 24 07:46 anaconda
drwxr-x---. 2 root root     22 Mar  5  2015 audit
-rw-r--r--. 1 root root   6998 Oct 31 10:15 boot.log
-rw-------. 1 root utmp      0 Oct 24 09:50 btmp
-rw-r--r--. 1 root root  14066 Oct 31 11:14 cron
-rw-r--r--. 1 root root  10625 Oct 25 03:41 cron-20151025
-rw-r--r--. 1 root root 112899 Oct 31 10:15 dmesg
-rw-r--r--. 1 root root 112825 Oct 24 13:52 dmesg.old
-rw-------. 1 root root   1370 Oct 24 09:50 grubby
-rw-r--r--. 1 root root 292000 Oct 31 10:17 lastlog
-rw-------. 1 root root    198 Oct 31 10:15 maillog
-rw-------. 1 root root    594 Oct 24 13:52 maillog-20151025
-rw-------. 1 root root 378914 Oct 31 11:24 messages
-rw-------. 1 root root 698853 Oct 25 03:30 messages-20151025
drwx------. 2 root root      6 Jun 10  2014 ppp
-rw-------. 1 root root   1043 Oct 31 10:17 secure
-rw-------. 1 root root   3333 Oct 24 13:52 secure-20151025
-rw-------. 1 root root      0 Oct 25 03:41 spooler
-rw-------. 1 root root      0 Oct 24 07:45 spooler-20151025
-rw-------. 1 root root      0 Oct 24 07:45 tallylog
drwxr-xr-x. 2 root root     22 Mar  6  2015 tuned
-rw-rw-r--. 1 root utmp  12672 Oct 31 10:17 wtmp
-rw-------. 1 root root  11128 Oct 31 10:18 yum.log
```

Configuring the `syslog` Service

As mentioned before, rsyslog is the default service for logging on most current Linux distributions. It allows administrators to specify what services should log which type of information to which destination. These three items are referred to as the facility (which service), the priority (the severity level that should be logged) and the destination (where the information should be logged to). Apart from these, rsyslogd can be configured with modules to further fine-tune the working of the log services. Modules are used for advanced configurations and for that reason are not discussed in this chapter.

The main rsyslog configuration file is /etc/rsyslog.cond. Apart from this file, you'll find the /etc/rsyslog.d directory. The contents of this directory is added to the configuration that is specified in /etc/rsyslog.conf, which allows RPM or Debian packages to extent the configuration without modifying the contents of the /etc/rsyslog.conf file. Listing 10-5 shows what the contents of the rsyslog.conf looks like.

Listing 10-5. Contents of the /etc/rsyslog.conf file

```
[root@localhost log]# cat /etc/rsyslog.conf
# rsyslog configuration file

# For more information see /usr/share/doc/rsyslog-*/rsyslog_conf.html
# If you experience problems, see http://www.rsyslog.com/doc/troubleshoot.html


#### MODULES ####

# The imjournal module bellow is now used as a message source instead of imuxsock.
$ModLoad imuxsock # provides support for local system logging (e.g. via logger command)
$ModLoad imjournal # provides access to the systemd journal
#$ModLoad imklog # reads kernel messages (the same are read from journald)
#$ModLoad immark  # provides -MARK- message capability

# Provides UDP syslog reception
#$ModLoad imudp
#$UDPServerRun 514

# Provides TCP syslog reception
#$ModLoad imtcp
#$InputTCPServerRun 514

#### GLOBAL DIRECTIVES ####

# Where to place auxiliary files
$WorkDirectory /var/lib/rsyslog

# Use default timestamp format
$ActionFileDefaultTemplate RSYSLOG_TraditionalFileFormat

# File syncing capability is disabled by default. This feature is usually not required,
# not useful and an extreme performance hit
#$ActionFileEnableSync on

# Include all config files in /etc/rsyslog.d/
$IncludeConfig /etc/rsyslog.d/*.conf
```

```
# Turn off message reception via local log socket;
# local messages are retrieved through imjournal now.
$OmitLocalLogging on

# File to store the position in the journal
$IMJournalStateFile imjournal.state


#### RULES ####

# Log all kernel messages to the console.
# Logging much else clutters up the screen.
#kern.*                                                 /dev/console

# Log anything (except mail) of level info or higher.
# Don't log private authentication messages!
*.info;mail.none;authpriv.none;cron.none               /var/log/messages

# The authpriv file has restricted access.
authpriv.*                                             /var/log/secure

# Log all the mail messages in one place.
mail.*                                                 -/var/log/maillog

# Log cron stuff
cron.*                                                 /var/log/cron

# Everybody gets emergency messages
*.emerg                                                :omusrmsg:*

# Save news errors of level crit and higher in a special file.
uucp,news.crit                                         /var/log/spooler

# Save boot messages also to boot.log
local7.*                                               /var/log/boot.log


# ### begin forwarding rule ###
# The statement between the begin ... end define a SINGLE forwarding
# rule. They belong together, do NOT split them. If you create multiple
# forwarding rules, duplicate the whole block!
# Remote Logging (we use TCP for reliable delivery)
#
# An on-disk queue is created for this action. If the remote host is
# down, messages are spooled to disk and sent when it is up again.
#$ActionQueueFileName fwdRule1 # unique name prefix for spool files
#$ActionQueueMaxDiskSpace 1g   # 1gb space limit (use as much as possible)
#$ActionQueueSaveOnShutdown on # save messages to disk on shutdown
#$ActionQueueType LinkedList   # run asynchronously
#$ActionResumeRetryCount -1    # infinite retries if host is down
# remote host is: name/ip:port, e.g. 192.168.0.1:514, port optional
#*.* @@remote-host:514
# ### end of the forwarding rule ###
[root@localhost log]#
```

The most important part of the rsyslog.conf configuration file is in the RULES section. In here the three elements facility, priority and destination are used to specify where information should be sent to

Facilities are a fixed part of rsyslog and you cannot easily add to them. The following facilities are available in syslog:

- auth: Facility that handles events related to authentication.

- authpriv: Facility that handles events related to authentication, as does auth. There is no difference between auth and authpriv.

- cron: Facility that handles messages generated by the cron subsystem (see Chapter 9 for more information about cron).

- daemon: Log messages that are generated by a daemon. No further subdivision can be made for system processes, with the exception of the daemons that have their own facility, such as ftp and mail.

- kern: Kernel-related messages. This facility also defines messages that are generated by the iptables kernel firewall.

- lpr: Messages related to the legacy lpr printing system.

- mail: Messages related to handling mail messages.

- mark: For internal use only. The syslog process can place a marker in syslog periodically. If your computer doesn't log a lot, this can help you make sure that logging is still enabled.

- news: Messages related to the Network News Transport Protocol (NNTP)-related services.

- security: Generic security-related messages.

- syslog: Messages that are related to the syslog process itself.

- user: User-related messages.

- uucp: Messages that are generated by the legacy Unix to Unix Copy Protocol (UUCP).

- local0-local7: Facilities that you can use for all other services. To use these facilities, you need to configure the service in its configuration file to log to the local facility. Consult the documentation for the service for more information on how to do this.

When writing log messages, the facilities produce messages with a given priority. When a priority is referred to, messages with this priority and all higher priorities are written to the destination that is specified. The following priorities are defined in syslog, listed in ascending order:

- debug: Relates to debug information. This gives you detailed information on everything the facility is doing. In general, this level of information is useful for programmers only in that it tells you exactly what system and library calls the facility performs.

- info: Gives all "normal" information about what the process is doing. This gives you information about files that are open, for instance, but does not give extensive information about system and library calls.

- `notice`: Gives information about noncritical errors. For instance, this can refer to a file that should exist, but because it didn't, it was created automatically.

- `warn/warning`: Give information about warnings that occurred when executing the process. Both `warn` and `warning` have the same meaning, but warning is deprecated. This means you can still use it, as Linux will understand it, but because it's "old school," so you shouldn't use it anymore. A warning defines a situation where normal functionality is disrupted, but the facility still operates.

- `err/error`: Give information about errors. Typically, `err`-level messages are about situations that interrupt normal functioning of the facility. The use of `error` is deprecated. Use `err` instead.

- `crit`: Gives information about critical situations that endanger normal operation of your computer.

- `alert`: Gives information about a situation that will cause your computer to stop.

- `emerg/panic`: Indicate normal operation of your computer has stopped. The use of `panic` is deprecated. Use `emerg` instead.

To define log events, in `rsyslog.conf` you'll refer to a facility combined with a priority. If no other exceptions are defined, the priority you mention includes all higher priorities as well. For instance, the following would refer to informational messages generated by the kernel and messages with a higher priority as well:

```
kern.info
```

You can also refer to multiple facilities in one line by specifying them in a comma- separated list. For instance, the following refers to both informational messages related to the kernel and informational messages related to the `cron` process:

```
kern,cron.info
```

Alternatively, you can refer to all facilities by using an asterisk, as in the following example line:

```
*.crit
```

When referring to a priority, normally by just mentioning the priority you will include all higher priorities as well. If you want to define what should happen just in case the specified priority occurs, use an equals sign, as in the following example line, which handles messages related to mail and not to messages with a higher priority:

```
mail.=info
```

You can also include a statement to exclude a priority and every priority beyond it by putting an exclamation mark in front of the name of the priority:

```
mail.!info
```

When a log event happens, an action is performed on it. This action typically means that a message is sent somewhere. In syslog, the available actions are also well defined. Multiple facilities and priorities can be specified in one line to log to the same destination. Listing 10-5 includes several examples of this. You can send log messages to the following:

- *Regular file*: When mentioning the name of a file, log messages are written to that file. You must specify this file name as an absolute path name. To prevent syslog from writing every single message to the configuration file immediately, you can put a - sign in front of the file name. This means that changes are buffered first before they are written to the actual configuration file. In Listing 10-5, this is used to handle logging of messages that have a debug status. The ; sign in this listing is used as the delimiter, and the \ sign makes sure that the next part is interpreted as belonging to the same line:

```
*.=debug;\
        auth,authpriv.none;\
        news.none;mail.none      -/var/log/debug
```

- *Named pipe*: By logging to a named pipe, you can pipe log messages to a device. To use a named pipe, you should put a pipe symbol in front of the device name. The following example from /etc/syslog.conf shows how to log to the xconsole device using a named pipe:

```
daemon.*;mail.*;\
        news.err;\
        *.=debug;*.=info;\
        *.=notice;*.=warn      |/dev/xconsole
```

- *Terminal or console*: If the file that you've specified as the actual log destination is a tty, syslog will handle it as a tty and log messages in real time to it. A very common tty to use for this purpose is /dev/console.

- *Remote machine*: A very useful feature that you can use with syslog is the option to configure one computer as the log host for all computers in the network. On this computer, you will see the name of the machine from which a message comes in the log files. To send log messages to a remote computer, you must meet two conditions:

  - Start syslog with the remote logging feature enabled. By default, the syslog process does not accept messages that come from other hosts. You can enable remote logging on the syslog process by starting it with the -r option. This tells your current machine that it should accept log messages coming from other machines.

  - In syslog.conf, specify the name of the machine you want to log to as the log destination by putting an @ sign in front of the machine name. For instance, you would use @RNA to log messages to a machine with the name RNA. This machine name must be resolvable if you want this to work.

- *User:* You can send messages directly to a user, who will receive this message in real time if he or she is logged in. To do this, just use the name of the user or a comma-separated list of multiple users. For instance, the following would make sure that all messages generated by the kernel and having a status of critical and higher are sent directly to the root user:

  ```
  kern.crit                    root
  ```

- *Everyone logged in:* If the log message is critical (for instance, because it disrupts all functionality of the system), it makes sense to send a message to all users who are currently logged in. To do this, specify an asterisk as the log destination.

EXERCISE 10-1: CONFIGURING RSYSLOG

In this exercise you'll learn how to configure rsyslog to send all messages that are generated to the file /var/log/all.

1. Open the /etc/rsyslog.conf file with an editor.

2. Locate the RULES section, and add the following line:

   ```
   *.* /var/log/all
   ```

3. Type **systemctl restart rsyslog**. Restarting the service is mandatory to make the changes effective.

4. Type **logger HELLO**

5. Type **tail -f /var/log/all**. You should see a line that has been added, displaying the text HELLO at the end of the /var/log/all file.

Configuring `syslog-ng`

Some years ago, syslog-ng has been introduced as the successor of the legacy syslog system. Even if most distributions have moved to rsyslog as the new next generation system logger, you may encounter syslog-ng as well. The following section describes how it is worked and configured.

In `syslog-ng` facilities, priorities and log destinations are also used; read the preceding section if you need to know more about these. The way they are used, however, is much different from standard `syslog`. In Listing 10-6, you see an example of `syslog-ng.conf`, which defines how logging should be handled.

Listing 10-6. Handling Logging with `syslog-ng`

```
nuuk:/etc/syslog-ng # cat syslog-ng.conf
#
# /etc/syslog-ng/syslog-ng.conf
#

#
# Global options.
#
```

```
options { long_hostnames(off); sync(0); perm(0640); stats(3600); };
#
# 'src' is our main source definition. you can add
# more sources driver definitions to it, or define
# your own sources, i.e.:
#
#source my_src { .... };
#
source src {
        #
        # include internal syslog-ng messages
        # note: the internal() source is required!
        #
        internal();

        #
        # the following line will be replaced by the
        # socket list generated by SuSEconfig using
        # variables from /etc/sysconfig/syslog:
        #
        unix-dgram("/dev/log");

        #
        # uncomment to process log messages from network:
        #
        #udp(ip("0.0.0.0") port(514));
};

#
# Filter definitions
#
filter f_iptables   { facility(kern) and match("IN=") and match("OUT="); };

filter f_console    { level(warn) and facility(kern) and not filter(f_iptables)
                      or level(err) and not facility(authpriv); };

filter f_newsnotice { level(notice) and facility(news); };
filter f_newscrit   { level(crit)   and facility(news); };
filter f_newserr    { level(err)    and facility(news); };
filter f_news       { facility(news); };

filter f_mailinfo   { level(info)     and facility(mail); };
filter f_mailwarn   { level(warn)     and facility(mail); };
filter f_mailerr    { level(err, crit) and facility(mail); };
filter f_mail       { facility(mail); };
filter f_cron       { facility(cron); };

filter f_local      { facility(local0, local1, local2, local3,
                               local4, local5, local6, local7); };
```

```
filter f_acpid       { match('^\[acpid\]:'); };
filter f_netmgm      { match('^NetworkManager:'); };

filter f_messages    { not facility(news, mail) and not filter(f_iptables); };
filter f_warn        { level(warn, err, crit) and not filter(f_iptables); };
filter f_alert       { level(alert); };


#
# Most warning and errors on tty10 and on the xconsole pipe:
#
destination console  { pipe("/dev/tty10"    group(tty) perm(0620)); };
log { source(src); filter(f_console); destination(console); };

destination xconsole { pipe("/dev/xconsole" group(tty) perm(0400)); };
log { source(src); filter(f_console); destination(xconsole


#
# News-messages in separate files:
#
destination newscrit   { file("/var/log/news/news.crit"
                              owner(news) group(news)); };
log { source(src); filter(f_newscrit); destination(newscrit); };

destination newserr    { file("/var/log/news/news.err"
                              owner(news) group(news)); };
log { source(src); filter(f_newserr); destination(newserr); };

destination newsnotice { file("/var/log/news/news.notice"
                              owner(news) group(news)); };
log { source(src); filter(f_newsnotice); destination(newsnotice); };


#
# Mail-messages in separate files:
#
destination mailinfo { file("/var/log/mail.info"); };
log { source(src); filter(f_mailinfo); destination(mailinfo); };

destination mailwarn { file("/var/log/mail.warn"); };
log { source(src); filter(f_mailwarn); destination(mailwarn); };

destination mailerr { file("/var/log/mail.err" fsync(yes)); };
log { source(src); filter(f_mailerr); destination(mailerr); };


#
# and also all in one file:
#
destination mail { file("/var/log/mail"); };
log { source(src); filter(f_mail); destination(mail); };
```

```
#
# acpid messages in one file:
#
destination acpid { file("/var/log/acpid"); };
log { source(src); filter(f_acpid); destination(acpid); flags(final); };

#
# NetworkManager messages in one file:
#
destination netmgm { file("/var/log/NetworkManager"); };
log { source(src); filter(f_netmgm); destination(netmgm); flags(final); };

#
# Some boot scripts use/require local[1-7]:
#
destination localmessages { file("/var/log/localmessages"); };
log { source(src); filter(f_local); destination(localmessages); };

#
# All messages except iptables and the facilities news and mail:
#
destination messages { file("/var/log/messages"); };
log { source(src); filter(f_messages); destination(messages); };

#
# Firewall (iptables) messages in one file:
#
destination firewall { file("/var/log/firewall"); };
log { source(src); filter(f_iptables); destination(firewall); };

#
# Warnings (except iptables) in one file:
#
destination warn { file("/var/log/warn" fsync(yes)); };
log { source(src); filter(f_warn); destination(warn); };
```

■ **Caution**   On SUSE Linux, you'll find the files /etc/syslog-ng/syslog-ng.conf and /etc/syslog-ng/
syslog-ng.conf.in. You should make all modifications to the /etc/syslog-ng/syslog-ng. conf.in file, and
after making the modifications, run the SuSEconfig command to write them to /etc/ syslog-ng/syslog-ng.conf.
This procedure is used because an update procedure to SUSE may alter the syslog-ng.conf file, which may
cause you to lose all changes that you've made to it.

In a syslog-ng configuration, three elements are combined in the log statement to define where
messages are logged to:

- source: Defines where messages are accepted from

- filter: Specifies what exactly the log message should match

- destination: Indicates where the message must be written to

To understand what's happening on your syslog-ng configuration, it makes sense to read the configuration file bottom up: at the bottom of the file, you'll find the log statement that defines how logging should be handled, and in the upper parts of the configuration file, you can find the different elements that make up this definition. Following is an example of such a log statement:

```
log { source(src); filter(f_warn); destination(warn); };
```

In this example, the first part that you see is the source specification, which is defined as (src). This refers to a definition that is made earlier in the same file, which you can see here:

```
source src {
        #
        # include internal syslog-ng messages
        # note: the internal() source is required!
        #
        internal();

        #
        # the following line will be replaced by the
        # socket list generated by SuSEconfig using
        # variables from /etc/sysconfig/syslog:
        #
        unix-dgram("/dev/log");
        #
        # uncomment to process log messages from network:
        #
        #udp(ip("0.0.0.0") port(514));
};
```

As you can see, the src definition by default accepts two sources: messages that are generated internally and messages for which the operating system uses the /dev/log device to process them. This definition handles all messages that are generated by your computer, but does not accept any messages from other computers. However, you may also include these easily. To accept messages from all computers, make sure the following line is enabled:

```
udp(ip("0.0.0.0") port(514));
```

Alternatively, you can refer to messages that come from one host or a range of hosts by mentioning the IP address of the host or the range from which you want this machine to accept messages. For instance, you could enable messages from all IP addresses in the network 192.168.1.0 by using the following:

```
udp(ip("192.168.1.0") port(514));
```

Looking back at the example, the second part of the log definition defines the filter, which in this case is f_warn, as shown here:

```
filter f_warn     { level(warn, err, crit) and not filter(f_iptables); };
```

In a filter definition, you can indicate what level the message should come from and also what facility should generate the message. As you can see in the preceding example, you can also tell the filter not to handle messages that come from another specific filter. Filters in syslog-ng are very flexible. This is because you can also use a match statement, which uses a regular expression to tell syslog-ng to look for specific text. Following is an example of this:

```
filter f_acpid     { match('^\[acpid\]:'); };
```

In this filter, a match is used to look for a regular expression. The regular expression defines that syslog-ng should handle all lines that start with the text [acpid], which enables you in this case to specify a specific log target for the acpid service. When building syslog-ng configurations, you will in particular like this match functionality.

As the last part of your syslog-ng configuration, you'll have to specify where to send the messages. You do this by defining a log destination. Following is an example of a destination:

```
destination newscrit   { file("/var/log/news/news.crit"
                        owner(news) group(news)); };
```

In syslog-ng destinations, you can use all log destinations that you've also seen in syslog. But here also, it is possible to be very specific. For instance, you can see that the example code defines not only the name of the file that syslog-ng has to write, but also the user owner and group assignments for that file.

■ **Tip**   Syslog-ng may look intimidating when you first start working with it. If you know it a little better, you will find out that it is not that hard. I recommend you to study the example syslog-ng.conf file thoroughly, because it has all the examples you need to build your own configuration.

Sending Logs Yourself with `logger`

Also very useful when handling logs is the logger command. This command sends messages to syslog by default, which makes it a useful command to include in scripts where no default logging is available. You can tell logger to use a certain priority, but normally you won't; if used in a syslog-ng environment, you'll just employ a matching filter to handle messages that are generated by the logger command. Using this command is very simple. For example, the following would write a message to your syslog:

```
logger hi
```

When using logger, you may like the option to mark every line you write to the log files with a specific tag. This makes it easier for you to recognize such lines later on. To do this, use the option -t tag. For instance, the command logger -t blah hi would tag the message hi in the log file with blah, which makes it easier for you to grep on messages that you've written with logger.

Rotating Old Log Files

Logging is good, but if your system writes too many log files, it can become rather problematic.

As a solution to this, you can configure the logrotate service. The logrotate service runs as a daily cron job and checks its configuration files to see whether any rotation has to occur. In these configuration files, you can configure when a new log file should be opened and, if that happens, what exactly should happen to the old log file: for example, whether should it be compressed or just deleted, and if it is compressed, how many versions of the old file should be kept.

logrotate works with two different kinds of configuration files. The main configuration file is /etc/logrotate.conf. In this file, generic settings are defined to tune how logrotate should do its work. You can see the contents of this file in Listing 10-7.

Listing 10-7. Contents of the logrotate.conf Configuration File

```
# see "man logrotate" for details
# rotate log files weekly
weekly

# keep 4 weeks worth of backlogs
rotate 4

# create new (empty) log files after rotating old ones
create

# uncomment this if you want your log files compressed
#compress

# uncomment these to switch compression to bzip2
compresscmd /usr/bin/bzip2
uncompresscmd /usr/bin/bunzip2

# former versions had to have the compresscommand set accordingly
#compressext .bz2

# RPM packages drop log rotation information into this directory
include /etc/logrotate.d

# no packages own wtmp - we'll rotate them here
#/var/log/wtmp {
#       monthly
#       create 0664 root utmp
#       rotate 1
#}

# system-specific logs may be also be configured here.
```

The code in Listing 10-7 includes some important keywords. Table 10-2 describes these keywords.

Table 10-2. logrotate *Options*

Option	Description
weekly	This option specifies that the log files should be created on a weekly basis.
rotate 4	This option makes sure that four old versions of the file are saved. If the rotate option is not used, old files are deleted.
create	The old file is saved under a new name and a new file is created. compress Use this option to make sure the old log files are compressed. compresscmd This option specifies the command that should be used for creating the compressed log files.
uncompresscmd	Use this command to specify what command to use to uncompress compressed log files.
include	This important option makes sure that the content of the directory /etc/logrotate.d is included. In this directory, files exist that specify how to handle some individual log files.

As you have seen, the logrotate.conf configuration file includes some generic code to specify how log files should be handled. In addition to that, most log files have a specific logrotate configuration file in /etc/logrotate.d/.

The content of the service-specific configuration files in /etc/logrotate.d is in general more specific than the contents of the generic logrotate.conf. In Listing 10-8, you can see what the configuration script that handles log files for /var/log/ntp looks like.

Listing 10-8. Example of the logrotate Configuration for ntp

```
/var/log/ntp {
    compress
    dateext
    maxage 365
    rotate 99
    size=+2048k
    notifempty
    missingok
    copytruncate
    postrotate
        chmod 644 /var/log/ntp
    endscript
}
```

Listing 10-8 demonstrates some additional options. Table 10-3 gives an overview of these options and their meaning.

Table 10-3. *Options in Service-Specific* logrotate *Files*

Option	Description
dateext	Uses the date as extension for old versions of the log files.
maxage	Specifies the number of days after which old log files should be removed.
rotate	Specifies the number of times a log file should be rotated before being removed or mailed to the address specified in the mail directive.
size	Logs files that grow bigger than the size specified here.
notifempty	Does not rotate the log file when it is empty.
missingok	If the log file does not exist, goes on to the next one without issuing an error message.
copytruncate	Truncates the old log file in place after creating a copy, instead of moving the old file and creating a new one. This is useful for services that cannot be told to close their log files.
postrotate	Specifies some commands that should be executed after performing the logrotate on the file.
endscript	Denotes the end of the configuration file.

Like the preceding example for the ntp log file, all other log files can have their own logrotate file. You can even create logrotate files for files that are not log files at all! More options are available when creating such a logrotate file; for a complete overview, check the man pages.

EXERCISE 10-2: CONFIGURING LOG ROTATION

In exercise 10-1 you have configured rsyslog to write all messages that are logged to the file /var/log/all. In this exercise you'll learn how to rotate that file based on specific criteria.

1. Open a root shell and use **cd /etc/logrotate.d** to go to the directory that contains log rotate files for specific services.

2. Type **cp syslog all** to copy the default syslog file to a new file with the name all. If you don't have a file with the name syslog, you can pick another file at your convenience.

3. Open the file with an editor and make sure it has the following contents:

```
/var/log/all {
        daily
        missingok
        rotate 1
        compress
        delaycompress
        copytruncate
        minsize 100k
}
```

4. Notice that you won't see the changes effective immediately. Logrotate is automatically scheduled through the cron service, and by default runs once a day.

5. Use **ls -l /var/log/all** to look at the current date and time stamp of the file.

6. To manually trigger a rotation, type **logrotate /etc/logrotate.conf**. Notice that it still is unlikely to see any effect, as the file doesn't meet the criteria for rotation yet.

Understanding Journald

With the release of systemd, a new logging service has been introduced as well. This is the journald service. Journald is not meant to replace rsyslog, but it is complementary to rsyslog. The main purpose of rsyslog is to log information that is generated by specific events and services and write that information to files in /var/log. Also, rsyslog allows you to set up a central log service in your network.

Journald is used to provide more information about working of services. It provides you with real-time information, which by default is cleared when your machine is restarted. Using journald allows you to query for specific information about services and their current operational state.

The easiest interface to information that is logged by journald, is through the **systemctl status** command, which you have seen before. This command automatically shows the last five lines that have been logged for a specific systemd unit file. Journald also has the **journalctl** command, that opens a pager in which you can read recent log messages. The pager is based on the less command, so to see the most recent lines that have been added to the log, use **G** to go to the bottom of the command output.

The journalctl also has many options to filter specific items out of the log. If the bash-completion package has been installed, you can easily use tab key command completion to work with these options. Listing 10-9 shows what the default options are, as shown by bash command line completion.

Listing 10-9. Using tab completion to show journalctl options

```
[root@workstation ~]# journalctl
_AUDIT_LOGINUID=              __MONOTONIC_TIMESTAMP=
_AUDIT_SESSION=               _PID=
_BOOT_ID=                     PRIORITY=
_CMDLINE=                     __REALTIME_TIMESTAMP=
CODE_FILE=                    _SELINUX_CONTEXT=
CODE_FUNC=                    _SOURCE_REALTIME_TIMESTAMP=
CODE_LINE=                    SYSLOG_FACILITY=
_COMM=                        SYSLOG_IDENTIFIER=
COREDUMP_EXE=                 SYSLOG_PID=
__CURSOR=                     _SYSTEMD_CGROUP=
ERRNO=                        _SYSTEMD_OWNER_UID=
_EXE=                         _SYSTEMD_SESSION=
_GID=                         _SYSTEMD_UNIT=
_HOSTNAME=                    _TRANSPORT=
_KERNEL_DEVICE=               _UDEV_DEVLINK=
_KERNEL_SUBSYSTEM=            _UDEV_DEVNODE=
_MACHINE_ID=                  _UDEV_SYSNAME=
MESSAGE=                      _UID=
MESSAGE_ID=
```

Particularly useful in the options listed above, is the _SYSTEMD_UNIT option. Using this option allows you to get the information you need about a specific systemd unit. Use for instance **journalctl _SYSTEMD_UNIT=sshd.service** to see all that has been logged by the SSH service recently.

EXERCISE 10-3: DISCOVERYIN JOURNALCTL OPTIONS

In this exercise you'll learn how to work with different journalctl options.

1. Type **journalctl**. You'll see the contents of the journal since your server last started, starting at the beginning of the journal. The contents is shown in **less**, so you can use common less commands to walk through the file.

2. Type **journalctl -f**. This opens the live view mode of journalctl, which allows you to see new messages scrolling by in real time. Use **Ctrl-C** to interrupt.

3. Type **journalctl -n 20**. The -n 20 option displays the last 20 lines of the journal (just like **tail -n 20**).

4. Now type **journalctl -p err**. This command shows errors only.

5. If you want to view journal messages that have been written in a specific time period, you can use the --since and --until commands. Both options take the time parameter in the format YYYY-MM-DD hh:mm:ss. Also, you can use yesterday, today and tomorrow as parameters. So type **journalctl --since yesterday** to show all messages that have been written since yesterday.

6. **journalctl** allows you to combine different options as well, so if you want to show all messages with a priority err that have been written since yesterday, use **journalctl --since yesterday -p err**.

7. If you need as much detail as possible, use **journalctl -o verbose**. This shows different options that are used when writing to the journal (see listing 13.3). All of these options can be used to tell the journalctl command which specific information you're looking for. Type for instance **journalctl _SYSTEMD_UNIT=sshd.service** to show more information about the sshd systemd unit.

Summary

In this chapter, you've learned how to handle logging. First, you've learned where you can find the default log files on your system and how you can have a look at them. Next, you've learned how to create your own rsyslog or syslog-ng configuration. You have also learned you how to configure log rotation to make sure that your computer's file system is not filled completely with log files by accident. At the end of this chapter you have read how journald and journalctl add another interface to get relevant information out of the system log files. The following commands have been covered in this chapter:

- rsyslog: Legacy process used for logging files

- syslog-ng: Newer process that offers more clever log services

- `tail -f /var/log/messages`: *The* way to see what's happening in /var/log/messages, the most important log file on your computer

- `logger`: Useful tool that lets you write messages to `syslog`

- `logrotate`: Command that helps you to prevent log files from growing too big and rotate them after a certain amount of time or once a given size has been reached

- **journalctl:** Versatile command that helps you getting information from the systemd related journald service.

In the next chapter, you'll learn how to configure networking on your computer.

■ ■ ■

## CHAPTER 11

Configuring the Network

Most Linux computers operate in a connected world. Therefore, configuring the network board is of highest importance. In this chapter, you'll first learn how to give your computer an IP address and related information. You'll also learn about some useful tools that will help you in analyzing and troubleshooting a failing network connection. The last part of this chapter is about Secure Shell (SSH), which helps you make secured connections to other computers.

A Quick Introduction to Computer Networking

Before looking at the specifics of network configuration, it's important you first have a general understanding of what it is all about. This section explains basic networking for people who are new to the subject; it's not a complete tutorial, but it tries to outline the most important concepts of networking for people who don't have much knowledge on the subject.

All networking starts with an address. The most basic address, which is on the network card, is called a Media Access Control (MAC) address. Every network card has a MAC address. This goes not only for the wired network card in your computer, but also for the mobile phone that you use to browse the Internet. These MAC addresses are unique worldwide.

Although it is possible to communicate based solely on the MAC address, such a solution would not be ideal. This is because a MAC address contains no information about where a specific computer is on the network. The only way to have communication based on the MAC address is by broadcasting to all computers in the network, querying them to find out which has the MAC address you are looking for. This works for a small local network (referred to as a LAN), but it doesn't work for a computer that is thousands of miles away over the Internet.

The solution for this problem is in the IP address. IP addresses make worldwide communication between computers possible, as each IP address contains information about the local computer (referred to as the node part of the IP address) as well as the network the computer is on. Since each IP address includes this network information, it is possible to address a computer at the other end of the world directly through an IP.

To connect different IP networks together, a *router* is used. This is a dedicated machine that knows how to reach other IP networks. Most routers just know a few other networks and contain a *default route*. This default route refers to all other IP network addresses. At the end, most routed network traffic is handled by one of the backbone routers on the Internet. These are huge machines that know how to find all IP network addresses.

As IP addresses are in a numeric format (such as 179.237.39.66), which is not easy to handle for humans, on the Internet, computers are addressed by their name instead of their IP address. This name is translated into an IP address by a Domain Name Service (DNS) server.

To make sure your computer can communicate with other computers on the Internet, your computer needs to have an IP address, and it needs to know where to find the default router and the DNS servers. You can enter all this information manually (which you'll learn how to do later in this chapter), but in many cases, a DHCP server is used to hand out this information automatically. If you are working on a workstation, your computer will by default contact a DHCP server, and you'll be fine. However, if you are an administrator who is responsible for having a server up and running in your network, you'll probably need to set all this information yourself. The next sections teach you how.

Understanding Network Device Naming

When working with network cards in Linux, you need to know a bit about network device naming. Older Linux systems used names such as eth0 for the physical network card in a system and wlan0 for a WiFi network card. As on some servers multiple network cards are used, this way of addressing network device names isn't efficient. For that reason the BIOS dependent network device names were introduced. When this feature is enabled, you'll see network device names that say something about the physical location of a network card in the machine.

If BIOS devicenames are used, you will see the name **em** for embedded network cards (em1 for instance), and p<slot>p<ethernet_port> (p6p1 for instance) for cards that are inserted in a PCI slot. In virtual machines and for network cards whose firmware doesn't support BIOS device names, you may still see the old eth<number> names.

For some administrators, using BIOS device names is a great improvement. Others sincerely hate it because it makes network device names inconsistent between machines. If you don't want to use BIOS device names, but rather use the old naming instead, make sure that the GRUB2 boot loader starts your server with the boot options bios.devname=0 and net.ifnames=0.

Setting the IP Address

On installation, all Linux distributions work with DHCP to get an IP address. DHCP offers a very convenient way of configuring the network card, as even simple Internet routers for home usage have an embedded DHCP server. In some cases, however, you'll need a fixed IP address. Let's see how this works.

Before starting our discussion about IP address manipulation, you should know that there are two methods to manage IP addresses. There is the **ifconfig** command, a command that has been in use for a very long period. For modern Linux distributions however, this command isn't efficient enough anymore, and therefore there is a new way of managing IP addresses, using the **ip** command. The **ip** command is the preferred way to manage IP addresses, and if you've never worked with **ifconfig**, I recommend skipping the section about **ifconfig** completely. As some administrators still like using this command, I'm including information on how to manage the IP stack with this command anyway.

Using the ip Tool

The **ip** tool is the default tool for managing IP address configuration. It has many options that allow you to manage virtually all aspects of the network connection. For example, you can use it to configure an IP address, but it manages routing as well. Other more advanced manipulations are supported through the **ip** tool as well.

The first option you use with the ip command determines exactly what you want to do with the tool. It is a reference to the so-called object; you can consider these objects the secondary command level that determines more precisely what you want to do. Each of the objects has different possibilities:

- link: Used to manage or display properties of a network device. Use this for monitoring the current state of a network interface.

- addr: Used to manage or display IPv4 or IPv6 network addresses on a device.

- route: Used to manage or display entries in the routing table.

- rule: Used to manage or display rules in the routing policy database.

- neigh: Used to manage or display entries in the ARP cache. ARP gives information about which IP address is used by which MAC address. By using this option, you can modify the ARP information or display it.

- netns: Used to manage IP network namespaces, a technology that is commonly used in cloud environment and which allows you to manage isolated network environments while using the same network interface.

- tunnel: Used to manage or display IP tunnels. This is something you'll only need when setting up Virtual Private Network (VPN) connections over the Internet. VPN technology is quite popular in enterprise environments to set up secure connections, but will not be discussed any further in this book.

- maddr: Used to manage or display multicast addresses for interfaces. A multicast address is a group address that you can add to a network card. Using multicast makes it possible for a user or an application to address all nodes that provide the same functionality simultaneously.

- mroute: Used to manage or display multicast routing cache entries.

- monitor: Used to monitor what happens on a given device.

For each of the objects, you'll have to use options. The easiest way to learn about these options is to use the ip command followed by the object followed by the keyword help. For example, ip address help provides information on how to use the ip address command, as shown in Listing 11-1.

Listing 11-1. The ip address help Command Gives Help on Configuring IP Addresses with the ip Tool

```
root@ZNA:~# ip address help
Usage: ip addr {add|del} IFADDR dev STRING
       ip addr {show|flush} [ dev STRING ] [ scope SCOPE-ID ]
                            [ to PREFIX ] [ FLAG-LIST ] [ label PATTERN ]
IFADDR := PREFIX | ADDR peer PREFIX
          [ broadcast ADDR ] [ anycast ADDR ]
          [ label STRING ] [ scope SCOPE-ID ]
SCOPE-ID := [ host | link | global | NUMBER ]
FLAG-LIST := [ FLAG-LIST ] FLAG
FLAG := [ permanent | dynamic | secondary | primary |
          tentative | deprecated ]
```

It can be quite a challenge to find out how the help for the ip tool works, so I'll give you some pointers on this feature. To understand what you need to do, you must first analyze the Usage: lines. In the example in Listing 11-1, you see two of them: a usage line that starts with ip addr {add|del}, and another that starts with ip addr {show|flush}. Let's have a look at the first one, which allows you to add or remove an IP address.

The complete usage line as described by ip address help is ip addr {add|del} IFADDR dev STRING. So you can add or delete an IP address that is referred to by IFADDR from a device (dev) that is referred to by STRING. Now, a string is just a string, and that can be anything (but normally will be something like eth0). The IFADDR part, which is the address that you'll assign to the string, offers more options, which are described in the next part. You can find an explanation of that part in the next section of the help output: IFADDR := PREFIX | ADDR peer PREFIX [broadcast ADDR] [anycast ADDR] [label STRING] [scope SCOPE-ID]. In this line, the help explains that you have to use a PREFIX or an ADDR statement, which may be followed by several options like the broadcast address, the anycast address, a label, or a SCOPE-ID.

But from the help also follows that you can just simply add an address. There is no further explanation of the other options, as this is information that you should know about when configuring IP addresses. This means ip address help can't tell you which IP address you need on which Ethernet interface. Now that you understand how the help works, let's have a look at some of the different ways you can use the ip command.

Tip! Using the **ip** command based on the help text alone is challenging. You might be better of just trying to remember the most important tasks that you can do with the ip command, and how you can accomplish them. Table 11-1 gives an overview of these commands.

Table 11-1. *ip command important examples overview*

Task	Command
show current configuration	ip addr show
add an IP address to eth0	ip addr add 10.0.0.10/24 dev eth0
show link statistics	ip link show
show the routing table	ip route show
add a default route	ip route add default via 10.0.0.1

Showing Ip addresses with `ip`

A common use of ip is to display information about the use of IP addresses for a given interface. The command to use is ip address show, or just ip address. Note that, if it is clear exactly what you want and there can be no confusion between options, you can specify the options used with the ip command in short form, such as ip a s, which accomplishes the same thing as ip address show. Listing 11-2 gives an example.

Listing 11-2. Showing ip Address Configuration with ip address show

```
root@ZNA:~# ip address show
1: lo: <LOOPBACK,UP,10000> mtu 16436 qdisc noqueue
    link/loopback 00:00:00:00:00:00 brd 00:00:00:00:00:00
    inet 127.0.0.1/8 scope host lo
    inet6 ::1/128 scope host
       valid_lft forever preferred_lft forever
2: eth0: <BROADCAST,MULTICAST,UP,10000> mtu 1500 qdisc pfifo_fast qlen 1000
    link/ether 00:0c:29:a0:a5:80 brd ff:ff:ff:ff:ff:ff
    inet 192.168.1.33/24 brd 192.168.1.255 scope global eth0
    inet 10.0.0.10/8 brd 10.255.255.255 scope global eth0:0
    inet 10.0.0.20/8 brd 10.255.255.255 scope global secondary eth0:1
    inet6 fe80::20c:29ff:fea0:a580/64 scope link
       valid_lft forever preferred_lft forever
```

As you can see, the **ip addr show** command is quite complete in what it is showing. In particular the part about eth0 (normally your fixed network card) is interesting. First, you can see that broadcast and multicast are enabled on this device, and that the network card is up. Next, it shows some other properties of the network card that are interesting if you need to troubleshoot the way a network card is functioning. However, if you just need to assign an IP address, you typically wouldn't care about these parameters. Last, the lines starting with inet show the addresses that are assigned to the network card, with their corresponding subnet masks.

Showing Device attributes

Another simple use of the ip tool is to show device attributes, which you can do with the ip link show command. This command shows usage statistics for the device you've specified but no address information, which is kind of obvious as well. ip link works on the link, ip address on the IP address. Listing 11-3 provides an example of its output.

Listing 11-3. Use the ip link show Command for an Overview of Link Attributes

```
root@ZNA:~# ip link show
1: lo: <LOOPBACK,UP,10000> mtu 16436 qdisc noqueue
    link/loopback 00:00:00:00:00:00 brd 00:00:00:00:00:00
2: eth0: <BROADCAST,MULTICAST,UP,10000> mtu 1500 qdisc pfifo_fast qlen 1000
    link/ether 00:0c:29:a0:a5:80 brd ff:ff:ff:ff:ff:ff
```

The information displayed by ip link show is related to the activity on the network board. Of particular interest are the device attributes returned for each of the devices (they're displayed in brackets right after the name of the device). You can see for instance the attributes BROADCAST,MULTICAST,UP for a normal network interface card. The BROADCAST attribute indicates that the device is capable of sending broadcasts to other nodes in the network, the MULTICAST attribute indicates that the device can also send multicast packets (a feature that is disabled in some networks), and the UP attribute indicates that the device is working. The command also shows all IP protocol attributes, such as the maximum transmission unit (mtu) that is used on the interface.

Setting the IP address

You can also use the ip tool to assign an IP address to a device. To do this, you could use a command like ip address add 10.0.0.10/16 dev eth0. This command sets the IP address for eth0 to 10.0.0.10. With this IP address, a 16-bit subnet mask is used, which is indicated by the CIDR notation of the subnetmask 255.255.0.0 (/16) directly behind the IP address. The broadcast address is calculated automatically, which you can specify by adding brd + to the command. Once you have set the IP address with the ip tool, you can use the following command to check if it's set correctly: ip address show dev eth0 (or just use ip a, which gives you the address configuration for all network cards).

You can add more than one IP address to a network interface when using the ip tool as well. And it isn't hard: just use ip address add 10.0.0.20/16 dev eth0, and 10.0.0.20 with its specified properties is added as a second IP address to eth0 (assuming that some other IP address was already defined for this network card). There is a difference between secondary IP addresses that are added with ifconfig and the IP addresses that are added with the ip tool. An address added with ip won't show up when you use ifconfig. So when using secondary IP addresses, make sure you use the right tool to check their properties, you might miss them when using the legacy **ifconfig** tool.

Using ifconfig

You can use ifconfig to manage and monitor a network interface card. The command has been around for years; although it's not the most flexible command, it'll still do the job. And the biggest advantage: it's a relatively easy command to use. If you use the ifconfig command without any parameters, you'll see information about the current configuration of the network cards in your computer. An example of this is in Listing 11-4.

Listing 11-4. The ifconfig Command Can Show Your Current Network Configuration Parameter

```
eth0       Link encap:Ethernet HWaddr 00:0C:29:A0:A5:80
           inet addr:192.168.1.33 Bcast:192.168.1.255 Mask:255.255.255.0
           inet6 addr: fe80::20c:29ff:fea0:a580/64 Scope:Link
           UP BROADCAST RUNNING MULTICAST MTU:1500 Metric:1
           RX packets:3035 errors:0 dropped:0 overruns:0 frame:0
           TX packets:199 errors:0 dropped:0 overruns:0 carrier:0
           collisions:0 txqueuelen:1000
           RX bytes:240695 (235.0 KiB) TX bytes:19035 (18.5 KiB)
           Interrupt:18 Base address:0x1400
Lo         Link encap:Local Loopback
           inet addr:127.0.0.1 Mask:255.0.0.0
           inet6 addr: ::1/128 Scope:Host
           UP LOOPBACK RUNNING MTU:16436 Metric:1
           RX packets:0 errors:0 dropped:0 overruns:0 frame:0
           TX packets:0 errors:0 dropped:0 overruns:0 carrier:0
           collisions:0 txqueuelen:0
           RX bytes:0 (0.0 b) TX bytes:0 (0.0 b)
```

Displaying Information with `ifconfig`

As you have seen in Listing 11-4, the ifconfig command provides different kinds of information about a network card. It starts with the name of the protocol used on the network card. The protocol is indicated by (for example) Link encap: Ethernet, which states that it is an Ethernet network board. Almost all modern LAN interfaces will show you Ethernet as the link encapsulation type, but on a WAN connection you may see other protocols such as PPP instead. Then the MAC address is given as the HWaddr (hardware address). This address is followed first by the IPv4-related address information (inet addr) and then the IPv6 address information, if IPv6 hasn't been disabled (inet6 addr). Then several statistics about the network board are given. Pay special attention to the RX packets (received packets) and TX packets (transmitted packets) because you can see from these statistics what the network board is doing and if any errors have occurred. Typically, there should be no errors here.

■ **Note** Currently, most computers use IP version 4 IP addresses. In version 4, approximately 4 billion IP addresses can be addressed. However, since the protocol specification is inefficient, there are almost no more free IPv4 addresses available. Therefore, IPv6 was developed (see www.ipv6.org). The most important purpose of IPv6 is to make (many) more IP addresses available. Migration to IPv6 goes slowly, however, as it requires quite a lot of work on the network infrastructure of companies that want to migrate. Linux offers full support for IPv6, and most distributions even enable it by default. An IPv6 address is represented in hexadecimal way, as in this example: feb0:ff66:ab08:0963:badc:afe0:3796:0012. Compare this to the typical IPv4 address, which looks like 129.13.57.192.

Apart from the information about the physical network boards that are present in your computer, you'll also always see information about the loopback device (lo), which is the network interface that's used for internal purposes on your computer. Your computer needs this loopback device because some IP-related services depend on it; for example, the graphical environment that's used on Linux is written on top of the IP stack offered by the loopback interface.

Configuring a Network Card with `ifconfig`

Although your system is provided with an IP address upon installation, it's important for you to be able to manage IP address configuration on the fly, using the `ifconfig` command. Fortunately, it's relatively easy to configure a network board in this way: just add the name of the network board you want to configure followed by the IP address you want to use on that network board (for example, `ifconfig eth0 192.168.1.125`). This command will configure eth0 with a default class C subnet mask of 255.255.255.0, which indicates that the first three bytes of the IP address are a part of the network address and that the last byte is the unique host identifier within that network.

■ **Tip** Not sure what eth device number is used? You can manage this via the udev mechanism. In the file `/etc/udev/rules.d/nn-persistent-net.rules` a mapping is made between the MAC address and interface number of your network boards. So if you want the eth1 device to be presented as eth0, this is the place where you can change it. Just change the current name (e.g., eth1) in the name you want it to be, and restart your computer to make the change effective.

If you need a custom subnet mask, add an extra parameter to `ifconfig`, as in the command `ifconfig eth0 172.16.18.18 netmask 255.255.255.0 broadcast 172.16.18.255`, which configures the eth0 device with the given IP address and a 24-bit subnet mask. If you work with a nondefault subnet mask, you have to specify the broadcast address that's used to address all nodes in the same network as well; the `ifconfig` command just isn't smart enough to realize that you're using a nondefault IP address and to calculate the right broadcast address accordingly.

■ **Note** In the IP protocol, subnet masks are used to distinguish the network part from the node part of the IP address. All IP addresses must have a subnet mask. To make working with IP easier, IP addresses do have a default subnetmask; for instance, IP addresses starting with 192, such as 192.1.2.3, have the default subnet mask 255.255.255.0, which tells the IP stack that the first three bytes are used to address the network, and the last byte only is used to address the node. In some situations, an administrator may choose to use nondefault subnet masks, for instance, if he or she needs to address more than one network but doesn't have enough network addresses available. There are two ways to write the subnet mask that is to be used: in the so-called dotted method (e.g., 255.255.255.0) or in the CIDR method. The latter uses a slash, followed by the number of bytes that are in the subnet mask. Consult `http://en.wikipedia.org/wiki/Subnetwork` for a more detailed explanation of subnet masks.

Bringing Interfaces Up and Down with `ifconfig`

Apart from adding an IP address to a network board, you can use the `ifconfig` command to bring a specific network board up or down. For example, `ifconfig eth0 down` shuts down the interface, and `ifconfig eth0 up` brings it up again with its default settings. This is useful if you want to test a new configuration, but you're not sure whether it's really going to work properly.

Instead of using `ifconfig` to bring the network card up and down, you can also use `ifup` and `ifdown`. These commands allow you to bring a network card up or down easily, without changing the configuration of a given network board. For example, to bring a network board down, use `ifdown eth0`; to bring it up again, use `ifup eth0`. In both cases, the default configuration for the network card is applied.

Using Virtual Ip addresses with `ifconfig`

In some cases, one network card may need multiple IP addresses. These are called virtual IP addresses, and you can set them with `ifconfig`. Using virtual IP addresses is useful if you are configuring services on your computer that all need their own IP address. Think, for example, of different virtual Apache web servers that are all reachable on their own IP address.

■ **Note** This doesn't mean that to run multiple instances of Apache, you'll always need a virtual IP address configuration. Using virtual IP addresses is just one way of doing this.

You can use the virtual IP address either within the same IP address range or on a different one. To add a virtual IP address, add :*n* where *n* is a number after the name of the network interface. For example, `ifconfig eth0:0 10.0.0.10` adds the address 10.0.0.10 as a virtual IP address to eth0. The number after the colon must be unique, so you can add a second virtual IP address with `ifconfig eth0:1 10.0.0.20`, and so on. When you use the `ifconfig` tool to display the current configuration of your computer, you'll see all virtual IP addresses that are configured, as shown in Listing 11-5.

Listing 11-5. The ifconfig Tool Shows Virtual IP Addresses As Well

```
root@ZNA:~# ifconfig eth0:0 10.0.0.10
root@ZNA:~# ifconfig eth0:1 10.0.0.20
root@ZNA:~# ifconfig
eth0      Link encap:Ethernet HWaddr 00:0C:29:A0:A5:80
          inet addr:192.168.1.33 Bcast:192.168.1.255 Mask:255.255.255.0
          inet6 addr: fe80::20c:29ff:fea0:a580/64 Scope:Link
          UP BROADCAST RUNNING MULTICAST MTU:1500 Metric:1
          RX packets:3035 errors:0 dropped:0 overruns:0 frame:0
          TX packets:199 errors:0 dropped:0 overruns:0 carrier:0
          collisions:0 txqueuelen:1000
          RX bytes:240695 (235.0 KiB) TX bytes:19035 (18.5 KiB)
          Interrupt:18 Base address:0x1400
eth0:0    Link encap:Ethernet HWaddr 00:0C:29:A0:A5:80
          inet addr:10.0.0.10 Bcast:10.255.255.255 Mask:255.0.0.0
          UP BROADCAST RUNNING MULTICAST MTU:1500 Metric:1
          Interrupt:18 Base address:0x1400
eth0:1    Link encap:Ethernet HWaddr 00:0C:29:A0:A5:80
          inet addr:10.0.0.20 Bcast:10.255.255.255 Mask:255.0.0.0
          UP BROADCAST RUNNING MULTICAST MTU:1500 Metric:1
          Interrupt:18 Base address:0x1400
          Link encap:Local Loopback
          inet addr:127.0.0.1 Mask:255.0.0.0
          inet6 addr: ::1/128 Scope:Host
          UP LOOPBACK RUNNING MTU:16436 Metric:1
          RX packets:0 errors:0 dropped:0 overruns:0 frame:0
          TX packets:0 errors:0 dropped:0 overruns:0 carrier:0
          collisions:0 txqueuelen:0
          RX bytes:0 (0.0 b) TX bytes:0 (0.0 b)
```

EXERCISE 11-1: MANAGING IP ADDRESSES

In this exercise you'll learn how to manage IP addresses. You'll work with the **ip** command and also will see why you shouldn't use the **ifconfig** command anymore.

1. Open a root shell on your machine. If you're working on Ubuntu, you can do so by using the **sudo su** command.

2. Type **ip addr show**. Look up the name of the network card in your machine. In the remainder of this exercise I'll assume it is eth0, make sure to replace that name with the name that is used in your configuration.

3. Type **ip link show** to show link statistics for your network card.

4. Type **ip addr add dev eth0 10.11.12.13/24** to add a secondary IP address.

5. Use **ping 10.11.12.13** to verify that this IP address is operational.

6. Type **ifconfig**. You won't see the secondary IP address that you have assigned. This is why you should not use **ifconfig** anymore.

Storing Address Configuration

When your computer boots, it normally loads its IP address configuration automatically. In the next sections you'll read how this works on the most important Linux distributions.

Storing IP Address Configuration on Ubuntu

When your computer boots, it starts the networking script from /etc/init.d. The script reads the configuration that is stored in the /etc/network directory or using the systemd script if you're on a newer version, paying particular attention to the /etc/network/interfaces file. This configuration file stores the entire configuration of the network board. Listing 11-6 shows an example configuration for a computer that has two Ethernet network cards.

Listing 11-6. Example Contents of the interfaces File on Ubuntu

```
root@ZNA:~# cat /etc/network/interfaces
# This file describes the network interfaces available on your system
# and how to activate them. For more information, see interfaces(5).
# The loopback network interface
auto lo
iface lo inet loopback

# The primary network interface
auto eth0
iface eth0 inet static
        address 192.168.1.33
        netmask 255.255.255.0
        network 192.168.1.0
        broadcast 192.168.1.255
        gateway 192.168.1.254
```

```
        # dns-* options are implemented by the resolvconf package, if installed
        dns-nameservers 193.79.237.39
        dns-search lan

#The second network board
auto eth1
iface eth1 inet static
        address 10.0.0.10
        netmask 255.255.255.0
        network 10.0.0.0
        broadcast 10.0.0.255
```

As you can see from the configuration file, the computer has activated three network interfaces. The first is lo, and this is the loopback interface. It's required for many services to function, even if your computer has no network connection at all. For instance, the X server that takes care of the graphical display on your computer uses the loopback interface to handle internal communication. The loopback interface always uses the IP address 127.0.0.1.

In most cases, an Ethernet network card is used to connect with the rest of the world. This network card is represented by the name eth0 if it's the first, and names like eth1 and so on for the next cards. The definition of each of the network boards starts with auto ethn, in which n is the number of the network interface. This line is used to start the network card automatically when your computer boots. You can omit this line, but if you do so, you'll need to use the ifup or ifconfig commands as described earlier to start the network card by hand. In most situations you don't want to do that, so make sure that the line that starts with auto is used at all times.

Following the auto line, there is a definition of the interface itself. In this example, a computer is configured with two static IP addresses. If you need DHCP on an interface, make sure the iface line reads iface ethn inet dynamic. Following that, there is the rest of the configuration for the network card. You'll need address, netmask, network, and broadcast in all cases. The other options are optional.

Storing IP Address Configuration on Red Hat

On Red Hat, fixed IP address configuration is stored in the /etc/sysconfig/network-scripts/ ifcfg-ethn file. One file is created for each Ethernet interface. In Listing 11-7, you can see what this file looks like.

Listing 11-7. Network Configuration As Stored on Red Hat

```
[root@workstation ~]# cat /etc/sysconfig/network-scripts/ifcfg-eno16777736
TYPE="Ethernet"
BOOTPROTO="none"
DEFROUTE="yes"
IPV4_FAILURE_FATAL="no"
IPV6INIT="yes"
IPV6_AUTOCONF="yes"
IPV6_DEFROUTE="yes"
IPV6_FAILURE_FATAL="no"
NAME="eno16777736"
UUID="67ef89fc-cf5f-449b-b92d-7f980951eace"
ONBOOT="yes"
HWADDR="00:0C:29:25:D0:71"
IPADDR0="192.168.4.9"
PREFIX0="24"
```

```
GATEWAY0="192.168.4.2"
DNS1="8.8.8.8"
IPV6_PEERDNS="yes"
IPV6_PEERROUTES="yes"
```

In this example configuration file, you can see several parameters. You can change them as needed and deactivate and activate the device after applying the changes with `ifdown ethn`, followed by `ifup ethn`. The following parameters are in the `ifcfg-ethn` file:

- DEVICE: The device name. This should be the `eth` name of the hardware device.

- HWADDR: The MAC address of the device. Make sure that it is unique for all devices you are using.

- ONBOOT: Whether or not the device must be activated when your computer boots. You normally want to set this parameter to `yes`.

- SEARCH: The default DNS search domain. If an incomplete DNS name is used (e.g., ping linda), the default DNS search domain is appended.

- BOOTPROTO: The specific boot protocol used, if any. Set this to DHCP if you want the network card to obtain an IP address automatically from a DHCP server when activated.

- NETMASK: The netmask that you are using with the IP address on this interface.

- IPADDR: The IP address used by this interface.

- USERCTL: Whether or not an end user is allowed to activate and deactivate this interface.

- PEERDNS: DNS information for the peer in a point-to-point setup.

- IPV6INIT: Whether or not you want to initialize the IPv6 protocol.

- NMCONTROL: As an alternative to manual device configuration, you can configure a network device with the network manager application. This parameter tells your system whether this applet should be used.

- GATEWAY: The IP address of the default router that is needed to connect to computers on other networks.

- TYPE: The protocol used by this network card.

Storing IP Address Configuration on SUSE

On SUSE Linux, the network information is stored in more or less the same way as on Fedora. The name of the configuration file is `/etc/sysconfig/network/ifcfg-nnn`, in which nnn represents the MAC address the network card uses. Listing 11-8 shows what the SUSE configuration file looks like. In this listing, you can see that the contents of the file `ifcfg-eth- id-00:0c:29:ae:e6:e5` is requested. In the file name, backslashes are used to make sure that the next character is not interpreted by the shell. You can change the SUSE configuration file by hand, or by using the YaST configuration tool.

Listing 11-8. Network Card Configuration As Stored on SUSE

```
nuuk:/etc/sysconfig/network # cat ifcfg-eth-id-00\:0c\:29\:ae\:e6\:e5
BOOTPROTO='dhcp'
BROADCAST=''
ETHTOOL_OPTIONS=''
IPADDR=''
MTU=''
NAME='AMD PCnet - Fast 79C971'
NETMASK='255.255.255.0'
NETWORK=''
REMOTE_IPADDR=''
STARTMODE='auto'
UNIQUE='rBUF.weGuQ9ywYPF'
USERCONTROL='no'
_nm_name='bus-pci-0000:02:00.0'
```

In the SUSE configuration file, multiple parameters are stored. A short explanation of each of them follows:

- BOOTPROTO: Indicates whether DHCP should be used or whether the interface has a static IP address assignment. Use either DHCP or STATIC.

- BROADCAST: Specifies the broadcast address of the network.

- ETHTOOL_OPTIONS: Specifies ethtool command arguments that will be interpreted by the ethtool utility. ethtool lets you set specific parameters, such as the link speed, duplex mode, or receive buffer size of your network card. You can read more about this utility in the section "Tuning the Network Card with ethtool" later in this chapter.

- IPADDR: Specifies which IP address is to be used.

- MTU: Specifies the maximum transmission unit. By default on Ethernet, it is 1500; set it to 9000 to enable jumbo frames, which are useful on links that work with large packets.

- NAME: Specifies a name for the interface. Enter a unique name here. * NETMASK: Indicates the netmask in dotted notation (255.255.255.0 and not /24).

- NETWORK: Allows you to specify the address of the network. This field is optional.

- REMOTE_IPADDR: Specifies the IP address of the remote node in a peer-to-peer connection.

- STARTMODE: Indicates whether this interface must be started automatically or manually.

- UNIQUE: Contains a unique ID that is used by the YaST management utility.

- USERCONTROL: Indicates whether or not an end user is allowed to stop and start this interface.

- _nm_name: Contains a reference to the hardware location of the NIC.

Configuring Routing

You've read about how a network interface is provided with an IP address. But, to be completely functional on the network, you have to specify some routes as well. These routes allow you to communicate with computers on other networks, and, conversely, they allow computers on other networks to communicate with your computer.

As a minimal requirement, you need a default route. This entry specifies where to send packets that don't have a destination on the local network. The router used as the default route is always on the same network as your computer; just consider it to be the door that helps you get out of the local network. Your computer typically gets the information about the default router that it should use from the /etc/network/interfaces Ubuntu file, /etc/sysconfig/network-scripts/ifcfg-eth0 on Fedora, or /etc/sysconfig/network/routes on SUSE. To set the default route yourself, two tools can be used: the ip tool and the route utility. In the next two sections, you'll read how to do this. The **ip** tool is the preferred utility to manage routes.

Managing the Default Route with route

The old command to set the default route is route. If no options are used, it will display a list of all routes that are currently defined on this host. Listing 11-9 provides an example. When using the route command without options, it will always try to resolve the name for a given IP address, which takes some time. If you don't want any name resolution to be performed, use the option -n, which makes the command a lot faster.

Listing 11-9. Use the route Command to Get an Overview of All Routes That Are Currently Configured

```
root@ZNA:~# route
Kernel IP routing table
Destination     Gateway         Genmask          Flags  Metric  Ref  Use  Iface

localnet        *               255.255.255.0    U      0       0    0    eth0
10.0.0.0        *               255.0.0.0        U      0       0    0    eth0
default         192.168.1.254   0.0.0.0          UG     0       0    0    eth0
```

In the output of the route command all information necessary for the routing process is provided, as you can see in Listing 11-9. The first column provides the destination, which is the network or host that a route is defined for. Typically, these are networks that your computer is connected to with its local interfaces and the default route. Next is the gateway, which is the router that needs to be contacted to reach the specified destination. An asterisk (*) in this field indicates that the local computer is the gateway for that destination. If an external router is used as the destination, you'll see the IP address (or name) of that router. Next is the genmask, which is the subnet mask used on the specified destination. Then come the flags, metric, ref, and use columns, all of which reveal more detailed information about this route. Finally, the iface column reveals what network interface is used to route packets.

To specify a route, you need to provide a minimum of two pieces of information: the IP address or name of the network you want to add, and the IP address of the default gateway. All the other information is added automatically. For example, if you want to specify that the router with IP address 192.168.1.254 should be used as the default gateway, use the command route add default gw 192.168.1.254.

If you need to change the default gateway, you should be aware that you first have to remove the old entry for this default gateway. Use the route del command to do this. For example, to remove the current setting for the default gateway, use route del default gw.

Managing the Default Route with the `ip` Tool

If you know what information to enter when defining a route, it's easy to do it with either the `ifconfig` or the `ip` tool. Only the syntax is different. To set the default gateway to 192.168.1.254 using the `ip` tool, use the `ip route add default via 192.168.1.254` command. This command makes sure that all packets sent to nonlocal destinations are sent through 192.168.1.254. Likewise, you can delete the default route with `ip route del default`.

Storing Routing Information

To make sure that your computer still knows the default route after a reboot, you should store it somewhere. In the next three sections, you'll read how to do this for the three main distributions.

Ubuntu

When you enter information, such as the default gateway, from the command line, it will be lost the next time you reboot your computer. To make sure that the information remains after a reboot, store it in the `/etc/network/interfaces` file on Ubuntu. This file is read every time the network is activated. The entry used in this file to store the default route isn't complex:

```
gateway 192.168.1.254
```

If you have more than one network card in your computer, it is enough to specify the information about the default route once only.

Red Hat

On Red Hat also, you specify the address of the default route in the file that stores the configuration of your network interface. See Listing 11-7 earlier in this chapter for an example. If you have more than one network card in your computer, you do not need to enter this information in the configuration file of each network card.

Resolving DNS Names to IP Addresses

If you want to manually configure a network connection as the last part, you need to specify what DNS name server to use. The DNS Server makes sure that names that are used on your local network and the Internet can be translated to the IP addresses your computer needs to make a connection.

To store the DNS information, you use the so-called DNS resolver. This DNS resolver is stored in the `/etc/resolv.conf` file; there is no command-line utility to configure it. Typically, the `/etc/resolv.conf` file will contain the IP address of at least two DNS name servers and a search domain. The name server specifications indicate what DNS name computer should be contacted to translate DNS names to IP addresses and vice versa. Typically, your Internet provider will get you this information. Specify at least two name servers so that if the first one cannot be reached, the second one can do the job.

The search domain specifies what domain name should be appended if an incomplete host name is used. It makes sense to use the name of your default DNS domain as the search domain. So if you computer's name is computer.example.com, set the search domain name to example.com. Listing 11-10 is an example of the content of the `/etc/resolv.conf` file.

Listing 11-10. Example of the /etc/resolv.conf File

```
nameserver 192.168.1.10
nameserver 193.79.237.39
search example.com
```

In this example, you see that name server 192.168.1.10 is used as the default name server, and all DNS requests will be sent to it. If this server cannot be reached, only then will the second server in the list (193.79.237.39) be contacted. The third line of the Listing 11-10 example specifies the search domain. For example, if a user uses the command ping ftp, which includes an incomplete host name, the name of the domain specified with the search option in resolv.conf is added automatically to it, so in this case the packet would be sent to ftp. example.com.

Notice that on none of the three major Linux distributions the /etc/resol.conf file should be edited directly. You'll have to include the DNS server configuration in the network card configuration file (/etc/sysconfig/network-scripts/ifcfg-eth0 on Red Hat or /etc/network/interfaces on Ubuntu). From there, the DNS name server will be written to the /etc/resolv.conf file. Any modification you make manually to the /etc/resolv.conf file risks getting lost after a restart of the network service.

The Role of the /etc/nsswitch.conf File

Most people take it for granted that DNS resolves host names to IP addresses, but this isn't necessarily so. Every Linux computer has the /etc/nsswitch.conf file that determines what exactly should happen when translating a host name to an IP address and vice versa. This file specifies many things (such as user configuration, which you read about in Chapter 6), but only the following lines are important for resolving host names:

```
hosts:          files dns
networks:       files
```

These two lines specify that, when resolving host names as well as network names, the (local) files should be searched first, and that the DNS subsystem should be used only if the files have no information about the given host. Thus, an administrator can make sure that frequently accessed host names are resolved locally, where the DNS is contacted only when the files don't have information about a particular host. The most important file used for resolving names to IP addresses is the /etc/hosts file, which is the file referred to by files on the hosts line in /etc/nsswitch.conf.

Using the /etc/hosts File

One of the oldest ways to resolve host names to IP addresses (and vice versa) is to use the /etc/hosts file. It's rather primitive because you have to maintain the file on every single computer where you need it, and no synchronization of entries in this file is established between computers. But it's also a very efficient way to supply information that needs to be available locally.

■ **Note** To resolve the problem of decentralized management, the Network Information Service (NIS, formerly known as Yellow Pages) was invented by Sun Microsystems. Nowadays, it's hardly ever used anymore, because most companies keep their hosts-related information in DNS.

Using the /etc/hosts file makes resolving names faster and reduces Internet traffic, and you can use it to add any host names that need to be available only locally. Listing 11-11 shows example contents of this file.

Listing 11-11. Example of the /etc/hosts File

```
[root@workstation ~]# cat /etc/hosts
127.0.0.1     localhost    localhost.localdomain    localhost4 localhost4.localdomain4
::1           localhost    localhost.localdomain    localhost6 localhost6.localdomain6
192.168.4.9  workstation  workstation.example.com
192.168.4.10 server1      server1.example.com
192.168.4.20 server2      server2.example.com
```

As you can see, the contents of this file is rather simple. First, you specify the IP address of the host, which can be an IPv4 or an IPv6 address. Next, the fully qualified host name of the host is specified. This is the name of the host itself followed by its DNS suffix. Last, the short host name is used. Alternatively, you can just provide the IP address followed by the name of the host you want to add, such as in the following line:

```
192.168.1.180     RNA
```

On a modern Linux computer, it's often not necessary to set up /etc/hosts except for local name resolving. Network name resolving is typically managed in DNS. So you'll always need your own host name and IP address in this file. This is configured automatically when installing your computer.

Tuning the Network Card with `ethtool`

At this point you know how to configure IP-related parameters. The network card itself also has settings that you may need to modify, and you'll use the `ethtool` command to do this. With this utility, you can change network board properties like link speed and duplex mode. Don't overestimate this tool though. Some Ethernet cards are not supported, and the only way to change settings on those may be through the network board's BIOS settings. Let's start by displaying some information: issue `ethtool -i eth0` to see an overview of driver properties that are currently used, as shown in Listing 11-12.

Listing 11-12. The ethtool -i Command Provides an Overview of Driver Properties

```
[root@lab ~]# ethtool -i eno1
driver: e1000e
version: 2.3.2-k
firmware-version: 0.6-4
bus-info: 0000:00:19.0
supports-statistics: yes
supports-test: yes
supports-eeprom-access: yes
supports-register-dump: yes
supports-priv-flags: no
```

To change duplex settings and link speed on your network board, you'll use the `-s` option, followed by one of these arguments:

- speed: This option changes the speed. Valid options are 10, 100, and 1000.

- duplex: This option changes the duplex settings. Set it to half or full.

- port: This specifies what port to use. This option is used for network interfaces with different ports available (which is not very common). Valid choices are tp, aui, bnc, mii, and fibre.

- autoneg: This option indicates whether you want to use autonegotiation to discover the settings that are used on the network.

So, for example, if you want to change the settings of your network card to full duplex and a link speed of 1000 Mbps, use ethtool -s eth0 speed 1000 duplex full. Now there is a problem when using ethtool like this: you need to enter these settings again the next time you start your computer. Only SUSE offers a solution for this problem; on SUSE you can store the ethtool configuration parameters in the configuration file for your network card. You have seen this in Listing 11-8. On other distributions that don't offer such a solution, you can include the ethtool command with all the parameters you need in the /etc/ init.d/boot.local script. Doing this, you'll make sure that ethtool settings are applied after a reboot as well.

In addition to the -i option with ethtool, which gives you a brief summary about your network board, are some other useful options. For instance, you can get some very detailed statistics about your network board when using ethtool -S as you can see in Listing 11-13.

Listing 11-13. ethtool -S Gives You Very Detailed Statistics About Your Network Card

```
[root@lab ~]# ethtool -S eno1
NIC statistics:
     rx_packets: 4423965
     tx_packets: 5086934
     rx_bytes: 2789043235
     tx_bytes: 4708139801
     rx_broadcast: 81778
     tx_broadcast: 4
     rx_multicast: 5044
     tx_multicast: 64
     rx_errors: 0
     tx_errors: 0
     tx_dropped: 0
     multicast: 5044
     collisions: 0
     rx_length_errors: 0
     rx_over_errors: 0
     rx_crc_errors: 0
     rx_frame_errors: 0
     rx_no_buffer_count: 0
     rx_missed_errors: 0
     tx_aborted_errors: 0
     tx_carrier_errors: 0
     tx_fifo_errors: 0
     tx_heartbeat_errors: 0
     tx_window_errors: 0
     tx_abort_late_coll: 0
     tx_deferred_ok: 0
     tx_single_coll_ok: 0
     tx_multi_coll_ok: 0
     tx_timeout_count: 0
     tx_restart_queue: 0
     rx_long_length_errors: 0
```

```
rx_short_length_errors: 0
rx_align_errors: 0
tx_tcp_seg_good: 718842
tx_tcp_seg_failed: 0
rx_flow_control_xon: 0
rx_flow_control_xoff: 0
tx_flow_control_xon: 0
tx_flow_control_xoff: 0
rx_csum_offload_good: 4325815
rx_csum_offload_errors: 3
rx_header_split: 0
alloc_rx_buff_failed: 0
tx_smbus: 0
rx_smbus: 0
dropped_smbus: 0
rx_dma_failed: 0
tx_dma_failed: 0
rx_hwtstamp_cleared: 0
uncorr_ecc_errors: 0
corr_ecc_errors: 0
tx_hwtstamp_timeouts: 0
```

Analyzing Network Connections

Once you have finished the setup tasks I've just described, you should have a working network connection. But, even if it's working fine right now, you may at some point need to perform some tuning and troubleshooting, and that's exactly what this section is about. Here, you'll learn how to test that everything is working the way it should and how to monitor what is happening on the network itself, as well as on the network interface. The tools I'm talking about in this section are the top-notch troubleshooting tools.

Testing Connectivity

After configuring a network card, you want to make sure it's working correctly. For this, the ping command is your friend, and more so because it's easy to use: enter the command followed by the name or address of the host you want to test connectivity to, such as ping www.ubuntu.com. This forces ping to start continuous output, which you can interrupt by using the Ctrl+C key sequence. You can also send a limited number of packets; for example, the command ping -c 3 192.168.1.254 sends just three packets to the specified host. If you use ping in a clever way, you can test a lot of things with it. I recommend using it in the following order:

1. Ping the localhost. If you pass this test, you've verified that the IP stack on your local machine is working properly.

2. Ping a machine on the local network by using its IP address: if this works, you've verified that IP is properly bound to the network board of your computer and that it can make a connection to other nodes on the network. If it fails, you need to check the information you've entered with the ifconfig or ip commands; you may have made an error entering the subnet mask for your network interface.

3. Ping a machine on the Internet using its IP address. A good bet is 8.8.8.8, which is a DNS server that hasn't failed me in the last 15 years. Of course, you can use any other host as long as you know its IP address. If the ping is successful, you've verified that the routers between the localhost and the destination are all working. If it fails, there's an error somewhere in the routing chain. Check route -n or ip route show on your localhost to see if the default route is defined.

4. Ping a machine on the Internet using its DNS name. If this succeeds, everything is working. If this step fails (but test 3 was successful), make sure you've entered the name of the DNS server that should be used in /etc/resolv.conf. If this is okay, check to see whether your DNS server is working.

In many cases, you'll use the ping command without options. But some options can be useful, and these are listed in Table 11-2.

Table 11-2. *Useful ping Options*

Option	Description
-c count	Specifies the number of packets to be sent. The ping command terminates automatically after reaching this number.
-l device	Specifies the name of the network device that should be used. Useful on a computer with several network devices.
-i seconds	Specifies the number of seconds to wait between individual ping packets. The default setting is 1 second.
-f	Sends packets as fast as possible, but only after a reply comes in.
-l	Sends packets without waiting for a reply. If used with the -f option, this may cause a denial-of-service attack on the target host, and the host may stop functioning properly or even crash. Apart from the unknown harm that this may do to the target computer, you may find yourself blacklisted or even charged with a criminal offense. Because this is such a very dangerous option, only the user root is allowed to use it.
-t ttl	Sets the time to live (TTL) for packets that are sent. This indicates the maximum number of routers that each packet may pass through on its way to a destination. The TTL is decremented by one by each router it passes until the TTL becomes 0, which means that the packet won't be routed any more.
-b	Sends packets to the broadcast address of the network. This prompts a reply from every host that's up and allowed to answer to ping packets. Don't use this unless you have a very good reason to use it, as this command generates large numbers of packets on your network.

■ **Note** To protect against a denial-of-service attack, many hosts are configured not to answer a ping request. Therefore, when testing connectivity, make sure that you use a host that's allowed to answer.

The ping command is not just used to test that a connection can be established; you can also use it to check the round-trip delay between your computer and a given host. The elapsed time is an important indication of the quality of the network connection. To check the round-trip delay, have a look at the time parameter that's listed in the result of the ping command. Listing 11-14 provides an example in which ping is used to send four packets to www.ubuntu.com.

Listing 11-14. Testing Connectivity to www.ubuntu.com

```
root@ZNA:~# ping -c 4 www.ubuntu.com
PING www.ubuntu.com (82.211.81.158) 56(84) bytes of data.
64 bytes from arctowski.ubuntu.com (82.211.81.158): icmp_seq=1 ttl=51 time=22.0 ms
64 bytes from arctowski.ubuntu.com (82.211.81.158): icmp_seq=2 ttl=51 time=10.7 ms
64 bytes from arctowski.ubuntu.com (82.211.81.158): icmp_seq=3 ttl=51 time=18.6 ms
64 bytes from arctowski.ubuntu.com (82.211.81.158): icmp_seq=4 ttl=51 time=20.8 ms

--- www.ubuntu.com ping statistics ---
4 packets transmitted, 4 received, 0% packet loss, time 3015ms
rtt min/avg/max/mdev = 10.741/18.092/22.057/4.417 ms
```

Testing Routing

If you can ping your default router but you can't ping a given host on the Internet, it's probably obvious that something is wrong with one of the routers between your network and the destination host. You can use the traceroute command to find out exactly where things are going wrong. The traceroute command uses the TTL value of the UDP datagrams it sends out.

■ **Note**   A datagram is a packet sent over the OSI model network layer.

The idea is that, when the TTL value reaches 0, the packet is discarded by the router, and a message is sent back to the sender. When starting, traceroute uses a TTL value of 0, which causes the packet to be discarded by the very first router. This is how traceroute identifies the first router. Next, it sends the packet to the target destination again, but with a TTL of 1, which, as you can see, causes the packet to be discarded by the second router. Things continue in this manner until the packet reaches its final destination.

To use traceroute, you normally put the host name as the argument, such as traceroute www.ubuntu.com. It's possible as well to use the IP address of a host, which will produce a result as shown in Listing 11-15.

Listing 11-15. Testing a Network's Route with traceroute

```
root@ZNA:~# traceroute www.ubuntu.com
traceroute to www.ubuntu.com (82.211.81.158), 30 hops max, 40 byte packets
1   192.168.1.254 (192.168.1.254) 72.668 ms 10.361 ms 176.306 ms
2   195.190.249.90 (195.190.249.90) 3.353 ms 9.199 ms 10.351 ms
3   42.ge-4-0-0.xr1.3d12.xs4all.net (194.109.5.49) 6.386 ms 7.237 ms 16.421 ms
4   0.so-6-0-0.xr1.tc2.xs4all.net (194.109.5.10) 11.407 ms 11.447 ms 9.599 ms
5   217.149.46.21 (217.149.46.21) 31.989 ms 29.321 ms 22.756 ms
6   sl-bb21-ams-11-0.sprintlink.net (217.149.32.41) 13.415 ms 13.244 ms 12.569 ms
7   213.206.131.46 (213.206.131.46) 11.147 ms 12.282 ms 11.222 ms
8   ae-0-56.mp2.Amsterdam1.Level3.net (4.68.120.162) 7.862 ms ae-0-54.mp2.Amster\
dam1.Level3.net (4.68.120.98) 11.796 ms ae-0-52.mp2.Amsterdam1.Level3.net\
   (4.68.120.34) 11.000 ms
9   as-0-0.bbr2.London2.Level3.net (4.68.128.110) 21.047 ms ae-1-0.bbr1.London2.\
Level3.net (212.187.128.46) 35.125 ms as-0-0.bbr2.London2.Level3.net\
   (4.68.128.110) 17.183 ms
```

```
10   ae-15-53.car1.London2.Level3.net (4.68.117.79) 18.917 ms 17.388 ms ae-25-52.\
car1.London2.Level3.net (4.68.117.47) 18.992 ms
11   tge9-3-146.core-r-1.lon2.\
mnet.net.uk (212.187.196.82) 14.699 ms 17.381 ms 15.293 ms
12   85.133.32.134 (85.133.32.134) 27.130 ms 33.310 ms 37.576 ms
13   82.211.81.76 (82.211.81.76) 16.784 ms 20.140 ms 17.556 ms
14   * * *
15   * * *
16   * * *
17   * * *
```

With the traceroute command, you'll see every router that's passed. For each router, the name of the router is displayed, followed by its IP address and then the round-trip times of the three packets that were sent to that router. You'll often see that a router replies with only a string of three asterisks (* * *), which indicates that the router forwards packets normally but is configured not to reply to ping packets for security reasons.

Testing Availability of Services

When the ping and traceroute commands show that everything is working, you're the proud owner of a working network interface. Next you can test the availability of two kinds of services: those on your computer itself and those on external computers. Because so many tools are available to test service availability, I won't try to cover them all, but I do want to discuss two of the most popular. First is the netstat tool, which you can use to test for the availability of services on the host where you run the command. And second is nmap, which is used to test availability on other hosts.

■ **Caution** Some administrators consider any use of nmap on their hosts or their network as an attack against their security, and therefore won't allow it. I once used it in a hotel room in the United States to see if my server in Amsterdam was still offering all its services, and the hotel network shut me off immediately. In these circumstances, it can be a real pain to get your connection back, so be careful.

Using netstat for Services on Your Computer

If you want to know what services are available on your computer and what these services are doing, the netstat command is an excellent choice. However, because many of its options require you to be root, I recommend that you use netstat as root only. To see the most useful information offered by netstat, use the -platune options, which make sure that you see information about programs connected to ports (-p) and what ports are actually listening (-l).

Other options show you everything there is to show (-a), do that for TCP (-t) as well as UDP (-u), without translating IP addresses to DNS names (-n), or with extended information (-e).

If you think that netstat -platune offers too much information, use netstat -tulp instead. The results are slightly less verbose, which makes it easier to get the data you really need. Listing 11-16 shows the first screen of output generated by netstat -platune.

Listing 11-16. The netstat -platune Command Provides an Exhaustive Overview of Everything Happening on Your Computer

```
root@ZNA:~# netstat -platune
Active Internet connections (servers and established)
Proto Recv-Q Send-Q Local Address     Foreign Address    State   User\ Inode    PID/Program name
tcp   0      0      127.0.0.1:3306    0.0.0.0:*   LISTEN    103\ 12937     3839/mysqld

tcp   0      0      0.0.0.0:80        0.0.0.0:*   LISTEN    0\ 13209       3965/apache2

tcp   0      0      10.0.0.20:53      0.0.0.0:*   LISTEN    104\ 13737     3737/named

tcp   0      0      10.0.0.30:53      0.0.0.0:*   LISTEN    104\ 13735     3737/named

tcp   0      0      10.0.0.10:53      0.0.0.0:*   LISTEN    104\ 13733     3737/named

tcp   0      0      192.168.1.33:53   0.0.0.0:*   LISTEN    104\ 12821     3737/named

tcp   0      0      127.0.0.1:53      0.0.0.0:*   LISTEN    104\ 12819     3737/named

tcp   0      0      127.0.0.1:953     0.0.0.0:*   LISTEN    104\ 12824     3737/named

tcp6  0      0      :::53             :::*        LISTEN\   104  12816     3737/named

tcp6  0      0      :::22             :::*        LISTEN\   0    13585     4150/sshd

tcp6  0      0      ::1:953     :::*  LISTEN\ 104    12825     3737/named

tcp6  0      0      ::ffff:192.168.1.33:22 ::ffff:192.168.1.6:4197 ESTABLISHED0\ 13761  4229/1

tcp6  0      164    ::ffff:192.168.1.33:22 ::ffff:192.168.1.7:9688 ESTABLISHED0\   13609  4158/0

udp   0      0      0.0.0.0:1024      0.0.0.0:*             104\ 12822     3737/named

udp   0      0      10.0.0.20:53      0.0.0.0:*             104\ 13736     3737/named

udp   0      0      10.0.0.30:53      0.0.0.0:*             104\ 13734     3737/named

udp   0      0      10.0.0.10:53      0.0.0.0:*             104\ 13732     3737/named

udp   0      0      192.168.1.33:53   0.0.0.0:*             104\ 12820     3737/named

udp   0      0      127.0.0.1:53      0.0.0.0:*             104\ 12818     3737/named

udp6  0      0      :::1025           :::*                  104\ 12823     3737/named

udp6  0      0      :::53             :::*                  104\ 12815     3737/named
```

As you can see, the netstat command yields a lot of information when used with the -platune options. Table 11-3 explains the information displayed in Listing 11-16.

Table 11-3. *Information Offered by* netstat -platune

Item	Explanation
Proto	The protocol that's used. Can be TCP or UDP.
Recv-Q	The number of packets waiting in the receive queue for this port at the moment that netstat was used.
Send-Q	The number of packets waiting to be sent from this port at the moment that netstat was used.
Local Address	The local socket address (the local IP address followed by the port number that's used).
Foreign Address	The address of the foreign host (if any) that currently has an open connection to this host.
State	The current state of the protocol connected to the mentioned port.
User	The numeric user ID of the user with whose permissions the process was started.
Inode	The inode(s) of files that currently are opened by the process.
PID/Program name	The PID and name of the program that has currently claimed the mentioned port.

As you can see, netstat provides a complete overview of what's happening on your computer. It's especially useful if you get error messages like "port already in use." In combination with the grep utility, it's easy to learn what port program is currently holding a port open and, if required, to terminate that program. For example, to find out what program is currently occupying port 80, use netstat -platune | grep 80. This returns a line like

```
root@ZNA:~# netstat -platune | grep 80

tcp    0    0 0.0.0.0:80    0.0.0.0:*    LISTEN    0\
    13209    3965/apache2
```

From this line, you can see that an Apache web server with a PID of 3965 is currently listening on port 80. Want to remove it and you don't know how to do that in a normal way? Use kill 3965 and it's gone.

Using nmap to Check Services on remote Computers

The netstat command is a useful tool, but it works only on the host where you run it. Sometimes, when you cannot connect to a given service on a given host, you'd like to know if the service is available at all. You can do this with the nmap command. Like most powerful network tools, nmap also works best if you are root.

The nmap command is an expert tool that helps you find out exactly what's happening at another host. If you use it properly, the owner of that host will never even know that you were there. However, you should be aware that running a so-called port scan to monitor open ports on a given host is considered an intrusion by many administrators, so be careful what you're doing with it because you may run into trouble if you use nmap on a host that isn't yours, and you haven't notified its owner.

If you really want to keep things simple, just use nmap without arguments. For example, nmap 192.168.1.69 performs a basic scan on host 192.168.1.69 to find what common ports are open on it. This gives good results for day-to-day use; see Listing 11-17 for an example.

Listing 11-17. The nmap Command Shows You What Services Are Offered by a Host

```
root@ZNA:~# nmap 192.168.1.69

Starting Nmap 4.20 ( http://insecure.org ) at 2007-011-01 11:08 EDT
Interesting ports on 192.168.1.69:
Not shown: 1693 closed ports
PORT STATE SERVICE
22/tcp open ssh
111/tcp open rpcbind
139/tcp open netbios-ssn
445/tcp open microsoft-ds
MAC Address: 00:18:8B:AC:C9:54 (Dell)
Nmap finished: 1 IP address (1 host up) scanned in 0.626 seconds
```

A very common reason why the test shown in Listing 11-17 could fail is that nmap normally tries to ping its targets first. On many hosts, ping commands are administratively prohibited, dropped, or ignored. And these hosts won't reveal anything when you issue nmap on them. To make sure that they're working even when you cannot ping, use the -P0 option to disable ping. Another useful option is -O, which tries to guess the operating system that is on the target host. And, if you want to make sure that both TCP and UDP ports are scanned, you should include -sT and -sU as well. So the command becomes somewhat longer: nmap -sT -sU -P0 -O 192.168.1.69 would scan the target host with all those options. You'll notice that, because nmap has to do a lot more work with these options, it takes considerably longer for the command to complete. Listing 11-18 shows the result of this scan.

Listing 11-18. You Have Lots of Options to Specify How nmap Should Do Its Work

```
root@ZNA:~# nmap -sT -sU -P0 -O 192.168.1.69

Starting Nmap 4.20 ( http://insecure.org ) at 2007-011-01 11:11 EDT
Interesting ports on 192.168.1.69:
Not shown: 3176 closed ports
PORT            STATE           SERVICE
22/tcp          open            ssh
111/tcp         open            rpcbind
139/tcp         open            netbios-ssn
445/tcp         open            microsoft-ds
68/udp          open|filtered   dhcpc
111/udp         open|filtered   rpcbind
631/udp         open|filtered   unknown
5353/udp        open|filtered   zeroconf
32768/udp       open|filtered   omad
MAC Address: 00:18:8B:AC:C9:54 (Dell)
Device type: general purpose
Running: Linux 2.6.X
OS details: Linux 2.6.14 - 2.6.17
```

```
Uptime: 0.176 days (since Wed Aug 1 07:23:05 2007)
Network Distance: 1 hop

OS detection performed. Please report any incorrect results at http://insecure.org/nmap/submit/ .
Nmap finished: 1 IP address (1 host up) scanned in 1482.860 seconds
```

In the last command, you'll most likely get a better result, but there's still a problem: the scan is rather noisy, and so the target host may log messages to tell its owner that you're using nmap on it. There's nothing wrong with this in most cases, but if you really want to put nmap through a thorough security test, you should use some stealth options like -sF (FINscan), -sX (X-mas tree scan), or -sN (NULL-scan). All of these use specific properties of the IP protocol to perform a stealth scan so that the target host never knows you were there. The disadvantage of these scan options is that they don't always work! On many modern operating systems, you'll find that the operating system ignores them, so you'll end up waiting a long time without a result.

EXERCISE 11-2: ANALYZING NETWORKING

In this exercise you'll analyze the current configuration of network in your network.

1. Type **ip route show**. This will show you the IP address of your router.

2. Ping the router, using **ping <router>**. (Replace <router> with the IP address you've just found.

3. Note the network address of your current configuration. Normally, the network address is the same as your IP address, but with a 0 in the last byte. So if your IP address is 192.168.1.10, the network address is 192.168.1.0. In this example I'll use 192.168.1.0 as the example network, replace this IP so that it matches your configuration. Use **nmap -sP 192.168.1.0/24** to scan your network for IP addresses.

4. Type **nmap <router>** (replace <router> with the IP address of your router. This shows all services that are currently being offered on your router.

5. Type **netstat -tulpen**. This gives a list of all services that are being offered on your local machine.

Connecting Remotely with Secure Shell

If you're in a network with multiple Linux computers, you'll occasionally need to make a shell connection to another computer. Secure Shell is just made for that. It also replaces the older telnet utility, which was used in the days that security was not the issue it is today. The essence of SSH is its security, and public and private keys naturally play an important role in it. On first making contact, the client and the host exchange public and private keys. In this communication, the host creates a key based on its private key—the so-called host key—and uses this as its proof of identity. When connecting, the host sends its public key to the client. If this is the first time the client has connected to this host, the host replies with the message that shown in Listing 11-19.

Listing 11-19. Establishing an SSH Session with an Unknown Host

```
root@ZNA:~# ssh 192.168.1.70
The authenticity of host '192.168.1.70 (192.168.1.70)' can't be established.
RSA key fingerprint is fd:07:f6:ce:5d:df:6f:a2:84:38:c7:89:f1:3a:a6:34.
Are you sure you want to continue connecting (yes/no)? yes
Warning: Permanently added '192.168.1.70' (RSA) to the list of known hosts.
Password:
Last login: Tue Jul 31 15:34:15 2007 from ida.lan
```

If the client trusts that this is really the intended host, it should answer yes to the request, in which case the host is then added to the .ssh/known_hosts file in the home directory of the user who initiated the SSH session. The next time the client connects to the host, this file is checked to see whether the host is already known. The check is based on the public key fingerprint of the host, which is a unique checksum related to the public key of the host. The connection is established only if this check matches the name and public key of the host that the client is connecting to. If these two pieces of data don't match, it's very likely that the host the client is trying to connect to isn't the intended host, and the connection is refused.

Once the identity of the host you want to connect to is established, a secured channel is set up between the client and host. These secured channels are established by a session key, which is an encryption key that's the same on both the host and the client and that encrypts all data sent between the two machines. The client and the host negotiate this session key based on their public keys. One of the things determined in this negotiation is the protocol that should be used. For example, session keys can use different encryption protocols like 3DES, Blowfish, or IDEA.

After establishing the secured channel, the user on the client is asked for credentials: if nothing is configured, a prompt asks the user to enter his or her username and password. Alternatively, the user can authenticate with his or her public/private key pair, thus proving he or she really is that user, but some more things have to be configured before that can happen.

All this may sound pretty complicated, but the nice thing is that the user doesn't notice any of it. The user just has to enter a username and a password. If, however, you want to move beyond simple password-based authentication, it's necessary to understand what's happening.

Working with Public/Private Key Pairs

The security of SSH relies on the use of public/private key pairs. By default, the client tries to authenticate using RSA or DSA key pairs. To make this work, the host must have the client's public key, which is something that you have to configure by hand, as you'll see later. When the client has a public/private key pair, it generates an encrypted string with its private key. If the host is able to decrypt this string using the client's public key, the client's identity is authenticated.

When using public/private key pairs, you can configure different things. First, the user needs to determine what cryptographic algorithm he or she wants to use. For this purpose, he or she can choose between RSA and DSA (of which DSA is considered stronger). Next, the user has to decide whether to protect his or her private key with a passphrase.

Using a passphrase is important because the private key really is used as the identity of the user. Should anyone steal this private key, it would be possible to forge the identity of the key's owner, and, for that reason, it's a very good idea to secure private keys with a passphrase.

Working with Secure Shell

Basically, Secure Shell is a suite of tools that consists of three main programs and a daemon, sshd. On Fedora/Red Hat and SUSE, SSH is installed by default. On Ubuntu, you'll need to install it first, using apt-get install openssh-server.

In SSH, three tools are available: ssh, scp, and sftp. The first, ssh, is used to establish a secured remote session. Let's say that it's like telnet but cryptographically secured. The second, scp, is a very useful command that's used to copy files to and from another computer where the SSH process is running. The third, sftp, is a secure FTP client interface. Using it establishes a secured FTP session to a computer that's running the sshd.

Two of the best things of all of these tools are that they can be used without any preparation or setup, and you can set them up to work entirely according to your needs. They are at once easy-to-use and very specialized tools.

Using the ssh Command

The simplest way to work with SSH is to just enter the ssh command, followed by the name of the host you want to connect to. For example, to connect to the host AMS.sandervanvugt.com, use ssh AMS.sandervanvugt.com.

Depending on whether you've connected to that host before, it may check the host credentials or just ask for your password. The ssh command doesn't ask for a username because it assumes that you want to connect to the other host with the same identity that you're logged in with locally. If you'd rather log in with another user account, you can indicate this intention in one of two ways: you can specify the username and follow it with an ampersand when establishing the connection to the remote host, or you can use the -l option followed by the name of the user account you want to use to connect to the other host. So, basically, ssh linda@AMS.sandervanvugt.com and ssh -l linda AMS.sandervanvugt.com accomplish the same thing. After establishing a session, use the exit command (or Ctrl+D) to close the session and return to your own machine.

Now, it seems a lot of trouble to log in to a remote host if you just need to enter one or two commands. If you face this situation often, it's good to know that you can just specify the name of the command at the end of the ssh command: ssh -l linda@AMS.sandervanvugt.com ls -l provides a long listing of files that user linda has in her home directory at the other host. Of course, this isn't the most realistic example of how to use "one command only" sessions to a host, but you probably can see its value when working from shell scripts.

Using scp to Copy Files Securely

The scp command is another part of the SSH suite that you'll definitely like. It's used to copy files securely. If you know how the cp command works, you'll know how to handle scp. The only difference is that it requires a complete network path name including the names of the host and the file you want to copy. Also, if you don't want to use the name of the user you are currently logged in as, a username should be included as well. Consider the following example:

```
scp /some/file linda@AMS.sandervanvugt.com:/some/file
```

This easy command copies /some/file to AMS.sandervanvugt.com and places it with the name file in the directory /some on that host. Of course, it's possible to do the opposite as well: scp root@SFO.sandervanvugt.com:/some/file /some/file copies /some/file from a remote host with the name SFO.sandervanvugt.com to the localhost. You're going to like the -r option as well, because it allows you to copy a complete subdirectory structure.

Using sftp for Secured Ftp Sessions

As an alternative to copying files with scp, you can use the sftp command. This command is used to connect to computers running the sshd program and to establish a secured FTP session with it. From the sftp command, you have an interface that really looks a lot like the normal FTP client interface. All the standard FTP commands work here as well, with the only difference that, in this case, it's secure. For example, you can use the ls and cd commands to browse to a directory and see what files are available and, from there, use the get command to copy a file to the current local directory. Once you've opened the sftp interface, you can use the following FTP commands to copy files to and from your computer:

- put: Copies a file from your computer to another computer

- mput: Copies multiple files from your computer to another computer

- get: Copies a file from another computer to your computer

- mget: Copies multiple files from another computer to your computer

Before establishing an FTP session to another computer, use the cd command on your local computer to change to the directory you want to copy files to or from. Your home directory might be a decent location. When using put, mput, get, and mget to transfer files, this directory is used as the default local directory. To establish an sftp session to the computer named nuuk, you would first use the following command:

```
sftp nuuk
```

This command assumes that you want to connect to the remote host using the same user account. If you want to connect with another user account, put it in front of the name of the remote server, as in the following command:

```
sftp sander@nuuk
```

You'll now see an SFTP prompt and will be in the root directory that was provided for the user on the remote host. Here, you can use standard Linux commands such as ls to show a list of files, pwd to print your working directory, and cd to change to another directory. You can now transfer files between your computer and the remote computer. For instance, the following command would use sftp to copy the /etc/hosts file to the current directory on your local computer:

```
get /etc/hosts
```

When finished copying files, use the quit or the exit command to terminate the sftp session.

Configuring SSH

In an SSH environment, a node can be client and server simultaneously. This means that your computer can provide SSH services to others, and use SSH to connect to others at the same time. So, as you can imagine, there's a configuration file for both of these aspects. The client is configured in /etc/ssh/ssh_config, and the host uses /etc/ssh/sshd_config. Setting options for the host isn't hard to understand: just put them in the configuration file for the daemon /etc/ssh/sshd_config. For the client settings, however, the situation is more complicated, because there are several ways of overwriting the default client settings:

- The generic /etc/ssh/ssh_config file is applied to all users initiating an SSH session. An individual user can overwrite these if he or she creates a .ssh_config file in the .ssh directory of his or her home directory.

- An option in /etc/ssh/ssh_config has to be supported by the sshd_config file on the host you are connecting to. For example, if you're allowing password-based authentication from the client side but the computer doesn't allow it, it won't work.

- Options in both files can be overwritten with command-line options.

Table 11-4 is an overview of some of the most useful options that you can use to configure the client in ssh_config.

Table 11-4. *Useful Options in* ssh_config

Option	Description
Host	This option restricts the following declarations (up to the next Host keyword) to a specific host. Therefore, this option is applied on a host that a user is connecting to. The host name is taken as specified on the command line. Use this parameter to add some extra security to specific hosts. You can also use wildcards such as * and ? to refer to more than one host name.
CheckHostIP	If this option is set to yes (the default value), SSH will check the host IP address in the known_hosts file. Use this as a protection against DNS or IP address spoofing.
Ciphers	This option, which takes multiple arguments, is used to specify the order in which the different encryption algorithms should be tried to use in an SSHv2 session (version 2 is the default SSH version nowadays).
Compression	The yes/no values for this option specify whether to use compression in your SSH session. The default is no.
ForwardX11	This very useful option specifies whether X11 connections will be forwarded. If set to yes, graphical screens from an SSH session can be forwarded through a secure tunnel. The result is that the DISPLAY environment variable that determines where to draw graphical screens is set correctly. If you don't want to enable X forwarding by default, use the -X option on the command line when establishing an SSH session.
LocalForward	This option specifies that a TCP/IP port on the local machine is forwarded over SSH to the specified port on a remote machine. (See "Generic TCP Port Forwarding" later in this chapter for more details.)
LogLevel	Use this option to specify the level of verbosity for log messages. The default value is INFO. If this doesn't go deep enough, VERBOSE, DEBUG, DEBUG1, DEBUG2, and DEBUG3 provide progressively more information.
PasswordAuthentication	Use this option to specify whether or not you want to use password authentication. By default, password authentication is used. In a secure environment in which keys are used for authentication, you can safely set this option to no to disable password authentication completely.
Protocol	This option specifies the protocol version that SSH should use. The default value is set to 2,1 (which indicates that version 2 should be used first and, if that doesn't work, version 1 is tried). It's a good idea to disable version 1 completely because it has some known security issues.
PubkeyAuthentication	Use this option to specify whether you want to use public key–based authentication. This option should always be set to the default value (yes) because public key–base authentication is the safest way of authenticating.

The counterpart of ssh_config on the client computer is the sshd_config file on the host. Many options that you can use in the ssh_config file are also available in the sshd_config file. However, some options are specific to the host side of SSH. Table 11-5 gives an overview of some of these options.

Table 11-5. *Important Options in* sshd_config

Option	Description
AllowTcpForwarding	Use this option to specify whether you want to allow clients to do TCP port forwarding. This is a very useful feature, and you'll probably want to leave it at its default value (yes).
Port	Use this option to specify the port that the SSH process is listening on. By default, sshd is listening on port 22. If the SSH process is connected directly to the Internet, this will cause many people to try a brute-force attack on your host. Consider running the SSH process on some other port for increased security.
PermitRootLogin	Use this option to specify whether you want to allow root logins. To add additional security to your host, consider setting this option to the no value. If set to no, the root user has to establish a connection as a normal user and from there use su to become root or use sudo to perform certain tasks with root permissions.
PermitEmptyPasswords	Use this option to specify whether you want to allow users to log in with an empty password. From a security perspective, this isn't a very good idea, and so the default no value is suitable in most cases. If, however, you want to run SSH from a script and establish a connection without entering a password, it can be useful to change the value of this parameter to yes.
ChallengeResponseAuthentication	This option specifies whether users are allowed to log in using passwords. If you want to add additional security to your host by forcing users to log in with public/private key pairs only, give this parameter the value no.
X11Forwarding	Use this option to specify whether you want to allow clients to use X11 forwarding. On most Linux distributions, the default value for this parameter is yes.

Using SSH Key-Based Authentication

Now that you know all about the basics of SSH, let's look at some of the more advanced options. One of the most important is key-based authentication, which SSH uses via public/ private key–based authentication. Before diving into the configuration of key-based authentication, let's first have a look on how these keys are used.

A Short Introduction To Cryptography

In general, you can use two methods for encryption: symmetric and asymmetric. Symmetric encryption is faster but less secure, and asymmetric encryption is slower but more secure. In a symmetric key environment, both parties use the same key to encrypt and decrypt messages. With asymmetric keys, a public and a private key are used, and this is the important technique that's used for SSH.

If asymmetric keys are used, every user needs his or her own public/private key pair, and every computer needs a pair of them as well. Of these keys, the private key must be protected at all times: if the private key is compromised, the identity of the owner of the private key is compromised as well. In short, stealing a user's private key is like stealing that user's identity.

Therefore, a private key is normally stored in a very secure place where no one other than its owner can access it; typically this is in ~/.ssh. The public key, on the other hand, is available to everyone.

Public/private keys are generally used for three purposes: encryption, authentication, and nonrepudiation.

To send an encrypted message, the sender encrypts the message with the public key of the receiver who can decrypt it with the matching private key. This scenario requires that, before sending an encrypted message, you have the public key of the person you want to send the message to.

The other options are to use public/private keys for authentication or to prove that a message has not changed since it was created. This method is known as nonrepudiation. In the example of authentication, the private key is used to generate an encrypted token, the salt. If this salt can be decrypted with the public key of the person who wants to authenticate, that proves the host really is dealing with the right person, and access can be granted. However, this technique requires the public key to be copied to the host before any authentication can occur, which is also the case when keys are used to prove that a message hasn't been tampered with.

Using Public/Private Key–Based Authentication in an SSh Environment

When SSH key-based authentication is used, you must make sure that, for all users who need to use this technology, the public key is available on the hosts they want to log in to. When logging in, the user creates an authentication request that's signed with the user's private key. This authentication request is matched to the public key of the same user on the computer where that user wants to be authenticated. If it matches, the user is allowed access; if it doesn't, user access is denied.

Public/private key–based authentication is enabled by default on all major Linux distributions, so it's only when no keys are present that the computer prompts users for a password. The following steps provide a summary of what happens when a user tries to establish an SSH session with a host:

1. If public key authentication is enabled (the default), SSH checks the .ssh directory in the user's home directory to see whether a private key is present.

2. If a private key is found, SSH creates a packet with some data in it (the salt), encrypts that packet with the private key, and sends it to the host. The public key is also sent with this packet.

3. The host now checks whether a file with the name authorized_keys exists in the home directory of the user. If it doesn't, the user can't be authenticated with his or her keys. If the file does exist and the public key is an allowed key (and also is identical to the key that was previously stored on the host), the host uses this key to check the signature.

4. If the signature is verified, the user is granted access. If the signature can't be verified, the host prompts the user for a password instead.

All this sounds pretty complicated, but it really isn't. Everything happens transparently, if it has been set up right. Also, there's hardly any noticeable delay when establishing a connection. It normally takes no more than a second.

Setting Up SSh for Key-Based Authentication

The best way to explain how to set up SSH for key-based authentication is by working through an example. In the following procedure, key-based authentication is enabled for the user root.

1. On the desktop where root is working, use the command ssh-keygen -t dsa -b 1024. This generates a public/private key pair of 1,024 bits. Listing 11-20 shows what happens.

Listing 11-20. Generating a Public/Private Key Pair with ssh-keygen

```
workstation # ssh-keygen -t dsa -b 1024
Generating public/private dsa key pair.
Enter file in which to save the key (/root/.ssh/id_dsa) :
Enter passphrase (empty for no passphrase):
Enter same passphrase again:
Your identification has been saved in /root/.ssh/id_dsa.
Your public key has been saved in /root/.ssh/id_dsa.pub.
The key fingerprint is:
59:63:b5:a0:c5:2c:b5:b8:2f:99:80:5b:43:77:3c:dd root@workstation
```

I'll explain what happens. The user in this example uses the ssh-keygen command to generate a public and a private key. The encryption algorithm used to generate this key is DSA, which is considered more secure than its alternative, RSA. The option -b 1024 specifies that 1024-bit encryption should be used for the key. You're possibly aware that the longer this number, the more secure it is. Notice, however, that a many-bits encryption algorithm also requires more system resources to use it. After generating the keys, the command prompts you to save it somewhere. By default, a directory with the name .ssh is created in your home directory and, within this directory, a file with the name id_dsa. This file contains the private key.

Next, you're prompted to enter a passphrase, which is an important extra layer of protection that can be added to the key. Because anyone who has access to your private key (which isn't that easy) can forge your identity, your private key should always be protected with a passphrase. After entering the same passphrase twice, the private key is saved, and the related public key is generated and saved in the file /root/.ssh/ id_dsa.pub. Also, a key fingerprint is generated. This fingerprint is a summary of your key, a checksum that's calculated on the key to alert you if the key has been changed. Make sure that your passphrase is not too easy to guess; a weak passphrase makes a strong key useless.

2. After creating the public/private key pair, you must transfer the public key to the host. The ultimate goal is to place the contents of the id_dsa.pub file in the /root/.shh/ authorized_keys file on the host. But you can't simply copy the file to the destination file authorized_keys because other keys may already be stored there. Therefore, first use scp to copy the file to a temporary location. The command scp /root/.ssh/id_dsa. pub root@host:/root/from_ workstation_key.pub would do the job.

3. Now that the public key is on the host, you have to put it in the authorized_keys file. Before doing this, though, make sure that the .ssh directory exists on the host in the home directory of the user root, and that it has user and group root as its owner and permission mode 700. Then, on the host with the directory /root as your current directory, use cat from_workstation_key.pub >> .ssh/ authorized_keys. This command appends the content of the public key file to the authorized_keys file, thus not overwriting any file that may have been there already.

4. Hopefully, no errors have occurred, and you've been successful. Go back to your workstation and start an SSH session to the host where you just copied your public key to the authorized_keys file. You'll notice that you are no longer prompted for a password, but for a passphrase instead. This proves that everything worked. Do notice, however, that you need to repeat this procedure for every key-secured host with which you want to be able to establish a session.

Working with keys as described in these steps is an excellent way to make SSH authentication more secure. But there's a drawback: if you need to establish an SSH session automatically from a shell script or cron job, it's not very handy if you're first prompted for a key. Therefore, some method is needed to execute such jobs automatically. One solution is to create a special user account with limited permissions and without a passphrase on its private key. Another solution is to run ssh-agent, which caches the keys before they are used, and you'll learn how to do this in the next section.

Caching Keys with ssh- ssh-agent

You can use ssh-agent to save yourself from constantly having to enter private keys. With this program, you can cache keys for a given shell environment. After starting ssh-agent from a shell prompt, you need to add the passphrase for the private key that belongs to it. This is something that you'll do for a specific shell, so after you close that specific shell or load another shell, you'll need to add the passphrase to that shell again.

After adding a passphrase to ssh-agent, the passphrase is stored in RAM, and only the user who added the key to RAM is able to read it from there. Also, ssh-agent listens only to ssh and scp commands that you've started locally, so there's no way that you can access a key that is kept by ssh-agent over the network. So you can be sure that using ssh-agent is pretty secure. Apart from being secure, it's pretty easy as well. Enabling ssh-agent and adding a passphrase to it is a simple two-step procedure:

1. From the shell prompt, use ssh-agent followed by the name of the shell you want to use it from. For example, use ssh-agent /bin/bash to activate ssh-agent for the Bash shell.

2. Now type ssh-add. You'll be prompted for the passphrase of your current private key, and you'll then see the message identity added, followed by the private key whose passphrase is added to ssh-agent.

■ **Tip**   Secure Shell is a great way of accessing other hosts. But did you know that you can also use it to mount a file system on a remote host? All modern versions of SSH support this feature: just use sshfs for access to all the files and directories on the remote host, just like a local user on that host. If you know how to mount a directory with the mount command, working with sshfs is easy. For example, the command sshfs linda@AMS:/data /mnt allows access to the /data directory on the remote host and connects that directory to /mnt on the local computer. Secure Shell is not installed by default, so use apt-get install sshfs to install it on your computer.

Tunneling Traffic with SSH

Apart from establishing remote login sessions, copying files, and executing commands on remote hosts, you can also use SSH for TCP port forwarding. When used like this, SSH is a simple VPN solution with the capability of tunneling to almost any unsecured protocol over a secured connection. In this section, I'll first talk about X forwarding, and then you'll see how to forward almost any protocol using SSH.

X Forwarding

Wouldn't it be useful if you could start an application on a host, where all the workload is performed by the host, while you control the application from your client? Well, you can with SSH X forwarding. To use X forwarding, you first must establish an SSH session to the host you want to connect to. Next, from this SSH session, you start the graphical application, which will draw its screen on your workstation while doing all the work on the host itself.

Sounds good? Establishing such an environment has only two requirements:

- Make sure the X11Forwarding option is set to yes in /etc/ssh/sshd_config on the host.

- Connect to the host with the ssh -X command from your client. Alternatively, you can set the X11Forwarding option in the client configuration file /etc/ssh/ssh_config, which allows you to forward graphical sessions by default. This poses a minor security problem, however, and so this setting is not enabled by default on most Linux distributions.

Now that you have established the SSH session with your host, start your favorite graphical program. The program itself will be executed at the remote host, and you'll see the screen locally.

■ **Note**   X-forwarding sessions with SSH is really cool, but there is a limitation: you need an X server on the client from which you are establishing the SSH session. This X server is used as the driver for your graphical hardware, and the application that you want to run on your client needs it to display its screens. On Linux, UNIX, or Macintosh machines, this won't be a problem because an X server is present by default. It's a problem on Windows, however. The most common SSH client for Windows is PuTTY, which, although very useful, doesn't contain an X server. A good X server for Windows is Xming, which is a free X server that you can download from the Internet.

Generic tCp port Forwarding

X is the only service for which port forwarding is hard-coded in the SSH software. For everything else, you need to do port forwarding by hand, using the -L (local forwarding) or the -R (remote port forwarding) options. Let's have a look at the example in Figure 11-1.

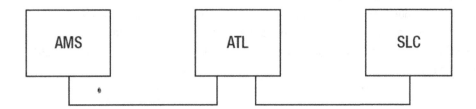

Figure 11-1. *Example network*

This example network has three nodes: AMS is the node where the administrator is working, ATL is the node in the middle, and AMS has a direct connection to ATL, but not to SLC, which is behind a firewall. ATL does have a direct connection to SLC and is not obstructed by any firewall.

The following command illustrates a simple case of port forwarding:

```
linda@AMS:~> ssh -L 4444:ATL:110 linda@ATL
```

In this example, user linda forwards connections to port 4444 on her localhost to port 110 on the host ATL as user linda on that host. This is how you would establish a secure session to the insecure POP service on that host, for example. The localhost first establishes a connection to the SSH host running on ATL. This SSH host connects to port 110 at ATL, whereas ssh binds to port 4444 on the localhost. Now an encrypted session is established between local port 4444 and host port 110: everything sent to port 4444 on the localhost really goes to port 110 at the host. If, for example, you configured your POP mail client to get its mail from local port 4444, it would really get it from port 110 at ATL.

Notice that a nonprivileged port is used in this example. Only user root can connect to a privileged port with a port number lower than 1024. No matter what port you are connecting to, you should always check in the services configuration file /etc/services, where port numbers are matched to names of services indicating what the port is normally used for (if anything), and use netstat -platune | grep <your-intended-port> to make sure that the port is not already in use.

A little variation on local port forwarding is remote port forwarding, which involves forwarding all connections on a remote port at a remote host to a local port on your machine.

To do this, use the -R option as in the following example:

```
linda@AMS:~> ssh -R 4444:AMS:110 linda@ATL
```

In this example, user linda connects to host ATL (see the last part of the command). On this remote host, port 4444 is addressed by using the construction -R 4444. This remote port is redirected to port 110 on the localhost. As a result, anything going to port 4444 on ATL is redirected to port 110 on AMS. This example would be useful if ATL is the client and AMS is the host running a POP mail server that user linda wants to connect to. Another instance when port forwarding proves useful is when the host you want to forward to cannot be reached directly, perhaps because it is behind a firewall. In this case, you can establish a tunnel to another host that is reachable with SSH. Imagine that, in Listing 11-6, the host SLC is running a POP mail server that our user linda wants to connect to. This user would use the following command:

```
linda@AMS:~> ssh -L 4444:SLC:110 linda@ATL
```

In this example, linda forwards connections to port 4444 on her localhost to host ATL, which is running SSH. This host, in turn, forwards the connection to port 110 on host SLC. Note that in this scenario, the only requirement is that ATL has the SSH service activated; no sshd is needed on SLC for this to work. Also note that there is no need for host AMS to get in direct contact with SLC, as that's what ATL is used for.

In these examples, you've learned how to use the ssh command to accomplish port forwarding, but this isn't the only way of doing it. If a port-forwarding connection needs to be available all the time, you can put it in the ssh configuration file at the client computer. Put it in .ssh/config in your home directory if you want it to work for your user account only, or in /etc/ssh/ssh_config if you want it to apply to all users on your machine. The parameter that should be used as an alternative to ssh -L 4444:ATL:110 would be LocalForward 4444 ATL:110.

EXERCISE 11-3: USING SSH

In this exercise you'll configure SSH. Make sure to change back the configuration if this doesn't match your operational needs.

1. Open a root shell.

2. Open the configuration file /etc/ssh/sshd_config with an editor and find the line that reads **Port 22**. Below this line, add the line **Port 2222**. This tells your server to offer services on two different ports.

3. Type **systemctl restart sshd** to restart the ssh server.

4. Type **ssh -p 2222 localhost** to connect as root to port 2222 on the server that is listening on localhost. We're using localhost here, because that allows you to do this exercise without the need of configuring an additional server.

5. Type **exit**. This closes the current SSH session.

6. Type **ssh-keygen**. This generates a pair of SSH keys.

7. Type **ssh-copy-id localhost** to copy the public key to the authorized_keys file on the target server.

8. Type **ssh -p 2222 localhost** again. This will now connect you to localhost without asking for a password.

Summary

In this chapter, you've learned how to set up a network connection. First, we explored how an IP address is assigned to a network interface card. We covered IPv4 addresses as well as IPv6 addresses. Following that, you read how to troubleshoot a network connection using basic commands such as ping and traceroute, or advanced tools like nmap. In the last part of this chapter, you've learned how to create a remote session with SSH. You have read about the following commands:

- ifconfig: Legacy command to monitor and set IP address and other network card- related information

- ip: Newer command to monitor and set IP address and other network card–related information

- route: Command that displays and sets routing information

- ethtool: Command that displays and sets settings related to the physical capabilities of a network card, such as duplex mode and speed

- ping: Tool to test connectivity to other computers

- traceroute: Utility that helps you analyzing reachability of hosts on the network

- nmap: Utility that helps you check which services are offered by an other host

- netstat: Utility that helps you find out which services are offered by the local host

- `ssh`: Command that helps you to establish a shell connection to a remote computer, secured wit cryptography

- `scp`: Command that securely copies files between hosts

- `sftp`: Secure FTP client

- `ssh-keygen`: Command that generates public/private keys you can use for automatic SSH connection establishments where keys are used for authentication

- `ssh-agent`: Command that caches the passphrase associated to a private key used by SSH

In the next chapter, you'll find out how to set up file services like Samba and NFS on your computer.

CHAPTER 12

Configuring a File Server

Avery common task that people use Linux for is to configure it as a file server. With regard to this task, Linux is very versatile; it offers support for all common protocols. In this chapter, you'll learn how to configure Linux as a file server using either Samba or NFS.

Operating File Servers Securely

To operate a file server in a secure way, modern Linux distributions are using advanced security solutions such as firewalls and methods for mandatory access control, such as SELinux or Apparmor. In this chapter we'll ignore these features completely and just focus on the functional part of the services involved. That means that you may need to shut off these services.

To ensure that no firewall rules are blocking access to your services, type **iptables -L**. If this command shows a lot of lines as output, you'll have a firewall that is operational and that needs to be configured to make the network services accessible. You can shut it off temporarily by using the **iptables -F** command.

On Red Hat and derivatives, SELinux is used to offer an enhanced security. On a production system, using SELinux is definitely recommended, but as the purpose of this chapter is to teach you how to configure NFS and Samba, you might want to start shutting off SELinux before you start. To do this on a temporary basis, type **setenforce 0**.

If AppArmor is used, you don't need to shut down anything. Apparmor is similar to SELinux, but not as restrictive. Notice that using the above commands to shut down the firewall and SELinux works on a temporary basis only. After a restart of your machine, these security mechanisms will be activated again automatically.

Creating a Samba File Server

In this section, you'll first read about the background of the Samba project. This helps you to better understand what Samba is all about. Following that, you'll read how to configure a Samba server to offer file services to end users using a Windows desktop. In the last part of this section, you'll read how to access files on a computer that provides SMB file services from the Linux command line.

Background of the Samba Project

In 1998, Microsoft released the specifications of its Server Message Block (SMB) protocol, which spurred the start of the Samba project. The goal of the Samba project was to implement a free file server that offers SMB functionality. With such a server in place, companies would be able to migrate away from Windows Servers to Linux, without any hassle. With Samba, the end user wouldn't notice the difference, as Samba can provide exactly the same services that Windows does.

Almost than twenty years on, the Samba project has made great progress. However, there are some problems also. The biggest challenge Samba team members have to face is that all they do is done by reverse engineering. Microsoft in general is not too willing to share the source code of the core functionality that is offered by Windows servers.

The result is that Samba functionality, in particular for advanced features such as Active Directory can appear a bit limited if compared to the Microsoft solutions. In comparison to Windows servers, you may find other functionality lacking as well. However, if you are looking for a fast and easy-to-configure file server that can replace such functionality on Windows, Samba offers a decent alternative.

Configuring a Samba File Server

Before you start configuring, make sure that Samba is installed on your computer. If which smb doesn't give you anything, it's not installed. In this case, install it with yum, zypper, or apt-get using yum | zypper | apt-get install samba. Configuring a Samba file server is not too hard, but you should know what this configuration is all about. The basic purpose of Samba is to offer access to shared directories over the network. To do so, you need a directory to share on the local Linux file system, and the share itself, which gives access to this directory over the network. The former is configured on Linux, the latter is configured in the main Samba configuration file /etc/samba/smb.conf. To get access to the Samba file server, you need two user accounts as well. First, there must be a Linux user who has Linux permissions to the Linux file system. Next, you need a user who has Windows-compatible credentials to access the share. After creating the share and the user account, you may need to configure some generic Samba parameters as well. Finally, when all this is done, you must start the processes that the Samba server needs. In the following sections, you'll find more details about all of these tasks.

■ **Note**   The topics in this chapter are about core Samba functionality. In the version 4 release of Samba, Samba can be configured as an Active Directory domain controller as well. The intention of this chapter is to provide you with basic information, and for that reason the Active Directory configuration is not covered.

Configuring the Share

The first part in the configuration of a Samba server is the share. You'll need the configuration file /etc/samba/smb.conf to do this. Before doing so, you need to create the directory you want to share in the Linux file system, and you need to configure access to the share. The following procedure describes how to do this for an imaginary share with the name /share. You will make this directory read/write accessible to members of the sales group. In this group, user linda needs special permissions to be able to do some application management. You'll notice that none of the tasks described here is really new, but you will need to perform all of them as a part of the Samba configuration. All of the tasks described here assume that you have root permissions.

1.   Use mkdir /share to create the shared directory in the Linux file system. It doesn't really matter what file system you are using on Linux, although I do recommend you work with a file system that has support for ACLs (see Chapter 7 for more on ACLs). Samba works with ACLs to enable Windows-like permission inheritance.

2. After creating the directory, you need to configure permissions on the share. You could, of course, work with the infamous Everyone Full Control that you encounter on older versions of Windows servers. If you want this, just use chmod 777 /share. It is nicer though if you apply more granularity in the file system permissions. In this scenario, you need to make the share read/write accessible for all users in the group sales. Also, user linda needs group management permissions. You can do this by changing ownership on the directory using the following command: chown linda.sales /share. This command assigns user linda and group sales as the owners of the share /share.

3. At this point, you have configured ownership but still are working with the default permissions, which normally don't allow group members to write to the share. To make sure that only user linda and members of the group sales can write to the share, use the following command: chmod 770 /share.

At this point, you have configured the Linux part of the file share. However, this doesn't make the directory accessible over the network. To do that, you need to modify the /etc/ samba/smb.conf file. Since you've already set permissions on the Linux file system, the configuration of the Samba share can be really simple. In Listing 12-1, you can see what the share configuration might look like. This listing contains some code that you need to include in the /etc/samba/smb.conf file.

Listing 12-1. Simple Share Configuration in /etc/samba/smb.conf

```
[share]
        comment = sales share
        path = /share
        read only = No
        inherit acls =yes
        create mask = 0660
```

In this share configuration, a few parameters are used:

-   comment: This parameter is used to provide a comment, which is shown to Windows users who browse to the share. It's a good idea always to use such a comment to make it clear to users what exactly they are connecting to.

-   path: This parameter, the only required one in the list, tells you what directory the Samba server should share.

-   read only: This parameter configures security on the Samba share. If you don't use it, the share will be read-only. In this example, it is set to no, which means that the share is writable by all users who also have write permissions on the underlying Linux file system.

-   inherit acls: This parameter tells Samba to honor Linux ACLs. This means that you can set ACLs on the Linux file system and benefit from them in the Samba environment.

-   create mask: If you don't use this parameter, Samba will use the default Linux umask when it creates new files on the Linux file system. Since the default umask gives read access to all users, this might not be a good idea. Therefore, in this example, a custom create mask is used to grant read/write permissions to the user and group owners, but no permissions at all to others. When specifying a create mask value, you have to enter the exact permissions you want to set. For instance, create mask 0660 would set read/ write permissions for the user and group and nothing for others.

At this point, you have configured all that needs to be configured to make the share accessible. In the next section, you'll read how to handle user access.

Creating the User Account

To access a Samba share, you need access to the share on the Linux file system, as well as on the share itself. You can compare this to a Windows server, where a user needs NTFS permissions as well as share permissions. Unfortunately, the way that Windows handles encryption is not compatible with the way Linux handles permissions. Therefore, you cannot access a Linux directory from a Windows workstation if you only have a Linux user account; you need Windows credentials as well. The simplest way to fix this problem is to create a Linux user account as well as a Windows user account, which is exactly what we'll do in this chapter.

When working in an enterprise environment where many users need to get access to a share, this may not be a workable solution, however. This is especially true if you have many servers with Samba shares. If your needs go beyond a situation where you can work with just a Linux and a Samba user account, there are some other options. As all are relevant in typical enterprise environments, none of these options are explained any further in this book:

- *Set up an OpenLDAP Directory server*: By using such a Directory server, you can create user accounts that have properties that make it a valid user in Linux, as well as properties that make it a valid user in Windows.

- *Configure Samba as a Windows NT-style Domain Controller*: When doing this, you still need Linux user properties to be able to access the Linux file system, but at least this method allows you to manage users in a centralized way. Another benefit is that you can configure end-user computers for domain logon, which is more flexible than local logon only.

- *Configure Samba as a member server in Active Directory*: This option is interesting in environments where an existing Active Directory environment is in use. If Samba is configured as a member server in Active Directory, it can get all user information from Active Directory, which means that you don't have to set up Windows user accounts at all. However, you will still need to set up Linux user accounts.

- *Use Winbind to get all required information from Active Directory*: Winbind also is a decent solution if you want to use Samba in an environment that mostly uses Active Directory. To accomplish this, you'll run the winbind service on the Linux computer. Winbind will authenticate user accounts against Active Directory, and once this authentication has happened successfully, the user account is authenticated on Linux as well. This solution therefore allows you to manage one user account only, centralized from Active Directory.

- *Use the security=server option*: This option allows you to configure one Samba server with user accounts. All other Samba servers can get the user information from this main Samba server.

In this book, I'll only cover the option where you'll create two different user accounts: the Linux user account and the Samba user account. The following procedure shows what you need to do to set up such an environment:

1. Create the Linux user account with the methods discussed in Chapter 6 of this book. For instance, to create a user linda and make sure that she has a home directory as well, use the following command (note that using the -m option is required on SUSE and not necessary on other Linux distributions):

```
useradd -m linda
```

2. There is no need to set a password for this user account as well. A Samba user typically connects to a share over the network and never accesses the console of your Linux computer. If your Samba user needs local access, you can give him or her a Linux password. However, if the user account is used on a Windows computer only, you don't have to do this.

3. Use the smbpasswd command to create the Samba user account. You can do this as follows:

```
smbpasswd -a linda
```

The smbpasswd command now asks you to enter a password for the Samba user. This Samba password conforms to all rules that Windows normally uses for password storage and is stored with the user account in the configuration file /etc/samba/smbpasswd. Listing 12-2 shows the contents of this file after creating the user linda.

Listing 12-2. Example /etc/samba/smbpasswd File

```
nuuk:~ # cat /etc/samba/smbpasswd
# This file is the authentication source for Samba if 'passdb backend' is set
# to 'smbpasswd' and 'encrypt passwords' is 'Yes' in the [global] section of
# /etc/samba/smb.conf
#
# See section 'passdb backend' and 'encrypt passwords' in the manual page of
# smb.conf for more information.
linda:1001:F6E8482239815354AAD3B435B51404EE:55DB0294BC42D6E1B81AE2B5C7F294
3F:[U        ]:LCT-49543651:
```

Apart from creating user accounts with smbpasswd, you can also use this command to manage user accounts. The command allows you to do this in local mode, as well as remote mode. The remote mode helps you in managing Samba user accounts on other computers. In local mode, you'll manage Samba users on your computer only. Following is a list of the most useful parameters that you can use in smbpasswd local mode:

- -a: Adds a user

- -d: Disables a user account without removing it from your configuration

- -e: Enables a user account after it has been disabled

- -m: Creates a machine account, which is required in setups where workstations need to authenticate to a domain

- -x: Removes the user account from the smbpasswd file

At this point, you have done all that is necessary to enable the Samba user account. In the next section, you'll read how to start Samba services.

Starting Samba Services

At this point all that you need to do to create a Samba file server has been done. It's time to start it now! To do this, you normally need to run two different services. First is the smbd service, which starts Samba file services. Next is the nmbd service. This service gives you NetBios name services; you'll only need to start it if you want to use NetBios for name resolution.

■ **Note**   In older Windows versions, NetBIOS was used to get the IP addresses belonging to a given name in the network. Modern Windows networks use DNS for this purpose. This means that you probably don't need NetBIOS name services anymore, because your DNS server takes care of name resolution already.

To start these services, on modern Linux distributions you'll use **systemctl start smb**; followed by **systemctl enable smb** to make sure it is automatically activated upon reboot. If you need the nmb naming services to be started also, use **systemctl start nmb; systemctl enable nmb**.

Working with additional parameters in `smb.conf`

Based on the information that was just discussed, you are able to configure a Samba server that offers a share on the network. However, hundreds of other parameters exist that you can use to tune and enhance your server. I won't cover every available parameter, but to give you an impression of some of the most important ones, Listing 12-3 shows an example `smb.conf` configuration file and an explanation of the parameters used in this file.

Before explaining the individual parameters, you should be aware of the main distinction used on the configuration file. There is a section with the name [global] as well as other sections. The section [global] contains global parameters. These are parameters that are not directly related to individual shares, but they define how your Samba server should behave in general. Most parameters used in this section are specific to the [global] section only; you can't use them in individual shares. (There are some exceptions to this rule, but they are rare.)

Following the [global] settings are some specific share settings. In this example file, some "normal" file shares are used, but some specific shares are included as well that help you in enabling specific functionality. Here's a list of the specific shares in Listing 12-3:

- [homes]: This share shares user home directories. When creating a Linux user, it normally gets a home directory in /home. This share makes sure that the Samba user can access the contents of this home directory as well.

- [profiles]: This share enables users to share their user profile on the Samba server.

- [printers]: This share makes a connection to the printing system, which on all current Linux distributions is the Common UNIX Printing System (CUPS).

- [print$]: This share enables access to printer drivers for end users. By using this share the way it is configured here, end users can install printer drivers directly from the Samba server.

Listing 12-3. Example `smb.conf` Configuration File

```
nuuk:/etc/samba # cat smb.conf
 [global]
        workgroup = WORKGROUP
        printing = cups
        printcap name = cups
        printcap cache time = 750
        cups options = raw
        map to guest = Bad User
        include = /etc/samba/dhcp.conf
```

```
        logon path = \\%L\profiles\.msprofile
        logon home = \\%L\%U\.9xprofile
        logon drive = P:
        usershare allow guests = Yes
[homes]
        comment = Home Directories
        valid users = %S, %D%w%S
        browseable = No
        read only = No
        inherit acls = Yes
[profiles]
        comment = Network Profiles Service
        path = %H
        read only = No
        store dos attributes = Yes
        create mask = 0600
        directory mask = 0700
[users]
        comment = All users
        path = /home
        read only = No
        inherit acls = Yes
        veto files = /aquota.user/groups/shares/
[share]
        comment = sales share
        path = /share
        read only = No
        inherit acls =yes
        create mask = 0660
[groups]
        comment = All groups
        path = /home/groups
        read only = No
        inherit acls = Yes
[printers]
        comment = All Printers
        path = /var/tmp
        printable = Yes
        create mask = 0600
        browseable = No
[print$]
        comment = Printer Drivers
        path = /var/lib/samba/drivers
        write list = @ntadmin root
        force group = ntadmin
        create mask = 0664
        directory mask = 0775
```

Following is a list of the options used in Listing 12-3 and a short explanation for each of these options. Of these options, the only one that is required is path. All others are optional.

- workgroup: This option specifies the workgroup name your Samba server uses, which serves not only as the workgroup name in Windows peer-to-peer networking, but also as the domain name in an environment where domains are used. This can be a Windows NT 4 environment, an Active Directory environment, or an environment where Samba is used to provide domain functionality.

- printing: This parameter tells Samba what local solution is used to handle printing. On Linux, this will normally be CUPS.

- printcap name: In pre-CUPS Linux printing, the printing system had its own configuration file, which had the name /etc/printcap. In CUPS printing, there is no longer such a file. Samba needs to know what to do with /etc/printcap though, and that's why in this example, cups is used as the value for this parameter.

- cups options: This parameter tells Samba how it should offer data to CUPS printers.

- map to guest: In a Windows environment, a guest user can be used. Therefore, the Samba server may receive requests addressed to the guest user. Using this parameter, you tell Samba how to handle such requests. For instance, you can map the Windows guest user to a local Linux user account that has limited permissions. In this example, the parameter has the value of Bad User, which completely disables the Windows guest user feature.

- include: Use this parameter if you also want to read the contents of an additional configuration file. In this example, the contents of a file with the name dhcp.conf is read. In this file, you'll need to specify additional Samba commands. Using an additional configuration file is useful in making sure that the main smb.conf configuration file doesn't grow too big.

- logon path: In a domain environment, workstations that are in the domain need to know where they can find system logon information. Samba makes that clear by using the logon path parameter. This parameter has as its argument the name of a share that this Samba server offers. In the share, %L is used to refer to the localhost name.

- logon home: In a Windows 9x environment, users may also use home directories. If this is the case, they'll use the logon home parameter to discover where to find all home directory related settings.

- logon drive: This parameter indicates which drive is used on the Windows workstation to map to the share that contains home directories. Make sure that this drive is not already in use by something else.

- usershare allow guest: This parameter indicates whether you allow guest users in user shares. If you want to maintain tight security, you should set this to no.

- comment: Use this parameter to make it clear what a share is used for. Users will see the value that you've used here when browsing the network environment.

- valid users: You can use this parameter to indicate which users are allowed access to this share. This is a very good measure for security: if a user is not on the list, he or she simply doesn't get access. You can also refer to all members of a group by using the @ sign. For instance, @sales would allow access to all users who are a member of the group sales.

- `browseable`: This parameter indicates whether you allow browse access to a share. A user who has browse access can see all contents of the share. It is typical to switch this off on home directories and shares that relate to printing.

- `read only`: This parameter sets basic security on a share. If not set, the share will be read only. Change this to `read only = no` (or `writeable = yes`, both work) to allow write access to the share.

- `inherit acls`: This parameter is used to let your Samba server cooperate with Linux ACLs. If this parameter is set to yes, Samba will honor ACLs and create new files according to the specification of the ACL setting.

- `path`: This parameter, which is required, indicates which path on the Linux file system is shared by this share.

- `store dos attributes`: If you want to store DOS attributes, make sure that this parameter is set to yes. As DOS attributes require additional disk space, they are not stored by default.

- `create mask`: This parameter is used to set a `create mask` for new files. The `create mask` determines permissions on new files. If you use `inherit acls`, you should not use this parameter because the settings in a default ACL and the settings in the `create mask` may conflict with one another.

- `directory mask`: This parameter accomplishes the same as the `create mask` parameter, with the only difference being that it works on directories.

- `printable`: This parameter is needed on a printer share to allow the CUPS printing sub- system to get files from this share and print them.

- `write list`: This parameter contains a list of users who have write access to a share. You can use it in combination with the `valid users` parameter for more strict security settings. Only valid users get access, and only users who are on the write list are able to write new files in the share.

- `force group`: This parameter tries to set the group owner to the group whose name is specified here. If the user is not a member of that group, the default primary group of that user is set as the owner. You don't need this parameter if you have already applied the SGID permission (see Chapter 7), or if you are working with a default ACL.

Accessing a Samba File Server

After applying all items that are discussed in the preceding sections, you should now have a decent Samba file server up and running. Time to test whether it works! You could, of course, use a Windows workstation and connect to the network share by using UNC naming. For example, if the name of your host is nuuk and the name of the share is share, you would try from Windows to map a network drive as \\nuuk\share. Windows would then ask you to enter a username and password and connect you to the share.

If you don't have a Windows workstation available at the moment, there is an alternative: you can connect to the share from the Linux command line. In the next two sections, you'll learn how to test the share and connect to it from the command line. Following that, you'll also read how to connect to the share automatically when starting your workstation by including it in the /etc/fstab startup file on your workstation.

Accessing Samba from the Command Line

There are two methods to connect to a Linux share from the command line. You can use the smbclient utility, which gives you an FTP-like interface to the Samba shared file system. This means that you would need to use FTP-like commands like put and get to transfer files to and from your local workstation. When working this way, the share doesn't really integrate smoothly to your file system, so you probably don't want to do that. To integrate the share in the Linux file system, you can mount it using the mount command.

Before connecting to a share, you might be interested to find out whether the share exists. Even if you have started the Samba server using systemctl start smb and not seen a failure, there may be another reason why accessing the share fails. Hence, you need to make sure that it works first. To do this, you can use the smbclient utility. Using this utility, you can ask the Samba server to get an overview (list) of all available shares. You do this by entering the following command:

```
smbclient -L //servername
```

The command next asks for a password, but you can ignore that and just press the Enter key, as no password is needed to get a mere overview of shares that are offered. Listing 12-4 shows the result of the smbclient -L command on the machine that uses the example Samba configuration file that you've seen in Listing 12-3.

Listing 12-4. With the smbclient -L Command, You Can Get an Overview of All Shares That Are Offered by Your Samba Server

```
nuuk:/etc/samba # smbclient -L //localhost
Password:
Domain=[NUUK] OS=[Unix] Server=[Samba 3.0.28-0.5-1657-SUSE-CODE10]

        Sharename       Type        Comment
        ---------       ----        -------
        profiles        Disk        Network Profiles Service
        users           Disk        All users
        share           Disk        sales share
        groups          Disk        All groups
        print$          Disk        Printer Drivers
        IPC$            IPC         IPC Service (Samba 3.0.28-0.5-1657-SUSE-CODE10)
Domain=[NUUK] OS=[Unix] Server=[Samba 3.0.28-0.5-1657-SUSE-CODE10]

        Server                  Comment
        ---------               -------

        Workgroup               Master
        ---------               -------
```

Given the output provided by the smbclient -L command, our test server is available, and it has some shares to offer. So it's time to connect now. To make a connection to a share by using the mount command, you first need a directory that is available to mount the file system on. For testing purposes, let's use the directory /mnt/samba. This directory doesn't exist by default, so make sure that you create it before you start, using mkdir /mnt/samba. To connect the Samba share to that directory, you need to use an option that tells mount that it should connect to a Samba share, which by the way can also be a share on a Windows machine. To make this clear to the mount command, you can use either the -t cifs option.

Next, you need to tell Samba what user credentials to use. You can do this by passing the username as a special option to the mount command, using -o username=. Using a special option, you can even pass the password directly on the command line to the mount command, but that is a very bad idea, since this password would be readable text on the command line with no encryption applied. This means that other users would be able to get the password by using such mechanisms as the history command. As the third and fourth arguments, you need to tell mount what share to connect to and where to mount this share. The result of all this is a command that looks like the following:

```
mount -t cifs -o username=linda //nuuk/share /mnt/samba
```

At this point, the directory /mnt/samba on your Linux computer is connected to the share on your Samba server. It looks a little weird to use a Windows protocol to connect one Linux machine to another Linux machine, but why shouldn't you? Samba is a fast, versatile solution that offers way more options to secure it than the alternative NFS file system. Also, using this solution, you can not only connect your Linux computer to a Samba server, but also to a share that is offered by a Windows machine, and that is useful if you need to exchange files between Windows and Linux computers.

Configuring Samba Access on Booting

In a test environment, an excellent solution is to perform a manual mount to connect to the Samba share. Once you have verified it's working, you probably want a solution that is more user friendly. You can do this by using the /etc/fstab file to mount the share automatically.

Before typing your share entry in /etc/fstab, however, you should have a plan. This plan is based on the answer to one question: what exactly are you going to do with your share?

There are three common scenarios:

- The share gives access to user home directories. If this is the case, you want to mount the contents of the home directory share on the /home directory of the local machine.

- The share gives access to a shared group directory. If this is the case, you may want to create a directory with the name /groups on the local workstation and mount the share in a subdirectory of that directory. For instance, if you want to mount //server/sales, you might want to do that on /groups/sales.

- It is another, more generic kind of share. If the share is not used in a specific user or group scenario, but is of a more generic kind, it is a good idea to mount it in the /srv directory. Many distributions have this directory by default now to allow you to access common server-based files. For example, if you have a tools directory on the Samba server that you want to make accessible on the local file system, it's a good idea to create a directory named /srv/samba/tools and mount it there. Of course, you may also use another solution—any solution that makes sense to you is fine.

After deciding where to mount the share, you just have to mount it. To do this for the share //nuuk/share that was discussed previously, you can add the following line to your fstab file (see Chapter 3 for more information about fstab and its contents):

```
//nuuk/share    /groups/sales    cifs _netdev,username=linda,password=secret    0    0
```

Since the same options are used as when you are performing the mount manually, there are only two items that need a little explanation. First is the option _netdev. This option tells fstab that the share is on the network. The result is that your computer will wait until the network is available before trying to mount this share. Next, the password of the user is in the fstab file in clear text. Since this is the case, you do want to apply some additional security to the fstab file. I recommend you at least remove the read permissions for the others entity.

Basic Samba Troubleshooting

Based on the preceding information, your Samba server should now be up and running. Sometimes it won't though. In case this happens, here is a basic troubleshooting procedure for you to follow, based on the problems I've seen people having with Samba:

1. Start by narrowing the scope: can you reach the Samba host with the ping utility? Try the command ping 1.2.3.4, and make sure to replace 1.2.3.4 with the IP address of the machine where the Samba server resides. Are you getting a reply? Then you know the problem is not on the network.

2. Now do some checks on the computer that runs the Samba server. The best check to start with is the smbclient -L //localhost command. This command gives an overview of all shares that are locally offered. If this command does not give anything that looks like Samba shares, proceed with Step 3. If this command does give you a list of available shares, proceed with Step 4.

3. If smbclient didn't return anything looking like Samba shares, the problem is probably in the service process. Make sure that it is up and running using ps aux | grep smb. In case this command doesn't give you any running Samba servers, start the Samba service now with the procedure that is appropriate for your distribution. This should fix the problem.

4. If smbclient -L did give a result, there can be two possible causes. First, you may have made a syntax error while writing the smb.conf file. Step 5 describes what to do in that case. Another reason can be an error in the user configuration. See Step 6 for more details on how to fix this.

5. Samba has an excellent tool that helps you look for syntax errors in the smb.conf configuration file. Its name is testparm, and you can just run it like that from the command line. The tool will first give you the results of its analysis and, after you press Enter, display all the effective parameters (which in fact is a dump of all active lines in smb.conf, excluding comment lines). In Listing 12-5, you can see an example of its output. In this output, the tool points out an unknown parameter directory mask, which in this case helps in fixing the problem.

Listing 12-5. The testparm Utility Analyzes smb.conf for Syntax Errors

```
nuuk:/etc/samba # testparm
Load smb config files from /etc/samba/smb.conf
Processing section "[homes]"
Processing section "[profiles]"
Unknown parameter encountered: "dictory mask"
Ignoring unknown parameter "diectory mask"
Processing section "[users]"
Processing section "[share]"
Processing section "[groups]"
Processing section "[printers]"
Processing section "[print$]"
Loaded services file OK.
Server role: ROLE_STANDALONE
Press enter to see a dump of your service definitions
```

6. If you still haven't found the problem, it is probably user related. In this case, the solution really depends on the way you've set up the user accounts. If you did it in the way described in this chapter, you can run a few checks to see whether the user setup still works. If you are using an external service for user authentication, check the configuration and availability of that service. The first thing to do if a user gives a problem is to check whether the user is available on your Linux computer. You can do this by using grep on /etc/passwd, which is shown in the following example code line:

```
grep linda /etc/passwd
```

If this command does not give you a result, use useradd -m to create the local user account. In case this command does give a result, it may help to reset the password for the user. The following command will do that for you:

```
smbpasswd linda
```

The smbpasswd command will now ask you to enter the password for your user twice. Once you've entered it, try again and see whether that has made the user account functional.

I am aware that this section on Samba troubleshooting was short. However, I've described the most common problems, which will help you in resolving these issues. Other problems are less common and therefore not covered in this chapter.

EXERCISE 12-1: CONFIGURING SAMBA

In this exercise you'll set up a Samba server and learn how to access it as well.

1. Install the Samba server packages on your server. On Red Hat for instance, use **yum install -y samba-common** to install the required packages.

2. To start with, create the Linux environment for the Samba share. Start creating a directory, using **mkdir /samba**.

3. Type **useradd daphne** to create a user daphne, and **groupadd sales** to create a group with the name sales as well. (You may get a message that this user and group already exist). Next, type **usermod -aG sales daphne** to make user daphne a member of the group sales.

4. Set group ownership for the directory /samba, using **chown daphne:sales /samba**.

5. Also make sure that the user and group owner have full access at a Linux level to the directory, using **chmod 3770 /sales**.

6. Now that the Linux part of the configuration is ready, start by making a Samba user account for user daphne, using **smbpasswd -a daphne**. Enter the password "password" and confirm this password by hitting enter.

7. Open the file /etc/samba/smb.conf with an editor and include the following at the end of the file:

    [sales]
    path=/sales
    writable = yes
    valid users = +sales
    write list = + sales

8. Start and enable the samba service, using **systemctl start smb; systemctl enable smb**. Also start and enable Samba naming services, using **systemctl start nmb; systemctl enable smb**.

9. Type **setenforce 0** to switch off SELinux security (applies to Red Hat and derivatives only).

10. Use **smbclient -L //localhost** to verify that the Samba share is correctly displayed.

11. Type **mount -o username=daphne //localhost/sales /mnt**. This mounts the share on the local directory /mnt.

12. Use **cd /mnt** and type **touch daphnes-file**. Type **ls -l** to verify ownership of the file. It should be set to user daphne, which proves that you've accessed the /mnt directory using the Samba protocol.

Configuring an NFS Server

The preceding part of this chapter described how to configure Samba to offer file access to mostly Windows users. In this section, you'll learn how to configure Network File System (NFS) services on your computer. Following a brief overview of the protocol, you'll next learn how to build a configuration to share NFS services and how to access these NFS shares.

NFS Backgrounds

NFS is an old protocol that allows you to share files on a UNIX/Linux network. It goes back to the days when you still had to wear a white coat before being allowed to approach the computer. In those days, computers that were networked were also computers that were trusted, because there was no such thing as the Internet that allowed everyone to connect to your computer. Given this environment, NFS was developed as a protocol that offers a fast-and-easy way to share files. Unfortunately, it was never developed with security in mind.

Security in NFS has always been based on hosts. When creating a share, you'll give access to a host, not to individual users. After the host has made contact, the users on that host will have the same permission as the users on the NFS server. That is, the user with user ID 501 (or any other user ID) on the NFS client will automatically get the permissions that user 501 has on the NFS server. You can imagine that there can be some serious problems with this. Since NFS was often used in conjunction with the NIS service, which allows for centralized user management (i.e., which takes care that the user with UID 501 is the same on all hosts involved), this feature was not really harmful.

In the recent version 4 of the NFS protocol, Kerberos security has been added as an option. Using Kerberos security allows you to use Kerberos tickets, which allows user-based access control as well. Setting up Kerberized NFS shares requires insight in the working of Kerberos and for that reason goes beyond the scope of this chapter. Version 4 has become the default NFS version on all Linux distributions, which is why in this chapter we'll be working with NFS version 4, even if Kerberos will not be used.

You may wonder, however, why people still want to use NFS. There are two main reasons: its speed and the ease with which you can set it up. As you will find out in the next sections, setting up an NFS share really is not hard to do, as is using the NFS environment.

Another reason why NFS is still being used, is because it is a default option in that is provided by many hardware storage appliances. These appliances are common in large corporate environments and are offering NFS because it's a simple protocol that is fast and not very difficult to configure.

Understanding NFS Processes

To use an NFS server, a couple of components are involved. First is the NFS server itself. This is provided by the Linux kernel. To offer its services, NFS uses another service, which is the NFS RPC (Remote Procedure Call) portmapper. Let's see what role this service plays first.

Most modern services have their own port number. Historically this has never been the case for NFS, as NFS was created at a time where TCP and UDP ports hadn't become the standard yet.

NFS was created a long time ago, when the Internet port numbers in use nowadays weren't yet common. As a result, NFS uses its own kind of port numbers, the so-called RPC program numbers.

Up to NFS version 3, to offer compatibility with the way that modern computers offer services on the network, these RPC numbers must be converted to an Internet port number. This is the task of the portmap program, which runs as a daemon to support your NFS server. When an RPC-based service, such as NFS, is started, it will tell portmap on what port number it is listening and what RPC program numbers it serves. When a client wants to communicate to the RPC-based service, it will first contact the portmapper on the server to find out the port number it should use. Once it knows about the port number, its requests can be tunneled over the Internet port to the correct RPC port.

To find out on which RPC program numbers your server is currently listening, you can use the rpcinfo -p command. In Listing 12-6, you can see an example of this command showing its results.

Listing 12-6. Displaying RPC Program Numbers with rpcinfo -p

```
SFO:~ # rpcinfo -p
   program    vers   proto   port
    100000     2      tcp    111  portmapper
    100000     2      udp    111  portmapper
    100003     2      udp    2049 nfs
    100003     3      udp    2049 nfs
    100003     4      udp    2049 nfs
    100003     2      tcp    2049 nfs
    100003     3      tcp    2049 nfs
    100003     4      tcp    2049 nfs
    100024     1      udp    1147 status
    100021     1      udp    1147 nlockmgr
    100021     3      udp    1147 nlockmgr
    100021     4      udp    1147 nlockmgr
    100024     1      tcp    2357 status
    100021     1      tcp    2357 nlockmgr
    100021     3      tcp    2357 nlockmgr
    100021     4      tcp    2357 nlockmgr
    100005     1      udp    916  mountd
    100005     1      tcp    917  mountd
    100005     2      udp    916  mountd
    100005     2      tcp    917  mountd
    100005     3      udp    916  mountd
    100005     3      tcp    917  mountd
```

As you can see in the output of the rpcinfo -p command, NFS is listening to Internet port 2049 for version 2, 3, and 4 calls. Internally, it is using RPC port 100003 as well. Before the NFS server is started, you must make sure that the portmapper is started. All of the main Linux distributions will take care of this automatically when you start the NFS server.

After starting the portmapper, the other NFS server components can be started. First is the rpc.nfsd program. This program makes sure that the portmapper is informed there is an NFS server present, and it will give the proper portmapper program number to the NFS server.

Next, the rpc.mountd program must be loaded. This program allows users to make NFS mounts to the NFS server. As the third component, the rpc.lockd program needs to be started. This program ensures that only one user can have access to a file at a time; when it is accessed, the nfs.lockd program locks access to the file for other users. You don't need to load all these programs individually; they are loaded automatically when the NFS server is started through its systemctl script.

Notice that things have changed significantly with the release of NFSv4. In NFSv4, NFS offers its services on port 2049 by default. This makes managing NFS a lot easier, especially in environments where firewalls are being used.

The last part of the NFS server consists of its configuration files. Two different files are involved. First is the /etc/exports file. In this file, the NFS shares are specified. Then on some distributions such as SUSE and Red Hat, there is also the /etc/sysconfig/nfs configuration file, where the number of NFS threads and other startup parameters are specified.

Configuring an NFS Server

On most distributions, two configuration files are involved if you want to manage the NFS server by hand. First and most important is the /etc/exports file. You will find it on all Linux distributions. This file is used to configure all NFS shares you want to offer from your NFS server. Apart from that, your distribution may use the /etc/sysconfig/nfs file, in which a couple of parameters is provided to the NFS server, determining the way that server offers its services.

In the file /etc/exports, the NFS shares are defined. The generic structure of the lines where this happens is as follows:

directory hosts(options)

In this, *directory* is the name of the directory you would like to share, for example, /share. Next, *hosts* refers to the hosts that you want to grant access to that directory. The following can be used for the host specification:

- The name of an individual host, either its short name or its fully qualified domain name

- The IP address of an individual host

- A network referred to by its name, for example, *.mydomain.com

- A network referred to by a combination of IP address and subnetmask, for example, 192.168.10.0/255.255.255.0

- All networks, referred to by an asterisk

After indicating which hosts are granted access to your server, you need to specify the options with which you want to give access to the NFS share. Some of the most used options are listed in Table 12-1.

Table 12-1. *Commonly Used NFS Options*

Option	Meaning
Ro	The file system is exported as a read-only file system. No matter what local permissions the user has, writing to the file system is denied at all times.
Rw	The file system is exported as a read-write file system. Users can read and write files to the directory if they have sufficient permissions on the local file system to do that. That is, this parameter makes the share writable, but to write files in the share, you still need permissions to the local file system as well.
root_squash	The user ID of user root is mapped to the user ID 65534, which is mapped to the user nobody by default. This means that you won't have write permissions, and depending on the permission configuration on your computer, probably you'll have no permissions at all. This default behavior ensures that a user who is mounting an NFS mount as user root on the workstation does not have root access to the directory on the server. Especially if you use NFS to give end users access to a share, you should at all times use this option.
no_root_squash	With this option, there is no limitation for the root user. He or she will have root permissions on the server as well. Use this option only if you want to create an NFS share only the user root has access to.
all_squash	Use this option if you want to limit the permissions of all users accessing the NFS share. With this option, all users will have the permissions of user nobody on the NFS share. Use this option if you want extra security on your NFS share, but realize that it may make your NFS share unworkable.
sync	This option makes sure that changes to files have been written to the file system before others are granted access to the same file. Although it doesn't offer the best performance, to avoid losing data to files, it is recommended you always use this option.

Following is an example of a configuration line that is quite common in /etc/exports. Check man 5 exports for more examples.

```
/       ilulissat(rw) kangerlussuaq(rw,no_root_squash)
```

In this line, the host ilulissat gets read/write access to the shared root file system, but root from that host will not get root permissions on the NFS server. The computer kangerlussuaq gets read/write access as well, but the user root will still have his root permissions when connecting to this share.

Tuning the List of Exported File Systems with exports

When the NFS server is activated, it keeps a list of exported file systems in the /var/lib/nfs/ xtab file (your distribution may use a different location). This file is initialized with the list of all directories exported in the /etc/exports file by invoking the exportfs -a command when the NFS server initializes. With the exportfs command, it is possible to add a file system to this list without editing the /etc/exports file or restarting the NFS server. For example, the following is used to export the directory /srv to all servers in the network 192.168.1.0:

```
exportfs 192.168.1.0/255.255.255.0:/srv
```

The exported file system will become available immediately, but will only be available until the next reboot of your NFS server, as it is not in the /etc/exports file. If you want it to be available after a reboot as well, make sure to include it in the /etc/exports file as well.

Configuring an NFS Client

Now that the NFS server is operational, you can configure the clients that need to access the NFS server. There are two ways to do so:

- Mount the NFS share by hand.

- Mount the NFS share automatically from fstab.

Mounting an NFS Share with the mount Command

The fastest way to get access to an NFS shared directory is by issuing the mount command from the command line. Just specify the file system type as an NFS file system, indicate what you want to mount and where you want to mount it, and you have immediate access. In the next example, you can see how to get access to the shared directory /opt on server STN via the local directory /mnt:

```
mount -t nfs STN:/opt /mnt
```

Notice the colon after the name of the server; this required element separates the name of the server from the name of the directory that you want to export. Although you can access an NFS shared directory without using any options, there are some options that are used often to make accessing an NFS mounted share easier. These options are summarized in Table 12-2.

Table 12-2. *Common NFS Mount Options*

Option	Meaning
Soft	Use this option to tell the mount command not to insist indefinitely on mounting the remote share. If after the default timeout value (normally 60 seconds) the directory could not be mounted, the mount attempt is aborted. Use this option for all noncritical mounts.
Hard	By using this option, you tell the mount command that it should continue trying to access the mount indefinitely. Be aware that if the mount is performed at boot time, using this option may cause the boot process to hang. Therefore, only use this option on directories that are really needed.
Fg	This default option tells the mount command that all mounts must be activated as foreground mounts. The result is that you can do nothing else on that screen as long as the mount could not be completed.
Bg	This performs the mount as a background mount. If the first attempt is unsuccessful, all other attempts are started in the background.
rsize=n	With this option, you can specify the number of bytes that the client reads from the server at the same time. For compatibility reasons, this size is set to 1024 bytes by default. NFS version 3 and later can handle much more than that. To increase the speed of your system, set it to a higher value, like 8192 bytes.

(*continued*)

Table 12-2. (*continued*)

Option	Meaning
wsize=*n*	Use this option to set the maximum number of bytes that can be written simultaneously. The default is 1024. NFS 3 and later can handle much more than that, so you should specify 8192 to optimize the write speed for your server.
retry=*n*	This option is used to specify the number of minutes a mount attempt can take. The default value is 10000 (which is 6.94 days). Consider setting it lower to avoid waiting forever on a mount that can't be established.
Nosuid	Use this option to specify that the SUID and SGID bits cannot be used on the exported file system. This is a security option.
Nodev	This option is used to specify that no devices can be used from the imported file system. This also is a security feature.
Noexec	Use this option to avoid starting executable files from the exported file system.

■ **Tip** NFS uses long timeouts to establish a connection. This may be very useful. Once I was installing a Linux machine by using an NFS installation server. The installation server was accidently rebooted during the installation, so the installation stopped. At the moment the installation server came back, it restarted the installation automatically.

Mounting an NFS Share automatically from `fstab`

Mounting an NFS share with the mount command will do fine for a mount you only need occasionally. If you need the mount more than once, it is better to automate it using /etc/fstab.

If you know how to add entries to /etc/fstab, it isn't difficult to add an entry that mounts an NFS share as well. The only differences with normal mounts are that you have to specify the complete name of the NFS share instead of a device, and that some NFS options must be specified. When mounting from fstab, you should always include the options rsize, wsize, and soft for optimal performance. To refer to the server, its name as well as its IP address can be used. The following line gives an example of what the line in fstab could look like:

```
server:/nfsshare    /mnt/nfsserver    nfs    rsize=8192,wsize=8192,soft    1 2
```

Getting a List of available NFS Shares

To mount an NFS share, you first must know what shares are offered by a machine. You can find that out using the showmount command. This command is fairly simple in use: just type showmount -e followed by the name of the host that you want to check. The example in Listing 12-7 shows what its result can look like.

Listing 12-7. To Find Out What Shares Are Offered, Use showmount -e

```
nuuk:/ # showmount -e localhost
Export list for localhost:
/share *
```

EXERCISE 12-2: CONFIGURING NFS

In this exercise you'll configure an NFS server. The procedure in this exercise is based on a Red Hat system, you may notice small differences if you're applying it on another Linux distribution.

1. Use **yum install -y nfs-utils** to install the NFS server package.

2. Create a directory with the name **/nfs**, using **mkdir /nfs**.

3. Open the file /etc/exports with an editor and add the following line:

    ```
    /nfs *(rw)
    ```

4. Type **systemctl start nfs-server**. This should start the nfs server. Use **systemctl status nfs-server** to verify that this was succesfull.

5. Use **showmount -e localhost** to verify that the export is indeed available.

6. If you have verified the availability of the export, try to mount it on the local file system. To start with, use **umount /mnt** to ensure that nothing else currently is mounted on it. Next, type **mount localhost:/nfs /tmp** and verify that the share is mounted.

7. Try to write a file in the /mnt directory, using **touch /mnt/afile**. Is this succesfull? Can you explain why?

In the previous exercise you have created an NFS share and mounted it. At the end of the exercise you have tried to write a file to the share but that didn't succeed. The reason is that user root by default is "squashed", which means that the UID 0 is mapped to the user nfsnobody, a user with no permissions whatsoever on the share. If you wanted to make it possible for this user to write to the NFS share anyway, you would need to grant access permissions on the mount point, for instance by making the user nfsnobody owner of the mount point and giving this user write permissions on it. Notice that it wouldn't be a good idea to use the mount option no_root_squash, as this would mean that everybody who connects to the share will get root permissions to the share. This is a major flaw in security and should be avoided at all times.

Summary

In this chapter, you've learned how to set up Linux as a file server. You've read about Samba, which nowadays is a kind of universal option for configuring a Linux file server. It works for Windows, but also for Apple and Linux users. You've also read how you can enable NFS file sharing, which is a useful method for file sharing if you want to share files between Linux computers. In this chapter, you've learned about the following commands and configuration files:

- smbd: The process responsible for Samba file sharing.

- nmbd: The process that offers NetBIOS-style name services.

- smb.conf: The main Samba configuration file.

- mount -t smbf/mount -t cifs/mount -t nfs: Specific options that specify the file system type that should be used when mounting a Samba or an NFS share.

- `testparm`: Command that does a syntax check on the `smb.conf` configuration file.

- `rpcinfo`: Command that gives information about mappings between NFS ports and RPC ports.

- `exports`: The main configuration file for your NFS server. All NFS shares are in this file.

- `exportfs`: Command that lets bypass the `/etc/exports` file if you need an NFS share for temporary use. Use `exportfs` with the name of the directory you want to export as its argument.

- `showmount`: Command that helps you discover which shares are available on any host offering NFS services.

In the next chapter, you will learn how to manage the kernel, its modules, and its hardware on your computer.

■ ■ ■

## CHAPTER 13

Working with the Kernel

The heart of your computer is the kernel. This kernel works with specific parameters and modules, and as a Linux user you need to have at least a minimal knowledge about them. In this chapter, you'll learn how to perform basic kernel management tasks and how to change parameters for your kernel. You'll also learn how to configure GRUB to load your kernel.

Understanding the Kernel

As mentioned, the Linux kernel is the heart of the operating system. It is the software that communicates directly to the hardware. The kernel is the only part of the operating system that communicates to the hardware directly; all other components that you use have to go through the kernel as shown in Figure 13-1.

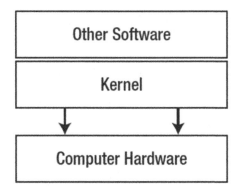

Figure 13-1. *Only through the kernel can all software communicate to the computer hardware*

To access the different hardware components, the kernel needs drivers. Every kernel driver is represented by a kernel module. Only the most essential drivers are directly compiled in the kernel itself. While booting, the kernel loads in initial RAM disk. This RAM disk contains drivers for hardware that may be present in your computer. These drivers are not included in the kernel itself, because these are non-essential drivers.

In general, drivers are loaded automatically when the computer boots through the kernel directly or by using the initial RAM disk or when new hardware is attached to the computer. The latter is done with the aid of the udev process, which is used by all modern distributions.

■ **Note**   In the old days, kernels were monolithic, meaning that all drivers were compiled directly into the kernel. This also meant that if a user needed a new driver, he or she had to enable the driver in the source code and recompile the entire kernel. Fortunately, this is no longer necessary; if a new driver is required, the user just has to load a new module. Therefore, situations where kernels need to be recompiled are pretty rare nowadays.

Managing Kernel Modules

To work with your computer's hardware, you need drivers to access the hardware. The role of the driver is to tell the kernel exactly how it should address the hardware. In general, you don't need to do anything for proper hardware access, but some cases will require your involvement, and Linux offers some commands to help you with that. These commands are discussed in the following sections.

Listing Modules with `lsmod`

Before doing any module management on your computer, you should know which modules are loaded. For this purpose, you can use the lsmod command. Listing 13-1 shows you the command and sample output.

Listing 13-1. Use `lsmod` to Get a List of All Loaded Modules

```
nuuk:/ # lsmod
Module                 Size   Used by
vfat                   11648  0
fat                    47132  1 vfat
usb_storage            72896  0
vmblock                15900  4
vsock                  41152  0
vmci                   32116  1 vsock
vmmemctl               11708  0
dock                    8840  0
button                  6672  0
battery                 9604  0
ac                      4996  0
apparmor               32420  0
piix                    9476  0 [permanent]
sd_mod                 19088  5
scsi_mod              127372  9
usb_storage,mptctl,ahci,libata,sg,mptspi,mptscsih,scsi_transport
_spi,sd_mod
ide_disk               14848 0
ide_core              117648 5 usb_storage,ide_cd,ide_generic,piix,ide_disk
```

The output of lsmod shows you not only which modules are loaded, but also what the modules are doing. In the first column of its output, you see the name of the module (for instance, on the last line, you see information about ide_core). Next is the amount of memory the module uses (117648 in the case of usb_core), followed by the number and names of the other modules that currently use this module. In particular, the latter part of this information is important to know about, because if a module has dependencies, you cannot just unload it before unloading the dependencies. Before doing anything, you should use lsmod to see what the modules are currently doing, after which you can use modprobe or modinfo on these modules.

Loading and Unloading Modules with modprobe

Basically, modules get loaded automatically. In some cases, however, you may need to unload and reload a module by hand. This may be required after changing options for a module (see the section "Changing Module Options" later in this chapter for more information). As modules normally get loaded automatically, you'll probably have to unload a module first before you can load it again. To unload a module that is currently loaded, use modprobe -r. For example, the following command would unload the fat32 module from your computer:

```
modprobe -r fat32
```

modprobe will not normally return any messages; it just does its job and quits. If you actually want to see what it is doing, you can add the -v option for verbosity. This can be especially useful when loading a module; for instance, it shows you what dependencies are automatically loaded with your module. Listing 13-2 gives an example of this. Notice that modules that are currently required by another kernel module as a dependency cannot be unloaded.

Listing 13-2. To See What Happens on Loading a Module, Use modprobe –v

```
nuuk:/ # modprobe -v vfat
insmod /lib/modules/2.6.16.60-0.21-default/kernel/fs/fat/fat.ko
insmod /lib/modules/2.6.16.60-0.21-default/kernel/fs/vfat/vfat.ko
```

Loading of a module may fail because of versioning errors. Typically, modules are written for a specific version of the kernel, and if the version in the module is wrong, it will fail to load. A bad solution to this problem is to disable version checking by using the -f (force) option. Notice that this should never happen for kernel modules that where installed with the kernel. Versioning problems can occur though if an administrator has manually installed Linux kernel modules that are not a part of the official Linux kernel, the proprietary kernel modules.

You may succeed in loading the module using the option -f, but it won't be stable. However, if this is your only option, you may need to use it. Before using modprobe -f, you should first check whether you can find the source code for your module, which you might want to compile again to make sure it works with your kernel. See the section "Compiling Modules" later in this chapter for more information.

Displaying Module Properties with modinfo

In some situations, you may just want to know more about a module that is currently loaded. To do this, you can use modinfo. This is a pretty straightforward command that gives you all available properties for a module, which may be useful for troubleshooting. For instance, modinfo also gives you the license that is used for the module in question. This allows you to recognize a proprietary module, which may possibly cause problems in your current kernel. In Listing 13-3, you can see the result of running the modinfo command on the vfat module.

Listing 13-3. Use modinfo to Find Out More About a Module

```
nuuk:/ # modinfo vfat
filename:       /lib/modules/2.6.16.60-0.21-default/kernel/fs/vfat/vfat.ko
author:         Gordon Chaffee
description:    VFAT filesystem support
license:        GPL
srcversion:     A7FE86D3A7ECDB19677320F
depends:        fat
supported:      yes
vermagic:       2.6.16.60-0.21-default 586 REGPARM gcc-4.1
```

Changing Module Options

When working with kernel modules, you can pass options to them. You would do this by editing the /etc/modprobe.conf configuration file or by adding module-specific files to /etc/modprobe.d. You can include lines for specific modules in modprobe.conf and specify all you need to do on one line per module, or alternatively you can create a configuration file for a specific module in /etc/modprobe.d. Note that the letter currently is the preferred method for loading kernel modules. Listing 13-4 shows partial sample contents of modprobe.conf.

Listing 13-4. Using modprobe.conf for Module-Specific Options

```
alias char-major-10-170 thinkpad
alias personality-13        abi-solaris
alias personality-14        abi-uw7
# required for DRI support on SiS chips
options sisfb               mode=none mem=12288
# ata_piix can't handle ICH6 in AHCI mode
install ata_piix /sbin/modprobe ahci 2>&1 |:; /sbin/modprobe\
  --ignore-install ata_piix
include /etc/modprobe.d
include /etc/modprobe.conf.local
```

As you can see, a few commands are used in modprobe.conf or the files in /etc/modprobe.d:

- **alias**: Use this to give an alternative name to a module. In the example line alias personality-14 abi-uw7, the alias name personality-14 is given to the real module name abi-uw7. This means that you can also load this module by referring to personality-14.

- **options**: This command is used to pass specific options to a module. In the example line options sisfb mode=none mem=12288, no specific mode is specified, and a memory address is added. Module options are normally module specific and in some cases are required to get the appropriate behavior from a module. You can find out which module options exist for a specific module by using the **modinfo** command. The last lines of the output of this command show which options are supported (if any) by lines that start with the text parm.

- **install**: Normally, a module is just added to the kernel. If your module needs more parameters and settings when it initializes, you can use the install command, which lets you use complete shell scripts to load a module. An example of this is in the line install ata_piix /sbin/modprobe ahci 2>&1 |:; /sbin/modprobe --ignore-install ata_piix, which tells modprobe that it should load the ata_piix module by doing a modprobe on the ahci module; if that fails, it should not load ata_piix at all. (More on the techniques that are used in a shell script like this will be discussed in the next chapter.)

- **remove**: Like install, this command allows you to pass specific options when unload- ing a module.

- **include**: By using the include command, you can tell modprobe to use an additional configuration file for loading modules. As you can see in Listing 13-4, the include command is used to include all configuration files in /etc/modprobe.d as well.

- `blacklist`: In some cases, a module is programmed to use internal alias names. These may conflict with an alias name that you have configured for the module. To prevent problems with this, you can use the `blacklist` command to indicate that all of the module's internal alias names should be ignored. Some distributions have an `/etc/modprobe.d/blacklist` configuration file in place by default to prevent certain alias names from being used.

Managing Module Dependencies

As you can see, when using the `lsmod` command, some modules depend on other modules to load successfully. Scanning for these module dependencies is the responsibility of the `depmod` command, which automatically loads when your computer boots. The result of this command is written to the `modules.dep` file, which you can find in the `modules` directory for your current kernel (`/lib/modules/...`). Notice that normally you should not need to manually use the depmod command as this command is automatically executed when the kernel is installed, or when kernel updates are installed.

Since this file just contains a long list of modules and their depen- dencies, it makes no sense to edit it yourself. In case a module has dependency problems, it can be useful to run the `depmod` command again from the command line. This command will generate a new `modules.dep` file automatically for you.

Legacy Commands for Module Management

Some older commands for module management don't take module dependencies in consid- eration. You should not use these commands, which I've listed here, because they most likely won't load and unload your modules correctly:

- `insmod`: Loads a module

- `rmmod`: Removes a module

EXERCISE 13-1: WORKING WITH KERNEL MODULES

1. Type **lsmod** to get an overview of currently loaded kernel modules. Check if the **vfat** module is loaded using **lsmod | grep vfat**. The next steps in this exercise assume that it has not been loaded.

2. Type **modprobe vfat** to manually load the vfat module.

3. Repeat the command **lsmod | grep vfat**. You will now see it loaded, and you'll also see that it has a dependency to the **fat** kernel module.

4. Type **modinfo vfat**. You won't see any kernel module options near the end of the result of this command.

5. Type **modinfo cdrom**. Notice the parm lines near the end of the output, which indicates the module options that can be used.

6. Type **modprobe -r vfat**. This unloads the vfat module.

7. Type **lsmod | grep fat**. Notice that not only the vfat module, but the fat module as well have been unloaded.

Finding the right Hardware Module

For hardware on your computer, the right modules should be loaded automatically. You can verify if this is the case using the **lspci -k** command. Listing 13-5 shows partial output of this command, notice the last line of every PCI address that mentions the name of the PCI module that is loaded.

Listing 13-5. Finding Which Hardware Module is Loaded

```
[root@localhost log]# lspci -k
00:00.0 Host bridge: Intel Corporation 440BX/ZX/DX - 82443BX/ZX/DX Host bridge (rev 01)
        Subsystem: VMware Virtual Machine Chipset
        Kernel driver in use: agpgart-intel
00:01.0 PCI bridge: Intel Corporation 440BX/ZX/DX - 82443BX/ZX/DX AGP bridge (rev 01)
00:07.0 ISA bridge: Intel Corporation 82371AB/EB/MB PIIX4 ISA (rev 08)
        Subsystem: VMware Virtual Machine Chipset
00:07.1 IDE interface: Intel Corporation 82371AB/EB/MB PIIX4 IDE (rev 01)
        Subsystem: VMware Virtual Machine Chipset
        Kernel driver in use: ata_piix
00:07.3 Bridge: Intel Corporation 82371AB/EB/MB PIIX4 ACPI (rev 08)
        Subsystem: VMware Virtual Machine Chipset
00:07.7 System peripheral: VMware Virtual Machine Communication Interface (rev 10)
        Subsystem: VMware Virtual Machine Communication Interface
        Kernel driver in use: vmw_vmci
00:0f.0 VGA compatible controller: VMware SVGA II Adapter
        Subsystem: VMware SVGA II Adapter
        Kernel driver in use: vmwgfx
```

In some cases you won't see any Kernel driver in use line. If this is the case, no kernel module could be found for this specific hardware. To fix this issue, you should try to find a proprietary driver with the vendor of the specific hardware.

Tuning Kernel Parameters

In the old days, tuning kernel parameters was hard. You needed to change parameters in the C language source files and recompile the kernel to make changes. Today this is no longer a requirement. Instead, you can write new parameters to the /proc file system. This file system contains several kernel settings, and by writing directly to some of the files in /proc, you will immediately change the setting.

You should never try to change settings in /proc without knowing what you are doing, because you may severely trash your system. However, /proc expertise requires deep insight into the working of Linux and the Linux kernel; hence, I won't give you a complete list of every parameter that you can change in /proc. I will give you some useful examples, however, as well as the method to make changes permanent.

Writing Changes to /proc

To write a change to a file in /proc, you need to echo the new value to the configuration file. All kernel-related configuration files are in /proc/sys. Let's consider an example: the con- figuration file /proc/sys/net/ipv4/ ip_forward indicates whether your computer can route packets between two network cards. Typically, this is not required for an end-user compu- ter, but you may choose to set this up if you want to use your computer as a wireless access point, for instance. You can show the default setting in this file by using cat /proc/sys/net/ ipv4/ip_forward, which will give you the value of 0, meaning that routing currently is disa- bled. To enable it, echo the value of 1 to this configuration file. Listing 13-6 shows how this procedure works.

Listing 13-6. Changing Parameters in /proc

```
nuuk:/proc/sys/net/ipv4 # cat ip_forward
0
nuuk:/proc/sys/net/ipv4 # echo 1 > ip_forward
nuuk:/proc/sys/net/ipv4 # cat ip_forward
1
```

The disadvantage of the procedure just described is that changes are not persistent when you reboot your computer. This means that after a reboot, you would have to apply all of these settings again. Fortunately, a workaround exists in the form of the sysctl package. If installed, sysctl runs as a service when your computer boots. When loaded, it reads its configuration file, /etc/sysctl.conf. This file contains a list of all parameters that have to be applied to the /proc file system. Listing 13-7 shows an example of what the contents of sysctl may look like. This example, which comes from an Ubuntu server, contains some valuable information on param- eters that you may want to change.

Listing 13-7. Applying Settings Permanently with sysctl

```
root@mel:/etc# cat sysctl.conf
#
# /etc/sysctl.conf - Configuration file for setting system variables
# See sysctl.conf (5) for information.
#

#kernel.domainname = example.com

# the following stops low-level messages on console
kernel.printk = 4 4 1 7

# enable /proc/$pid/maps privacy so that memory relocations are not
# visible to other users. (Added in kernel 2.6.22.)
kernel.maps_protect = 1

# Increase inotify availability
fs.inotify.max_user_watches = 524288
# protect bottom 64k of memory from mmap to prevent NULL-dereference
# attacks against potential future kernel security vulnerabilities.
# (Added in kernel 2.6.23.)
vm.mmap_min_addr = 65536

###############################################################3
# Functions previously found in netbase
#

# Comment the next two lines to disable Spoof protection (reverse-path filter)
# Turn on Source Address Verification in all interfaces to
# prevent some spoofing attacks
net.ipv4.conf.default.rp_filter=1
net.ipv4.conf.all.rp_filter=1
```

```
# Uncomment the next line to enable TCP/IP SYN cookies
# This disables TCP Window Scaling (http://lkml.org/lkml/2008/2/5/167)
#net.ipv4.tcp_syncookies=1

# Uncomment the next line to enable packet forwarding for IPv4
#net.ipv4.ip_forward=1

# Uncomment the next line to enable packet forwarding for IPv6
#net.ipv6.ip_forward=1


###################################################################
# Additional settings - these settings can improve the network
# security of the host and prevent against some network attacks
# including spoofing attacks and man in the middle attacks through
# redirection. Some network environments, however, require that these
# settings are disabled so review and enable them as needed.
#
# Ignore ICMP broadcasts
#net/ipv4/icmp_echo_ignore_broadcasts = 1
#
# Ignore bogus ICMP errors
#net/ipv4/icmp_ignore_bogus_error_responses = 1
#
# Do not accept ICMP redirects (prevent MITM attacks)
#net/ipv4/conf/all/accept_redirects = 0
# _or_
# Accept ICMP redirects only for gateways listed in our default
# gateway list (enabled by default)
# net/ipv4/conf/all/secure_redirects = 1
#
# Do not send ICMP redirects (we are not a router)
#net/ipv4/conf/all/send_redirects = 0
#
# Do not accept IP source route packets (we are not a router)
#net/ipv4/conf/all/accept_source_route = 0
#
# Log Martian Packets
#net/ipv4/conf/all/log_martians = 1
#
# Always defragment packets
#net/ipv4/ip_always_defrag = 1
```

In /etc/sysctl.conf, configuration files in /proc/sys are referred to by using relative path names. As you can see in the last line, for instance, the setting net/ipv4/ip_always_defrag is used, which refers to the file with the complete name of /proc/sys/net/ipv4/ip_always_ defrag. Instead of using the notation with slashes that you see in this example listing, your distribution may use the dotted notation, which would in this case be net.ipv4.ip_always_ defrag. It doesn't matter which you choose, as both are compatible.

When changing kernel settings, you should know where to find which kind of settings. In /proc/sys, different subdirectories are used to group different kinds of configuration files. The following subdirectories are used:

- debug: Contains parameters related to kernel debugging

- dev: Contains parameters related to devices and their working

- fs: Contains file system parameters

- kernel: Contains kernel-related parameters

- net: Contains network-related settings

- vm: Contains settings that relate to memory management

Some Useful /proc Parameters

As mentioned before, tuning the kernel by modifying the /proc file system is not easy to do and requires deep insight in the working of the kernel. Therefore, I will not go into that here. To give you an impression of the possibilities, I've included a short list of some of the options in /proc:

- /proc/sys/net/ipv4/ip_forward: Determines whether your computer has to route packets between network cards. Use this if you are setting up your computer as a router on a network.

- /proc/sys/dev/cdrom/autoeject: Tells the kernel whether it should automatically eject the optical disk after unmounting it.

- /proc/sys/dev/scsi/logging_level: Determines the logging level that SCSI devices should use. A higher log level means more intensive logging. Only use values here that are the double or the half of the previous value; for example, 1, 2, 4, 8, 16, 32, 64, 128, 256. Tune this if you want more (or less) SCSI-related logging.

- /proc/sys/fs/file-max: Gives the maximum number of files that can be opened simultaneously.

- /proc/sys/kernel/hostname: Contains the name of the computer as it is known by your kernel.

- /proc/sys/kernel/osrelease: Contains the current kernel version. This file is read when displaying the current version on the command line with the uname -r command.

- /proc/sys/net/core/rmem_max: Sets the maximum amount of memory that the kernel should reserve to buffer incoming network packets.

- /proc/sys/vm/laptop_mode: Tells the kernel whether it should run in laptop mode. When enabled with the value 1, it will use settings that are more energy efficient.

- /proc/sys/vm/swappiness: Tells the kernel how fast it should start swapping. A higher value in here indicates a higher willingness on the part of your kernel to start swapping.

EXERCISE 13-3: MAKING KERNEL CHANGES THROUGH /PROC

1. Open a root shell.

2. Type **sysctl -a | grep icmp**. This shows all current ICMP related proc settings. Notice that the parameter icmp_echo_ignore_all should be set to 0.

3. Type **ping localhost**. You are getting a reply because ICMP traffic is allowed.

4. Type **echo 1 > /proc/sys/net/ipv4/icmp_echo_ignore_all**

5. Repeat step 3. You should no longer be able to ping localhost.

Compiling Your Own Kernel and Kernel Modules

Among the advantages of using Linux is that you can create new functionality based on the source files of kernel as well as other programs. In this section, you'll read how compiling is used to get things going, first as it applies to the kernel, and second as it applies to new kernel modules.

To be able to build and compile your own software, you must have a C compiler installed on your computer. Typically, the GNU C compiler, which is in the gcc package, is used for this purpose. Make sure that it is installed, as well as all the packages that depend on it, before pro- ceeding. Read Chapter 8 for more information about the installation of new software packages on your distribution.

Note: On enterprise Linux distributions such as SUSE and Red Hat, it is not common to compile your own kernel. The kernel source files often aren't even included. This is because for those distributions the supportability is very important. By recompiling your own kernel, you'll break support as you are going to include options that haven't been verified by the vendor. So if you're using an enterprise Linux distribution, don't compile changes into your kernel.

Understanding Make

To compile software, you need a C compiler, which is in the gcc package. To compile C files successfully, generically speaking you'll use one of two approaches; the one you use depends on which way the source program files have been delivered. If your source file is one file only, you could compile it directly, using the gcc command. When dealing with Linux kernels and drivers, this never is the case; you don't work with one single source file, but with lots of source files that are all linked to each other and, depending on your current configuration, have to behave differently. As it would be virtually impossible to compile all of these one by one, most source files come with a file that helps with the compilation process, named Makefile. You will find it after extracting the source files from the software package.

The Makefile contains specific instructions that tell the C compiler exactly what it has to do when compiling the software. To start compiling the software against this Makefile is not too hard: you just run the make command. However, since there can be different Makefiles on your computer, you should always run the make command from the directory that contains the Makefile you need to start compiling your software.

If the software in question is very complex, the Makefile may contain instructions to run the compiling job for different scenarios. This is the case when working with the kernel, where you can run make with different arguments to tell the compiler exactly what it has to do. These arguments are not specific to make but are defined in the Makefile itself. If you're not afraid of complicated scripts, you can even read the Makefile to try to find out exactly what it accomplishes. (See http://www.gnu.org/software/make/manual/make.html for more information on make.)

Modifying and Compiling the Kernel

Before the Linux kernel was modular and before it was easy to write new kernel options to the /etc/sysctl.conf file to change settings dynamically, you needed to change kernel settings and recompile a new kernel after making your setting changes. Nowadays, there is hardly a reason to proceed in this way. Nevertheless, this section gives some insight into what is needed to configure and compile your own kernel, which will result in a new kernel. Before you start, make sure that the kernel source files are installed on your computer. Read Chapter 8 for more details on how to install software.

It only makes sense to compile a kernel if you have changed settings to the kernel. The next section shows you how to do so, and the section after that discusses how to compile the kernel after making these changes.

Modifying the Kernel

The current kernel configuration is normally stored in the .conf file in the directory /usr/ src/linux, which contains the source files of your current kernel. To create this file, different options are available, of which two will be covered here:

- Create the .conf file from scratch.

- Create the .conf file based on the default configuration.

Creating a .config file from Scratch

To create a .config file from scratch, you need to run the make config command or one of the related commands. This command starts a script that asks for every single piece of kernel functionality how you want to configure it, which is very user unfriendly. Some alternatives exist that are easier to use: make menuconfig and make xconfig. Both offer a menu interface that enables you to specify what you need in your new kernel configuration. As they offer the same functionality, I will cover the make menuconfig command only; you can run it from the console, which is not the case for make xconfig.

You must run the make config commands from the /usr/src/linux directory, so before you start, make sure that you are in this directory. Next, type make menuconfig to start the menu-based kernel configuration. Figure 13-2 shows what the interface looks like.

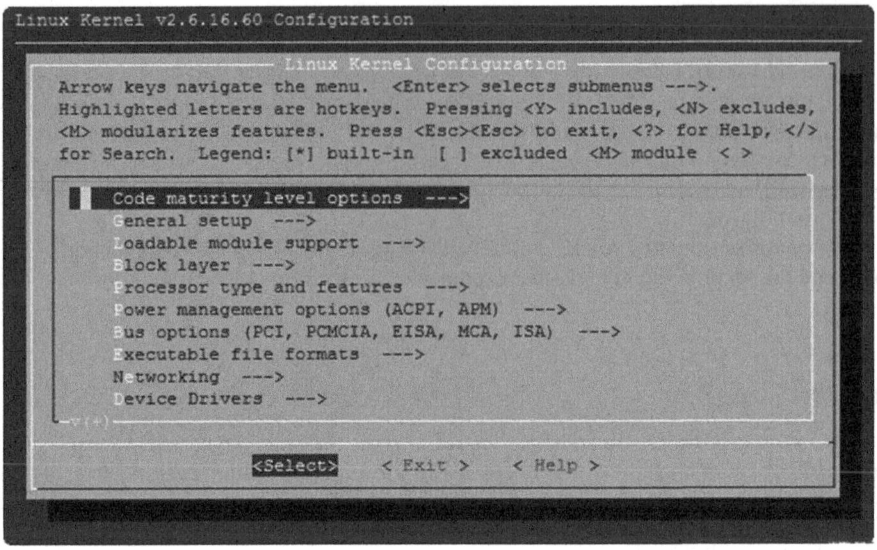

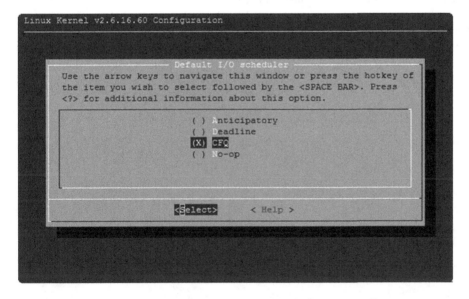

Figure 13-2. *make menuconfig offers a menu interface that allows you to change kernel options*

In the make menuconfig interface, all options are subdivided in different modules that allow you to find specific functionality easily. You can select an option by navigating to it with the arrow keys and pressing Enter to select it. Some options can just be switched on or off, whereas other options can be enabled as a module as well. For the latter option type, you can toggle between selected, unselected, or an M, which indicates that you want to use the option as a module (see Figure 13-3). You can also get more details about what functionality is related to a given option: select it first and then use the Tab key to navigate to the Help option. Select- ing Help will show you a description of the selected function.

Figure 13-3. *From make menuconfig, it is easy to switch options on or off*

Once you are finished creating the configuration you need with make menuconfig, you can browse back to the top of the menu interface by selecting Exit until you are back in the main menu. This offers you the screen shown previously in Figure 13-2. From there, select Exit once more. You will now be prompted to save the current selection. Select Yes to write the current selection to a configuration file. Read the section "Compiling a New Kernel" later in this chap- ter for information on how to proceed from this point.

Creating a .config Based on the Default Configuration

Every kernel also contains a default configuration, which according to the kernel maintainer contains the best options for the architecture that you are using. You can easily write this default configuration to the /usr/src/linux/.config file by using the make defconfig com- mand. Make sure that you use this command from the /usr/src directory, as it otherwise won't work.

After starting the make defconfig command, lots of options will scroll over your screen (see Listing 13-8), and the result is written to the new .config file.

Listing 13-8. Using make defconfig, You Can Write the Favorite Options of the Kernel Developer to a Configuration File

```
TEA, XTEA and XETA cipher algorithms (CRYPTO_TEA) [M/n/y/?] m
ARC4 cipher algorithm (CRYPTO_ARC4) [M/y/?] m
Khazad cipher algorithm (CRYPTO_KHAZAD) [M/n/y/?] m
Anubis cipher algorithm (CRYPTO_ANUBIS) [M/n/y/?] m
Deflate compression algorithm (CRYPTO_DEFLATE) [M/y/?] m
Michael MIC keyed digest algorithm (CRYPTO_MICHAEL_MIC) [M/y/?] m
CRC32c CRC algorithm (CRYPTO_CRC32C) [M/y/?] m
Camellia cipher algorithms (CRYPTO_CAMELLIA) [M/n/y/?] m
Testing module (CRYPTO_TEST) [M/n/?] m
*
* Hardware crypto devices
*
Support for VIA PadLock ACE (CRYPTO_DEV_PADLOCK) [M/n/y/?] m
   PadLock driver for AES algorithm (CRYPTO_DEV_PADLOCK_AES) [M/n/?] m
   PadLock driver for SHA1 and SHA256 algorithms (CRYPTO_DEV_PADLOCK_SHA) [M/n/?] m
*
* Library routines
*
CRC-CCITT functions (CRC_CCITT) [M/y/?] m
CRC16 functions (CRC16) [M/y/?] m
CRC32 functions (CRC32) [Y/?] y
CRC32c (Castagnoli, et al) Cyclic Redundancy-Check (LIBCRC32C) [M/y/?] m
```

Compiling a New Kernel

Now that you have created the /usr/src/linux/.config file, it's time to compile the new ker- nel, or better, build the new kernel. Whereas previously several commands were needed to do this, nowadays you can perform this task by running one simple command from the /usr/src/ linux directory:

make

Completing the build of a new kernel can take awhile. make will show you the names of all the individual source files that it is currently is working on and display any warning or status errors related to these files. Listing 13-9 gives you an impression of what you see at this point.

Listing 13-9. Run make from /usr/src/linux to Build the New Kernel

```
nuuk:/usr/src/linux # make
  CHK      /usr/src/linux-2.6.16.60-0.21/include/linux/version.h
  SPLIT    include/linux/autoconf.h -> include/config/*
  CC       arch/i386/kernel/asm-offsets.s
  GEN      include/asm-i386/asm-offsets.h
  HOSTCC   scripts/genksyms/genksyms.o
  SHIPPED  scripts/genksyms/lex.c
  SHIPPED  scripts/genksyms/parse.h
  SHIPPED  scripts/genksyms/keywords.c
  HOSTCC   scripts/genksyms/lex.o
  SHIPPED  scripts/genksyms/parse.c
  HOSTCC   scripts/genksyms/parse.o
  HOSTLD   scripts/genksyms/genksyms
  CC       scripts/mod/empty.o
  HOSTCC   scripts/mod/mk_elfconfig
  MKELF    scripts/mod/elfconfig.h
  HOSTCC   scripts/mod/file2alias.o
  HOSTCC   scripts/mod/modpost.o
  HOSTCC   scripts/mod/sumversion.o
```

Compiling Modules

Although you won't often have to recompile the kernel very often, the same is far from true for kernel modules. The issue is that many hardware vendors refuse to publish the source code for their drivers under open source licenses. Instead, they will make some proprietary Linux drivers available only. These proprietary Linux drivers are generic, but to be fully functional, drivers have to be developed for your specific kernel. The only way to meet this requirement is to compile these drivers for your machine.

Speaking in a generic way, there are two methods to install such drivers on your com- puter: the easy way and the hard way. When choosing the easy way, you'll have to integrate the web site where the vendor made his or her drivers available as a package repository on your computer. When choosing the hard way, you'll have to download and compile the drivers yourself. The exact procedure to do this is different for each driver. What is described in the following procedure is a generic way that will work in most cases:

1. Download the driver and store it somewhere on your computer. Let's assume that the driver you want to install is driver.tgz, and you have stored it in the home directory of the user root. You should also make sure that you have acquired root permissions before starting.

2. Extract the tar archive using tar zxvf driver.tgz. Normally, this creates a sub- directory in the current directory, which would be /tmp/driver in this case. Use cd to change to this directory.

3. In the driver subdirectory, you'll normally find some files. One of them is the configure file (which may also have the name install, setup, or something similar). Often you'll also find a file with the name Makefile, and in most cases there's also a file with the name README. Be aware that exact file names may vary, so check to be sure that you are using the right files. It's a good idea to start by reading the README file, as it may contain useful tips on how to install the driver.

4. After reading the README file, run the generic setup script, which is normally configure. To run it from the current directory, run it as ./configure, and not just configure.

5. The configure script makes sure that all conditions have been met to start compiling the driver.

6. From the directory where you've extracted the driver files, run make to start the com- piling process. The make command will follow the instruction in the Makefile in the directory and compile the driver for your current kernel.

7. After running make, you'll need to make sure that all drivers are copied to the correct location. To do this, run make install, still within the directory that contains the driver files as the current directory.

This generic procedure should help you in compiling and installing the driver for your kernel. It is a very generic procedure, however: in all cases, you should check the documenta- tion that comes with the driver to see whether it contains any specific instructions.

Managing the Grub2 Bootloader

When your computer starts up, a Linux kernel has to be loaded. On most Linux distributions, this is accomplished by the Grub 2 boot loader. This boot loader shows a configuration while it starts, and from this startup menu it allows you to specify specific options that should be used when booting (see Figure 13-4). It also has a configuration file that can be used to make startup parameters persistent.

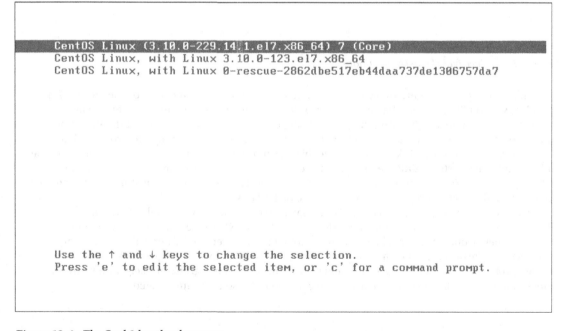

Figure 13-4. *The Grub2 bootloader menu*

The Grub 2 boot menu shows the different kernel versions that are available. After software updates have been installed, you normally will see a few kernel version, which allows you to select an older version, or a troubleshooting kernel in case you have problems starting the default kernel. From the Grub 2 boot loader menu, you can press the **e** key on a highlighted item. This opens the screen that you can see in Figure 13-5, where kernel boot options can be specified. To do this, find the line that starts with the text Linux and add the boot parameters to the end of the line.

```
        insmod xfs                                                            ↑
        set root='hd0,msdos1'
        if [ x$feature_platform_search_hint = xy ]; then
            search --no-floppy --fs-uuid --set=root --hint-bios=hd0,msdos1 --hin\
t-efi=hd0,msdos1 --hint-baremetal=ahci0,msdos1 --hint='hd0,msdos1'  b3ed3d66-8\
9a6-4e44-86c1-ddb964fc7fea
        else
            search --no-floppy --fs-uuid --set=root b3ed3d66-89a6-4e44-86c1-ddb9\
64fc7fea
        fi
_       linux16 /vmlinuz-3.10.0-229.14.1.el7.x86_64 root=/dev/mapper/centos-ro\
ot ro rd.lvm.lv=centos/swap vconsole.font=latarcyrheb-sun16 rd.lvm.lv=centos/r\
oot crashkernel=auto  vconsole.keymap=us rhgb quiet LANG=en_US.UTF-8
        initrd16 /initramfs-3.10.0-229.14.1.el7.x86_64.img



    Press Ctrl-x to start, Ctrl-c for a command prompt or Escape to
    discard edits and return to the menu. Pressing Tab lists
    possible completions.
```

Figure 13-5. *Specifying kernel boot options*

In the example from figure 13-4 you can see that many arguments are provided on the line that starts with **linux16**. You'll also notice that different Linux distributions are using different options. In this case for instance the options **rhgb** and **quiet** are used to indicate that the system should not show any startup messages. If you rather do want to see startup messages, you can remove these options from this line.

Also, you can add specific kernel options to this line. If your machine fails to start for instance, you can add the argument **systemd.unit=rescue.target** to enter rescue mode. This brings you in a minimal mode where you can repair settings on your system. Notice that all changes you're making from here are once only. To start with the modified kernel arguments, use the **Ctrl-X** key stroke.

If you want to make changes to the GRUB 2 boot loader permanent, you should include them in the file /etc/default/grub. In this file you'll find a line GRUB_CMDLINE that contains all kernel arguments that are used when booting. You can add to or remove from this line as required. After making modifications, you need to write the changes to the Grub 2 configuration. You can do so using **grub2-mkconfig -o /boot/grub2/grub.cfg**. Notice that you should never write to the /boot/grub2/grub.cfg file directly, as all modifications to it will be overwritten if the kernel or the Grub 2 software are updated.

EXERCISE 13-3: MODIFYING GRUB2 ARGUMENTS

In this exercise you'll learn how to enter rescue mode.

1. Use **echo b > /proc/sysrq-trigger** to reset your system. By writing a b to this file, you're giving the system a hard reset.

2. When the Grub 2 boot menu appears, select the default kernel entry and press **e** to open the edit mode.

3. Find the line that starts **linux16** and move your cursor to the end of this line. Add the text **systemd.unit=rescue.target**.

4. Use the **Ctrl-x** key stroke to boot your system with these options. After logging in as root, you'll be in a minimal troubleshooting mode.

5. To enter a normal operational mode from troubleshooting mode, type **systemctl isolate multi-user.target**. This starts the normal multi-user mode on your system. Alternatively, you can type **reboot** to reboot your system.

Summary

In this chapter, you have learned how to work with the kernel. You've read how to manage ker- nel modules, as well as how to change kernel parameters. The following commands have been covered in this chapter:

- modprobe: Allows you to load and unload kernel modules

- modinfo: Provides information about kernel modules

- lsmod: Lists loaded modules

- insmod: Allows you to load kernel modules (legacy command)

- rmmod: Removes currently loaded modules from memory (legacy command)

- depmod: Creates the modules.dep configuration file, which makes sure that module dependencies are loaded automatically

- gcc: Refers to the GNU C compiler, used to convert source files into program files

- make: Works with the Makefile to make compiling software easier

- sysctl: Allows you to load kernel parameters while booting

- **grub2-mkconfig**: Writes changes from the /etc/default/grub file to the Grub 2 boot loader configuration.

In the next and final chapter of this book, you will read how to create shell scripts.

■ ■ ■

## CHAPTER 14

Introduction to Bash Shell Scripting

Once you really get to be at ease working on the command line, you'll want to do more than what the previous chapters have taught you. You've already learned how to combine commands using piping, but if you really want to get the best out of your commands, there is much more you can do. In this chapter, you'll get an introduction to the possibilities of Bash shell scripting, which really is the command line on steroids; piping and redirection just is not enough if you need to do really complex tasks. As soon as you really understand shell scripting, you'll be able to automate many tasks, and thus do your work at least twice as fast as you used to do it.

Basic Shell Script Components

A shell script is a text file that contains a sequence of commands. So basically, anything that can run a bunch of commands can be considered a shell script. Nevertheless, some rules exist for making sure that you create decent shell scripts, scripts that will not only do the task you've written them for, but also be readable by others. At some point in time, you'll be happy with the habit of writing readable shell scripts. As your scripts get longer and longer, you will notice that if a script does not meet the basic requirements of readability, even you yourself won't be able to understand what it is doing.

Elements of a Good Shell Script

When writing a script, make sure that you meet the following requirements:

- Give it a unique name.

- Include the *shebang* (#!) to tell the shell which subshell should execute the script.

- Include comments—lots of them.

- Use the exit command to tell the shell that executes the script that the script has executed successfully.

- Make your scripts executable.

Let's start with an example script (see Listing 14-1).

Listing 14-1. Make Sure Your Script Is Well Structured

```
#!/bin/bash
# this is the hello script
# run it by typing ./hello in the directory where you've found it
clear
echo hello world
exit 0
```

Let's talk about the name of the script first: you'll be amazed how many commands already exist on your computer. So you have to make sure that the name of your script is unique. For instance, many people like to give the name test to their first script. Unfortunately, there's already an existing command with that name (see the section "Using Control Structures" later in this chapter). If your script has the same name as an existing command, the existing command will be executed, not your script (unless you prefix the name of the script with ./). So make sure that the name of your script is not in use already. You can find out whether a name already exists by using the which command. For instance, if you want to use the name hello and want to be sure that it's not in use already, type which hello. Listing 14-2 shows the result of this command.

Listing 14-2. Use which to Find Out Whether the Name of Your Script Is Not Already in Use

```
nuuk:~ # which hello
which: no hello in
(/sbin:/usr/sbin:/usr/local/sbin:/opt/gnome/sbin:/root/bin:/usr/local/bin:/usr/bin:/
  usr/X11R6/bin:/bin
:/usr/games:/opt/gnome/bin:/opt/kde3/bin:/usr/lib/mit/bin:/usr/lib/mit/sbin)
```

In the first line of the script is the shebang. This scripting element tells the shell from which this script is executed which subshell should be executed to run this script. This may sound rather cryptic, but is not too hard to understand. If you run a command from a shell, the command becomes the child process of the shell; the pstree command will show you that perfectly. If you run a script from the shell, the script becomes a child process of the shell. This means that it is by no means necessary to run the same shell as your current shell to run the script. To tell your current shell which subshell should be executed when running the script, include the shebang. As mentioned previously, the shebang always starts with #! and is followed by the name of the subshell that should execute the script. In Listing 14-1, I've used /bin/bash as the subshell, but you can use any other shell if you'd like.

You will notice that not all scripts include a shebang, and in many cases, even if your script doesn't include a shebang, it will still run. However, if a user who uses a shell other than /bin/bash tries to run a script without a shebang, it will probably fail. You can avoid this by always including a shebang.

The second part of the example script in Listing 14-1 are two lines of comment. As you can guess, these command lines explain to the user what the purpose of the script is and how to use it. There's only one rule about comment lines: they should be clear and explain what's happening. A comment line always starts with a # followed by anything.

▨ **Note** You may ask why the shebang, which also starts with a #, is not interpreted as a comment. That is because of its position and the fact that it is immediately followed by an exclamation mark. This combination at the very start of a script tells the shell that it's not a comment, but a shebang.

Following the comment lines is the body of the script itself, which contains the code that the script should execute. In the example from Listing 14-1, the code consists of two simple commands: the first clears the screen, and the second echoes the text "hello world" to the screen.

The last part of the script is the command exit 0. It is a good habit to use the exit command in all your scripts. This command exits the script and next tells the parent shell how the script has executed. If the parent shell reads exit 0, it knows the script executed successfully. If it encounters anything other than exit 0, it knows there was a problem. In more complex scripts, you could even start working with different exit codes; use exit 1 as a generic error message and exit 2 , and so forth, to specify that a specific condition was not met. When applying conditional loops later (see the section "Using Control Structures" later in this chapter), you'll see that it may be very useful to work with exit codes.

Executing the Script

Now that your first shell script is written, it's time to execute it. There are different ways of doing this:

- Make it executable and run it as a program.

- Run it as an argument of the bash command.

- Source it.

Making the Script Executable

The most common way to run a shell script is by making it executable. To do this with the hello script from the example in Listing 14-1, you would use the following command:

chmod +x hello

After making the script executable, you can run it, just like any other normal command. The only limitation is the exact location in the directory structure where your script is. If it is in the search path, you can run it by typing just any command. If it is not in the search path, you have to run it from the exact directory where it is. This means that if linda created a script with the name hello that is in /home/linda, she has to run it using the command /home/linda/hello. Alternatively, if she is already in /home/linda, she could use ./hello to run the script. In the latter example, the dot and the slash tell the shell to run the command from the current directory.

■ **Tip** Not sure whether a directory is in the path or not? Use echo $PATH to find out. If it's not, you can add a directory to the path by redefining it. When defining it again, you'll mention the new directory, followed by a call to the old path variable. For instance, to add the directory /something to the path, you would use PATH=$PATH:/something.

Running the Script as an Argument of the bash Command

The second option for running a script is to specify its name as the argument of the bash command. For instance, our example script hello would run by using the command bash hello. The advantage of running the script in this way is that there is no need to make it executable first. Make sure that you are using a complete reference to the location where the script is when running it this way; it has to be in the current directory, or you have to use a complete reference to the directory where it is. This means that if the script is /home/linda/hello, and your current directory is /tmp, you should run it using the following command:

bash /home/linda/hello

Sourcing the Script

The third way of running the script is rather different. You can source the script. By sourcing a script, you don't run it as a subshell, but you are including it in the current shell. This may be useful if the script contains variables that you want to be active in the current shell (this happens often in the scripts that are executed when you boot your computer). Some problems may occur as well. For instance, if you use the exit command in a script that is sourced, it closes the current shell. Remember, the exit command exits the current script. In fact, it doesn't exit the script itself, but tells the executing shell that the script is over and it has to return to its parent shell. Therefore, you don't want to source scripts that contain the exit command. There are two ways to source a script. The next two lines show how to source a script that has the name settings:

```
. settings
source settings
```

It doesn't really matter which one you use, as both are equivalent. When discussing variables in the next section, I'll give you some more examples of why sourcing may be a very useful technique.

Working with Variables and Input

What makes a script so flexible is the use of variables. A *variable* is a value you get from somewhere that will be dynamic. The value of a variable normally depends on the circumstances. You can have your script get the variable itself, for instance, by executing a command, by making a calculation, by specifying it as a command-line argument for the script, or by modifying some text string. In this section, you'll learn all there is to know about variables.

Understanding Variables

A variable is a value that you define somewhere and use in a flexible way later. You can do this in a script, but you don't have to, as you can define a variable in the shell as well. To define a variable, you use *varname=value*. To get the value of a variable later on, you call its value by using the echo command. Listing 14-3 gives an example of how a variable is set on the command line and how its value is used in the next command.

Listing 14-3. Setting and Using a Variable

```
nuuk:~ # HAPPY=yes
nuuk:~ # echo $HAPPY
yes
```

■ **Note**   The method described here works for the Bash and Dash shells. Not every shell supports this method, however. For instance, on tcsh, you need to use the set command to define a variable: set happy=yes gives the value yes to the variable happy.

Variables play a very important role on your computer. When booting, lots of variables are defined and used later when you work with your computer. For instance, the name of your computer is in a variable, the name of the user account you logged in with is in a variable, and the search path is in a variable as well. These are the *shell variables*, the so-called environment variables you get automatically when logging in to the shell. As discussed earlier, you can use the env command to get a complete list of all the variables that are set for your computer. You will notice that most environment variables are in uppercase. However, this is in no way a requirement; an environment variable can be in lowercase as well.

The advantage of using variables in shell scripts is that you can use them in three ways:

- As a single point of administration for a certain value

- As a value that a user provides in some way

- As a value that is calculated dynamically

When reading some of the scripts that are used in your computer's boot procedure, you will notice that the beginning of the script features a list of variables that are referred to several times later in the script. Let's have a look at the somewhat silly example in Listing 14-4.

Listing 14-4. Understanding the Use of Variables

```
#!/bin/bash
#
# dirscript
#
# Silly script that creates a directory with a certain name
# next sets $USER and $GROUP as the owners of the directory
# and finally changes the permission mode to 770
DIRECTORY=/blah
USER=linda
GROUP=sales

mkdir $DIRECTORY
chown $USER $DIRECTORY
chgrp $GROUP $DIRECTORY
chmod 770 $DIRECTORY

exit 0
```

As you can see, after the comment lines, this script starts by defining all the variables that are used. I've specified them in all uppercase, because it makes it a lot easier to recognize the variables when reading a longer script. In the second part of the script, the variables are referred to by typing in their names with a $ sign in front of each.

You will notice that quite a few scripts work in this way. There is a disadvantage though: it is a rather static way of working with variables. If you want a more dynamic way to work with variables, you can specify them as arguments to the script when executing it on the command line, for instance.

Variables, Subshells, and Sourcing

When defining variables, you should be aware that a variable is defined for the current shell only. This means that if you start a subshell from the current shell, the variable won't be there. And if you define a variable in a subshell, it won't be there anymore once you've quit the subshell and returned to the parent shell. Listing 14-5 shows how this works.

Listing 14-5. Variables Are Local to the Shell Where They Are Defined

```
nuuk:~/bin # HAPPY=yes
nuuk:~/bin # echo $HAPPY
yes
nuuk:~/bin # bash
nuuk:~/bin # echo $HAPPY

nuuk:~/bin # exit
exit
nuuk:~/bin # echo $HAPPY
yes
nuuk:~/bin #
```

In Listing 14-5, I've defined a variable with the name HAPPY, and next its value is correctly echoed. In the third command, a subshell is started, and as you can see, when asking for the value of the variable HAPPY in this subshell, it isn't there because it simply doesn't exist. But when the subshell is closed by using the exit command, we're back in the parent shell where the variable still exists.

Now in some cases, you may want to set a variable that is present in all subshells as well. If this is the case, you can define it by using the export command. For instance, the following command would define the variable HAPPY and make sure that it is available in all subshells from the current shell on, until you next reboot the computer. However, there is no similar way to define a variable and make that available in the parent shells.

```
export HAPPY=yes
```

■ **Note**   Make sure that you include the definition of variables in /etc/profile so that the new variable will also be available after a reboot.

Listing 14-6 shows the same commands as used in Listing 14-5, but now with the value of the variable being exported.

Listing 14-6. By Exporting a Variable, You Can Make It Available in Subshells As Well

```
nuuk:~/bin # export HAPPY=yes
nuuk:~/bin # echo $HAPPY
yes
nuuk:~/bin # bash
nuuk:~/bin # echo $HAPPY
yes
nuuk:~/bin # exit
exit
nuuk:~/bin # echo $HAPPY
yes
nuuk:~/bin #
```

So that's what you have to do to define variables that are available in subshells as well.

A technique you will see often as well that is related to variables is the sourcing of a file that contains variables. The idea is that somewhere on your computer you keep a common file that contains variables. For instance, consider the example file vars that you see in Listing 14-7.

Listing 14-7. By Putting All Your Variables in One File, You Can Make Them Easily Available

```
HAPPY=yes
ANGRY=no
SUNNY=yes
```

The main advantage of putting all variables in one file is that you can make them available in other shells as well by sourcing them. To do this with the example file from Listing 14-7, you would use the following command (assuming that the name of the variable file is vars):

```
. vars
```

■ **Note**   . vars is not the same as ./vars. With . vars, you include the contents of vars in the current shell. With ./vars, you run vars from the current shell. The former doesn't start a subshell, whereas the latter does.

In Listing 14-8, you can see how sourcing is used to include variables from a generic configuration file in the current shell. In this example, I've used sourcing for the current shell, but the technique is also quite commonly used to include common variables in a script.

Listing 14-8. Example of Sourcing Usage

```
nuuk:~/bin # echo $HAPPY

nuuk:~/bin # echo $ANGRY

nuuk:~/bin # echo $SUNNY

nuuk:~/bin # . vars
nuuk:~/bin # echo $HAPPY
yes
nuuk:~/bin # echo $ANGRY
no
nuuk:~/bin # echo $SUNNY
yes
nuuk:~/bin #
```

Working with Script Arguments

In the preceding section, you have learned how you can define variables. Up to now, you've seen how to create a variable in a static way. In this section, you'll learn how to provide values for your variables in a dynamic way by specifying them as an argument for the script when running the script on the command line.

Using Script arguments

When running a script, you can specify arguments to the script on the command line. Consider the script dirscript that you've seen previously in Listing 14-4. You could run it with an argument on the command line as well, as in the following example:

```
dirscript /blah
```

Now wouldn't it be nice if in the script you could do something with the argument /blah that is specified in the script? The good news is that you can. You can refer to the first argument that was used when launching the script by using $1 in the script, the second argument by using $2, and so on, up to $9. You can also use $0 to refer to the name of the script itself. The example script in Listing 14-9 shows how it works.

Listing 14-9. Showing How Arguments Are Used

```
#!/bin/bash
#
# argscript
#
# Silly script that shows how arguments are used

ARG1=$1
ARG2=$2
ARG3=$3
SCRIPTNAME=$0

echo The name of this script is $SCRIPTNAME
echo The first argument used is $ARG1
echo The second argument used is $ARG2
echo The third argument used is $ARG3
exit 0
```

The example code in Listing 14-10 shows how dirscript is rewritten to work with an argument that is specified on the command line. This changes dirscript from a rather static script that can create one directory only to a very dynamic script that can create any directory and assign any user and any group as the owner to that directory.

Listing 14-10. Referring to Command-Line Arguments in a Script

```
#!/bin/bash
#
# dirscript
#
# Silly script that creates a directory with a certain name
# next sets $USER and $GROUP as the owners of the directory
# and finally changes the permission mode to 770
# Provide the directory name first, followed by the username and
# finally the groupname.

DIRECTORY=$1
USER=$2
GROUP=$3
```

338

```
mkdir /$DIRECTORY
chown $USER $DIRECTORY
chgrp $GROUP $DIRECTORY
chmod 770 $DIRECTORY

exit 0
```

To execute the script from Listing 14-10, you would use a command as in this example:

```
dirscript /somedir kylie sales
```

This line shows you how the dirscript has been made more flexible now, but at the same time it also shows you the most important disadvantage: it has become somehow less obvious as well. You can imagine that it might be very easy for a user to mix up the right order of the arguments and type dirscript kylie sales /somedir instead. So it becomes important to provide good information on how to run this script.

Counting the Number of Script Arguments

On some occasions, you'll want to check the number of arguments that are provided with a script. This is useful if you expect a certain number of arguments, for instance, and want to make sure that the required number of arguments is present before running the script.

To count the number of arguments provided with a script, you can use $#. Basically, $# is a counter that does no more than show you the exact number of arguments you've used when running the script. Used all by itself, that doesn't really make sense. Combined with an if statement (about which you'll read more in the section "Using if ... then ... else" later in this chapter) it does make sense. For example, you could use it to show a help message if the user hasn't provided the correct number of arguments. Listing 14-11 shows the contents of the script countargs, in which $# is used. Directly following the code of the script, you can see a sample running of it.

Listing 14-11. Counting the Number of Arguments

```
nuuk:~/bin # cat countargs
#!/bin/bash
#
# countargs
# sample script that shows how many arguments were used

echo the number of arguments is $#

exit 0
nuuk:~/bin # ./countargs a b c d e
the number of arguments is 5
nuuk:~/bin #.
```

Referring to all Script Arguments

So far, you've seen that a script can work with a fixed number of arguments. The example in Listing 14-10 is hard-coded to evaluate arguments as $1, $2, and so on. But what if the number of arguments is not known beforehand? In that case, you can use $@ or $* in your script. Both refer to all arguments that were specified when starting the script, although there is a difference. To explain the difference, I need to show you how a for loop treats $@ or $*.

A for loop can be used to test all elements in a string of characters. Now what I want to show you at this point is that the difference between $@ and $* is exactly in the number of elements that each has. But let's have a look at their default output first. Listing 14-12 shows version 1 of the showargs script.

Listing 14-12. Showing the Difference Between $@ and $*

```
#!/bin/bash
# showargs
# this script shows all arguments used when starting the script

echo the arguments are $@
echo the arguments are $*

exit 0
```

Now let's have a look at what happens if you launch this script with the arguments a b c d. You can see the result in Listing 14-13.

Listing 14-13. Running showargs with Different Arguments

```
nuuk:~/bin # ./showargs a b c d
the arguments are a b c d
the arguments are a b c d
```

So far, there seem to be no differences between $@ and $*, yet there is a big difference: the collection of arguments in $* is treated as one text string, whereas the collection of arguments in $@ is seen as separate strings. In the section "Using for" later in this chapter, you will see some proof for this.

At this moment, you know how to handle a script that has an infinite number of arguments. You can tell the script that it should interpret them one by one. The next subsection shows you how to count the number of arguments.

Asking for Input

Another elegant way to get input is just to ask for it. To do this, you can use read in the script. When using read, the script waits for user input and puts that in a variable. The sample script askinput in Listing 14-14 shows a simple example script that first asks for the input and then shows the input that was provided by echoing the value of the variable. Directly following the sample code, you can also see what happens when you run the script.

Listing 14-14. Asking for Input with read

```
nuuk:~/bin # cat askinput
#!/bin/bash
#
# askinput
# ask user to enter some text and then display it
echo Enter some text
read SOMETEXT
echo -e "You have entered the following text:\t $SOMETEXT"
```

```
exit 0
nuuk:~/bin # ./askinput
Enter some text
hi there
You have entered the following text: hi there
nuuk:~/bin #
```

As you can see, the script starts with an echo line that explains what it expects the user to do. Next, with the line read SOMETEXT, it will stop to allow the user to enter some text. This text is stored in the variable SOMETEXT. In the following line, the echo command is used to show the current value of SOMETEXT. As you see, in this sample script I've used echo with the option -e. This option allows you to use some special formatting characters, in this case the formatting character \t, which enters a tab in the text. Formatting like this ensures that the result is displayed in a nice manner.

As you can see, in the line that has the command echo -e, the text that the script needs to be echoed is between double quotes. This is to prevent the shell from interpreting the special character \t before echo does. Again, if you want to make sure the shell does not interpret special characters like this, put the string between double quotes.

You may get confused here, because two different mechanisms are at work. First is the mechanism of escaping characters so that they are not interpreted by the shell. This is the difference between echo \t and echo "\t". In the former, the \ is treated as a special character, with the result that only the letter t is displayed; in the latter, double quotes tell the shell not to interpret anything that is between the double quotes, hence it shows \t.

The second mechanism is the special formatting character \t, which tells the shell to display a tab. To make sure that this or any other special formatting character is not interpreted by the shell when it first parses the script (which here would result in the shell just displaying a t), you have to put it between double quotes. In Listing 14-15, you can see the differences between all the possible commands.

Listing 14-15. Escaping and Special Characters

```
SYD:~ # echo \t
t
SYD:~ # echo "\t"
\t
SYD:~ # echo -e \t
t
SYD:~ # echo -e "\t"

SYD:~ #
```

When using echo -e, you can use the following special characters:

- \0NNN: The character whose ASCII code is *NNN* (octal).

- \\: Backslash. Use this if you want to show just a backslash.

- \a: Alert (BEL, or bell code). If supported by your system, this will let you hear a beep.

- \b: Backspace.

- \c: Character that suppresses a trailing newline.

- \f: Form feed.

- \n: Newline.

- \r: Carriage return.
- \t: Horizontal tab.
- \v: Vertical tab.

Using Command Substitution

Another way of getting a variable text in a script is by using *command substitution*. In command substitution, you'll use the result of a command in the script. This is useful if the script has to do something with the result of a command. For instance, by using this technique, you can tell the script that it should only execute if a certain condition is met (you would have to use a conditional loop with if to accomplish this). To use command substitution, put the command that you want to use between backquotes (also known as back ticks). The following sample code line shows how it works:

```
nuuk:~/bin # echo "today is `date +%d-%m-%y`"
today is 27-01-09
```

In this example, the date command is used with some of its special formatting characters. The command date +%d-%m-%y tells date to present its result in the day-month-year format. In this example, the command is just executed; however, you can also put the result of the command substitution in a variable, which makes it easier to perform a calculation on the result later in the script. The following sample code shows how to do this:

```
nuuk:~/bin # TODAY=`date +%d-%m-%y`
echo today=$TODAY
today is 27-01-09
```

Substitution Operators

Within a script, it may be important to check whether a variable really has a value assigned to it before the script continues. To do this, Bash offers *substitution operators*. By using substitution operators, you can assign a default value if a variable doesn't have a value currently assigned, and much more. Table 14-1 provides an overview of the substitution operators with a short explanation of their use.

Table 14-1. Substitution Operators

Operator	Use
${parameter:-value}	Shows the value if a parameter is not defined.
${parameter=value}	Assigns the value to the parameter if the parameter does not exist at all. This operator does nothing if the parameter exists but doesn't have a value.
${parameter:=value}	Assigns a value if the parameter currently has no value or if parameter doesn't exist at all.
${parameter:?somevalue}	Shows a message that is defined as the value if the parameter doesn't exist or is empty. Using this construction will force the shell script to be aborted immediately.
${parameter:+somevalue}	Displays the value if the parameter has one. If it doesn't have a value, nothing happens.

Substitution operators can be hard to understand. To make it easier to see how they work, Listing 14-16 provides some examples. In all of these examples, something happens to the $BLAH variable. You'll see that the result of the given command is different depending on the substitution operator that's used. To make it easier to discuss what happens, I've added line numbers to the listing. Notice that, when trying this yourself, you should omit the line numbers.

Listing 14-16. Using Substitution Operators

```
1. sander@linux %> echo $BLAH
2.
3. sander@linux %> echo ${BLAH:-variable is empty}
4 variable is empty
5. sander@linux %> echo $BLAH
6.
7. sander@linux %> echo ${BLAH=value}
8. value
9. sander@linux %> echo $BLAH
10. value
11. sander@linux %> BLAH=
12. sander@linux %> echo ${BLAH=value}
13.
14. sander@linux %> echo ${BLAH:=value}
15. value
16. sander@linux %> echo $BLAH
17. value
18. sander@linux %> echo ${BLAH:+sometext}
19. sometext
```

The example of Listing 14-16 starts with the following command:

```
echo $BLAH
```

This command reads the variable BLAH and shows its current value. Because BLAH doesn't have a value yet, nothing is shown in line 2. Next, a message is defined in line 3 that should be displayed if BLAH is empty. This happens with the following command:

```
sander@linux %> echo ${BLAH:-variable is empty}
```

As you can see, the message is displayed in line 4. However, this doesn't assign a value to BLAH, which you see in lines 5 and 6 where the current value of BLAH is asked again:

```
3. sander@linux %> echo ${BLAH:-variable is empty}
4 variable is empty
5. sander@linux %> echo $BLAH
6.
```

In line 7, BLAH finally gets a value, which is displayed in line 8:

```
7. sander@linux %> echo ${BLAH=value}
8. value
```

The shell remembers the new value of BLAH, which you can see in lines 9 and 10 where the value of BLAH is referred to and displayed:

```
9. sander@linux %> echo $BLAH
10. value
```

In line 11, BLAH is redefined but it gets a null value:

```
11. sander@linux %> BLAH=
```

The variable still exists; it just has no value here. This is demonstrated when echo ${BLAH=value} is used in line 12; because BLAH has a null value at that moment, no new value is assigned:

```
12. sander@linux %> echo ${BLAH=value}
13.
```

Next, the construction echo ${BLAH:=value} is used to assign a new value to BLAH. The fact that BLAH really gets a value from this is shown in lines 16 and 17:

```
14. sander@linux %> echo ${BLAH:=value}
15. value
16. sander@linux %> echo $BLAH
17. value
```

Finally, the construction in line 18 is used to display sometext if BLAH currently does have a value:

```
18. sander@linux %> echo ${BLAH:+sometext}
19. sometext
```

Notice that this doesn't change anything for the value that is assigned to BLAH at that moment; sometext just indicates that it has a value and that's all.

Changing Variable Content with Pattern Matching

You've just seen how substitution operators can be used to do something if a variable does not have a value. You can consider them a rather primitive way of handling errors in your script.

A pattern-matching operator can be used to search for a pattern in a variable and, if that pattern is found, modify the variable. This can be very useful because it allows you to define a variable exactly the way you want. For example, think of the situation in which a user enters a complete path name of a file, but only the name of the file itself (without the path) is needed in your script.

The pattern-matching operator is the way to change this. Pattern-matching operators allow you to remove part of a variable automatically. Listing 14-17 is an example of a script that works with pattern-matching operators.

Listing 14-17. Working with Pattern-Matching Operators

```
#!/bin/bash
# stripit
# script that extracts the file name from one that includes the complete path
# usage: stripit <complete file name>
```

```
filename=${1##*/}
echo "The name of the file is $filename"

exit 0
```

When executed, the script will show the following result:

```
sander@linux %> ./stripit /bin/bash
the name of the file is bash
```

Pattern-matching operators always try to locate a given string. In this case, the string is */. In other words, the pattern-matching operator searches for a /, preceded by another character (*). In this pattern-matching operator, ## is used to search for the longest match of the provided string, starting from the beginning of the string. So, the pattern-matching operator searches for the last / that occurs in the string and removes it and everything that precedes the / as well. You may ask how the script comes to remove everything in front of the /. It's because the pattern-matching operator refers to */ and not to /. You can confirm this by running the script with /bin/bash/ as an argument. In this case, the pattern that's searched for is in the last position of the string, and the pattern-matching operator removes everything.

This example explains the use of the pattern-matching operator that looks for the longest match. By using a single #, you can let the pattern-matching operator look for the shortest match, again starting from the beginning of the string. If, for example, the script in Listing 14-17 used filename=${1#*/}, the pattern-matching operator would look for the first / in the complete file name and remove that and everything before it.

You should realize that in these examples the * is important. The pattern-matching operator ${1#*/} removes the first / found and anything in front of it. The pattern-matching operator ${1#/} removes the first / in $1 only if the value of $1 starts with a /. However, if there's anything before the /, the operator will not know what to do.

In these examples, you've seen how a pattern-matching operator is used to start searching from the beginning of a string. You can start searching from the end of the string as well. To do so, a % is used instead of a #. This % refers to the shortest match of the pattern, and %% refers to its longest match. The script in Listing 14-18 shows how this works.

Listing 14-18. Using Pattern-Matching Operators to Start Searching at the End of a String

```
#!/bin/bash
# stripdir
# script that isolates the directory name from a complete file name
# usage: stripdir <complete file name>

dirname=${1%%/*}
echo "The directory name is $dirname"

exit 0
```

While executing, you'll see that this script has a problem:

```
sander@linux %> ./stripdir /bin/bash
The directory name is
```

As you can see, the script does its work somewhat too enthusiastically and removes everything. Fortunately, this problem can be solved by first using a pattern-matching operator that removes the / from the start of the complete file name (but only if that / is provided) and then removing everything following the first / in the complete file name. The example in Listing 14-19 shows how this is done.

Listing 14-19. Fixing the Example from Listing 14-18

```
#!/bin/bash
# stripdir
# script that isolates the directory name from a complete file name
# usage: stripdir <complete file name>

dirname=${1#/}
dirname=${1%%/*}
echo "The directory name is $dirname"

exit 0
```

As you can see, the problem is solved by using ${1#/}. This construction starts searching from the beginning of the file name to a /. Because no * is used here, it looks for a / only at the very first position of the file name and does nothing if the string starts with anything else. If it finds a /, it removes it. So, if a user enters usr/bin/passwd instead of /usr/bin/passwd, the ${1#/} construction does nothing at all. In the line after that, the variable dirname is defined again to do its work on the result of its first definition in the preceding line. This line does the real work and looks for the pattern /*, starting at the end of the file name. This makes sure that everything after the first / in the file name is removed and that only the name of the top-level directory is echoed. Of course, you can easily edit this script to display the complete path of the file: just use dirname=${dirname%/*} instead.

So, to make sure that you are comfortable with pattern-matching operators, the script in Listing 14-20 gives another example. This time, though, the example does not work with a file name, but with a random text string.

Listing 14-20. Another Example with Pattern Matching

```
#!/bin/bash
#
# generic script that shows some more pattern matching
# usage: pmex
BLAH=babarabaraba
echo BLAH is $BLAH
echo 'The result of ##ba is '${BLAH##*ba}
echo 'The result of #ba is '${BLAH#*ba}
echo 'The result of %%ba is '${BLAH%ba*}
echo 'The result of %ba is '${BLAH%%ba*}

exit 0
```

When running it, the script gives the result shown in Listing 14-21.

Listing 14-21. The Result of the Script in Listing 14-20

```
root@RNA:~/scripts# ./pmex
BLAH is babarabaraba
The result of ##ba is
The result of #ba is barabaraba
The result of %%ba is babarabara
The result of %ba is
root@RNA:~/scripts#
```

Performing Calculations

Bash offers some options that allow you to perform calculations from scripts. Of course, you're not likely to use them as a replacement for your spreadsheet program, but performing simple calculations from Bash can be useful. For example, you can use calculation options to execute a command a number of times or to make sure that a counter is incremented when a command executes successfully. The script in Listing 14-22 provides an example of how counters can be used.

Listing 14-22. Using a Counter in a Script

```
#!/bin/bash
# counter
# script that counts until infinity
counter=1
     counter=$((counter + 1))
     echo counter is set to $counter
exit 0
```

This script consists of three lines. The first line initializes the variable counter with a value of 1. Next, the value of this variable is incremented by 1. In the third line, the new value of the variable is shown.

Of course, it doesn't make much sense to run the script this way. It would make more sense if you include it in a conditional loop, to count the number of actions that is performed until a condition is true. In the section "Using while" later in this chapter, I have an example that shows how to combine counters with while.

So far, we've dealt with only one method to do script calculations, but you have other options as well. First, you can use the external expr command to perform any kind of calculation. For example, the following line produces the result of 1 + 2:

```
sum=`expr 1 + 2`; echo $sum
```

As you can see, a variable with the name sum is defined, and this variable gets the result of the command expr 1 + 2 by using command substitution. A semicolon is then used to indicate that what follows is a new command. (Remember the generic use of semicolons? They're used to separate one command from the next command.) After the semicolon, the command echo $sum shows the result of the calculation.

The expr command can work with addition, and other types of calculation are supported as well. Table 14-2 summarizes the options.

Table 14-2. *expr Operators*

Operator	Meaning
+	Addition (1 + 1 = 2).
-	Subtraction (10 – 2 = 8).
/	Division (10 / 2 = 5).
*	Multiplication (3 * 3 = 9).
%	Modulus; this calculates the remainder after division. This works because expr can handle integers only (11 % 3 = 2).

When working with these options, you'll see that they all work fine with the exception of the multiplication operator, *. Using this operator results in a syntax error:

```
linux: ~> expr 2 * 2
expr: syntax error
```

This seems curious but can be easily explained. The * has a special meaning for the shell, as in ls -l *. When the shell parses the command line, it interprets the *, and you don't want it to do that here. To indicate that the shell shouldn't touch it, you have to escape it. Therefore, change the command as follows:

```
expr 2 \* 2
```

Another way to perform some calculations is to use the internal command let. Just the fact that let is internal makes it a better solution than the external command expr: it can be loaded from memory directly and doesn't have to come all the way from your computer's hard drive. Using let, you can make your calculation and apply the result directly to a variable, as in the following example:

```
let x="1 + 2"
```

The result of the calculation in this example is stored in the variable x. The disadvantage of working this way is that let has no option to display the result directly as can be done when using expr. For use in a script, however, it offers excellent capabilities. Listing 14-23 shows a script in which let is used to perform calculations.

Listing 14-23. Performing Calculations with let

```
#!/bin/bash
# calcscript
# usage: calc $1 $2 $3
# $1 is the first number
# $2 is the operator
# $3 is the second number

let x="$1 $2 $3"
echo $x

exit 0
```

Here you can see what happens if you run this script:

```
SYD:~/bin # ./calcscript 1 + 2
3
SYD:~/bin #
```

If you think that we've now covered all methods to perform calculations in a shell script, you're wrong. Listing 14-24 shows another method that you can use.

Listing 14-24. Another Way to Calculate in a Bash Shell Script

```
#!/bin/bash
# calcscript
# usage: calc $1 $2 $3
# $1 is the first number
# $2 is the operator
# $3 is the second number

x=$(($1 $2 $3))

echo $x
exit 0
```

You saw this construction before when you read about the script that increases the value of the variable counter. Note that the double pair of parentheses can be replaced by one pair of square brackets instead, assuming the preceding $ is present.

Using Control Structures

Up until now, you haven't read much about the way in which the execution of commands can be made conditional. The technique for enabling this in shell scripts is known as *flow control*. Flow control is about commands that are used to control the flow of your script based on specific conditions, hence the classification "control structures." Bash offers many options to use flow control in scripts:

- if: Use if to execute commands only if certain conditions were met. To customize the working of if some more, you can use else to indicate what should happen if the condition isn't met.

- case: Use case to work with options. This allows the user to further specify the working of the command when he or she runs it.

- for: This construction is used to run a command for a given number of items. For example, you can use for to do something for every file in a specified directory.

- while: Use while as long as the specified condition is met. For example, this construction can be very useful to check whether a certain host is reachable or to monitor the activity of a process.

- until: This is the opposite of while. Use until to run a command until a certain condition has been met.

The following subsections cover flow control in more detail. Before going into these details, however, I want to first introduce you to the test command. This command is used to perform many checks to see, for example, whether a file exists or if a variable has a value. Table 14-3 shows some of the more common test options. For a complete overview, consult its man page.

Table 14-3. *Common Options for the* test *Command*

Option	Use
test -e $1	Checks whether $1 is a file, without looking at what particular kind of file it is.
test -f $1	Checks whether $1 is a regular file and not (for example) a device file, a directory, or an executable file.
test -d $1	Checks whether $1 is a directory.
test -x $1	Checks whether $1 is an executable file. Note that you can test for other permissions as well. For example, -g would check to see whether the SGID permission (see Chapter 7) is set.
test $1 -nt $2	Controls whether $1 is newer than $2.
test $1 -ot $2	Controls whether $1 is older than $2.
test $1 -ef $2	Checks whether $1 and $2 both refer to the same inode. This is the case if one is a hard link to the other (see Chapter 5 for more on inodes).
test $1 -eq $2	Checks whether the integers $1 and $2 are equal.
test $1 -ne $2	Checks whether the integers $1 and $2 are not equal.
test $1 -gt $2	Gives true if integer $1 is greater than integer $2.
test S1 -lt $2	Gives true if integer $1 is less than integer $2.
test $1 -ge $2	Checks whether integer $1 is greater than or equal to integer $2.
test $1 -le $2	Checks whether integer $1 is less than or equal to integer $2.
test -z $1	Checks whether $1 is empty. This is a very useful construction for finding out whether a variable has been defined.
test $1	Gives the exit status 0 if $1 is defined.
test $1=$2	Checks whether the strings $1 and $2 are the same. This is most useful to compare the value of two variables.
test $1 != $2	Checks whether the strings $1 and $2 are not equal to each other. You can use ! with all other tests as well to check for the negation of the statement.

You can use the test command in two ways. First, you can write the complete command, as in test -f $1. This command, however, can be rewritten as [-f $1]. (Don't forget the spaces between the square brackets—the script won't work without them!) Most of the time you'll see the latter option only because people who write shell scripts like to work as efficiently as possible.

Using if ... then ... else

Possibly the classic example of flow control consists of constructions that use if ... then ... else. This construction offers various interesting possibilities, especially if used in conjunction with the test command. You can use it to find out whether a file exists, whether a variable currently has a value, and much more. Listing 14-25 provides an example of a construction with if ... then ... else that can be used in a shell script.

Listing 14-25. Using `if` to Perform a Basic Check

```
#!/bin/bash
# testarg
# test to see if argument is present

if [ -z $1 ]
then
      echo You have to provide an argument with this command
      exit 1
fi

echo the argument is $1

exit 0
```

The simple check from the Listing 14-25 example is used to see whether the user who started your script provided an argument. Here's what you see if you run the script:

```
SYD:~/bin # ./testarg
You have to provide an argument with this command
SYD:~/bin #
```

If the user didn't provide an argument, the code in the `if` loop becomes active, in which case it displays the message that the user needs to provide an argument and then terminates the script. If an argument has been provided, the commands within the loop aren't executed, and the script will run the line `echo the argument is $1`, and in this case echo the argument to the user's screen.

Also notice how the syntax of the `if` construction is organized. First, you have to open it with `if`. Then, separated on a new line (or with a semicolon), then is used. Finally, the `if` loop is closed with an `fi` statement. Make sure all those ingredients are used all the time, or your loop won't work.

■ **Note** You can use a semicolon as a separator between two commands. So `ls;` who would first execute the command `ls` and then the command `who`.

The example in Listing 14-25 is rather simple; it's also possible to make `if` loops more complex and have them test for more than one condition. To do this, use `else` or `elif`. Using `else` within the control structure allows you to not only make sure that something happens if the condition is met, but also check another condition if the condition is not met. You can even use `else` in conjunction with `if` (`elif`) to open a new control structure if the first condition isn't met. If you do that, you have to use `then` after `elif`. Listing 14-26 is an example of the latter construction.

Listing 14-26. Nesting `if` Control Structures

```
#!/bin/bash
# testfile

if [ -f $1 ]
then
      echo "$1 is a file"
elif [ -d $1 ]
```

```
then
        echo "$1 is a directory"
else
        echo "I don't know what \$1 is"
fi

exit 0
```

Here you can see what happens when you run this script:

```
SYD:~/bin # ./testfile /bin/blah
I don't know what $1 is
SYD:~/bin #
```

In this example, the argument that was entered when running the script is checked. If it is a file (if [-f $1]), the script tells the user that. If it isn't a file, the part under elif is executed, which basically opens a second control structure. In this second control structure, the first test performed is to see whether $1 is perhaps a directory. Notice that this second part of the control structure becomes active only if $1 is not a file. If $1 isn't a directory either, the part after else is run, and the script reports that it has no idea what $1 is. Notice that for this entire construction, only one fi is needed to close the control structure, but after every if (that includes all elif as well), you need to use then.

You should know that if ... then ... else constructions are used in two different ways. You can write out the complete construction as in the previous examples, or you can employ constructions that use && and ||. These so-called logical operators are used to separate two commands and establish a conditional relationship between them. If && is used, the second command is executed only if the first command is executed successfully (in other words, if the first command is true). If || is used, the second command is executed only if the first command isn't true. So, with one line of code, you can find out whether $1 is a file and echo a message if it is:

```
[ -f $1 ] && echo $1 is a file
```

Note that this can be rewritten as follows:

```
[ ! -f $1 ] || echo $1 is a file
```

■ **Note**   This example only works as a part of a complete shell script. Listing 14-27 shows how the example from Listing 14-26 is rewritten if you want to use this syntax.

In case you don't quite follow what is happening in the second example: it performs a test to see whether $1 is not a file. (The ! is used to test whether something is not the case.) Only if the test fails (which is the case if $1 is indeed a file) does the command execute the part after the || and echoes that $1 is a file. Listing 14-27 shows how you can rewrite the script from Listing 14-26 with the && and || tests.

Listing 14-27. The Example from Listing 14-26 Rewritten with && and ||

```
([ -z $1 ] && echo please provide an argument; exit 1) || (([ -f $1 ] && echo $1 is\
a file) || ([ -d $1 ] && echo $1 is a directory || echo I have no idea what $1 is))
```

■ **Note** You'll notice in Listing 14-27 that I used a \ at the end of the line. This slash makes sure that the carriage return sign at the end of the line is not interpreted and is used only to make sure that you don't type two separated lines. I've used the \ for typographical reasons only. In a real script, you'd just put all code on one line (which wouldn't fit on these pages without breaking it, as I've had to do). I'll use this convention in some later scripts as well.

It is not really hard to understand the script in Listing 14-27 if you understand the script in Listing 14-26, because they do the same thing. However, you should be aware of a few differences. First, I've added a [-z $1] test to give an error if $1 is not defined.

Next, the example in Listing 14-27 is all on one line. This makes the script more compact, but it also makes it a little harder to understand what is going on. I've used parentheses to increase the readability a little bit and also to keep the different parts of the script together. The parts between parentheses are the main tests, and within these main tests some smaller tests are used as well.

Let's have a look at some other examples with if ... then ... else. Consider the following line:

```
rsync -vaze ssh --delete /srv/ftp 10.0.0.20:/srv/ftp || echo "rsync failed" | mail
admin@mydomain.com
```

Here, the rsync command tries to synchronize the content of the directory /srv/ftp with the content of the same directory on some other machine. If this succeeds, no further evaluation of this line is attempted. If something happens, however, the part after the || becomes active and makes sure that user admin@ mydomain.com gets a message.

The following script presents another example, a complex one that checks whether available disk space has dropped below a certain threshold. The complex part lies in the sequence of pipes used in the command substitution:

```
if [ `df -m /var | tail -n1 | awk '{print $4} '` -lt 120 ]
then
      logger running out of disk space
fi
```

The important part of this piece of code is in the first line, where the result of a command is included in the if loop by using backquoting, and that result is compared with the value 120.

If the result is less than 120, the following section becomes active. If the result is greater than 120, nothing happens. As for the command itself, it uses df to check available disk space on the volume where /var is mounted, filters out the last line of that result, and from that last line filters out the fourth column only, which in turn is compared to the value 120. And, if the condition is true, the logger command writes a message to the system log file. This example isn't really well organized. The following rewrite does exactly the same, but using a different syntax:

```
[ `df -m /var | tail -n1 | awk '{print $4}'` -lt $1 ] && logger running out of
disk space
```

This shows why it's fun to write shell scripts: you can almost always make them better.

Case

Let's start with an example this time (see Listing 14-28). Create the script, run it, and then try to figure out what it's done.

Listing 14-28. Example Script with Case

```
#!/bin/bash
# soccer
# Your personal soccer expert
# predicts world championship football

cat << EOF
Enter the name of the country you think will be world soccer champion in 2010.
EOF

read COUNTRY
# translate $COUNTRY into all uppercase
COUNTRY=`echo $COUNTRY | tr a-z A-Z`

# perform the test
case $COUNTRY in
     NEDERLAND | HOLLAND | NETHERLANDS)
     echo "Yes, you are a soccer expert "
     ;;
     DEUTSCHLAND | GERMANY | MANNSCHAFT)
     echo "No, they are the worst team on earth"
     ;;
     ENGLAND | AUSTRALIA)
     echo "hahahahahahaha, you must be joking"
     ;;
     *)
     echo "Huh? Do they play soccer?"
     ;;
esac

exit 0
```

In case you haven't guessed, this script can be used to analyze the next World Cup championship (of course, you can modify it for any major sports event you like). It will first ask the person who runs the script to enter the name of the country that he or she thinks will be the next champion. This country is put in the $COUNTRY variable. Notice the use of uppercase for this variable; it's a nice way to identify variables easily if your script becomes rather big.

Because the case statement that's used in this script is case sensitive, the user input in the first part is translated into all uppercase using the tr command. Using command substitution with this command, the current value of $COUNTRY is read, translated to all uppercase, and assigned again to the $COUNTRY variable using command substitution. Also notice that I've made it easier to distinguish the different parts of this script by adding some additional comments.

The body of this script consists of the case command, which is used to evaluate the input the user has entered. The generic construction used to evaluate the input is as follows:

```
alternative1 | alternative2)
command
;;
```

So, the first line evaluates everything that the user can enter. Notice that more than one alternative is used on most lines, which makes it easier to handle typos and other situations where the user hasn't typed exactly what you were expecting him or her to type. Then on separate lines come all the commands that you want the script to execute. In the example, just one command is executed, but you can enter a hundred lines to execute commands if you like. Finally, the test is closed by using ;;. Don't forget to close all items with the double semicolons; otherwise, the script won't understand you. The ;; can be on a line by itself, but you can also put it directly after the last command line in the script.

When using case, you should make it a habit to handle "all other options." Hopefully, your user will enter something that you expect. But what if he or she doesn't? In that case, you probably do want the user to see something. This is handled by the *) at the end of the script. So, in this case, for everything the user enters that isn't specifically mentioned as an option in the script, the script will echo "Huh? Do they play soccer?" to the user.

Using while

You can use while to run a command as long as a condition is met. Listing 14-29 shows how while is used to monitor activity of an important process.

Listing 14-29. Monitoring Process Activity with while

```
#!/bin/bash
# procesmon
# usage: monitor <processname>

while ps aux | grep $1
do
     sleep 1
done

logger $1 is no longer present

exit 0
```

The body of this script consists of the command ps aux | grep $1. This command monitors for the availability of the process whose name was entered as an argument when starting the script. As long as the process is detected, the condition is met and the commands in the loop are executed. In this case, the script waits 1 second and then repeats its action. When the process is no longer detected, the logger command writes a message to syslog.

As you can see from this example, while offers an excellent method to check whether something (such as a process or an IP address) still exists. If you combine it with the sleep command, you can start your script with while as a kind of daemon and perform a check repeatedly. For example, the script in Listing 14-30 would write a message to syslog if the IP address suddenly gets lost due to an error.

Listing 14-30. Checking Whether the IP Address Is Still There

```
#!/bin/bash
# ipmon
# script that monitors an IP address
# usage: ipmon <ip-address>

while ip a s | grep $1/ > /dev/null
do
      sleep 5
done

logger HELP, the IP address $1 is gone.

exit 0
```

Using until

Whereas while does its work as long as a certain condition is met, until is used for the opposite: it runs until the condition is met. This can be seen in Listing 14-31 where the script monitors whether the user, whose name is entered as the argument, is logged in.

Listing 14-31. Monitoring User Login

```
#!/bin/bash
# usermon
# script that alerts when a user logs in
# usage: ishere <username>

until who | grep $1 >> /dev/null
do
      echo $1 is not logged in yet
      sleep 5
done

echo $1 has just logged in

exit 0
```

In this example, the who | grep $1 command is executed repeatedly. In this command, the result of the who command that lists users currently logged in to the system is grepped for the occurrence of $1. As long as that command is not true (which is the case if the user is not logged in), the commands in the loop will be executed. As soon as the user logs in, the loop is broken, and a message is displayed to say that the user has just logged in. Notice the use of redirection to the null device in the test, ensuring that the result of the who command is not echoed on the screen.

Using for

Sometimes it's necessary to execute a series of commands, whether for a limited or an unlimited number of times. In such cases, for loops offer an excellent solution. Listing 14-32 shows how you can use for to create a counter.

Listing 14-32. Using for to Create a Counter

```
#!/bin/bash
# counter
# counter that counts from 1 to 9

for (( counter=1; counter<10; counter++ )); do
    echo "The counter is now set to $counter"
done

exit 0
```

The code used in this script isn't difficult to understand: the conditional loop determines that, as long as the counter has a value between 1 and 10, the variable counter must be automatically incremented by 1. To do this, the construction counter++ is used. As long as this incrementing of the variable counter continues, the commands between do and done are executed. When the specified number is reached, the loop is left, and the script will terminate and indicate with exit 0 to the system that it has done its work successfully.

Loops with for can be pretty versatile. For example, you can use it to do something on every line in a text file. The example in Listing 14-33 illustrates how this works (as you will see, however, it has some problems).

Listing 14-33. Displaying Lines from a Text File

```
#!/bin/bash
# listusers
# faulty script that tries to show all users in /etc/passwd

for i in `cat /etc/passwd`
do
    echo $i
done

exit 0
```

In this example, for is used to display all lines in /etc/passwd one by one. Of course, just echoing the lines is a rather trivial example, but it's enough to show how for works. If you're using for in this way, you should notice that it cannot handle spaces in the lines. A space would be interpreted as a field separator, so a new field would begin after the space.

Listing 14-34 shows one more example with for: in this example, for is used to ping a range of IP addresses. This is a script that one of my customers likes to run to see whether a range of machines is up and running. Because the IP addresses are always in the same range, starting with 192.168.1, there's no harm in including these first three bits in the IP address itself. Of course, you're free to work with complete IP addresses instead.

Listing 14-34. Testing a Range of IP Addresses

```
#!/bin/bash
for i in $@
do
    ping -c 1 192.168.1.$i
done
```

Notice the use of $@ in this script. This operator allows you to refer to all arguments that were specified when starting the script, no matter how many there are. Let's have a closer look at this.

Remember $* nd $@, used when treating arguments within a script? Time to show you exactly what the difference is between the two by using a for loop. Using for, you can perform an action on each element in a string. Listing 14-35 provides a simple example that demonstrates this.

Listing 14-35. Using for to Distinguish Different Elements in a String

```
nuuk:~/bin # for i in 1 2 3; do echo $i; done
1
2
3
```

The example command line in Listing 14-35 consists of three different parts, which are separated by a semicolon. The first part is for i in 1 2 3, which you can interpret as "for each element in the string 1 2 3." While evaluating the for loop, each of these elements is stored in the temporary variable i. In the second part, for each of these elements a command is executed. In this case, the command do echo $i echoes the elements one by one, which you can clearly see in the output of the command used in Listing 14-35. Finally, the third part of this for loop is the word done, which closes the for loop. Every for loop starts with for, is followed by do, and closes with done. Now let's change the showargs script that appeared earlier in this chapter in Listing 14-12 to include a for loop for both $@ and $*.

Listing 14-36 shows what the new script looks like.

Listing 14-36. Evaluating $@ and $* Using for

```
#!/bin/bash
# showargs
# this script shows all arguments used when starting the script

echo showing for on \$@
for i in "$@"
do
       echo $i
done

echo showing for on \$*
for i in "$*"
do
       echo $i
done

exit 0
```

Let's consider a few comments before running this script. In this script, a technique called escaping is used. The purpose of escaping is to make sure that the shell doesn't interpret certain elements. For instance, consider this line:

```
echo showing for on $@
```

If you run this line as shown, the shell will interpret $@ and show you its current value. In this case, we want the shell to display the characters $@ instead. To do so, the shell should not interpret the $ sign, which we make clear by adding a slash in front of it. By using a slash, we tell the shell not to interpret the next character.

Later in the script, notice the lines for i in "$@" and for i in "$*". In here, I've used double quotes to prevent the shell from interpreting $@ and $* *before* executing the code lines in the script. We want the shell to interpret these at the moment it runs the script, and therefore I put both between double quotes. At this point, I recommend you try running the script once without the double quotes and once with the double quotes to see the difference yourself.

When you run the script without the double quotes and start the script with a command like ./showargs a b c d, the shell has already interpreted $* before it comes to the line for i in $*. So it would in fact execute for i in a b c d and next show a, b, c, and d, each displayed on its own line. But that's not what we want—we want the shell to show the result of for i in $*. To make sure this happens, put $* between double quotes. In Listing 14-37, you can see the result of running the example script from Listing 14-36.

Listing 14-37. Result of Running the Example Script in Listing 14-36

```
nuuk:~/bin # ./showargs a b c d
showing for on $@
a
b
c
d
showing for on $*
a b c d
nuuk:~/bin #
```

Summary

In this chapter, you've learned how to write a Bash shell script. Having mastered shell scripting, you are well on your way to becoming a real expert on the Linux command line. The following common Bash shell script elements have been covered:

- #!/bin/bash: Represents a shebang. Every script should start with a shebang, which tells the parent shell what shell should be used to interpret the script.

- #: Indicates a comment line. Use comments to explain to the user of a script what exactly the script ought to be doing.

- exit: Informs the parent shell whether the script executed successfully. It is good practice to include exit at the end of scripts.

- echo: Displays text on the STDOUT while executing the script.

- source: Includes a script in the current shell environment without launching a subshell.

- .: Operates the same way as source.

- read: Stops the script to read user input and put that into a variable.

- which: Searches the path to see where an executable file exists. Issue this before giving a name to a script to avoid using a name already in use.

- $0: Refers to the script name.

- $1, $*n*: Refer to arguments that were employed when starting the script.

- $@: Refers to all arguments.

- $#: Gives the number of arguments used when starting the script.

- $*: Refers to all arguments.

- \: Escapes the next character so that it is not interpreted by the shell.

- "...": Escapes the next string so that some characters are not interpreted by the shell.

- Generally, this is used when a string contains spaces.

- '...': Escapes the next string so that no characters are interpreted by the shell at all.

- expr: Performs calculations.

- let: Performs calculations.

- test: Performs tests, for instance, to see whether a file exists or a value is greater or smaller than another value.

- if ... then ... else: Executes a command when a certain condition has been met.

- while ... do ... done: Executes as long as a certain condition has been met.

- until ... do ...done: Executes until a certain condition has been met.

- case ... esac: Checks different options and, depending on the option that is true, executes a command.

- for ... do ... done: Executes a command for a range of items.

This was the last chapter. After reading all chapters in this book, you should now be capable of working efficiently from the Linux command line.

APPENDIX A

■ ■ ■

Installing Linux

In this appendix you'll learn how to install Linux. We're covering two popular distributions. You'll first learn how to install CentOS; next you'll read how to install the Ubuntu Server 14.04 LTS release on your computer.

While writing this book, I have primarily focused on CentOS 7.0 and Ubuntu Server 14.04 LTS. Of course you're free to use any other Linux distribution, but you will notice that a larger amount of differences exists when using another distribution. I have tried to write the book in a manner that differences between Linux distributions don't matter too much, but there will always be some items that don't work as well when using another distribution.

Installation Requirements

To install Linux, you don't need much advanced hardware. An amount of 512 MB RAM suffices, and apart from that, you'll do well with as little as 4 GB of disk space. You will need a 64 bits platform though to run a modern Linux server operating system where all features are supported. This shouldn't be a problem, because nearly all CPUs that have been released in the last decade offer support for 64 bits instructions.

To learn Linux and to be able to work through the exercises that are described in this book, I would recommend using virtualization software. A desktop virtualization solution such as VMware Workstation / Player for Windows or VMware Fusion for Apple will do well. An alternative solution is offered by Oracle VirtualBox. Most people like the VMware software better as it is well organized, but you will need to pay for it. Given the low hardware requirements, it will work well on older computer hardware also.

Installing CentOS

The following procedure walks you through a basic installation of CentOS with a configuration that works well for learning the items that are discussed in this book.

1. Boot CentOS from the installation media. This will show you the screen in figure A-1. Select Install CentOS 7 and press enter to start the installation.

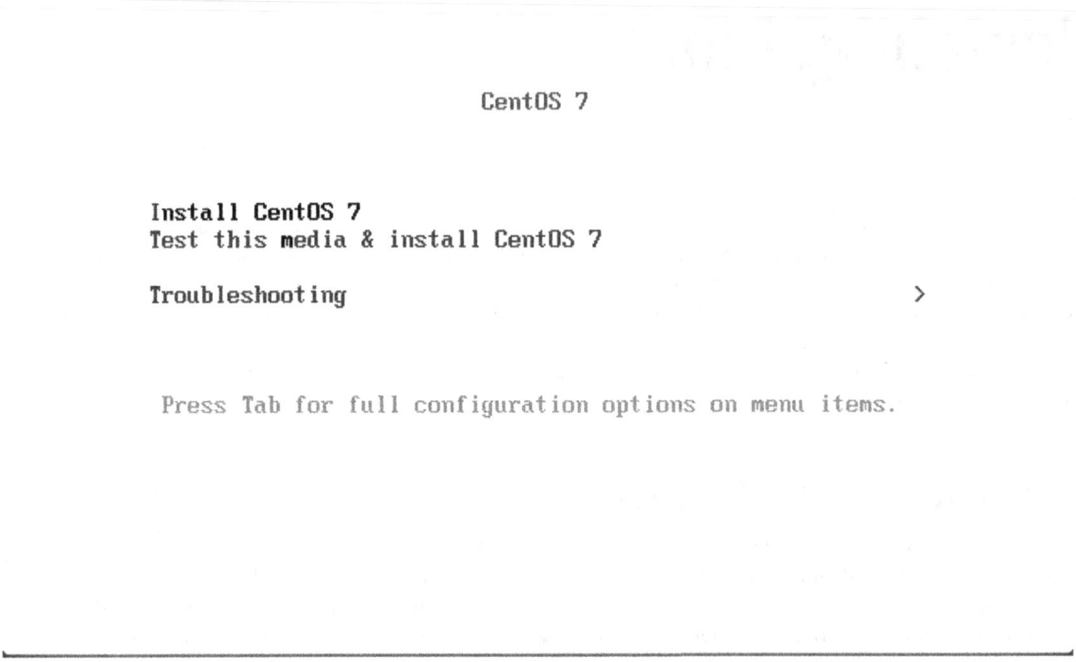

```
                          CentOS 7


          Install CentOS 7
          Test this media & install CentOS 7

          Troubleshooting                                    >


          Press Tab for full configuration options on menu items.
```

Figure A-1. *Starting the CentOS installation*

2. Once the installation program has been loaded, you'll see the Welcome to
    CentOS screen where you can select the language and keyboard settings. I
    recommend installing CentOS in English, but other languages are offered as well.
    After making your selection, press Continue to proceed.

Figure A-2. *Selecting language and keyboard settings*

3. In the next screen you'll see the installation summary (see figure A-3). From this screen you'll make all required choices to start the installation of your Linux distribution.

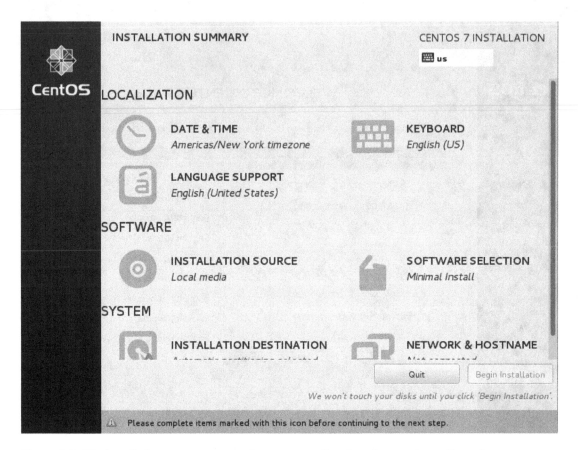

Figure A-3. *The installation summary screen gives access to all options that require configuration*

4. To start with, you can have a look at the software selection link. Click it, and it will open the screen that you can see in figure A-4. You can do very well with a minimal installation, which installs no graphical user interface and just a minimal set of packages. It is also perfectly fine to select the "Server with GUI" installation pattern. This does install a graphical user interface, which allows you to easily open multiple terminal windows on the same desktop. For this book both choices work well, so the choice is entirely up to you.

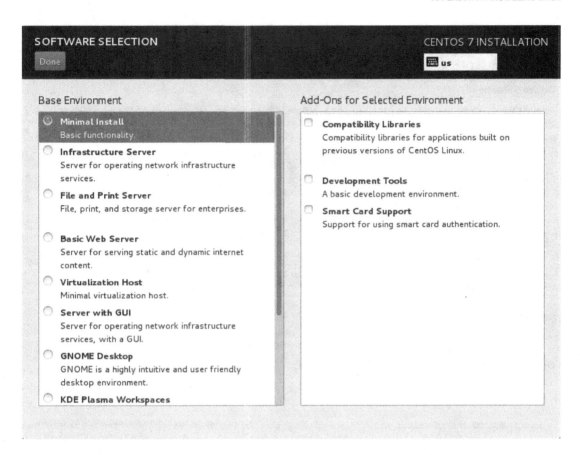

Figure A-4. *Selecting the basic software installation pattern*

5. Next you must click the Installation Destination link. This will open the screen that you can see in Figure A-5. You just have to click the Done button from this screen to confirm that you really want to use the selected disk device for your Linux installation. You don't have to do anything difficult with the hard disk, just select the default disk lay-out.

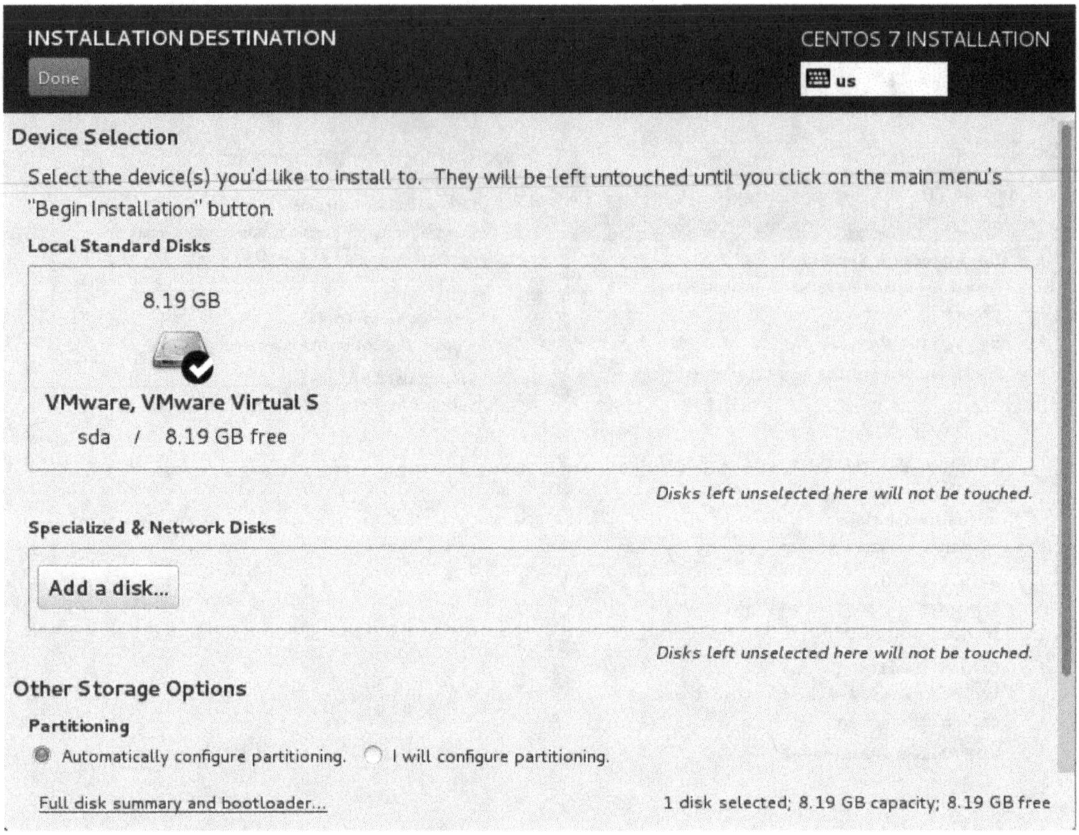

Figure A-5. *Selecting the hard disk for installation*

6. The last step before starting the installation is the configuration of network and hostname. Click the link to ensure that the network card is enabled, and here also, you can leave all default settings, which configures your network to get an IP address from a DHCP server. Close this screen; at this point you can start the installation.

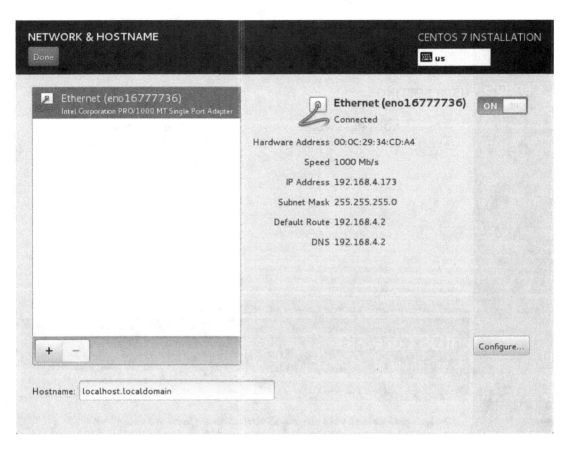

Figure A-6. Switch on the network card before starting the installation

7. The installation will start immediately now (see Figure A-7). While packages are being installed, you can enter a root password and create a user as well.

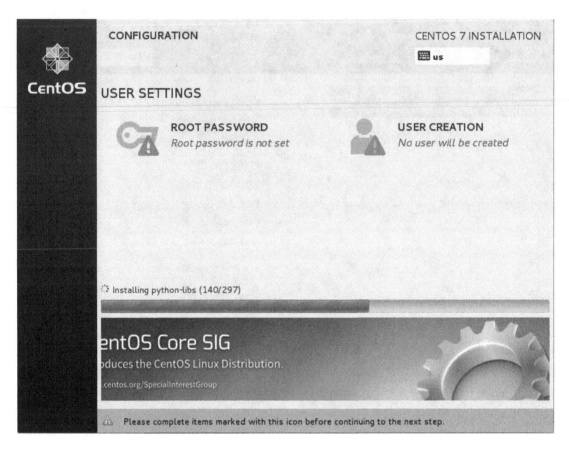

Figure A-7. *While the software packages are written to your system, you can set the root password and create a user*

8. In figure A-8 you see the screen where you have to enter a root password. Enter the same password twice to avoid any mistakes while typing the password and then click Done to write the configuration to disk. Optionally you can create a user account as well. If you don't create a user now, that's fine, you'll be instructed how to do that while working through the chapters in this book.

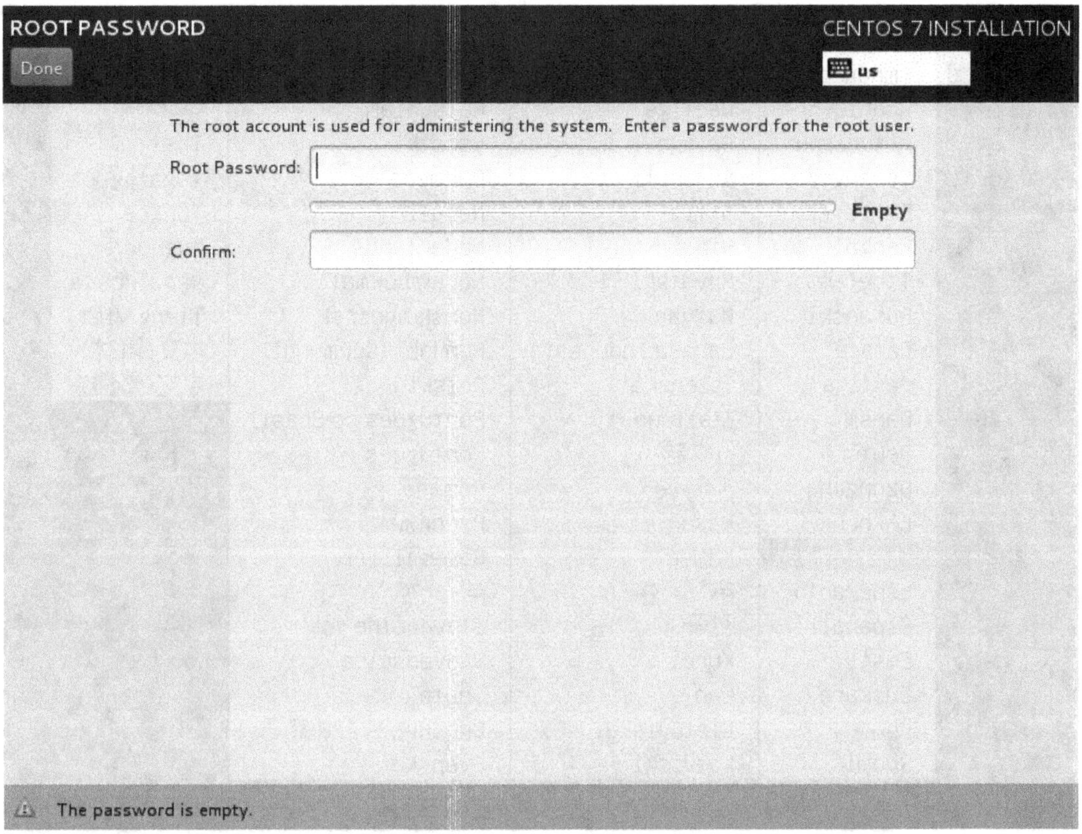

ROOT PASSWORD   CENTOS 7 INSTALLATION

Done   ⌨ us

The root account is used for administering the system. Enter a password for the root user.

Root Password: |

Empty

Confirm:

⚠ The password is empty.

Figure A-8. Enter the root password twice

9. When the installation has finished, this will be indicated. At that point you can click Finish the installation to write the final configuration to disk. Next Reboot, to start working on your freshly installed system. That was all!

Installing Ubuntu Server

While the Ubuntu desktop edition was designed for being easy to use, the Ubuntu server edition is designed to be as efficient as possible. You won't get a graphical interface at all, you'll just get a text based interface that allows you what needs to be done on the server. This procedure describes how to install an Ubuntu Server that can be used to work your way through this book.

1. Boot from the installation media. This will show the screen that you can see in Figure A-9, from which you can select the language that will be used in the enxt screen. I recommend using an English language installation.

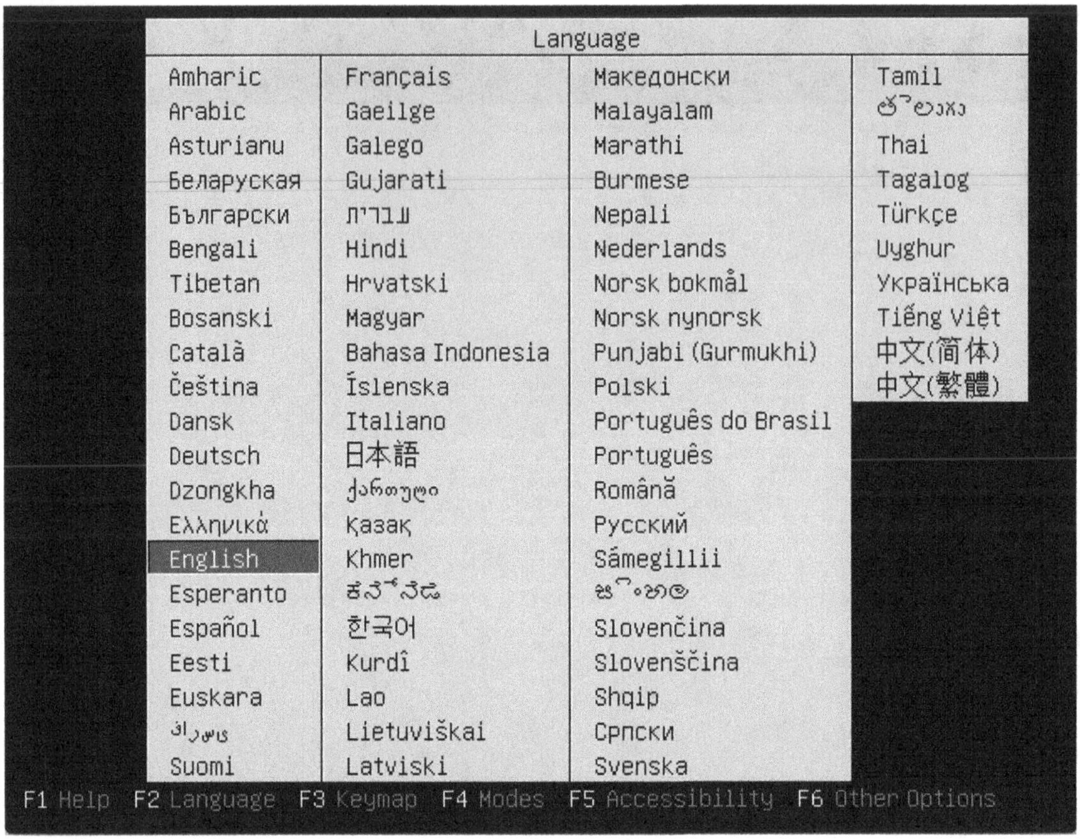

Language			
Amharic	Français	Македонски	Tamil
Arabic	Gaeilge	Malayalam	తెలుగు
Asturianu	Galego	Marathi	Thai
Беларуская	Gujarati	Burmese	Tagalog
Български	עברית	Nepali	Türkçe
Bengali	Hindi	Nederlands	Uyghur
Tibetan	Hrvatski	Norsk bokmål	Українська
Bosanski	Magyar	Norsk nynorsk	Tiếng Việt
Català	Bahasa Indonesia	Punjabi (Gurmukhi)	中文(简体)
Čeština	Íslenska	Polski	中文(繁體)
Dansk	Italiano	Português do Brasil	
Deutsch	日本語	Português	
Dzongkha	ქართული	Română	
Ελληνικά	Қазақ	Русский	
English	Khmer	Sámegillii	
Esperanto	ಕನ್ನಡ	ಜ°ಾಲ	
Español	한국어	Slovenčina	
Eesti	Kurdî	Slovenščina	
Euskara	Lao	Shqip	
اردو	Lietuviškai	Српски	
Suomi	Latviski	Svenska	

F1 Help   F2 Language   F3 Keymap   F4 Modes   F5 Accessibility   F6 Other Options

Figure A-9. *To start with, select the language that you want to be using for installation*

2. Next you'll need to indicate what you want to do. Multiple options are suggested; select Install Ubuntu Server to start the installation procedure.

Figure A-10. *Select Install Ubuntu Server*

3. You'll now see another screen where you need to select the language and keyboard disposition. That may seem redundant, but in this screen you'll determine the language the server will be installed in, as well as the keyboard layout that will be used.

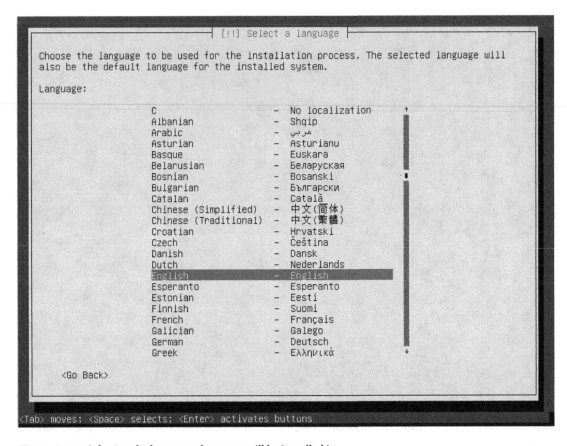

```
                         ┤ [!!] Select a language ├
Choose the language to be used for the installation process. The selected language will
also be the default language for the installed system.

Language:

                     C                    -   No localization          ↑
                     Albanian             -   Shqip
                     Arabic               -   عربي
                     Asturian             -   Asturianu
                     Basque               -   Euskara
                     Belarusian           -   Беларуская
                     Bosnian              -   Bosanski              · ▪
                     Bulgarian            -   Български
                     Catalan              -   Català
                     Chinese (Simplified)  -  中文(简体)
                     Chinese (Traditional) -  中文(繁體)
                     Croatian             -   Hrvatski
                     Czech                -   Čeština
                     Danish               -   Dansk
                     Dutch                -   Nederlands
                     English              -   English
                     Esperanto            -   Esperanto
                     Estonian             -   Eesti
                     Finnish              -   Suomi
                     French               -   Français
                     Galician             -   Galego
                     German               -   Deutsch
                     Greek                -   Ελληνικά              ↓

     <Go Back>

<Tab> moves; <Space> selects; <Enter> activates buttons
```

Figure A-11. *Selecting the language the server will be installed in*

4.   Before the actual installation is started, you'll need to make a couple more
     choices. To start with, you have to indicate your geographical area, which will be
     used to configure system time correctly.

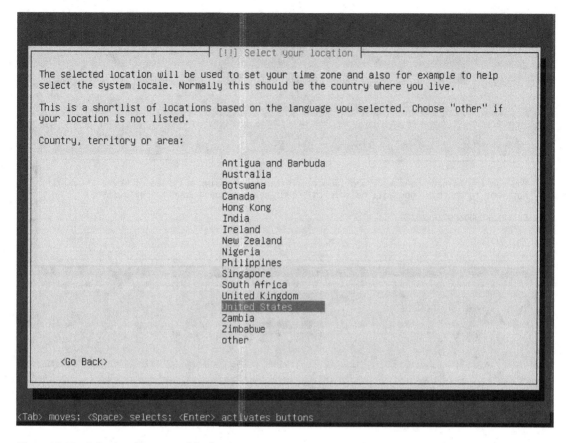

```
                    ┤ [!!] Select your location ├
The selected location will be used to set your time zone and also for example to help
select the system locale. Normally this should be the country where you live.

This is a shortlist of locations based on the language you selected. Choose "other" if
your location is not listed.

Country, territory or area:

                        Antigua and Barbuda
                        Australia
                        Botswana
                        Canada
                        Hong Kong
                        India
                        Ireland
                        New Zealand
                        Nigeria
                        Philippines
                        Singapore
                        South Africa
                        United Kingdom
                        United States
                        Zambia
                        Zimbabwe
                        other

    <Go Back>


<Tab> moves; <Space> selects; <Enter> activates buttons
```

Figure A-12. *Selecting the geographical area*

5. In the next screen you can indicate how you want to define the keyboard on your
   system. To do so, you may just select the keyboard from a list, or you can press a
   couple of keys so that the installation program will detect the type of keyboard
   you are using for you. Personally, I think selecting the keyboard layout from a list
   is easier, so select No to display the list and select your keyboard type.

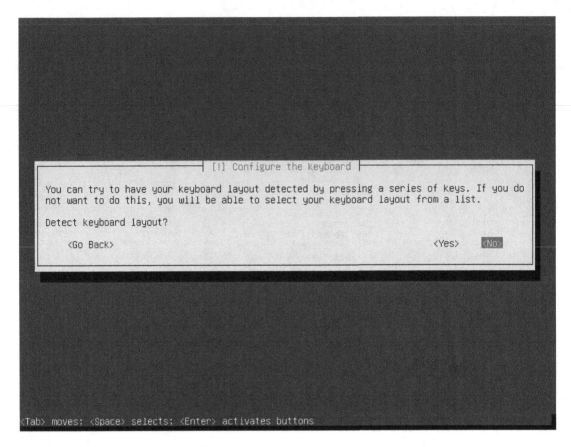

Figure A-13. *Selecting the keyboard disposition*

6. After selecting the keyboard, additional components are loaded that are required to complete the installation. To load these additional components, you'll need network access. So if you see something that doesn't match the next figure at all, make sure you're connected to the network and try again. Once that has been done, you'll need to select a name for your system. If you don't do anything, the system will be called ubuntu. It's a good idea to change that name into something a bit more meaningful.

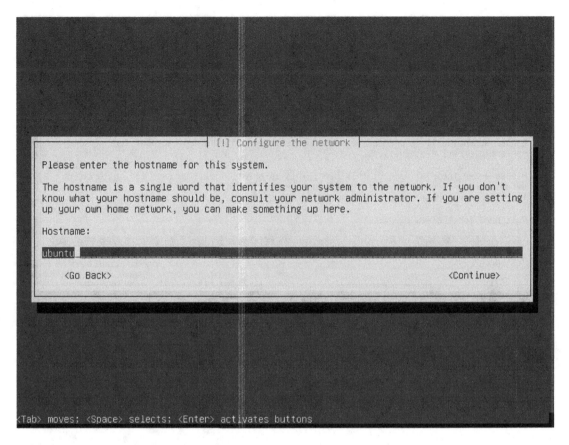

Figure A-14. Setting the system name

7. On Ubuntu you'll have to create a user, because root login is disabled by default. In the next screen you can enter the desired user name. This user will automatically be created as the administrative user, which means that this user account will have sudo access to all administrator commands.

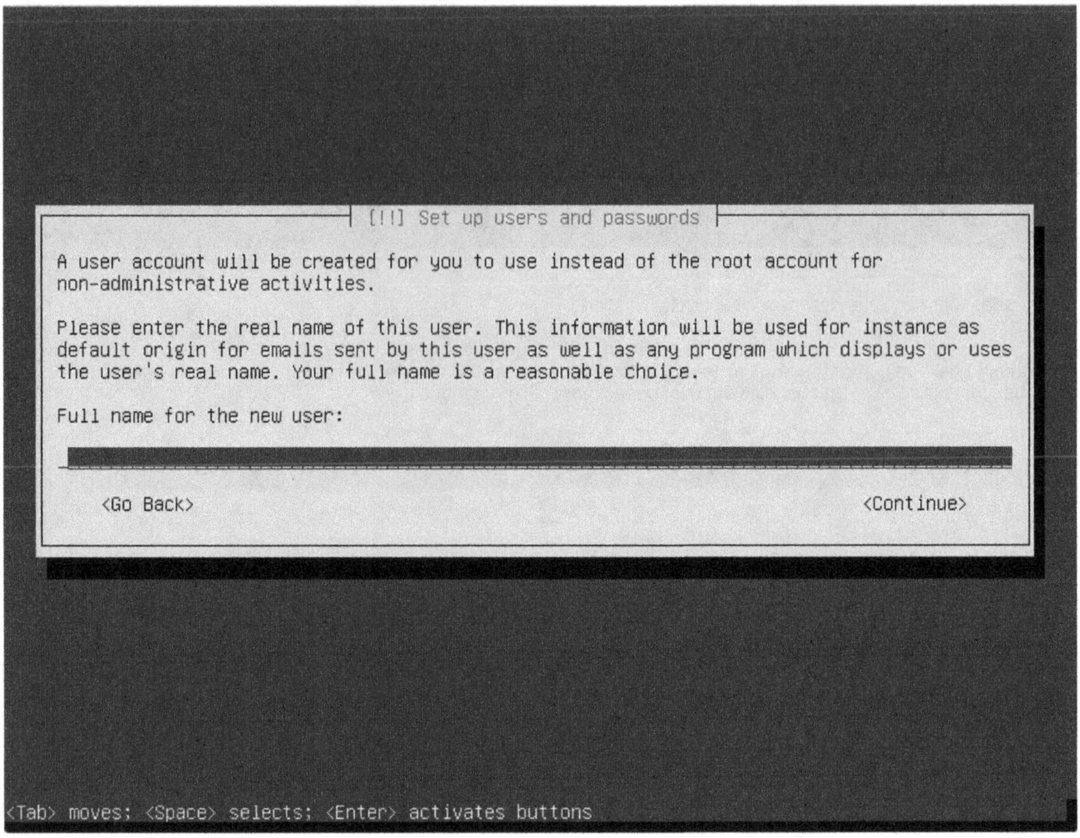

```
                    ┤ [!!] Set up users and passwords ├

 A user account will be created for you to use instead of the root account for
 non-administrative activities.

 Please enter the real name of this user. This information will be used for instance as
 default origin for emails sent by this user as well as any program which displays or uses
 the user's real name. Your full name is a reasonable choice.

 Full name for the new user:

 _____

    <Go Back>                                                          <Continue>




<Tab> moves; <Space> selects; <Enter> activates buttons
```

Figure A-15. *Creating the admin user*

8. After choosing the user name, you'll have to enter a password. Do this twice, to prevent any typos from locking you out from the system.

9. The last part of the user-related configuration asks you if you want to encrypt the contents of your home directory. While this is a good idea for a typical laptop user to prevent unauthorized access to personal files, on a server it's not really necessary to use an encrypted home directory.

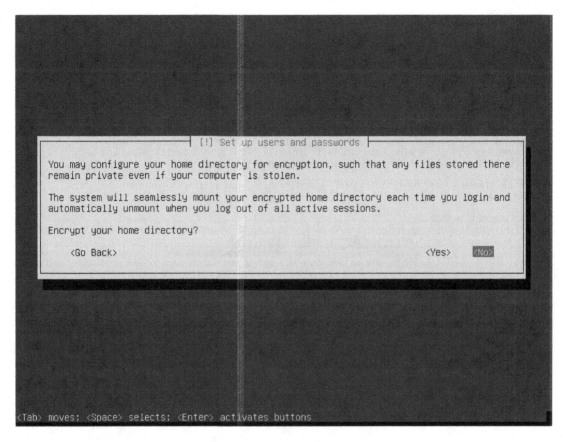

```
                    ┤ [!] Set up users and passwords ├
 You may configure your home directory for encryption, such that any files stored there
 remain private even if your computer is stolen.

 The system will seamlessly mount your encrypted home directory each time you login and
 automatically unmount when you log out of all active sessions.

 Encrypt your home directory?

    <Go Back>                                             <Yes>      <No>
```

```
<Tab> moves; <Space> selects; <Enter> activates buttons
```

Figure A-16. *On a server there's no real need to use an encrypted home directory*

10. In the next screen, you'll be prompted to confirm the time zone that is selected. Select yes if it is correct to move on to the next screen.

11. You'll now be asked how you want to organize disk lay-out (see Figure A-17). For an easy configuration of partitions on your hard disk, select the Guided - use entire disk and set up LVM option.

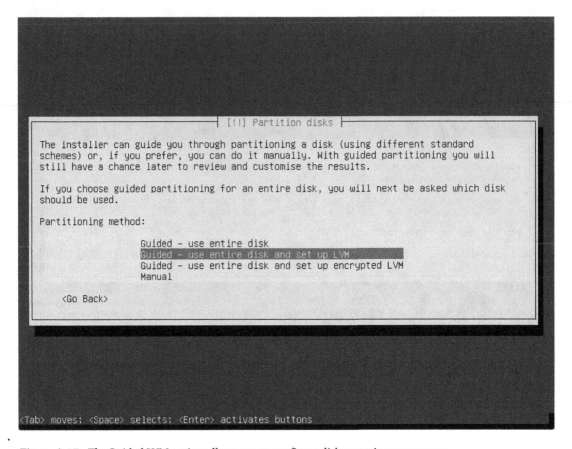

Figure A-17. *The Guided LVM option allows you to configure disk usage in an easy way*

12. The screen that you can see in Figure A-18 shows which disk will be used. Make sure that you're using the right disk, and if that is the case, press Enter to continue.

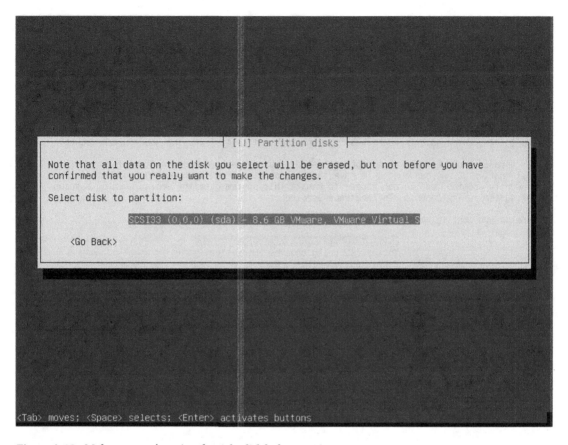

```
                    ┤ [!!] Partition disks ├

Note that all data on the disk you select will be erased, but not before you have
confirmed that you really want to make the changes.

Select disk to partition:

              SCSI33 (0,0,0) (sda) - 8.6 GB VMware, VMware Virtual S

     <Go Back>


```

```
<Tab> moves; <Space> selects; <Enter> activates buttons
```

Figure A-18. *Make sure you're using the right disk before moving on*

13. Before the configuration is actually written to disk, you need to confirm three more times in three different screens. Do this, which allows your disk to be formatted and a first set of files to be copied to disk.

14. You can now indicate if a proxy needs to be used for Internet access. For a simple home configuration, typically no proxies are used, so you can leave this field empty and just select Continue to move on.

15. In the next screen (see Figure A-19) you can indicate how you want to update your system. By default no automatic updates will be done, which is fine for what you need to do with Ubuntu server in this book. On a real server you might want to consider installing at least security updates automatically.

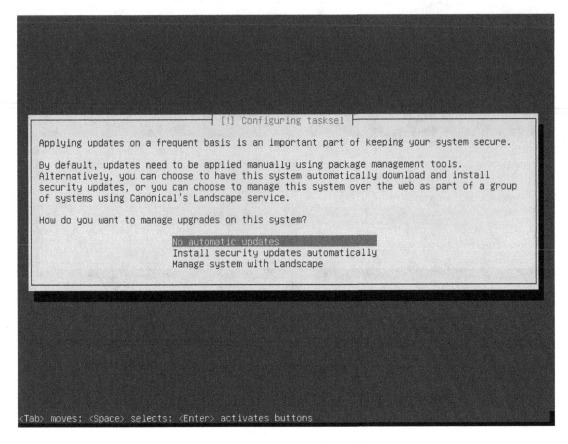

Figure A-19. *Defining how you want to deal with automatic updates*

16. You now can install some additional services as well. It is a good idea at least to install the SSH Server, everything else can be installed later as well.

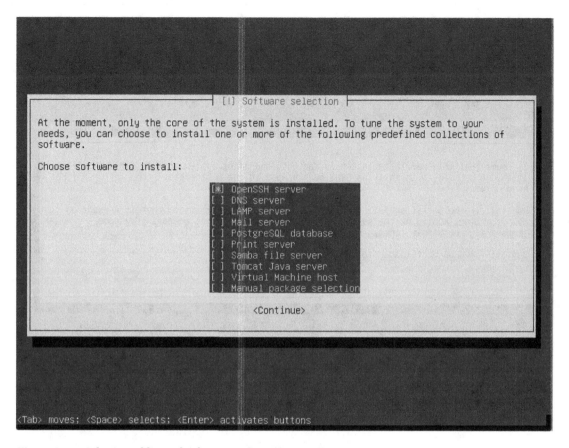

Figure A-20. *Selecting additional software packages for installation*

17. After the installation of selected packages, the installer will ask if you want to install the Grub 2 boot loader to disk (see Figure A-21). Select Yes and press Enter to confirm. Once that has been done, you'll see the Installation Complete message. Press enter one more time and your newly installed Ubuntu server will start booting.

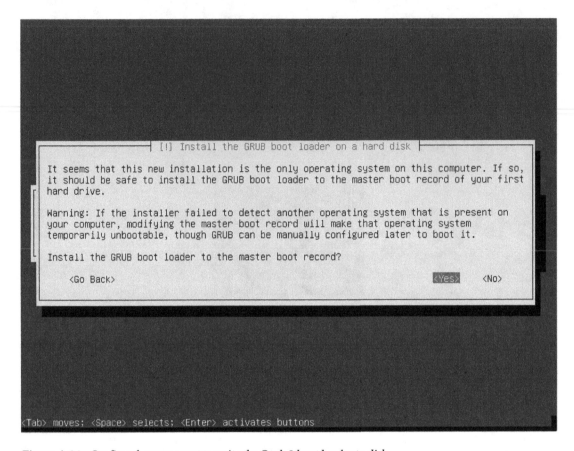

Figure A-21. Confirm that you want to write the Grub 2 boot loader to disk

Index

Get the eBook for only $5!

Why limit yourself?

Now you can take the weightless companion with you wherever you go and access your content on your PC, phone, tablet, or reader.

Since you've purchased this print book, we're happy to offer you the eBook in all 3 formats for just $5.

Convenient and fully searchable, the PDF version enables you to easily find and copy code—or perform examples by quickly toggling between instructions and applications. The MOBI format is ideal for your Kindle, while the ePUB can be utilized on a variety of mobile devices.

To learn more, go to www.apress.com/companion or contact support@apress.com.

Apress®
THE EXPERT'S VOICE™

All Apress eBooks are subject to copyright. All rights are reserved by the Publisher, whether the whole or part of the material is concerned, specifically the rights of translation, reprinting, reuse of illustrations, recitation, broadcasting, reproduction on microfilms or in any other physical way, and transmission or information storage and retrieval, electronic adaptation, computer software, or by similar or dissimilar methodology now known or hereafter developed. Exempted from this legal reservation are brief excerpts in connection with reviews or scholarly analysis or material supplied specifically for the purpose of being entered and executed on a computer system, for exclusive use by the purchaser of the work. Duplication of this publication or parts thereof is permitted only under the provisions of the Copyright Law of the Publisher's location, in its current version, and permission for use must always be obtained from Springer. Permissions for use may be obtained through RightsLink at the Copyright Clearance Center. Violations are liable to prosecution under the respective Copyright Law.

Printed in the United States
By Bookmasters

Printed in the United States
By Bookmasters